D-Day Remembered

D-DAY
REMEMBERED

The Normandy Landings
in American Collective Memory

MICHAEL R. DOLSKI

LEGACIES OF WAR
Series Editor, G. Kurt Piehler

THE UNIVERSITY OF TENNESSEE PRESS / *Knoxville*

The Legacies of War series presents a variety of works—from scholarly monographs to memoirs—that examine the impact of war on society, both in the United States and globally. The wide scope of the series might include war's effects on civilian populations, its lingering consequences for veterans, and the role of individual nations and the international community in confronting genocide and other injustices born of war.

First Edition.

The paper in this book meets the requirements of American National Standards Institute / National Information Standards Organization specification Z39.48-1992 (Permanence of Paper). It contains 30 percent post-consumer waste and is certified by the Forest Stewardship Council.

LIBRARY OF CONGRESS CATALOGING-IN-PUBLICATION DATA

Dolski, Michael, 1978-

D-Day remembered : the Normandy landings in American collective memory / Michael R. Dolski. — First edition.

pages cm. — (Legacies of war)

Includes bibliographical references and index.

ISBN 978-1-62190-218-8 (hardcover : alk. paper)

1. World War, 1939-1945—Campaigns—France—Normandy.

2. World War, 1939-1945—Campaigns—France—Normandy—Social aspects.

3. Nationalism and collective memory—United States.

I. Title.

D756.5.N6D65 2016

940.54'21421—dc23 2015024787

To the soldiers and civilians caught
in the path of war

CONTENTS

ILLUSTRATIONS

FOREWORD

The Allied invasion of Normandy, France, on June 6, 1944, has become central to American memory of World War II. Hundreds of books, ranging from official histories to self-published memoirs, have been published about the events of this day. Hollywood has made several critically acclaimed films that have garnered large audiences at home and abroad. Americans have built memorials not just in France to commemorate this overseas battle, but also in the small town of Bedford, Virginia. American Presidents visit Normandy regularly while in office and, beginning in 1984, have taken part in international ceremonies marking major anniversaries of the landing.

There are good reasons why D-Day has been remembered. The opening of a second front was a major issue that divided the Grand Alliance of the Soviet Union, Great Britain, and the United States. Soviet leader Joseph Stalin pressed for a second front as early as 1942, and a combination of inadequate resources and differences between British Prime Minister Winston Churchill and U.S. President Franklin D. Roosevelt regarding the strategic direction of the war delayed the much-sought after invasion for two years. Neptune and Overlord, the code names given to the naval and amphibious components of the war effort, represented the apex of Allied cooperation between the British Commonwealth and the United States. The foundation for this cooperation began with a multinational command structure that placed an American, U.S. Army General Dwight D. Eisenhower, as Supreme Commander of the Allied Expeditionary Force and senior British military leaders as his principal subordinates. The staging for this immense operation turned southern England into one huge military base as men and women gathered to mount the attack. The naval armada assembled for the invasion would be the largest in history. While the bulk of ground and naval forces were American, British, and Canadian, a total of sixteen nations took part. This truly was an operation for the ages.

Yet in many respects, D-Day was not unprecedented. There had been an earlier D-Day in Europe and dozens more in the Pacific. Why have Americans largely forgotten about the amphibious landings at North Africa, Sicily, Salerno, and Anzio, or the final one in Europe that took place in August 1944 in the south of France? Despite all the superlatives accorded to the heroic events on the beaches of Normandy, more soldiers fought in the snow during the Battle of the Bulge. Strategically, American British, Canadian, and Free French Forces forces at Normandy or the battles that followed never confronted the bulk of the German army. In terms of forces engaged and the casualties suffered, the Eastern Front dwarfed the efforts of the Western Front until V-E Day. Our memories have indeed been selective.

In *D-Day Remembered: The Normandy Landings in American Collective Memory*, Michael Dolski examines why D-Day has emerged as central to the memory of World War II. Like many scholars who write about memory and commemoration, Dolski demonstrates that collective memory is malleable and shaped by a range of constituencies. Historians have played an important role in influencing the memory of D-Day, most notably Cornelius Ryan and Stephen E. Ambrose. But equally pivotal were the roles played by veterans themselves, film makers, politicians, and average Americans. Unsurprisingly, interest in D-Day waned in the late 1960s and 1970s due to changing attitudes influenced by the course of the Vietnam War and general cultural upheaval. There also remained a strong generational impetus regarding commemoration. For instance, during the late 1940s and 1950s, when Dwight Eisenhower served as a general, college president, and U.S. president, he gave D-Day only passing attention. But in his retirement in the 1960s, Eisenhower played a significant role in formulating distinctive memories of D-Day that underscored the good war narrative of brave, democratic Americans selflessly rescuing captive Europe. In the 1980s and 1990s, the junior officers and enlisted personnel then reaching retirement age began to embrace and often promote a collective memory of D-Day that made it one of the preeminent events in the history of World War II.

The diminishing ranks of the World War II generation does not appear to have dimmed interested in commemorating the Allied invasion at Normandy. D-Day is likely to take its place among the pantheon of events—the first Thanksgiving, Valley Forge, Gettysburg, and Martin Luther King's *I Have a Dream Speech*—that successive generations of Americans remember and commemorate. At the same time, Michael Dolski observes the meaning attached to D-Day has evolved, especially with regard to attitude toward our former adversary, Germany, and former ally, the Soviet Union. While historians should be cautious about predicting the future, it is certain that successive generations of Americans will remember D-Day in their own unique ways. *D-Day Remembered* is indispensable in helping us understand why.

G. KURT PIEHLER
Florida State University

ACKNOWLEDGMENTS

Scholarship hangs upon the assistance of many people, often without any demand of compensation other than a simple thank you. These acknowledgments afford the opportunity to make good on the many debts of gratitude that have piled up in the course of this marathon effort. For nearly a decade, D-Day commemoration has been a large part of my life. Mentioned below are some of the most important people who made this journey possible, who tolerated my odd lapses into hermetic contemplation, or who helped keep me sane.

The basis for this book resides in my doctoral work at Temple University. The environment there was conducive to a life of academic pursuits and that surely helped start this project on the right foot. Primacy of place in my recognition must go to Gregory J. W. Urwin. As my advisor, he has championed my cause, and that of many others, even when such a stance may have seemed ill advised. Greg's wide-ranging knowledge, exacting standards for thought and expression, and rebukes for missteps have greatly improved my abilities as a historian. Without his guidance, none of this would have been possible. Jay Lockenour has also been a consistent mentor and friend. Indeed, it was a conversation between the two of us that first gave life to the idea of a project on D-Day remembrance. Ever since, Jay has been ready to offer assistance when needed. Also at Temple, Beth Bailey cheerfully agreed to push a bull-headed military history student to think beyond the confines of his preferred subject matter. Kurt Piehler provided sage counsel for my research and writing and willingly traveled to Philadelphia to be there in person for the completion of the first stage of this D-Day project. With their help, I completed my dissertation, "'To Set Free a Suffering Humanity': D-Day and American Remembrance," in 2012.

While at Temple, I made many lifelong friends who shared the joys and sorrows of graduate life. Jason Smith was there with me from the first day. I am proud to say that I know this most impressive historian and generous spirit. Josh Wolf provided comic relief at crucial moments and then, when back to business, some extremely provocative questions to mull over. Martin Clemis, Earl Catagnus, Jean-Pierre Beugoms, and Michael Lynch were all steadfast companions. These individuals continue to be, each in his own way, an influence on my scholarship, as is Ryan Johnson, who is sadly no longer with us. David Ulbrich was and is a true paragon of selflessness in the desire to assist other scholars. Dave provided a ready example of how people should help one another and how a true sense of fellowship can and will lead to better scholarship. He has become a very successful scholar in the time that I have known him, yet he is always ready to give advice, introduce me to "the right" people, or try to finagle some new opportunity. At Temple, I also had the distinct pleasure to meet and subsequently grow close in friendship with Eric Klinek. Since then, Eric has become like a brother and has generously invited me into his life with Adrienne, Amelia, and the rest of the family. His mastery of military history's minutia is only matched by his deep personal attachments that prove so endearing. Through many arcane, intense, and often humorous conversations, Eric has played a role in shaping this project.

Eric and I also had the good fortune to work together for some time at the Joint POW/MIA Accounting Command, the U.S. military's agency tasked with finding, recovering, identifying, and sending home the remains of missing service personnel. My time with JPAC has been extremely rewarding and just as humbling. Every day I am struck by the passionate dedication of civilians and military personnel who, despite hostile scrutiny and too-easy dismissal of their task, perform to the highest standards possible in an extremely difficult mission. James Rose brought me into the fold at JPAC and since has proven a steady friend and an outstanding historian. Conversations with Derek Congram were particularly rewarding and always provided a completely different frame of reference for any topic. Rebecca Dutton, a great historian and archivist in her own right, helped keep me on track, especially with questions pertaining to the *Chicago Manual of Style*. Colin Colbourn, Julian Saltman, Rob Shafer, and Aelwen Wetherby all provided stimulating discussions on a variety of historical topics. They are a fantastic group of scholars and great people with whom to simply sit and have a conversation. Debbi Prince-Zinni, Greg Berg, Bill Belcher, John Byrd, and Tom Holland all supported a convivial and open atmosphere of scholarly inquiry which rivals that of any academic department. Last but not least, Andrew Heuer's eagerness to read, discuss, and especially question historical matters provided a regular sense of refreshment. He also is a master of digital imagery and readily lent assistance and advice for this project.

I met Sam Edwards on a bus tour to Thomas Jefferson's Monticello home in Virginia. Since that encounter, we have become friends and collaborators on several projects. Sam and I, along with our esteemed colleague John Buckley, edited the entirety of and authored portions of a book titled *D-Day in History and Memory: The Normandy Landings in International Remembrance and Commemoration,* published by the University of North Texas Press in 2014. I developed some of my thoughts on American remembrance practices during the process of writing and editing that volume. Portions of my sections in that work appear, in revised form, in this book. I must extend my thanks to the other contributors to that project, as well as Ron Chrisman at UNT Press, for steering us through to completion. In addition, counsel from the expert outside readers, Edward T. Linenthal and Kurt Piehler, enabled me to improve my own work.

Interactive dialogue can greatly benefit any author by providing different perspectives on material that becomes too familiar over the years. To that end, I would like to thank commentators and audiences from the following conferences: the Barnes Club Conference, Temple University, April 2006; the D-Day Conference, Liberty University, June 2009; the Society for Military History Conference, Virginia Military Institute, May 2010; the Society for Military History Conference, the University of Southern Mississippi and the National World War II Museum, March 2013; the Seventy Years On Conference, Sandhurst Royal Military Academy, April 2014; and the D-Day at 70 Conference, National World War II Museum, June 2014. Regarding the last one, I would like to thank Keith Huxen at the museum for arranging everything and making my trip an extremely pleasant and productive one. Hal Winton, at an earlier conference, suggested the Periclean oratory that I use in the conclusion to this book.

Financial assistance made possible the travel, research, reading, and writing required for this project. Temple University granted several semesters of assistantships. John Votaw, a Temple alumnus, contributed to a research fellowship and freely answered questions on his own work. Finally, the Cantigny First Division Foundation honored me with a one-year fellowship that provided a generous financial allotment and an even more meaningful behind-the-scenes access to the collections and staff at the First Division Museum. I would like to thank Paul Herbert, Eric Gillespie, Andrew Woods, Kate Kleiderman, Melissa Tyer, Keith Gill, and Teri Bianchi for their assistance during my repeated trips to Cantigny.

The assistance of staff at archival or other research-related institutions is a foundational requirement for any project of this nature. This book depended greatly on the willing support and professional expertise consistently demonstrated by the personnel at a number of fine organizations. I would like to thank the following people: Doug McCabe at the Mahn Center for Archives and Special Collections, Ohio University Libraries; April Cheek-Messier at the National D-Day Memorial Foundation; the staff at the National Archives and Records Administration's College Park facility; Alan Raphael at the National World War II Museum in New Orleans; Rich Baker at the Army Heritage and Education Center in Carlisle, Pennsylvania; Virginia Lewick at the Franklin D. Roosevelt Presidential Library in Hyde Park, New York; Valoise Armstrong at the Dwight D. Eisenhower Presidential Library in Abilene, Kansas; Jennifer Mandel at the Ronald W. Reagan Presidential Library in Simi Valley, California; Mark Quigley at the UCLA Film and Television Archive; and Lea Whittington and Jenny Romero at the Margaret Herrick Library in Beverly Hills, California. I would also like to acknowledge the time taken by Karl Weissenbach, the director of the Eisenhower Library, to discuss with me President Eisenhower's Second World War and presidential campaign experiences.

This project benefited from the professional, timely, and expert advice offered by Thomas Wells at the University of Tennessee Press. Thomas was always quick to respond to any inquiry and provided constant feedback, all of which was much appreciated. He employed the right mix of prodding and disengagement to push this work to conclusion. Many thanks are due to Thomas for bringing to this project the outstanding editorial input of Gene Adair and Emily Huckabay. Thomas also employed the services of two outstanding external readers who delivered useful comments and corrections. For that, I would like to thank Allan Winkler and Kurt Piehler. As may be obvious at this point, Kurt has been a continuing source of encouragement and well-reasoned recommendations over the years. His book on American military commemoration profoundly shaped my own thoughts on the matter, as is evident in the text that follows. Thank you, Kurt, for all the help.

I would also like to thank Kristine Sordelet and Mackenzie Moss for their support during the early phases of this project.

Finally, my father, mother, and stepfather all instilled in me a desire to work hard, do better, and ask questions. Their love and support got me started on and maintained me as I progressed down the track that ends here. Emily Wilson entered my life in an unexpected way during this project. Ever since, she has been a continuous source of encouragement and relief. She had read, commented upon, helped correct, and even (painfully, one supposes) sat through presentations on material discussed here. Thank you for making this journey worthwhile.

Although my work has relied upon the contributions of everyone mentioned above, any errors of content or interpretation remain mine alone.

NOTE ON METHODS AND SOURCES

There is a large historiographical field for studies of collective remembrance. The daunting range of this work holds true even for the more confined branch of military history topics. What that thought fails to convey, however, is the vast gulf separating many authors, based not only on subject matter but also with methodologies and evidentiary base. Indeed, one sharp critic of this whole memory boom, Alon Confino, has astutely challenged the broad field of interested scholars by noting a lack of rigor with terms and lackadaisical engagement with theory.[1] That commentator, however, still readily admitted to the potential value of investigating remembrance patterns. Collective memory offers a fruitful path for looking at social groups and individuals in a new frame of reference. As I argue, this particular case will add further dimensions to larger stories about American society in the twentieth century. Nevertheless, taking a moment to explain the methodological approach, some key terms, and the evidence employed will help avoid some confusion.

First off, to be frank, societies do not remember the past, people do. Yet people encounter the past in a social environment that influences what they think, how they think, and even why they think as they do. At many points throughout this book, we see individuals reacting to larger social pressures by tapping their constructions of memory. This serpentine process is mutually influential between individuals and their parent society. It is iterative, feeding off prior versions of the past bandied about in the "marketplace of ideas," and therefore a chronological orientation to the material seems most fitting.

Some of these iterations will amount to sharp breaks from prior memories, while other versions will simply recycle old constructions or slightly refine and update them. Throughout, people have employed intriguingly similar versions of the D-Day paradigm to make sense of their world and also to foment or forestall changes.

The object of this study does have real-world implications. The memories connected to D-Day, in part, have ennobled military violence in ways that we must at least ponder. While describing the development of these memories, though, we must remain fair. The tension between honoring those who served and glorifying violence is palpable, particularly in light of America's recent season of war. Some myths and constructions are not necessarily wrong, nor do only those with base motives advance them. The eminent historian Gordon Wood recently cautioned critics overly intent on deconstructing national myths. As he warned, "We tamper with our heritage, our memory, at our peril."[2] Perhaps there is a distinction between scholars who are useful and those who are merely sensationalistic revisionists. The useful ones seek to foster deeper understanding of the past, fill in blanks, or smooth out edges. Sensationalists go for tabloid-style revelations and employ grandiose claims.[3] Regardless, scholars seeking to destroy national myths face a tough task. National myths burrow into culture and resiliently ward off frontal assaults. Stridently attacking the constructed memories of D-Day may stoke flames of controversy, but such an approach would likely remain unconvincing to most. Illumination, not quite eradication, is the goal here.

In historiographic terms, this work sides with those scholars who seek to avoid an overly fine distinction between history and memory. Some, like Pierre Nora, argue that history has a scientific objectivity about it that memory, particularly public memory, simply lacks.[4] Following the lead of others like Emily Rosenberg, the argument here finds "that memory and history are blurred forms of representation whose structure and politics need to be analyzed not as oppositional but as interactive forms."[5] Formal "histories" of the battle coexist with, draw from, and influence the "memories" held by the wider public. In fact, histories and memories are reasonably symbiotic, each empowering the other even as their edges blend into one another.

Aside from explaining the approach, defining a few terms used frequently in this venture will forestall confusion over meaning. *Monument* signifies a single structure intended to celebrate, honor, educate, or aid memory recall.

Memorial is a bit more fluid, meaning both an area set aside for remembrance (possibly with multiple monuments) or an honorific designation bestowed upon something extant. *Remembrance* indicates the act of recall, the process of constructing the past for present/future purposes. *Commemoration* implies an open, public, and often celebratory approach to remembering the past. *Collective* here stands for, broadly put, a group of varied size. When used in the phrase "collective memory" without elaboration, the intended meaning is that of dominant or mainstream society. *Memory* refers to the socially constructed versions of the past that derive shape from longer trends in a society, relate to the specific events referenced, and serve as a means for using the past to influence the present as well as the future. *Consciousness* points to the memories that the collective group keeps readily in circulation. Finally, as will be evident throughout this work, *freedom* is a concept often linked to D-Day as in the Allies fought for freedom, or fought to liberate others from oppression. Here, freedom and liberty will serve interchangeably to denote the absence of oppressive and destructive rule (namely, Nazi tyranny).[6]

The evidentiary trail with memory formation proves somewhat eclectic in nature. Traditional archival materials inform this study. Institutions like the National Archives, presidential libraries, or other public and privately based collections contain a wealth of documents related to the writing of speeches, the organization of public ceremonies, or the construction of monuments and museums. Films serve as an excellent means to study how society interacts with the past since so many people "learn" history through such visual media. Numerous mainstream movies, documentaries, and television programs appear herein and serve both as representations of and inputs into the collective remembrance process. The news media, print and broadcast, offer another potential resource for examining the way that society reconstructs the past. Keeping the nebulous relationship between history and memory in mind, a plethora of books—both academic and popular histories—populates this research. Memory studies are, in essence, forays into cultural history. As a result, a wide array of cultural artifacts, from physical traces to ephemeral celebratory events, from individual actions to society-wide activities, all come together in this story on D-Day remembrance.

D-Day Remembered

INTRODUCTION

Return to the Familiar

On June 6, 1944, a storm was coming to a close. Crossing the choppy waters of the English Channel, a vast armada bore down on the coast of German-occupied France. The amphibious element of this invasion force would join up in a matter of hours with airdropped units deposited behind enemy lines shortly after midnight. In the next twenty-four hours, more than 150,000 men of the Allied forces, primarily coming from the United States, Great Britain, and Canada, would touch French soil. Thousands of tanks, trucks, specialized vehicles, and the overwhelming array of matériel required by a twentieth-century invasion force also made the journey. Taken altogether, this constituted a veritable overseas migration in force. Allied leaders had given the operation the codename Overlord. D-Day, the launching date of the operation, soon passed into history and popular imagination as the shorthand reference, the epithet for this great and awful event.

D-Day. The term evokes images of men huddled in landing craft approaching a hazy and ominous shore. As the craft drew near the beaches and disgorged their human cargo, the full horrors of modern industrial warfare erupted into a frenzied hecatomb. Despite the difficulties of the action and the tenacity of the enemy, somehow these men won the battle and, as a result, the war. Most Americans now think of D-Day in terms similar to these. D-Day often signifies heroism and sacrifice for the greater good. It recalls the shining moment of Allied reentry into northwestern Europe and the beginning of the end of America's last "good war."

While the American military has long used the term "d-day" to indicate the launching date of any military operation, most Americans link it to one specific event. For them, D-Day signifies the invasion of Normandy, France, on June 6, 1944. Even more specifically, D-Day usually stands for the American experience of combat on the beaches and in the scattered areas beyond peppered with airborne troops. Despite attempts by some to point out the many d-days of the Second World War, D-Day in the public consciousness refers to the action in Normandy.[1]

Operation Overlord opened a new front that would advance during the succeeding eleven months into the heart of Germany. Besides this battle's role in achieving final victory, its importance partly stems from the awesome spectacle of a large invading force conquering both natural obstacles and a resolute enemy. Casualty figures for this action are still difficult to assess because of the hectic combat that day and in the weeks that followed. Charles MacDonald, a Second World War veteran and U.S. Army historian, estimated the total casualties for the Allies on D-Day at about 9,000, with 3,000 of that figure killed. More recently, the National D-Day Memorial Foundation has identified over 4,000 Allied dead (including approximately 2,500 Americans).[2]

Owing in part to the drama of the hard-fought battle and its function in determining the final verdict of the war, superlatives abound in characterizations of D-Day. General Dwight D. Eisenhower, supreme Allied commander in charge of the operation, commended his soldiers for embarking on a "great crusade" in the order of the day that he released prior to the battle.[3] Vietnam veteran and independent researcher Carlo D'Este described the invasion as "the most complex and daring military operation in the history of modern warfare."[4] Well-known military historian and perfervid D-Day popularizer Stephen E. Ambrose enthused, "The lesson of Normandy is that there is nothing a democracy cannot do once it agrees on what needs to be done."[5] Descriptions of the battle often include fustian like Eisenhower's "great crusade" or what one recent book called "the greatest invasion."[6] In the midst of all these assertions, though, several prevailing themes emerge even as other aspects of the operation fall to the side. Americans prefer to focus on the heroism of their soldiers and the latter's achievement of collective victory in the face of extreme adversity. Facets of the battle that seem to detract from the nobility of American military might, such as the contributions of Allied forces or the costs borne by civilians in the conflict zone, get shrouded in a veil of obscurity.[7]

Is another book on D-Day even necessary? The quick response is that this work does not focus on D-Day, per se. Rather, the investigation herein centers on the presence of D-Day in American memory, or, more aptly, it consists of an evaluation of the means, methods, and meanings implicit in the collective remembrance of this battle. The commemorative approach to D-Day opens a window through which to view American thinking connected to warfare, national identity, and America's place in the world.

The past, as William Faulkner famously wrote, is never truly dead.[8] The way people and societies see themselves depends largely upon understandings of the past. These conceptualizations are not static. They change, evolve, and adapt in ways that reflect the influence of the present on our views of the past. D-Day emerged as a major reference in American society because popular interpretations of the battle seemed to confirm cherished national self-perceptions. As Americans faced new foes or difficulties after the war, D-Day reaffirmed positive aspects of their society. Collective understandings of D-Day produced a *constructed* version of the past that may not have been wrong, yet nevertheless represented selective interpretations that narrowed the story to certain key elements. D-Day represented a morality tale of America's selfless sacrifice to restore order in the world. The stories told often stressed the moral fervor, and divine favor in many cases, as Americans, foremost among the Allies, struck a mighty blow against tyranny on D-Day. The liberation of Europe began that day, the benefits of which America, Europe, and the world still enjoy seven decades later. Challenges to this rousing assessment of one battle have surfaced. As America faced numerous postwar tensions, D-Day's presence vacillated, going from widely extolled to seemingly forgotten. Its return in the 1980s shows that mediated use of the past carries immense political significance. D-Day helped reunify America following the Vietnam era. Some political and cultural leaders also cited its "lessons" when asserting the country's prerogative to leadership in world affairs.

Over time, D-Day came to symbolize supposed American values. The battle seemed to indicate a unique American regard for freedom, the efficacy of American combat arms, and divine sanction for an American quest to confront evil. Implicitly, wartime glory produced national greatness, led to good times, and ensured liberties at home and abroad. Such conceptions furthered a militarization of American society in the second half of the twentieth century. The D-Day stories that Americans liked to hear created an ennobled understanding of warfare that had real-world effects.

History and Memory

Social or public memory can be a rather vague concept, loosely defined because of the varied nature of the plentiful studies that examine this phenomenon. The diversity breeds lexical fuzziness, particularly because of the multiplicity of ways available to approach the subject. Thus, public memory stands alongside other terms and phrases such as *social memory, collective memory, popular memory,* just plain *memory,* or *history and memory.* All these terms convey the implication that groups of individuals construct understandings of the past. Such constructions help define group identity.[9]

I use social, collective, and public memory interchangeably in this book. My intent is *not* to investigate a phenomenon of physiological recall taking place within an individual's unique mental faculties. Instead, the subject of study consists of the way in which individuals, groups, and institutions attempt to mediate the way others think about a major event in the past, specifically D-Day. Collective memory in this sense indicates a process of group engagement with the past shaped by social environment, conducted for a variety of present-minded (often political) reasons.[10]

As far back as the 1920s, French sociologist Maurice Halbwachs began pondering the nature and significance of collective memory. His insistence that memories of the past are largely constructed, and that the interaction between individuals and collectives shapes that constructive process, proved "pathbreaking" and of enduring value.[11] In the many decades between Halbwachs's work and the explosion in memory-history studies of late, scholarly attention to collective memory was fitful, but certainly present in various guises. Scholars such as Joseph Campbell, Roland Barthes, and Richard Slotkin plumbed the depths of myth formation in societies. Collectively, these and other authors highlighted the ways in which groups compose understandings of the past and then transmit those myth-memories to subsequent generations. As Richard Slotkin perceptively stated, "Myth . . . is a narrative formulation of a culture's world view and self-concept, which draws both on the historical experience of that culture and on sources of feeling, fear, and aspiration (individual and universal/archetypal) deep in the human subconscious and which can be shown to function in that culture as a prescription for historical action and value judgment."[12] Myths, in this formulation, function precisely as Halbwachs's collective memory. This conception of myth suitably characterizes the commemoration of D-Day in American society. Mythic, as employed by these authors, does not imply fable or fantastical yarn. Historian Mary Roberts maintained that "myth describes a type of speech, both visual and textual, which is able to transform history into idealized form" as it serves to "organize a world that is without depth or contradictions; they purify, simplify, and depoliticize"[13] As used in this work, mythic collective memories represent socially derived renderings of the past, influenced by present conditions, employed to satisfy a variety of personal and group needs. Myth also implies something greater—a depiction of the past that is widely accepted and no longer rigorously challenged.

Historians have explored an intriguing diversity of topics using the collective memory framework.[14] For instance, Benedict Anderson described modern nations as "imagined political communities" that linked their diffuse peoples through a variety of shared cultural features such as language, belief systems, and history.[15] D-Day remembrance exemplifies this thought as the tales told reflected the communal assessment of past, present, and future. Furthermore, as argued below, D-Day memories helped reunite the American imagined community torn asunder during the tumultuous Sixties era.

By the 1990s, many scholars were paying attention to what historians Geoff Eley and Jay Winter identified as a "memory boom" attracting academics as well as the public at large.[16] Perhaps the most expansive and ambitious book to arise out of this new fascination came with Michael Kammen's exhaustive study of American tradition and public memory. As Kammen explained, "societies in fact reconstruct their pasts rather than faithfully record them, and . . . they do so with the needs of contemporary culture in mind—manipulating the past in order to mold the present." While his work ranged widely over time, space, and topic, Kammen still indicated, "Wars have played a fundamental role in stimulating, defining, justifying, periodizing, and eventually filtering American memories and traditions."[17] This last point received added support and elaboration a few years later in Kurt Piehler's work on American war remembrance. According to Piehler, "Almost as important as the fighting itself is how Americans have assimilated the experiences of particular wars into their national consciousness and culture. The American national identity remains inexorably intertwined with the commemoration and memory of past wars."[18] Kammen and Piehler also explored the contests that erupted over differing constructions of the past. The competition for authority to commemorate D-Day fit into the overall framework of American military memories developed by these two authors.[19]

Concomitant with the emergence of this memory boom, by the 1980s many Americans developed a renewed interest in the Second World War.

Studs Terkel, famed oral historian, inspired a subfield of historical studies and coined a new phrase for popular usage with his 1984 book, *"The Good War": An Oral History of World War II.* Terkel set out to reverse what he termed the "disremembrance of World War II" by compiling oral histories from its American participants.[20] In the same year that Terkel's book appeared, President Ronald Reagan delivered speeches at Pointe du Hoc and the Normandy American Cemetery, both scenes of combat on D-Day, to commemorate the fortieth anniversary of the landings. On June 6, 1984, Reagan proclaimed:

> We're here to mark that day in history when the Allied armies joined in battle to reclaim this continent to liberty. For 4 long years, much of Europe had been under a terrible shadow. Free nations had fallen, Jews cried out in the camps, millions cried out for liberation. Europe was enslaved, and the world prayed for its rescue. Here in Normandy the rescue began. Here the Allies stood and fought against tyranny in a giant undertaking unparalleled in human history.[21]

Reagan's emphasis on American triumphalism, collective honor, nostalgic veneration of past heroes and the call for future successes resonated in a divided, post-Vietnam society. Significantly, these positive references to the Second World War pertained to the European Theater of Operations. Glowing odes to a "good war" failed to materialize in the same manner regarding the Pacific Theater because of its racist-fueled brutality and America's use of atomic bombs. Although there were many d-days in the Pacific, only the Normandy landings seemed to fit the comforting image of America as a benevolent liberator, one that guaranteed freedom for (white) others.[22]

The collective response to these interpretations of the wartime generation and the meaning of the war itself produced an explosion of movies and books, as well as an astounding array of commemorative activities throughout the 1980s and 1990s. Longtime NBC anchorman Tom Brokaw epitomized this trend in his immensely popular 1998 book, *The Greatest Generation,* which cast the wartime experience of Americans in romanticized tones. Brokaw's work reduced the complex motives and actions of the entire generation to simple honor and heroism. The Hollywood blockbuster *Saving Private Ryan* debuted the same year as Brokaw's book. *Saving Private Ryan* thrust the viewer into the midst of the D-Day landings a couple minutes into the movie. Spectacular special effects portrayed the horrors of warfare in shocking and at times thrilling ways.[23] Nevertheless, the prevailing theme depicted ordinary Americans as the heroic men of honor celebrated by Reagan and Brokaw.[24]

Interestingly enough, despite the increased attention, no major work on memory has solely examined the European Theater of Operations in the Second World War. This historiographical gap is important because although the war in the Pacific has received coverage, many of the factors that shape American remembrance of those events, such as racism or the use of atomic weapons, are not usually associated with the European area of operations. As Michael Adams aptly labeled it, the European war remains "the best war ever" in American popular remembrance while debates about the *Enola Gay,* Hiroshima, and Japanese-American internment challenge that conception for the Pacific Theater.[25]

One explanation for this lacuna may be simply that many people tend to narrow their concern to a few aspects of any specific event. In the case of the Second World War, Americans seem to meditate on its traumatic beginning at Pearl Harbor and the terrifying atomic firestorms at the war's end that gave birth to a new era of fear. These events merged in the public mind as an abiding dread of nuclear surprise attack and annihilation.[26] Even with the enormous degree of attention attracted by Pearl Harbor, Hiroshima, and Nagasaki, D-Day still stands as a pivotal moment in the public's conception of the war. When the Allies invaded Normandy, many contemporaries hailed this battle as the surge to the end of the war in Europe.[27] Because of such claims, D-Day has captured public and scholarly attention, despite periodic lulls, ever since.

Notwithstanding the numerous books, movies, and memorials focusing on D-Day, few people have attempted to analyze this phenomenon in the history-and-memory framework. Journalist Alex Kershaw's book, *The Bedford Boys,* covered the sacrifices made by a small town in Virginia, which lost nineteen local residents on D-Day. Kershaw offered a brief concluding section on the attempt to memorialize the loss after the war.[28] Rice University history professor Douglas Brinkley analyzed Reagan's 1984 speeches commemorating D-Day in *The Boys of Pointe du Hoc.* Brinkley, however, repeatedly shifted from describing the commemoration of D-Day as a whole to focusing solely on the remembrance of the 2nd Ranger Battalion at Pointe du Hoc.[29] Aside from recounting the dramatic Ranger assault, Brinkley was more concerned with depicting the speeches President Reagan delivered on D-Day's fortieth anniversary as the pivotal moment in the birth of a politically conservative "New Americanism."[30] In the end, Brinkley decontextualized the fortieth anniversary celebrations, as if past understandings of the events never existed. Brinkley, therefore, missed a key opportunity to explore the full scope of politicized memory centered on D-Day, which was his ostensible concern.

Such a gap in the coverage of American war memory is quite noticeable at this time. Public commemoration of the Second World War has experienced significant shifts over the past seventy years, permutations that certainly influenced the conceptualization of D-Day. D-Day stood out to Americans in June 1944 because it seemed to promise a quick end to the war in Europe. This lasting conception of D-Day as a turning point has placed it in the forefront of American memories of the Second World War's European component. The truly intriguing factors to consider, though, are the various peaks and lulls the public consciousness of D-Day has experienced in the intervening years since the day of battle. During the early Cold War years, D-Day served to remind Americans that their country protected freedom, even in foreign lands, while enemies past and present threatened liberties worldwide. The Vietnam morass called into question roseate views of American diplomatic and military policies. In the soul searching that attended that conflict, the glorification of former wars fell to the wayside. D-Day, however, returned in force during the 1980s and the 1990s as politicians, veterans, scholars, and other interested citizens emphasized the positive implications of this battle drawn from history. Casting about for a new national project after the conclusion of the Cold War, President Clinton's avowed intention to preserve and extend democracy abroad accorded well with the supposed lessons of D-Day. The barrage of militant language extolling the use of force for moral purposes, such as liberating the oppressed, fostered acceptance of new military ventures espoused in the name of liberty.

Day of Days in the American Century

D-Day has served as a defining moment in American intervention in European and world affairs. While profiling the role of individuals and organizations in shaping remembrance of the battle, this work will keep the larger social context as a constant source of reference. Beyond a mere listing of celebrations or cultural artifacts connected to the battle, the real value of this approach resides with the act of teasing out the meanings ascribed to D-Day. American memories of D-Day have tended to slant the story in rather interesting ways. The honor and glory of the fighting men are standard themes, but that fixation served to crowd out consideration of other vital, albeit noncombatant, roles in the operation. While extolling the moral virtues of the operation, Americans have also downplayed the disturbing aspects of the gruesome fighting. American stories of the battle usually have depicted the U.S. soldiers as saviors of world civilization while quickly passing over the necessary contributions of other countries before, during, and after this single day. The French served in a passive capacity here as the liberated. The implication that they owe a debt of gratitude has overwhelmed consideration of their destructive experience of liberation.[31] D-Day remains a story of Americans fighting in a good cause. These interpretive shadings are not necessarily *wrong,* but as a whole they simplify, sanitize, and, taken to extremes, misconstrue the awful reality of the battle. In the end, American notions of D-Day have evolved over time into a set of conceptions that romanticize the use of military force in beguiling ways because they seem so nonpolitical in orientation.

To fixate solely on the conceptualizations of D-Day would miss part of the story. Throughout this book, I devote effort to analyzing how and why people use these renderings of the past for present purpose. Thus, an evident tension permeates this book as the text shifts between constructions of the past and their employment in the present. The ramifications of such activities often provoke historical reassessments and, therefore, start the process over again.

All this commemorative activity takes place in, and at the same time serves as an influence upon, national culture. For our purposes, the most relevant characteristics of that culture include a fixation on a generalized notion of freedom, a conception of America as a nonmilitaristic (though militarily competent) society, certainty in the redemptive power of violence, and belief in the providential or exceptional nature of America itself. If, as Anderson maintained, the nation is essentially an "imagined community," these mythic constructions constitute some of the most potent glue binding together disparate Americans.[32] The very act of understanding or navigating the present often leads individuals, and entire collective groups, to rely upon interpretations of the past. These views assume mythic nature when they embed in a culture, bear frequent repetition, and move from the realm of something provable to become something a priori taken for granted.

Master narratives of the past act as framing devices: they are the overriding moral of the story. Often these master narratives emphasize breakpoints or key turning moments. In the twentieth century, it is hard to find a more significant and influential event than the Second World War. Yet even this obviously pivotal conflict is by itself such a vast complex of experiences that further reduction to a few moments of supreme importance seems almost inevitable. For American society as a whole, the Second World War has become an integral part of a national success story epitomized by certain iconic moments like D-Day. As will be demonstrated at length throughout the rest of this work, American myths centering on freedom, nonmilitarism, the utility of violence, and exceptionalism all conveniently fit into stories about the war, this battle, and the development of the rest of the century.[33]

Historian Eric Foner cogently noted, "No idea is more fundamental to Americans' sense of themselves as individuals and as a nation than freedom." The story of freedom constitutes the standard metanarrative for American history to most Americans, even in the face of quite the opposite condition prevailing at times, such as with the institution of chattel slavery.[34] Michael Sherry, on the other hand, has extensively explored the militarization of American society in the twentieth century. While claiming that Americans lived "under the shadow of war" and that "militarization reshaped every realm of American life," Sherry described a self-denial process. American conceptualizations of war cast the country always as a passive victim, never eager to fight, but hesitantly taking up the call to arms when provoked.[35] The militarization of American culture and society stemmed in part from real-world pressures, such as Cold War-related threats, yet it also connected to deeper views on the use of violence in general. To borrow from Richard Slotkin, a belief in the regenerative power of violence may not be a uniquely American cultural characteristic, but it is something certainly worth keeping in mind while studying American history. The larger pattern, with interesting abeyances, shows American society has perceived a moral as well as a political utility in the use of violence.[36] Finally, these concepts all come together—the notion of a commitment to freedom, the alleged disavowal of militarism coinciding with an embrace of violence—in what stands as a belief in American exceptionalism. George Herring recently described this concept by noting that Americans sustain faith in a providential mission of their country to lead the world. This divinely sanctioned role lends itself to the use of violence, though, when confronted with serious challenges or threats.[37]

These diffuse strands of thought help demonstrate deeply held beliefs that have had, and continue to hold, much purchase in American society. Recent trends in diplomatic history have lent further force to this assertion by showing the intertwined nature of "foreign" and "domestic" political culture. For instance, Michael Hunt's incisive probing of American foreign policy emphasized the ideological continuities stemming from cultural tendencies and pressures at home. Hunt demonstrated the subtle, yet pervasive presence of rhetorical code words that almost transcend politics of the moment because of their normative nature. The pursuit of stability, the quest for "liberties," the belief in a providential world mission all become *standards* or baseline points in the American worldview.[38] Frank Ninkovich likewise emphasized the role of ideology in American self-perceptions and policy formation. The twentieth century presented so many new challenges that political leaders had to rely upon underlying ideological precepts. Wilsonians, named after President Woodrow Wilson, depicted the world as a dangerous area requiring active American interventionism.[39] Michael Hogan argued that a Wilsonian worldview preceded and enabled the media mogul Henry Luce to proclaim the "American Century" in 1941. In the pages of *Time* magazine, Luce intently urged "the American people to accept their destiny and use their influence to remake the world according to their own values."[40]

Notwithstanding Luce's stirring arguments, his fellow Americans required some prodding to embrace their so-called century. Wilsonianism had arisen as a crisis response to a world beset by a multitude of threats.[41] Despite the dark horizons, Wilsonian solutions to the perceived world challenge of economic decay and military aggression did not convince everyone. From the disillusioned Lost Generation in the 1920s, to the neutrality proponents in the 1930s, and extending to the anti-internationalists in the 1940s and beyond, there were plenty of countercurrents in the policymaking seas.[42] These dissenters from the active interventionist streak of American foreign policy, however, faced an uphill battle from mid-century on. The Second World War overwhelmed such arguments by revitalizing and expanding Wilsonian proclivities in America. While the war did not create a clean break, as the above-mentioned myths and self-conceptualizations amply demonstrate, it did radically alter the cultural landscape. In the years after, the war has maintained a prominent place in stories and understandings of the century as a whole. The larger stories and the trends in their development not only helped people at the time make sense of this most destructive war, but they also offer an opportunity to view changes and continuities in the society that spawned such tales.

This analysis will follow the lead of other scholars who have seen politicized framings shape the public consciousness of battles and wars.[43] The first chapter provides a baseline explanation of the Second World War and the role of D-Day in the European Theater. Immediately upon hearing of the invasion, presidential commentary, public gatherings, and news-media stories began shaping wider perceptions of the battle. Many of these initial characterizations held D-Day as an indicator of American martial and moral strength in a world-saving quest for freedom. Such assertions set the tone for long-term public memories of the Normandy landings and the larger war. When the predicted triumph of arms in Europe took longer to achieve than anticipated, the public's attention switched back to ongoing wartime anxieties. The apocalyptic conclusion of the war, hastened by the twinned use of atomic bombs, caused Americans to focus on the possibility of future atomic war rather than pay extended homage to the recently won conflict and particular successes like D-Day.

The second chapter examines the first decade that followed the war. With economic concerns, European turbulence, and the Korean War clamoring for popular attention, the Second World War did not captivate the American people any longer. D-Day did not totally lapse from public consciousness. The groundwork for the mid-1950s revival was already evident, for instance, in the appellation of "The Great Crusade" that Eisenhower gave to the European war with his 1948 memoir. D-Day constituted the kickoff to the crusade in this framework.

Once the Cold War stabilized into a fact of daily life and the immediacy of nuclear warfare seemed to die down, some people began to refocus their attention on the Second World War. Addressed in the third chapter, the resultant reconceptualization of the past conflict elicited themes of glory, honor, and sacrifice for the greater good. D-Day figured prominently in this drive, as seen in various media. The real explosion in popular awareness and identification with the battle, however, stemmed from the efforts of Cornelius Ryan. His popular book *The Longest Day* came out in 1959 and translated into an extremely successful movie in 1962.[44]

D-Day tales of liberating the oppressed enjoyed widespread circulation in the mid-1960s just as America entered the Vietnam War. Political and military figures drew upon the supposed lessons of the past to reassure the public that America fought for freedom before and should do so once more. The flurry of renewed pride in D-Day, however, was not powerful enough to withstand the impact of social dislocation and antimilitarism that accompanied the Vietnam War. Throughout that divisive conflict, many individuals muted their references to D-Day, and commemorative activities appeared rather constrained. D-Day did not completely disappear from public consciousness, as shown in chapter 4. Still, there was a remarkable change of course in terms of popular focus on the battle when compared to what happened in the mid-1950s to mid-1960s. Prior attempts to cast the battle and the Second World War in terms that furthered Cold War priorities of the American cultural and political elite worked against D-Day celebration in the late 1960s and 1970s. Linking D-Day to the destruction of tyranny (and in the Cold War context this also overtly implied Soviet rule) produced distaste for the events previously commemorated as the superficially consensual society disintegrated. As America's failings in terms of racial, social, or gender equality became increasingly evident, praise for saving the world in a "good war" dwindled away. Moralistic conceptions of America's past rang less true, including the honor supposedly accrued for the sacrifices made on D-Day.[45]

Following chapter 4's examination of the decline in awareness and celebration, chapter 5 explains how D-Day came to serve as an important component for the reunification of American society after Vietnam. Douglas Brinkley was not wrong in asserting this point. He erred in overemphasizing Reagan's speeches in 1984. Without a doubt, those speeches served as vital pieces in the reemergence of D-Day consciousness. In them, Reagan's call for liberty from tyranny reinforced the attempted linkage of an earlier glorious struggle to the Cold War, which spiked once again in confrontational intensity in the early 1980s. Americans could look to their honorable and ultimately successful performance in the Second World War and hope for eventual triumph against the current foe. The war thus became a means to reunify a divided country behind themes of past heroism and glory alongside a renewed commitment to winning the Cold War. The 1980s, however, witnessed many different commemorative activities that sought to restore a sense of glory and honor to constructions of the American past.

D-Day memorialization benefited from a level of nostalgia wrought by growing chronological distance from the Second World War. With key anniversary dates in 1984 and 1994 passing along with a growing number of the wartime generation, the hazy tint of long-past glories acquired even more warmhearted tones. Chapter 6 describes the growing wave of D-Day-related commemorative activity following the fortieth anniversary. These efforts increased in speed as younger generations sought to honor passing elders by trumpeting their youthful gallantry as a golden period before current troubles. With the gala fiftieth anniversary celebrations in 1994, as covered in chapter 7, D-Day reassumed a prominent place in American society. Stephen Ambrose's books, which celebrated wartime heroism in general and that of D-Day in particular, epitomized this trend. His influence also spread across popular media. Ambrose consulted for the movie *Saving Private Ryan.* The opening of the National D-Day Museum in New Orleans on June 6, 2000, stemmed from his efforts. A 2001 HBO miniseries titled *Band of Brothers* followed Ambrose's book of the same name by depicting an airborne unit from training through D-Day to the end of the war.[46]

An explosion of references to the battle suffused popular culture and the political arena by the dawn of the new millennium, as discussed in chapter 8. Reconstructing the battle became a way to recast America's past in glowing terms. A partial effect of this trend was the insistence upon the valor of American society in the past and implicit call for heroic emulation in the present. This particular use of D-Day gained renewed fervor with the terrorist attacks on America that took place on September 11, 2001. Following that shocking assault, Americans drew frequently on a moralistic reading of the past to validate a global fight for freedom. D-Day commemorative activities have enshrined the past and legitimated America's world position, especially regarding the use of military force. Yet the divided reactions to the so-called Global War on Terror present counter tendencies for Second World War memorialization. Drawing on past glory could bolster support for current military actions if the two connect in the public mind. The danger of a backlash, however, emerged with some critics claiming by 2004 that political figures had adversely politicized D-Day memories for crass purposes.[47]

The conclusion discusses the particularized factors in the American approach to national-memory formation. The tendency in the years since 1944 has been to Americanize D-Day by minimizing the role of others. In the process, D-Day served as a confirmation of selected, yet supposedly inherent characteristics of America.[48] These traits, as constructed, ultimately glorified the use of arms.

The Utility of History

Certain longer-standing tendencies in the dominant American cultural landscape preceded the Second World War. These influences shaped the ways in which mainstream society conceptualized and reconceptualized D-Day both during the war and then in the period that followed. Prevalent mythic tropes emphasized America's commitment to freedom, nonmilitarism—yet capable employment of violence when necessary—and exceptional leadership role in the world. After the war concluded, an interesting process of thinking through the Second World War took place in ways that largely restructured it according to these perceptual frameworks. Kurt Piehler reminded us, "No generation of Americans has managed to avoid fighting a major war. How we have remembered these conflicts [has] played a crucial role in shaping the American national identity over time."[49] Because of its epic nature, conceptions of the Second World War, and America's role in the war, heavily influenced postwar society. With America's long history of trying to scope out a place in the world, the Second World War served as a major coming-of-age because of the economic-, political-, cultural-, and military-leadership functions the country assumed. Perforce, the rendering of the war changed to meet a transitioning society's changing needs. One result of this dynamic, as historian Michael C. C. Adams described it, is that "World War II . . . has been converted over time from a complex, problematic event, full of nuance and debatable meaning, to a simple, shining legend of the Good War."[50]

In the effort to draw upon this particular past, certain components of the story acquired greater importance as they more easily demonstrated the arguments advanced by individuals and groups. The commemorations of and meanings ascribed to D-Day played fundamental roles in the development of the Second World War into the "good war."[51] As a dramatic moment and turning point in the war, one that involved the liberation of territory held by the enemy, D-Day offered much to memorialists in the postwar years. Compared to more negative or darker moments in that war, D-Day's magnetism stems in part from such appealing aspects of the battle.[52]

In the chapters that follow, the evolution of certain themes attributed to this battle will coincide with larger changes suffusing America, and the world, in the decades after the war. Individuals play a large role in this story as veterans, their family members, government officials, and authors, scholars, and journalists all proffer their interpretations in the great "marketplace of ideas" that forms the public sphere.[53] While some views clashed with others, the general casting of this battle as a prime example of American benevolence, morality, and military capability—often to the exclusion of other countries—confronts us rather consistently. Because of the uncertainties inspired by the Cold War, falling back on a previous victory that issued forth from the depths of initial defeat and despair proved reassuring. The ideological confrontation of the Cold War also spurred many commentators to draw on the "obvious" moral lessons that the battle of D-Day offered. The affirmative role of D-Day for American identity issues did not die away with the demise of the Soviet Union. Rather, this role expanded as the Cold War conflict wound down, presenting renewed lessons for Americans in an even less stable world.

Decades after the Allied victory in Normandy, this battle has continued to ripple throughout American society, sometimes arising in odd places. D-Day's cultural resonance would have been neither as persistent nor as forceful if the battle had failed to conform to popular American self-conceptions. Significantly, as Herring wrote, "The American mood at the end of the century was one of triumphalism and smug, insular complacency."[54] The story of D-Day remembrance will shed light on how and why that triumphalist outlook developed.

Henry Luce sought to embolden Americans, to push them to accept global responsibilities in a bid to remake the world into a more "American" place. Americaness, however, could and did mean different things over time to various individuals. As people living through the so-called American Century encountered challenges and obstacles, reliance upon the record of benevolence and gallantry accruing from Second World War sacrifices settled in as a recurrent rhetorical device. This trope served to explain to the outside world why it should defer to the United States. It also acted as instruction for Americans at home on the supposedly proper understanding of what the nation symbolized. Naturally, with such bold intentions, friction, argument, and outright rejection all emerged in a dynamic, iterative process of thinking through the past. Depictions of D-Day in American society influenced and, in turn, evolved alongside this sometimes heated, sometimes low-key, but always interesting process of rethinking that past while living through a continuously changing present.

CHAPTER 1
D-DAY, JUNE 6, 1944

A Presidential Prayer

President Roosevelt came on the radio at 10:00 p.m. Eastern War Time to address the nation as he had done so often before. In this broadcast, he was going to lead Americans in a collective prayer for the fighting men then engaged in a suspenseful battle. After beseeching "Almighty God," Roosevelt focused attention on the tremendous task facing the men as they fought in France. He presented a clear-cut lesson in morality regarding this phase of the war. Roosevelt explained that these peace-loving forces "fight not for the lust of conquest. They fight to end conquest. They fight to liberate."[1] Realizing the enormity of the moment, the administration prereleased copies of the prayer. Congressional representatives in both chambers read the address into the record. Newspapers across the land printed the orison so that people could follow along with the president. One journalist, writing the next day, insisted that the American people had done exactly as intended.[2]

Drawing meaning out of battlefield carnage presented an age-old opportunity for American political leaders. Eighty-one years earlier, in November 1863, Abraham Lincoln recast the purpose of the Civil War in his honorific speech at the commemoration of the Gettysburg battle site. Lincoln used the Gettysburg Address to reaffirm America's national mission as the unique guarantor of freedom in the world.[3] In the 1940s, Franklin Roosevelt readily pointed to wartime achievements. The D-Day prayer, however, also represented a dignified attempt to connect with Americans. With it, Roosevelt would instruct them on the battle's meaning—not only for the war's progress but also as an indicator of what America itself represented. More than four score years after Lincoln spoke at Gettysburg, Roosevelt drew on another major battle to assert that America's unique world mission continued.

Roosevelt's address about what he called the "mighty endeavor" needed to do several things at once. Not only did he have to acknowledge the sacrifices of American combatants, but he also had to soothe their loved ones on the home front. In addition, this prayer presented yet another chance to indicate what the Allies fought for and how they differed from their opponents. Stressing the Allies' intent "to set free a suffering humanity" could serve to honor the soldiers, inspire civilians, reassure those in Nazi-occupied lands, and rhetorically strike once more at the enemy. Interestingly, an earlier draft of the prayer contained a significant difference in the opening lines. That version said America's sons were "set upon a mighty endeavor, a struggle to preserve our Republic and our civilization, and to set free millions of other human beings." In subsequent revisions, "our religion" also materialized as something preserved by force of arms and the concluding words of that first line changed to the more ringing phrase of a "suffering humanity."[4] Religious overtones suffused the final variant of what was, after all, a prayer. The president invoked Almighty God, Father, and the Lord, while instructing Americans to rely on their faith to ease the hard path ahead. When families throughout the United States, such as in the small town of Bedford, Virginia, gathered around the radio to listen to Roosevelt's benediction, this message struck home.[5] The president assured all that American soldiers fought in Normandy for a righteous cause, one that would save their country and world civilization.

From the very day the Allies stormed the Normandy beaches, efforts to ascribe meaning to D-Day arose in a number of forms. Certain characterizations of the battle and its significance proved more durable than others. Roosevelt's enticing emphasis on the moral authority of these forces and their fight for liberation coincided with similar messages. Collectively, this high-toned rhetoric began setting the temper in American collective memory regarding this battle, the larger war, and, indeed, the entire direction of the American Century.

The Second World War

The Second World War was the most destructive self-inflicted catastrophe in human history. Despite the enormity of devastation and worldwide nature of the fighting, it was hardly foreordained or even immediately apparent that the United States would intervene as a belligerent. While wars broke out in Africa, Asia, and Europe in the 1930s, Americans remained far more intent on dealing with the Great Depression than with ensuring international well being. President Franklin D. Roosevelt may have seen the likelihood of American involvement with the 1939 outbreak of war in Eastern Europe, but he faced a difficult task in persuading the populace that this European conflict warranted national participation and the attendant sacrifices. As one Nazi triumph followed upon another, leading to an isolated yet truculent British resistance by mid-1940, Japanese-American relations foundered upon the shoals of mutual mistrust and clashes of interest. The stunning Japanese air raid on Pearl Harbor on December 7, 1941, removed from Roosevelt's hands the problem of convincing the American people to fight. Hitler's declaration of war on the United States four days later made the task even easier.[6]

With the United States formally engaged in war, an intensive program of national mobilization took shape. The first peacetime draft in the form of the Selective Service Act of 1940 had helped push the American military up to roughly 460,000 personnel by the end of that year. Nevertheless, the dilapidated state of equipment, training deficiencies, lackluster officers, and the stunning success of potential opponents worried military planners and the public alike. Much hard work remained to forge a military instrument likely to produce desirable results on the battlefield. Once actively in the war, the military swelled to a massive 12 million persons at its height. The accompanying expansion of industry to equip, sustain, transport, and employ these forces only makes the wartime effort seem all the more awesome in retrospect.[7]

Expanding manpower and production capabilities represent frequently mentioned and celebrated aspects of America's Second World War experience. Even these factors, though, can present their own obfuscations. One apt reminder indicated that "all of the immense weight of matériel produced by the industrial strength of the United States was just so much junk without trained soldiers to operate it and bring it to bear against the enemy, a coherent doctrine for its employment, and leaders who could command the formations into which it was organized."[8] For military success, American leadership had to translate latent resources and productive power into real-world capability. The armed forces and war-related matériel also required competent employment.[9]

With the abrupt entry into war occasioned by the Japanese attack on Pearl Harbor, President Roosevelt and his advisors faced several acute dilemmas. In addition to the obvious need for a rapid expansion of military manpower and equipment, these men also had to consider how best to fight the dual war situation confronting the country across the Atlantic and Pacific Oceans. Roosevelt pledged support for a "Europe first" focus in the event of any outright war just months prior to Pearl Harbor in a face-to-face meeting with England's Winston Churchill. Agreeing to fight Germany first, however, was something the president could contemplate in August 1941 without the tremendous rage and public outcry for retribution that followed the Japanese surprise attack a few months later. As the dual wars developed in the ensuing years, the United States fought far more closely to equivalence in each of the two main theaters. The fact that the United States did not go all out for a "Japan first" strategy stems in large part from Roosevelt's geopolitical views concerning the importance of Europe and from his chief U.S. Army advisors, who argued for a showdown in Europe.[10]

Europe loomed large in the war councils held in the winter of 1941–42. Deciding on the most expeditious way to defeat Germany and its partners, however, produced several sharp disputes. General George C. Marshall, the U.S. Army chief of staff, consistently pushed for a rapid invasion of northwest Europe to defeat the German army as quickly as possible. While this outlook became the preferred army strategy, dissenters bandied about countervailing options. Many in the U.S. Navy pined for a Pacific focus, the U.S. Army Air Forces hoped to demonstrate the war-winning capabilities of airpower, the British longed for an indirect and ostensibly less costly route to victory in Europe, and the Soviets demanded some immediate and direct contribution to the fight to pull pressure off their front. Out of this clamor, political and military leaders of several nations had to forge a workable plan for victory.

The actual course of the war in Europe is a much-repeated tale. The Allies worked out a series of plans over time that encompassed a multipronged effort to secure the Atlantic, take control of the Mediterranean, provision the Soviet juggernaut, build up forces in the West for knockout blows against subsidiary powers like Italy, and then liberate German-occupied lands and finally destroy the Nazi state. While the basic tempo of these developments is now rather straightforward, varying emphases and interpretations have heightened some aspects or obscured other parts of this story. Furthermore, looking back on such a huge, hard-fought, and destructive war more than half a century later, several stark contingencies should draw our attention. The ultimate triumph of the Allies in Europe, and specifically the form of that triumph, carried no automatic guarantee. Even though today we know what did happen, many things were not set in stone in the dismal initial months of America's war experience. Without spending too much space stressing the obvious, suffice it to say here that with the American people calling out for vengeance against the Japanese, the seeming miracle of Midway in June 1942 provided time and opportunity for European operations to commence. That stunning success enabled Marshall and Roosevelt to adhere to the Europe-first provisions of the Atlantic Conference. Nevertheless, the president did diverge from army counsels when he astutely realized that to keep the American people and the powerbrokers in Washington committed to Europe, some sort of action, virtually *any* sort of action, had to take place in that theater as soon as possible.

While Marshall knew that success demanded a direct clash of arms with the key power in Europe, Roosevelt felt that delaying action until the military felt completely ready to conduct such a campaign would pose an unacceptable risk. Further, invading the European mainland required quite a few preliminary developments that had yet to take place in 1942. In addition to winning the battle of the Atlantic to ensure a more secure transport link from America to Europe, the Allies had to soften up Axis defenders while the American military in particular needed to earn its combat stripes.[11] As events would show in North Africa, the U.S. Army suffered personnel, doctrinal, and equipment shortcomings that proved almost criminally deficient when thrust up against the battle-hardened Wehrmacht.

While the Soviets reeled under a series of pummeling blows inflicted by Axis forces along the Eastern Front, the Western Allies struggled to come up with a coherent plan of action. The U.S. Army's official historian of the Normandy invasion, Gordon Harrison, succinctly described the process of seemingly interminable negotiation, preparation, and adjustment as real-world events unfolded in the several years prior to D-Day. Harrison noted the squabbling that divided British and American leaders at first but also pointed to the slow coming together of minds on the feasibility and necessity of this operation as the war continued its grinding course.[12]

Reaching that point, however, required tremendous work. Operation Torch, the invasion of Northern Africa, began on November 8, 1942, and despite several serious setbacks, saw the defeat of German and Italian forces in that region by the following May. The Allies followed up on that success by invading Sicily (Operation Husky, July 10, 1943) and then the Italian peninsula itself (Operation Avalanche, September 3). These actions led to Italy's surrender and subsequent occupation by its former German ally. The Red Army at the same time blunted a major German offensive in the East and responded with a successful counteroffensive around the city of Kursk. In contrast to the tremendous geographic gains made by the Red Army, the Western Allies quickly bogged down in a grueling fight northward through Italy that would last almost another two years. The cross-channel invasion, from the United Kingdom into German-occupied France, only came into being because of these prior developments. With the Atlantic relatively secure and the U-boat offensive beaten, Italy knocked out of the war (and German forces tied down fighting there), the Red Army pushing the Wehrmacht back into Central Europe, and Germany itself subject to around-the-clock aerial bombing, the Western Allies felt the need and opportunity for the vaunted "second front" to open in France.

The rest of the primary story from this point to the end of the war has grown into a staple of popular American renderings of the Second World War over the past few decades. As noted before, despite having a basic outline of events readily available, the focal point of discussion with this war—the war in Europe—tends to narrow down to a few specific moments. The work of the eminent historian Russell F. Weigley serves as an indicator of this selective coverage. Though far from oblivious to what came before, Weigley's well-received narrative of the European war picked up the story with the planning and preparation for the D-Day invasion.[13] It seems that even in the face of the obvious need to acknowledge earlier operations, many historians and storytellers of the war have felt that the "real" fighting began only with the clash of arms in Normandy.

Operation Overlord, the code name for the Normandy invasion, *was,* in fact, an extremely important component in the overall march towards victory. The Allied disputes over the need for the invasion offered a degree of uncertainty and tension even before the killing on the beaches began. An enormous level of difficulty on the day of battle and in the campaign that followed only added to the drama of this operation. One well-reasoned reminder cautioned that "an amphibious operation is the most difficult and complex of military maneuvers. And no amphibious operation was more difficult or complex than the invasion of Normandy on 6 June 1944."[14]

This operation included intricate naval and aerial support plans, far-flung bombardment activities, airborne assaults, and multiple amphibious landings—all this happening far from base areas in the face of an entrenched and experienced enemy. Unlike island hopping in the Pacific, once ashore the Allies had to face the real prospect of losing the race to reinforce any beachhead if the Wehrmacht reacted rapidly enough. To overcome these challenges, Allied forces had to display a tremendous level of ingenuity.

The threat of failure was real, even as the enormity of Allied success in Normandy at times risks post facto miscasting of the outcome as predetermined. German defensive preparations had strengthened what their military planners deemed the most likely invasion route. They focused on the Pas de Calais area of France, which had the shortest distance from England and offered the greatest air coverage for the invading fleet. Privy to German plans, thanks to a series of intelligence successes, the Allies decided to avoid that more accessible and more dangerous landing area. Meanwhile, they added to the likelihood for initial gains by spreading out the defenders through deception operations. Double agents, false signals traffic, fake armies, and deliberately scattered aerial bombing operations all confounded the defense. The Allies, on the other hand, focused their attention on preparing for the inevitably difficult task of landing on hostile shores. The preparatory planning agency, Chief of Staff to the Supreme Allied Command (COSSAC), headed by British lieutenant general Frederick Morgan, selected the location based on an array of factors. Tide tables, beach composition, transportation routes inland, distance from air and sea bases in England, and the German defensive preparations all factored into the choice. Southwest of Calais, Normandy became the optimal site based on these calculations.

Normandy was optimal, but it also was far from an easy landing location. Learning from the disastrous Dieppe experience in 1942, military planners sought to avoid the formidable defenses built up around any major port location. Still, the Normandy area was hardly bereft of defensive features by mid-1944. Hitler had assigned Field Marshal Erwin Rommel as head of Army Group B, under Field Marshal Gerd von Rundstedt's German Army Command in the West (OB West), early in the year. With typical energy, Rommel instituted a program for strengthening existing fortifications, leading to millions of mines, flooded river regions, and a host of nasty surprises for potential invaders throughout France and the Low Countries.[15] By June 1944 the Norman landscape contained a number of what the Germans called defense points (*Wiederstandsnesten*), antitank obstacles, reinforced gun emplacements, and presighted weapons ranging over potential air or seaborne landing sites. Aerial reconnaissance, along with covert fact-finding missions and information provided by the French Resistance, painted an increasingly grim picture for Allied planners.[16] Chances for a successful operation decreased each day that German preparations continued.

With several years of intensive combat operations behind them, however, Allied military officers could face such a daunting task with a reasonable sense of confidence. By the early part of 1944, when the final planning for the invasion came together, the Western Allies had fought in tandem across the globe, with setbacks and fiascos, but also relentlessly wearing away at formidable opponents. Global warfare demanded tremendous industrial output and logistical organization, areas that these countries displayed a great deal of skill in mastering. Not everything was a glowing success story. Production bottlenecks in vital equipment like the Landing Ship Tank (LST) pushed cautious leadership to postpone the original landing date in Normandy from May to June, which acutely displeased Soviet leadership. Yet the underlying point is that Americans, Canadians, British, and even their subordinate partners in this venture *did* produce thousands of naval craft, planes, tanks, motor vehicles, and sufficient food, equipment, and ammunition to equip a multimillion-man force ready to invade and expand inland. For some men, like the members of the U.S. Army's 29th Infantry Division, the training had consumed years of their lives—and many were ready to make their contribution to victory. Others, such as the battle-hardened veterans of the U.S. 1st Infantry Division or the British 50th Division, glumly anticipated the carnage and bloodletting that awaited them in France. All throughout the belligerent countries, people waited, watched for news, and prayed for those they loved to make it through the coming storm.

Depicting the clash as a storm is particularly apt since the one thing all the planning, training, and preparations could not conclusively settle was how nature itself would influence the coming battle. As it turned out, environmental factors intervened in a near-disastrous manner, as discerned in the oft-recounted tale of General Dwight D. Eisenhower's lonely hours in command prior to the invasion. After delaying a month for more shipping, the operation had to start soon to leave sufficient clear-weather months for the follow-up campaign. The weather took a drastic turn for the worse late on June 4, threatening one of the two acceptable windows to launch in that month. Eisenhower had to make the tough choice of starting in a less-than-opportune moment—and risk disaster in an already challenging maneuver—or stalling for a few more weeks while hoping for clear weather. After reconvening for a more up-to-date forecast, Ike's response was simply to go for it, thus setting the sixth of June as D-Day. If Eisenhower had delayed, the next invasion window would open two weeks later. That period witnessed one of the most powerful channel storms of the past century, which surely would have foundered any attempted invasion. More than one commentator noted the incredible fortune, or divine assistance, that pushed Eisenhower to act in early June despite the dire weather.[17]

His go order pushed the vast machinery of invasion into action. Ships milling about filled to the brim with a soaking, miserable cargo of amphibious forces began moving to rendezvous points for the landings to start early that Tuesday morning. The potential for a naval attack or aerial harassment by the Germans ratcheted up tensions. The main dangers that the vast Allied armada faced, however, came from the large number of mines strewn throughout these waters and the dislocation that nighttime operations on such a vast scale threatened. As it turned out, a small squadron of German motor torpedo boats did attack the fleet, sinking the Norwegian destroyer *Svenner* in the process.[18] In the aftermath of the battle, many Allied personnel expressed wonderment that the Germans did not take a proactive defense and try to disrupt seaborne operations more forcefully. Because of ceaseless defensive preparation, their German opponents had whittled away operational strength and possessed few naval or aerial resources available to confront the armada's protection. Those units the Germans had in place were lulled into a false sense of security because of inclement weather in the channel.

The first Allied soldiers to face sustained hostile fire on D-Day were the airborne forces and those that transported them to France. As one historian asserted, "The great invasion started on the wings of the troop carriers."[19] The initial airborne assault employed three specially trained divisions: the British 6th and the U.S. 82nd and 101st. To quote the title of another book on their exploits, these were "the first men in."[20] Aside from the intensity of dropping into battle, behind enemy lines, to face a determined foe with the mere *hope* that your seaborne comrades would make it in to you in time, these divisions had important missions to fulfill in the fleeting hours before the beach landings. The British superbly secured their planned-for objectives shortly after midnight, succeeding in a *coup de main* blow that took control of two important bridges on the eastern flank of the invasion area. Holding onto those bridges, while neutralizing another threatening artillery battery and other targets, produced some confused reactions from the Germans. Local commanders assumed that major landings were occurring even farther to the east. Their misapprehension was minimal, however, compared to the German bewilderment over the American landings in the Cotentin Peninsula. The two American divisions had the difficult task of securing ingress routes from the beaches inland for the westernmost seaborne forces. Unfortunately for them, the lay of the land beckoned an airborne landing, and flooded rivers, deadly anti-landing obstacles, and stout defenders awaited the men as they floated to ground in the dark amid a hail of gunfire. German anti-air activity had been so intense that it, combined with heavy clouds and less than fully trained pilots, led to a huge dispersion of the airborne forces. The unintended benefit came with the confusion as local packets of Germans dealt with smatterings of Americans in their midst. Despite misdrops and deadly opposition, certain key sites like the town of Sainte-Mère-Église and the causeways in from the beaches fell to American control.[21]

Owing to the particulars of tides and coastal conditions, the American beaches (Utah and Omaha) had earlier start times than the three British-Canadian beaches (Gold, Juno, and Sword). The American amphibious forces had a 6:30 a.m. kickoff, whereas their fellow combatants would start an hour later. Preceding the waterlogged men themselves, a furious naval and aerial bombardment of the beach area served to ease the way in for the amphibious units. The battle of D-Day serves as ample proof of the old axiom that the plan never survives contact with the enemy. The breakdown between plan and reality with this initial bombing effort threatened to derail the entire operation. Although the opening arpeggio of fire from huge battlewagons and smaller naval craft of all sizes proved heartening to the amphibious troops as they dutifully headed towards shore, the sad fact is that this storm of shell accomplished little. Coupled with ineffectual aerial bombardment, caused in large part by the cautious bomb-release delay to avoid friendly fire incidents, the defenses remained fairly intact, manned by stunned but still very much active opponents.[22]

Naval support proved important in several different ways, however. First, accompanying ships occupied and distracted German defenders in a series of duels spread across the invasion area. This attention came at a cost, as indicated by Lieutenant (JG) Howard A. Anderson's description of the final minutes on the USS *Corry,* which sank after hitting a mine while maneuvering to avoid battery fire. Anderson helped treat men horribly burned "from swimming in burning oil or . . . scalded by hot steam escaping from ruptured boilers."[23] The second contribution of naval forces came as the meticulous landing schedule broke down in the chaos of battle. When essential tanks and artillery failed to materialize on the beaches, several destroyer skippers ordered their ships in to act as invaluable close-order support for the men on the beaches. Beholding this vital assistance, Major General Leonard Gerow, who commanded the U.S. V Corps assaulting Omaha Beach, exulted, "Thank God for the U.S. Navy!"[24]

The men on the beaches fortunate to remain among the living by that evening certainly had good reason to be in an appreciative mood. A clear indicator of the fighting's intensity comes from the jarring fact that, in the years since the war, the storming of Utah Beach pales in comparison to the far more famous action at Omaha because "only" several hundred men lost their lives for the former strip of sand. The Utah assault force caught a major break when tides and battlefield smoke led it away from the intended landing area—to a section of beach with weaker defenses. Rather quickly, Major General Raymond O. Barton's 4th Infantry Division streamed inland, joined up with airborne forces, and began a slow thrust across the Cotentin Peninsula.[25] Omaha Beach, "Bloody Omaha" as often remembered, presented a more sobering view of the D-Day invasion. In contrast to Utah's low casualty rate and relatively easy advance, Omaha exacted the highest number of losses and demanded the hardest fighting of the five landing beaches. Owing to a recent German redeployment and some deadly defensive fieldworks that took excellent advantage of the concave beach and its high bluffs, the 1st Infantry Division (with attached elements of the 29th) faced a tough day. As Staff Sergeant John J. Moglia of the 16th Infantry, 1st Infantry Division, wrote years later, "It's still hard to believe that we were able [to] fight through it."[26] Moglia and his comrades did fight through the hard shell of German defenses, at the cost of approximately three thousand casualties, and they held on grimly to a small bubble of territory by nightfall.[27] Even though the commander of the invasion's American component, Lieutenant General Omar N. Bradley, briefly considered evacuating the Omaha beachhead at midday, the primary mission of landing—and staying—was a success.

The British, Canadians, and small groups of other nationalities were just as determined, and experienced the same mix of achievement and frustration on D-Day. Running west to east, the three beaches of Gold, Juno, and Sword led to a more densely settled area of the Norman coastline. Blending in with the buildings provided some coverage for the defense while beach obstacles added to Allied difficulties. Of the three British Commonwealth divisions, the Canadian 3rd Division had the roughest landing at Juno, where the early assault looked eerily similar to the near-catastrophe at Omaha. Determined to avenge the humiliation at Dieppe, this force smashed through the German resistance and made notable advances inland before halting that night in the area west of the Norman town of Caen.[28] The British 50th and 3rd Divisions, bracketing the Canadians at Gold and Sword beaches respectively, also made commendable initial gains, but likewise stopped short of their primary objectives. Because of these less-than-anticipated gains, the British and Americans failed to unite Omaha and Gold beaches, leaving a series of isolated landing sites vulnerable to piecemeal destruction by a concerted counterattack. Fortunately, none materialized. One controversy stemmed from the inability to take Caen on the eastern zone of the invasion area. Initial plans called for the city's capture on D-Day. Despite the general Allied failure to reach ambitious objectives along the entire battlefront, this particular lapse produced a great deal of recrimination at the time and since.[29]

Setbacks and backbiting aside, the main issue was decided in favor of the Allies. At the end of the day, roughly 150,000 men stood on French soil ready to continue the fight. In the face of extreme challenges, the Allies had prevailed. Hitler's vaunted Atlantic Wall shattered—quickly in most places—within a few hours in the most staunchly held sectors. With fighting on the Eastern Front soon to be renewed in a major Soviet offensive, the Germans had precious few resources to shift to Normandy. Deception operations continued to tie down significant German forces in other areas, such as Pas de Calais, in the advent of another potential invasion.[30] Nevertheless, D-Day was but one day of hard fighting and the Germans were far from capitulating at night's end. The Normandy campaign that followed exposed a host of problems within the Allied forces as well as the continued fortitude and capability of the Wehrmacht. Despite major interruptions, such as Operation Market Garden in September and the Battle of the Bulge in December, the Allies continued a slow yet unyielding advance into Germany. Though it took almost another year for completion, the Normandy landings ushered in the final stage of the war in Europe. Maybe D-Day was not *the* turning point of the war, as the collective Allies had succeeded in wearing away their foes since 1942. Still, D-Day was certainly *a* turning point, and an important one at that.[31]

Home-Front Perceptions of D-Day

Invasion jitters abounded in the United States well before June 6, 1944. As a result, the American public was primed to react to the earliest indication that fighting had erupted in Normandy. The news of D-Day broke early, too. Shortly after the aerial bombardment and airborne drops began, Berlin radio acknowledged the commencement of some action in France.[32] Nevertheless, a paucity of concrete details would characterize much of the reporting about the battle throughout June 6. Without satellite feeds, cable news, or the Internet to transmit firsthand information, there was little to pass on other than the obvious—the invasion had begun. Despite the dearth of hard material, American radios and printing presses repeatedly presented what little had been released about the fighting in France. At roughly 1:30 a.m. Eastern War Time, the *New York Times* issued an early morning edition with a bold announcement of the landings. By 2:00 that morning, radio announcers added to the clamor. The furor increased with the transmission of an Associated Press recording of Colonel Ernest Dupuy, Eisenhower's press aide, reading a prepared statement.[33] Rather quickly, word spread across the United States that D-Day had arrived.

The abrupt disclosure of this much-anticipated event triggered a cathartic release of pent-up tension. Throughout the country, Americans paid homage in varying ways to the men of their fighting forces. Residents of New York City halted for minor observances, including a two-minute moment of silence before the opening of the Stock Exchange, which then went on to a new high for the year. Work absences were low, while bond sales and blood donations hit tremendous highs. Returning to work, buying a bond, or giving blood all served as ways to feel connected to the war. That night, as the Statue of Liberty lit up for the first time since the institution of the war-enforced blackout, fifty thousand people gathered in Central Park for a prayer. Congress also paused to pray for America's fighting men and then returned to the business of the day. The legislators held hearings to extend the statute of limitations for courts-martial of the American commanders in charge during the Japanese raid on Pearl Harbor. Officials often cancelled or at least postponed sports and leisure activities, although the gambling dens in Reno, Nevada, could only restrain themselves until 6:00 p.m. Movie theaters continued playing films but usually in conjunction with prayer services and bond sales. Some theater managers halted films to announce the invasion and then joined audiences in singing the national anthem. In some theaters, people gathered to listen to Roosevelt reading his prayer. Mayor James Rhodes of Columbus, Ohio, had air-raid sirens blaring across the city to call people to prayer. Philadelphia's mayor, Bernard Samuel, carefully rang the cracked Liberty Bell with a wooden mallet and prayed "for the success and welfare of the men engaged in this mission of freedom."[34]

Most of these displays of support came before Roosevelt's prayer that evening. Even though the prayer would serve as a framing device for people to make sense of D-Day, the themes Roosevelt raised would not have proved so powerful had they eschewed accepted views of the day. The president lent his authority, his insight, and his eloquence to the process of shaping D-Day in the wider public understanding. His interpretation, however, hardly arose in isolation.

General Dwight D. Eisenhower's order of the day, issued before the landings, has surfaced frequently in films, books, and stories devoted to D-Day. Through it, he attempted to impress soldiers soon to engage in battle with the importance of their mission. Eisenhower's words also received wide distribution right away. Someone read them to the aforementioned crowd that gathered in Central Park. In this order, Eisenhower expressed a paradigm that would characterize D-Day, the American involvement in the Second World War, and the man himself for a long time. He called the Allied invasion the "great crusade," a resonant phrase that he would tap into for the title of his 1948 book on the war. Eisenhower used such high-minded adjectives as "liberty-loving," "free," and "noble" to describe the Allied peoples or their wartime purpose.[35]

Surprisingly, perhaps, not everyone on the Allied side was thrilled with Eisenhower's crusade. Lieutenant General Mark Clark, commander of the U.S. Fifth Army in Italy, had pushed his forces to capture Rome, succeeding on June 4. Supposedly, upon hearing of the Normandy landings, he exploded, "The sons-of-bitches. They didn't even let us have the newspaper headlines for the fall of Rome for one day."[36] Newspaper articles of the time make it appear that Clark's rant was right.[37] Two days after the Normandy invasion began, the U.S. Office of War Information (OWI) added to the deflation of Clark's ego. The OWI oversaw distribution of war-related information in the United States. This agency pressured theater owners to display on June 8 a short Frank Capra film portraying the extensive preparations for the cross-channel attack. The newsreel bumped out of the lineup for Capra's film had covered Mark Clark and the liberation of Rome.[38]

Almost immediately upon hearing of the landings, a barrage of laudatory commentary on D-Day blanketed the home front, crowding out other considerations. Clark's self-centered ranting and the more justified feeling of non-appreciation by his soldiers serve as suitable reminders of American society's immediate obsession with the battle in Normandy.[39] Even Earl Browder, then general secretary of the Communist Party USA, bought into the excitement and sent a letter to Eisenhower offering congratulations. After an obligatory reminder to the general of the Red Army's important role in the war, Browder described the Normandy landings as "history's greatest test, which will decide in battle the destiny of our nation and of the world."[40]

Feeding and drawing from this frenzy of interest, the news media set certain points about the invasion more firmly in the public consciousness. Within a week of D-Day, newsreels of the landings honored the American forces in France. The *News of the Day* clip that began playing on Thursday, June 15, opened with a dedication to those men fighting and dying for liberty in northwest Europe. This clip highlighted their "weapons of freedom," and wrapped up by proclaiming, "On their gallantry and their strength our hopes now rest."[41] The newsreel had taken only a week to produce. Yet in that relatively short period, its producers gathered aerial gun camera shots, footage from incoming landing craft, and even captured German film stock to create a stirring visual presentation of the battle.[42] Running throughout the weekend, this newsreel presented images to the public that have remained in circulation ever since. A fast-paced presentation maintained the hype of D-Day's importance. The newsreel's focus on common soldiers from across the country emphasized the democratic ethos of the fighting forces.

Beyond this one news film, a number of programs related to D-Day crowded American airwaves in the ensuing weeks. Journalist George Hicks's radio report, recorded on the USS *Ancon* off Omaha Beach during the invasion, presented an eyewitness account of the battle that aired on the evening of D-Day. The sounds of combat in the background and a sense of immediacy made this, arguably, "the most widely listened-to account of the D-Day landings."[43] Hicks's broadcast conveyed a sense of the action that characterized the first day's fighting.[44] Other radio transmissions that followed in his wake sought to give meaning to those events. Roosevelt's D-Day prayer was but one instance of the president's radio presence. In fact, his thirtieth, and final, fireside chat occurred on June 12. In that radio address, Roosevelt helped open the Fifth War Loan (Bond) Drive. He averred that "the chief interest tonight is centered on the English Channel and on the beaches and farms and the cities of Normandy" but also noted that the war was far from finished. The president reminded his audience that more sacrifice was necessary to complete the global quest for liberty.[45]

The print media reinforced themes linked to the battle that would linger in the public sphere for years to come. War correspondents imparted a basic understanding of the events that composed D-Day and what they meant. Don Whitehead, or "beachhead Don" (so named because of his many amphibious landings), accompanied the troops who stormed Omaha Beach.[46] In dispatches later filed that Whitehead dated between June 5 and 9, he cast the invasion as a major turning point, highlighted the immense logistical effort involved, and recounted tales of heroism on the beaches.[47] Famed author Ernest Hemingway wrote a widely read article on the invasion that appeared in *Collier's* the following month. In it, he told of problems with amphibious tanks, the desperate fighting on shore, and the American grit that overcame every challenge.[48]

Popular reporter Ernie Pyle landed on June 7 to find "bodies, uncollected, still sprawling grotesquely in the sand or half hidden by the high grass beyond the beach." He stood there shocked by the detritus of battle, the carnage filling his eyes, and wondered how the American troops had overcome such fierce resistance. Pyle wanted to tell people at home "what the opening of the second front in this one sector entailed, so that you can know and appreciate and forever be humbly grateful to those both dead and alive who did it for you."[49] In another piece, Pyle focused on the wreckage of the battle strewn about the shore as a way to make real the enormity of what had just happened. Emotionally drained by the costs and consequences of armed conflict, Pyle scornfully noted, "War is so romantic—if you're far away from it."[50]

The impressions journalists conveyed helped people at home understand at least some aspects of the invasion. Several of these radio, film, or print constructions would percolate through succeeding decades. The relatively few still photos of the invasion constitute, perhaps, one of the more resounding early influences on the wider understanding of D-Day. By far the most powerful photos come from the few surviving images taken by combat photographer Robert Capa. A self-deprecating Capa would mock his own fears as he went into the battle. Yet go he did, refusing a safer assignment. Capa felt that in order to capture war with the camera, he had to plunge into the midst of danger (and excitement). Upon landing on Omaha Beach, Capa snapped a series of photos before boarding a craft full of wounded men returning to the channel. Unfortunately, his darkroom assistant back in London exposed the film to excessive heat and destroyed most shots. All of the remaining eleven salvageable shots came out blurred. Still, as one of Capa's biographers astutely put it, "Ironically, the blurring of the surviving images may actually have strengthened their dramatic impact, for it pervades them with an almost tangible sense of urgency and explosive reverberation."[51] The hazy images of men huddled behind beach obstacles, confronting the frightening firepower of the entrenched enemy, encapsulated the high drama of the day.

From the outset of the invasion and in the following weeks, the impact of front-line reporting began setting the framework for D-Day in the public consciousness. President Roosevelt provided high-sounding rhetorical flourishes, but the main points he made reinforced the messages conveyed across the media. A bifurcated focus emerged that acknowledged the high Allied military leadership, particularly Eisenhower, but also emphasized that this was ultimately a soldier's battle. This split focus helps corroborate the concept of a democratization of American memory.[52] Stressing the collective achievements of common men, bonded together in the face of enormous difficulties, presented a way to celebrate supposed American values. This celebration stood out even more clearly when pitted against the authoritarian system of the Nazi regime. These early depictions of the battle, then, cast Americans and their allies as the heroes in a divinely sanctioned quest to liberate the oppressed.

Veterans of the battle also validated certain elements of this developing picture. As long as the war raged, they obviously had less freedom to communicate with friends and family. Nevertheless, letters from the front reached loved ones, reporters recorded soldiers' experiences and opinions in countless articles, and precious few visits home all acted as opportunities to talk about D-Day. Robert Huch's efforts to convey his experience back to family required several letters. Lieutenant Huch served as an assault section leader on D-Day from E Company, 16th Infantry, 1st Infantry Division. His unit landed on the eastern end of the section of Omaha Beach labeled Easy Red, almost directly in front of a major German defensive position. The three letters Huch penned between June 12 and 26 repeatedly invoked divine favor as an explanation for his survival. At one point, he exclaimed, "I'm convinced that I'm one of the most *luckiest* persons around." A sure sense of duty, even with "people dying all over the place—the wounded unable to move and being drowned by the incoming tide," suffused his letters home as well. Pride in the men who accomplished so much despite unremitting fire, deadly obstacles, and confused landings also surfaced in Huch's letters.[53] Huch's writing reinforced themes bandied about in the various news accounts of the battle.

A sharp eye can discern a small but important distinction emerging at this early point. As with all wars, things appear differently depending upon the observer's position. War correspondents and servicemen described the battle in articles, letters, and diary entries. They mentioned the tremendous difficulties confronting them, pride in a job well done, and regret that a necessary task cost so much. What is missing from these renderings emerges when looking at news stories or pronouncements that originated stateside. Few actual participants in the day's events, at this stage, tried matching the grandiloquent statements made by the *Atlanta Daily World,* whose editorial writers called D-Day "a last gamble for LIBERTY AND JUSTICE ON THIS EARTH!"[54] The men who fought in Normandy were too tired, too busy, and often too jaded to characterize the battle in such hyperbolic terms. Fatigued GIs celebrated their success, but moved on with the larger task at hand: winning the war and coming home alive.

The Sound of Silence? Fading into the (Immediate) Past

Even as those D-Day participants still able to stand on June 7 redirected their energy towards winning the war in Europe, the fanfare that attended D-Day soon subsided at home. If the public arena operates as a marketplace, with competing items jockeying for finite attention, then this turn away from the "last gamble for liberty and justice" made sense. Silences or gaps in historical memory often emerge over time.[55] This silencing does not even have to be an intentional process.

Despite the florid rhetoric in the initial burst of enthusiasm, the war did not end on June 6, 1944. As Bob Sales, a D-Day veteran, remarked years later, "D-Day was the longest day, there's no doubt about that . . . but for those who survived, it was just one day. I had a hundred and eighty to go."[56] D-Day, although of crucial importance, was still just the beginning of a new phase in the European war. Enlisted man Bruce Bliven came ashore the day after the initial assault. Bliven served with the 111th Artillery Battalion, attached to the 29th Infantry Division. Even one day later, he noted, "No one was talking about D-Day. That was history."[57] It would require a bitterly contested and tremendously painful eleven additional months to wrap up the conflict in Europe. The Normandy campaign alone, running from June through the end of August, produced roughly 225,000 casualties for the Allies. Even as a battered Third Reich tottered on the precipice of destruction in April 1945, American losses amounted to 10,677 that month. The ghastly toll prompted sharp analysts of the war to observe, "The simple truth was that the real German collapse did not come until the last week of April. As long as the Germans had guns and ammunition, they died for the Führer."[58] Thus, in the United States, paeans to an important battle rapidly fell to the wayside as the war continued its relentless course. Roosevelt's fight for liberty and Eisenhower's crusade began to wear a little thin as the contest against a stubborn foe racked up mounting casualties.

General Eisenhower issued an order of the day in 1945 in preparation for the anniversary of D-Day. This order acknowledged the significance of the battle but also sought to avoid any ostentatious displays. Even though the war had recently ended in Europe with Germany's surrender on May 8, fighting continued in the Pacific. Eisenhower appropriately decreed subdued anniversary observances. "Formal ceremonies will be avoided, but insofar as is consistent with the performance of essential duties, June 6 will be observed as a holiday by the Allied Expeditionary Forces."[59] Celebrations also remained somewhat muted outside of Europe, as demonstrated by the small Virginia town that had nineteen of its sons killed on D-Day. As Alex Kershaw explained, "The [first] anniversary passed quietly in Bedford. There were no special services. America was still at war with Japan and hundreds of Bedford County's sons were still fighting in the Pacific."[60] The pain was still too fresh for those who had lost someone, the battle against Japan wore on, and needs of the moment eclipsed thoughts of anniversary celebrations.

A year after D-Day, journalist Don Whitehead returned to Normandy. He informed his readers, "Time and the endless tides mercifully have wiped out most of the signs of death and destruction along this invasion beach hallowed by the deaths of so many American youths." Consequently, Whitehead felt "a curious sense of unreality to the scene for anyone who remembered that D-Day carnage." Yet he quickly pointed out that although the war had long since left the area, French civilians still remembered their liberation.[61]

For the French residents of the area, "liberation came . . . in a storm of destruction and death."[62] The fact that the fighting occurred in their homeland perforce led to a greater degree of engagement with the battle. French locals in Normandy made efforts to commemorate D-Day.[63] These actions accorded with the intentions of some American veterans' groups and various government organizations. Yet most Americans, far removed from the European battle zone, did not have the same sense of intimate familiarity with D-Day. They, instead, turned away from the battle. Michael Kammen insisted that "we increasingly tend to measure how we are doing (in terms of collective knowledge) by how well we commemorate anniversaries."[64] His point indicates that during good times, people have the luxury and inclination to celebrate events from the past. The relative absence of major D-Day commemorative activities in this period showed this dictum in operation. With challenges abounding in virtually every facet of life and the pain of the war still so fresh, extolling the heroism of soldiers on one single day failed to carry much allure.

With victory achieved in 1945, Americans seemed eager to embrace a well-earned peace. As with all major wars, hard times did not end with the fighting. The son of one veteran explained, "As many veterans would quickly discover, the last daunting challenge of the war, for those fortunate enough to survive it, was coming home."[65] Veterans of even the "good war" faced the challenging task of transitioning back to civilian society. This required a herculean effort. Beyond the veterans and the families of the more than 400,000 Americans who died in the war years, society also confronted a host of strains in the postwar period. Insufficient clothing, lack of housing, fears of a new depression, concern over returning veterans (or "trained killers" as sometimes labeled), and the whole array of everyday-life matters demanded attention. Such affairs directed people away from remembering the war recently won.[66]

In mainstream society, then, D-Day experienced a rapid flux. In the months prior to the assault, many anticipated it as a decisive battle, a coming turning point in the war. On June 6, 1944, D-Day stood as the day of days, a shining example of American and, to a lesser degree, Allied military capability applied to a moral purpose. This focus lasted for a few weeks as additional news filtered in, revealing the severity of the battle. Nevertheless, as a grueling conflict continued on its course, D-Day quickly became just another day in a long and hotly contested struggle. By the end of the war, the battle increasingly seemed part of the *past*. It came from a period that was important but not of immediate relevance because of new challenges.

CHAPTER 2
TO MOURN OR CELEBRATE?
D-DAY IN A POSTWAR MOMENT

Bedford as a National Metaphor?

Following the conclusion of the Second World War, there were small-scale, local-community efforts to memorialize D-Day in the United States. Staged in locations such as Bedford, Virginia, these early commemorations would not resonate with much force throughout American society. In a period that witnessed the return of soldiers' bodies from overseas, public attention fixed on the losses and anguish of war. The resultant somber mood dampened feelings of success as individuals coped with the pain of lives torn apart by the Second World War. Nevertheless, the hesitant embrace of victory in mainstream society during these early postwar years proffered some sense of meaning for these losses. The mixture of personal suffering and the celebration of national success set the path for a later explosion in D-Day memorialization that eventually reverberated throughout the country. This process developed in the initial stages of the Cold War. The avowed morality of the Allied cause in the Second World War, especially when connected to the purported liberating intent of D-Day, served to legitimize American actions in this new confrontation. Likewise, fear of far more devastating losses in any new clash shaped public reactions to the series of crises that characterized this era.

Even though national attention turned elsewhere, local communities were left to confront the holes wartime losses had torn through their social fabric. Great Depression–related penury and a local martial tradition motivated Bedford residents, such as brothers Ray and Roy Stevens, to join the National

Guard before the war. With the outbreak of hostilities came mobilization and unit reconfigurations. The 29th Infantry Division consisted mainly of National Guard forces mobilized from Virginia and Maryland. Many Bedford men—including Ray and Roy—had ended up in A Company, 116th Infantry, which assaulted Omaha Beach in the initial waves on D-Day.[1] The company landed on the far western end of the beach. Isolated from other units by general confusion, A Company faced a formidable German strong point with no other American targets in view. Nearly 100 of the company's 155 men who struggled shoreward died in mere minutes, 19 of them from Bedford County. Roy Stevens survived most likely because his landing craft hit a mine, which left the waterlogged men stranded until picked up and returned to England by a passing vessel. Ray was not so fortunate; he died on the beaches that day.[2]

Bedford residents did not immediately commemorate the battle that claimed so many of their neighbors or loved ones. People instead dwelt on their own private grief, which began hitting home one day in July 1944 with a deluge of War Department telegrams notifying families of the dead. As one description of these events poignantly noted, "All across Bedford County, joy died that summer." By the first anniversary, little enthusiasm had materialized for any public monument to commemorate the losses of D-Day.[3]

Within a few years, individuals like D-Day veteran Lieutenant Elisha "Ray" Nance pushed for a commemorative display. The impetus to mark the community's link to D-Day gained strength over the following years as the bodies of those killed returned home for burial. Because of the violent chaos that defined the Normandy campaign, graves registration personnel took several years after the war to locate, identify, and then dispose of what American remains they could find. Official U.S. policy permitted next of kin to decide on final resting grounds for their loved ones. Either the body remained with fellow soldiers in American cemeteries abroad or returned for burial in the United States. Initially, almost 95 percent of respondents sought the body's return home, with the final number by the next decade settling near 70 percent.[4] Brief ceremonies accompanied these returns in Bedford, yet Nance in particular felt dissatisfied with the lack of a permanent marker dedicated to the war dead.

By the end of the decade, Bedford township officials opted to install a plaque at the courthouse that listed the names of all local residents killed in either World War.[5] On May 30, 1949, Memorial Day, approximately two hundred citizens of Bedford dedicated a $500 plaque bearing 174 names of men killed in both wars. As one scholar described the scene, "Lucille Hoback Boggess, a Bedford resident who lost two brothers on D-Day, unveiled the plaque." Fittingly, the late May dedication occurred in time for D-Day's fifth anniversary the following week.[6]

In Bedford, where so many losses hammered a small community, commemorative activity centered on D-Day remained rather muted. Instead of highlighting the local connection to D-Day, residents at first focused on private mourning, often leaning on religion for support. Some people censured Eisenhower or Roosevelt, blaming them for the deaths. Only later did the community turn to public commemorations as a way to deal with the hole left by those killed in France.[7] Significantly, D-Day did not stand out from the two overall World Wars in these activities. The 1949 plaque mourned the loss of men in a variety of battles over a thirty-year period. Bedford residents, in an area devastated by the losses from one day of combat, proved reluctant to commemorate D-Day. At the national level, where D-Day's impact was far more diffuse, even less of an impulse to memorialize the battle emerged.

Popular consciousness is, however, a malleable phenomenon. D-Day impressed Americans as a major turning point in an important war. Although popular attention shifted to other pressing matters in the period following the assault landings, some people worked to keep the meaning of the day's events alive. Naturally, those involved in the actual operation formed one group of D-Day memory activists. Government officials, concerned citizens, and even a growing body of scholars and media personalities all played a role in these early years. These individuals, as demonstrated below, imprinted certain themes onto D-Day, many of which had already surfaced in the initial stories and pronouncements pertaining to the battle. While some themes received affirmation, other aspects of the day fell to the wayside. As the late 1940s turned into the early 1950s, D-Day appeared with increasing frequency in a variety of settings as an exemplar of selected American values. Like water heating to boil, a mention of the battle here and a ceremony there all bubbled up until the mixture burst over in the next decade.

Even as mainstream society moved on to other concerns, D-Day did not completely disappear from the cultural landscape. To be sure, the major news media still fitfully honed in on D-Day topics throughout the initial postwar years.[8] Eisenhower, for his part, began paying "tribute to the American fighting man," whose efforts on D-Day in particular determined "the future of the free world," as the general stated in one 1946 address.[9] Different forms of remembering the battle cropped up across the United States. Although less prevalent than today, D-Day still commanded a certain presence in American society. What D-Day *meant,* however, was still somewhat mutable at this point. Did it stand for something more than just another clash of arms? Was it merely a battle, or *the* battle in Europe? Certain individuals and groups began staking out firm positions on these questions for public consideration.

Honoring Those Lost: D-Day in the Late 1940s

The postwar period saw the rise of more concerted efforts by the federal government to shape public memories of the past.[10] Bedford residents understandably focused on their personal experiences or losses on D-Day. Their local take on the battle did not shape national perceptions of D-Day—yet. Instead, federal entities such as the American Battle Monuments Commission (ABMC) sought to influence national views by overseeing the commemorative interpretation of Second World War battle sites. The commission, formed after the First World War, held federal authority for maintaining American overseas battle sites and cemeteries.[11] The ABMC determined the commemorative display on battlegrounds ceded to American oversight by European governments. Once France granted control over parts of the battle zone, the commission's interpretations of artistic merit and its desire to avoid cluttering up sacred space influenced commemorative activities in Normandy. The ABMC, however, did not exercise inceptive memorial control over the D-Day landscape.

The U.S. Army's graves registration units held early de facto commemorative authority over the Normandy battle sites. These units began their grim task in Normandy on June 6, 1944, and they erected a temporary cemetery for the Omaha Beach area two days later. Owing to the enormity of the fighting on D-Day and the weeks that followed, many bodies remained scattered throughout the region. William Siebert, an enlisted man with one graves unit, landed on Omaha Beach on July 3. In the subsequent days of frenetic activity, Siebert found himself hard pressed "to accept that much death."[12] In the months and years that followed, the arduous task of collecting, identifying, and reinterring and/or repatriating these bodies demanded a great deal of work. That task continued even as the pressing need for European rebuilding competed for scarce material and labor resources. To simplify matters, grave-detail units consolidated cemetery locations while minimizing ornamentation. In fact, it took until December 1945 for the American Graves Registration Command (AGRC) to decide upon the exact location for the Normandy American Cemetery. The current St. Laurent site of the cemetery did not appear, incidentally, on the original list of priority cemetery sites in Europe.[13] Selecting St. Laurent proved a genuine boon in the long term as its proximity to "Bloody Omaha" makes a powerful impression on visitors.

A process of honoring the dead took place in Normandy. It began with the AGRC's erection of temporary cemeteries, followed by the acquisition of permanent resting places for the dead. Identifying those buried in the hectic aftermath of combat consumed a great deal of time, as did disinterring and repatriating those whose next of kin wanted the bodies to be returned home. Consolidation, dedication, construction, and opening ceremonies for the Normandy American Cemetery spanned more than a decade. Unlike the post-First World War period, the U.S. government now pushed families to leave the bodies of their loved ones abroad. Historian Kurt Piehler explained why: "The overseas cemeteries served to symbolize U.S. global military commitments undertaken after 1945. The army, by placing most of the cemeteries in Europe, indicated that it wished to have even greater ties with the Continent."[14] Twelve of the fourteen Second World War cemeteries constructed abroad stood in Europe.[15] Choosing where to deposit American war dead and where to honor their sacrifice acquired political significance. Americans alive and dead remained in Europe to show a commitment to defend freedom there.[16]

An important transfer of power occurred when the AGRC, a military command, handed over responsibility for the cemeteries to the ABMC, a public organization led by presidential appointees.[17] The ABMC significantly influenced subsequent views of D-Day. Control over the sacred space shaped wider views of the battle. The ABMC oversaw the creation of monuments, the selection of inscriptions, and the conduct of ceremonies held on sites in the Normandy region. With all these activities, honoring the soldiers, extolling their liberating intent, and mourning their sacrifice formed repeated themes. The liberation paradigm stressed in the commission's works tied to

Normandy gave meaning to the losses while it likewise burnished America's credentials as a beneficent world power.

While still undergoing reinterments and construction, in fact, the Normandy American Cemetery became a site of symbolic activity. On Memorial Day in 1946, ceremonies held at the cemetery drew a small contingent of Americans and up to thirty-two thousand French people. As reported by one member of the AGRC, several speeches honored the liberation of France and stressed the glory earned by Americans fighting for others in a civilization-saving effort.[18] By the following year, regular tours came to the area by the busload. These excursions brought French people as well as Americans, the latter often including military personnel stationed in Europe. These visitors usually walked the Omaha Beach area and examined the still-forming cemetery.[19] The year 1947 also saw several large events at the cemetery site, including a benediction ceremony on September 14 that marked the final interment in front of an estimated crowd of five thousand French and American people.[20]

The ABMC sought to provide ready answers as to what D-Day meant in the monuments it erected and the design of the Normandy American Cemetery. The commissioners, such as the secretary, Brigadier General Thomas North, began setting the scope of official and public memories connected to these battles and the overall war. One of the inscriptions prominently displayed at the Normandy American Cemetery set the tone for remembering D-Day: "This embattled shore, portal of liberation, is forever hallowed by the ideals, the valor and the sacrifice of our fellow countrymen." Highlighting the "hallowed" grounds and the "valor" of the soldiers and honoring their "sacrifice" echoed the language enshrined at other ABMC sites in Europe. The difference here, however, related to the unique function of the Normandy area as the "portal of liberation." D-Day often gained traction in American public conversations as the start of the end in a just war. The ABMC, as North wrote, sought not only to instill reverence in Americans but also to impress "upon alien people . . . the sacrifices made by Americans."[21]

In the process, the Omaha Beach area became the focal point of official commemoration for D-Day. Omaha saw the bloodiest fighting and thus offered an obvious stage for commemorative efforts. As one of the architects involved in the construction programs explained, "Here, on this cliff, overlooking . . . the scene of heroic conflict on the beaches, lies the American Military Cemetery."[22] Harbeson, Hough, Livingston and Larson Architects secured the primary contract for the cemetery; depicting D-Day as a heroic battle for freedom met with ABMC approval. The payment made for the cause seemed greater when fixating on the compact and deadly Omaha area in lieu of other sectors of the day's assault. The inscriptions and public activities held at the cemetery reminded all that *here* common Americans died as heroes.

As noted by other scholars, the twentieth century witnessed a widespread democratization of memory, specifically military memory and the focus on wartime losses.[23] Remembrance activities in Normandy, however, concentrated particularly on *American* stories when commemorating what was an international event. All nations mourn their own losses first, which is understandable. The point here moves beyond a postwar focus on those lost in strife. Rather, presentations like the ABMC inscriptions attribute a specific meaning to this loss, and that meaning stemmed from the repeated mantra of liberation. These men died so that others could live in freedom.

There were those, however, who were far from content to let the ABMC solely dictate the shape of D-Day commemoration in the area. Throughout the years, the correspondence of the commission's secretary bore witness to the power struggles that raged between this and other groups with alternate commemorative ideas. In an early postwar meeting, one commissioner insisted that "the Commission's primary responsibility at this time was to see that unauthorized monuments and memorials were not erected by various organizations." Brigadier General North heartily concurred, and he would maintain that outlook while serving as the commission's secretary over the next two decades.[24] The impetus for these words came from groups other than the ABMC, particularly those representing veterans, as they attempted to commemorate Second World War battles. The ABMC blocked proposed plans by members of the 90th Infantry Division to erect a monument in its honor in the region. The commissioners also tried, less successfully, to prevent the creation of a marker recognizing the 1st Infantry Division's role on D-Day. The Society of the First Division asserted its prerogative as keeper of the flame for the division's memory. Well organized and possessing a decent budget, the society had the resources and determination to buy a plot of land and finance its monument. The ABMC could do little to halt this juggernaut.[25] The marker, a column listing the name of each 1st Infantry Division man killed in Normandy, still overlooks Omaha Beach.

These struggles to define a suitable commemorative approach in the Normandy region showed that D-Day remained an event of concern to some government officials or veterans of the battle. Yet these occurrences took place far removed from the United States and the forefront of American public consciousness. The disputed construction of a monument, for instance, vexed active and veteran members of units that had fought at D-Day. The letters and conferences that resolved the resulting contretemps did not air in public venues. Members of the 1st Infantry Division asserted their right to commemorate the battle in which they had fought while also noting that their monument conformed to ABMC strictures of solemnity and unobtrusiveness. These arguments persuaded the ABMC to relent in the face of a fait accompli. Nevertheless, commemorative activities overseas did not draw a great deal of public attention at this time. People disconnected from events taking place so far away. Americans remained untroubled by the rather benign interpretations of the battle either group offered in Normandy.

As an example of more accessible treatments of D-Day and its meaning, some books, films, and speeches emerged in this period. These works, although relatively sparse, served as early promoters of the battle's importance. Common themes also appeared among them concerning the moral implications of this battle. For instance, famed war photographer Robert Capa, whose grainy pictures still usually accompany any treatment of the battle, released his book, *Slightly Out of Focus,* in 1947. Capa recounted how he had bested his own fears on D-Day, went in with the initial waves of troops, took his pictures amid horrendous confusion, and then returned to England for the problematic film development.[26] Far more prominent, however, stood books authored by combatants. At this time, the major books on the war came from the "great men," namely senior Allied military leaders. Eisenhower's *Crusade in Europe* came out in 1948. In that work, Eisenhower framed the invasion as the kickoff to a great crusade for civilization. The religious allusion stuck to the battle during the war and ever since. Through its use, Eisenhower here drew on popular understandings of their country's place in the war, while also strengthening such convictions. He reassured readers that "because only by the utter destruction of the Axis was a decent world possible, the war became for me a crusade."[27]

The American public, however, preferred to engage with history by watching films rather than reading books. Rather significantly, D-Day figured in the movies even in the initial post-battle period. As pointed out earlier, newsreels circulated a week after D-Day showing some of the frenetic combat action. Many of the shots featured in these productions became stock footage for later works. *News of the Day* newsreel stories covering the battle did appear in the years after, presenting more detail on the planning, conduct, and aftermath of D-Day.[28]

Going beyond news pieces, *The True Glory* (1945) formed one of the last theater-specific documentaries before the dominance of television.[29] The script that Paddy Chayefsky coauthored for this joint British and American production touted the themes of Allied cooperation in a momentous undertaking—one that was both just and necessary. *The True Glory* opened with Eisenhower dedicating the film to the "really important men of this campaign," the junior ranks who, as the narrator explained, fought for freedom and civilization. On screen, the black-and-white film mixed Allied and German stock along with reenacted scenes, making it one of the first documentaries to use such a technique. Its depiction of frantic combat on D-Day contrasted sharply with flashes to placid London. These peaceful scenes drove home what the Allied troops were fighting to protect. Rousing music accompanied the action, with breaks in the score allowing veterans speaking off-camera to interject their thoughts. The twenty-four minutes directed towards D-Day was enough to drill home the major points regarding the battle. D-Day was the beginning of the end of the war, it was a hard-fought battle, and the sacrifices made on June 6 represented the noblest qualities of Western civilization. The film closed with shots from German concentration camps that reaffirmed the moral superiority of the Allied cause. *The True Glory* captured the sense of moral justification, world-saving significance, and celebration of the common man that began appearing as standardized themes linked to D-Day.[30]

The True Glory came together as a wartime project, a piece of propaganda and reassurance. Yet many of its points concerning D-Day were echoed in postwar productions. After a brief hiatus of several years, other documentaries appeared in the late 1940s and early 1950s. The twenty-six-episode *Crusade in Europe,* based on Eisenhower's book, aired on television in 1949. The episode covering D-Day focused much attention on Eisenhower's role in the period prior to the invasion. The fickle weather and its potentially abortive impact on the invasion also stood out as a major point of emphasis. The fourteen minutes devoted to combat action on D-Day split coverage among various units—all with dubbed-over sounds of gunfire contributing a sense of excitement. The brief treatment of D-Day itself, which zeroed in on Omaha Beach and the fighting to secure it, ended by avowing that there, "our victory in World War II hung in the balance."[31] In the year that witnessed the Soviet testing of an atomic bomb and the "fall" of China to Communism, this tale of recent martial success shaded with moral overtones reassured Americans that their military could protect them against aggressors.

These documentaries set the tone for later educational and entertainment pieces that covered D-Day. Recycled film stock began circulating through these pieces since there was only so much relevant footage available. All these early documentaries also firmed up certain stylistic conventions. They offered intense action and, therefore, focused on the activities of those in the most dangerous roles. Airborne and amphibious units figured most prominently, and the naval and aerial units less so. These productions also tended to feature the Allied component of the fight less notably in their story lines. D-Day became an increasingly American event. Throughout such filmic treatments, the morality of the cause, the nobility of sacrifices, and the common bravery of the American fighting men remained conspicuous.

These themes also appeared in early Hollywood films devoted to D-Day. As discussed earlier, Americans turned to face a challenging postwar period with an uncertain economy and new global threats. The result, as several film scholars have argued, was that mainstream movies avoided the Second World War as subject matter for a brief period. It took until the end of the 1940s, with the success of *The Sands of Iwo Jima,* starring John Wayne, and that of several other major films, to revive Hollywood's fixation with the Second World War.[32]

Right in the middle of the war's artistic resurrection came one film that depicted aerial combat in the European Theater, including that on D-Day. The 1948 movie, *Fighter Squadron,* was not a blockbuster success. In fact, with campy jokes and strained dialogue, little of substance emerges in the film. In a melodrama with errant flyboys fighting the Germans in the skies and cowardly, inept leadership manning desks on base, the real focus remains on the machines themselves. The outcome on D-Day seemingly depended entirely upon the efforts of flying knights jocularly facing the worst the enemy threw at them.[33]

Aside from documentaries and films of varying quality, exultant victory parades, speeches, and ceremonies paid public tribute to D-Day.[34] With these activities, the linkage of D-Day to the preservation of freedom stood reaffirmed. On the anniversary of D-Day in 1945, to cite but one example, a journalist who heard Omar Bradley speaking to the graduating class at West Point wrote, "It was not an Army, nor a Navy, that sailed, but a nation. He said that the ships were filled with the achievements and hopes of the American people."[35] The entire country could bask in such honor.

A handful of books, filmic depictions, and public speeches that mention D-Day hardly seem the stuff of silence. Yet individuals like Bradley or Eisenhower would refer to D-Day, particularly on anniversary dates, and then move quickly to a more generalized discussion of the war. This happened in the following years as these two generals and former top Allied commanders suddenly faced new, demanding situations. Eisenhower could linger over D-Day, but he had pressing duties awaiting him first as army chief of staff, then as president of Columbia University, and then as supreme commander of NATO forces in Europe. Bradley rapidly fell into dealing with the needs of millions of former warriors as head of the Veterans Administration. Problems did not go away, and as the United States and the Soviet Union faced off against each other, urgent demands pulled attention away from one battle in a past war. D-Day still popped up in conversations, speeches, and ceremonies as the Cold War unfolded. The battle stood as a symbol of alliance unity and potency, even in the face of the grave challenges now facing Western Allies. Nevertheless, with new global threats stemming from the unleashed destructive power of the atom, D-Day faded from public focus.

A Korean Surprise

The fluctuating degree of public attention accorded to D-Day over the past seventy years experienced several notable turns in direction. Americans shifted their perceptions of D-Day in part because of wars that followed the Second World War. That influence makes sense since, as Michael Kammen wrote, "wars have played a fundamental role in stimulating, defining, justifying, periodizing, and eventually filtering American memories and traditions."[36] Several conflicts in particular stand out in the story of American D-Day remembrance, and the first important one in this regard is the Korean War. Without delving into the historical debates over the genesis of the Cold War, here it suffices to say that the Korean conflict made the danger of this new world ever more apparent to the average American. Atomic fear now combined with the dread of land wars across the globe—wars fought with great ferocity but offering little in meaningful result.

With the outbreak of a new war through a jolting surprise attack on June 25, 1950, the federal government attempted, noted Kurt Piehler, "to emphasize the continuity between World War II and Korea."[37] This ploy sought to legitimize a confusing struggle in a strange land. Mainstream American opinion perceived the Second World War as a justified conflict that indicated American strengths. Unintentionally, this linkage ended up shunting Korea into a nether region of public memory, as the eventual "Forgotten War," because of its less decisive outcome.[38] The Korean War often stood the lesser when compared to the Second World War and, as a result, fell rapidly from the public consciousness.[39] Interestingly, D-Day gained newfound relevance in American commemorative practice because of this new war.

The one phase of the Korean War that most resembled D-Day was the amphibious landings at Inchon in September 1950. Inchon constituted a bold operational stroke. General Douglas MacArthur landed his X Corps behind the North Korean main battle line to drive the invaders from South Korea and, hopefully, end the war. Reversing the humiliating course of the war over the preceding three months, Inchon seemed to turn the tide in Korea. One reporter, in fact, compared the Second World War's amphibious operations, including that of D-Day, with Inchon. The author of this *New York Times* article drew upon D-Day as a widely recognized component of the former war.[40] When hearing of MacArthur's invasion plans, U.S. Army Chief of Staff and D-Day VII Corps commander James Lawton Collins exclaimed to the briefing officer, "This is D-Day isn't it, Colonel?"[41] Using analogies to the previous conflict, however, threatened to cast Korea in a less gloried light. D-Day helped lead to the end of the Second World War. Inchon did not turn out to be decisive. Instead, it ushered in an entirely new and more deadly phase of fighting that only ended in stalemate over two and a half years later.

By the early 1950s, D-Day acquired added importance in American society. This development accompanied a renewal of attention for the Second World War as a whole. For a brief period following 1945, as Americans faced the fear of atomic devastation, the war seemed to fade in importance. With the return of conventional combat in Korea, however, the Second World War once again beckoned as an event offering practical lessons for a major current concern. As before, discussions of that complex event boiled down to a few key moments or themes. D-Day reemerged as a seminal moment in the American war experience, serving as an example of American martial prowess, which held obvious significance in a war setting. The event's moral implications loomed larger as America's resolve to wage the intensifying Cold War depended in great part on public opinion. The D-Day paradigm that identified Americans as liberators stood in stark contrast to the continued Soviet occupation of foreign lands.

As America sank into a new conventional war across the Korean Peninsula, stories of success in the large-scale combat of D-Day offered lessons and reassurance.[42] Members of the U.S. military had struggled since the dropping of the atomic bombs in 1945 to determine the future course of warfare. While the threat of atomic war pushed major reorganizations in the nation's military apparatus, indeed throughout the entire society, there were many people arguing that old staples of warfare had not faded into obscurity.[43] One D-Day veteran wrote an argumentative piece in 1950 insisting that land combat was still the key determinant in wars. Derrill M. Daniel, a lieutenant colonel at the time, had led the 2nd Battalion, 26th Infantry Regiment, 1st Infantry Division, on D-Day. He would soon test out his assertions in Korea.[44] The institutional memory of the armed forces fed into larger collective memories as America turned to a new war.

The desire to draw on D-Day for lessons and reassurance transcended the military and captured popular attention. As before, several key books came out during the Korean War that offered interesting commentary on D-Day. Omar Bradley released *A Soldier's Story* in 1951. Bradley's work differed from Eisenhower's earlier depiction of the Normandy invasion in one major way. Although *Crusade in Europe* pointed out, repeatedly, the British reluctance to embrace the cross-channel invasion, Bradley went a step farther in critiquing British strategy, capabilities, and especially military leaders. *A Soldier's Story* fueled the growing controversy between the British and Americans, especially because of heated recriminations over mistakes made in the battle.[45] Furthermore, Bradley emphasized American actions, plans, and desire to best the Germans face-to-face, all the while, naturally, focusing on his own role in what transpired. Following Bradley's lead, Americans increasingly Americanized D-Day as an event. As the United States assumed leadership in the fight against Communism, stressing its primacy in the earlier conflict fit into a narrative of America's premier role in world affairs.

The same year that Bradley's self-promoting book appeared, the U.S. Army released its official history of the Normandy invasion, *Cross-Channel Attack*. The author, Harvard-trained historian Gordon Harrison, captured the prevailing sense of grandiosity by noting that Operation Overlord "was the supreme effort of the Western Allies in Europe—the consummation of the grand design to defeat Germany by striking directly at the heart of Hitler's Reich." After describing the planning and preparatory period, Harrison's narrative papered over the difficulties caused by ineffective bombing, airborne misdrops, and even the baleful impact of confusion in battle that tore apart the overly constrictive landing schemes. In the overall assessment, Harrison argued that "the success achieved by Allied combined arms outstripped the plan." Despite praising the plan, he acknowledged that the actions and initiative of junior-ranking men produced the gains, as they adapted to extreme challenges.[46]

For an official history, Harrison's battle narrative is engaging. As a testament to this book's strengths and widespread influence, one can still find it in popular bookstores to this day. *Cross-Channel Attack* serves as an early indicator concerning the role of the historian in collective remembrance. Harrison did not necessarily identify public remembrance activities as his primary target. He sought to capture the U.S. Army's official understanding of the battle while also distilling lessons for the future. In the process, however, Harrison transcended dry "history" and instead entered into the public sphere by dint of his accessible narrative. As one commentator averred, "The public historian . . . is someone who writes compelling tales, communicating effectively through their personal style and clarity of expression."[47] Approachability meant a wider audience and ensured the longevity of this particular work. As a result, Harrison's characterizations of D-Day and its meaning influenced many at the time and since. He emphasized the American role in the battle, fixated on the carnage of Omaha Beach, and touted D-Day as the beginning of the end—all in a way that lent an official imprimatur to coalescing popular ideas on the battle.

Some of these thoughts appeared across the spectrum of popular media during the early 1950s. For instance, the battle once again became a subject of interest to filmmakers. The Korean War, however, interceded. The new conflict forced director Sam Fuller to alter one intended film project from a standard Second World War story into a piece about Korea. Writing decades later, the D-Day veteran indicated his view on war movies in general by noting that "there's no way you can portray war realistically, not in a movie nor in a book. You can only capture a very, very small aspect of it."[48] Fuller would talk about D-Day for the rest of his life; he would write a book on his experiences with the U.S. 1st Infantry Division in the war; and his directorial masterwork focused on his beloved "Big Red One." The Big Red One was the nickname for the 1st Infantry Division because of its shoulder patch, a large red number one.

In the late 1940s, Fuller wanted to make a film on the Second World War. With the outbreak of the Korean War in June 1950, Fuller changed the storyline for his movie, *The Steel Helmet,* which he then filmed in one week that October. The men, thrown together after one clash with the enemy, attempt to survive while holed up in a Buddhist temple behind North Korean battle lines. The embittered sergeant in the group is a veteran of the Second World War and had landed, as Fuller did, on Omaha Beach. In a moment of high tension, this sergeant berates the green lieutenant who randomly joined the group as an inept bumbler and who could not measure up to the noble men who had fought on D-Day. In this way, Fuller elevated D-Day service as the standard of comparison: those who saw combat in Normandy could instruct or belittle others. Fuller even indicated that the final scene of the movie, a frenzy of destructive chaos, served as a reimagining of the fighting on Omaha Beach.[49]

Fuller's movie did not release until 1951, several months after completion. This was due, in some part, to the changes required for the switch to the Korean War. Interestingly, Warner Brothers had issued a D-Day movie the previous year called *Breakthrough.* This film depicted the preparation for and the conduct of the Normandy campaign. *Breakthrough*'s black-and-white format helped blend actual footage of the battle with re-created scenes. The central character in *Breakthrough* is Lieutenant Joe Mallory, a reticent high school English teacher who struggles to lead his men through enormous events. Mallory succeeds as his platoon lands on Easy Red, one of the blood-soaked sectors of Omaha Beach, and then battles its way inland. The fighting in this production is reduced to a small-scale brawl between a few groups of men. The Germans surrender almost immediately after the American forces approach unmolested over the beach. Nevertheless, the movie does convey a sense of the difficult task Mallory and his men face.

There are several points worth noting with this film. On the journey across the Channel, the ship's PA system airs Eisenhower's famed order of the day in full. The production rejects any critique of higher command for the difficulties the men face in combat.[50] The end of the film comes with a voiceover from one off-screen soldier, who declares, "I'd sure hate to have to go through it again. But if we have to, our experience and know-how will make the job easier." Once again, in the year of the Korean intervention, the implication stood out here that prior war experience made a tough, and necessary, task of policing the world easier to handle.[51]

These films demonstrated prevalent American perceptions of D-Day. In addition, their messages confirmed the notion that, in cultural historian Thomas Doherty's words, "World War II films painted a portrait of victory and competence, of American true grit overpowering stormtrooper discipline and samurai fanaticism."[52] These films conveyed a triumphal depiction of American martial prowess. However, they always reminded viewers that unlike the enemy, the American soldier was not a militarist and fought only to make the world right. Their focus on the common man exemplified the democratic self-view of America, matching its professed wartime and Cold War goals. Such themes also carried over to the 1952–53 television series *Victory at Sea.* Although the D-Day episode depicts the Normandy invasion from the U.S. Navy's point of view, it still offers moral assessments of the day's meaning. The final comment in this episode proclaims, "Behind the survivors lie those who died to enslave the world, and those who died to free it."[53] World saviors battling tyranny constituted the prevailing American view of their D-Day military forces by the early 1950s.

For one veteran, however, a couple of ephemeral ceremonies, books, and questionable movies seemed insufficient tributes to the sacrifices made on D-Day. Residents of Bedford, Virginia, erected a small plaque in 1949 to commemorate the local dead from both World Wars. Yet Ray Nance lobbied hard for years to push Bedford County towards a more fitting marker of just D-Day. In his view, the plaque honoring those killed in both wars failed to acknowledge the devastating impact of nineteen locals killed in only one day of fighting. Initially, Nance's proposal for a D-Day marker attracted limited enthusiasm. His constant lobbying eventually won the support of a few key people, such as the editor of the local newspaper. Bedford then decided to erect a monument to its D-Day dead. This new marker consisted of a slab of rock cut from the bluffs in Normandy that overlooked the assault beaches. The French provided the rock, the funds, and a suitable escort for the official dedication ceremony held on June 6, 1954. A crowd of over five thousand people gathered to hear of the gallant sacrifice of men sent to save France from barbaric despotism. General Charles Gerhardt, a major general when he had led the 29th Infantry Division on June 6, 1944, helped dedicate the new monument in 1954. Summarizing Gerhardt's speech, one author wrote, "The Bedford boys had been engaged in a great crusade, an ultimately glorious battle to preserve the very foundations of Western civilization of Christendom itself."[54]

Earlier, a plaque proved sufficient as a marker for most local residents. Ten years after D-Day, however, enough people supported Nance's personal quest to ensure the creation of a major monument that celebrated Bedford's contribution to a vital battle. Even with this victory, one dark cloud hung over the dedication. Bedford residents also looked forward to a major *Life* article on the area and its contribution to D-Day. The story fell to the wayside as other matters took hold of national interest. Photographer Robert Capa had recently died while covering events in Vietnam.[55] Capa's death combined with the culminating phase of the infamous Army-McCarthy hearings to yank national attention away from the town's D-Day memorial.[56] For the moment, however, Bedford residents could appreciate a monument that marked the role their loved ones had played in a great event.

During these early postwar years, as Bedford created its first D-Day monument, Dwight Eisenhower remained an important figure in national life. Serving as Supreme Allied Commander on D-Day, he retained a special link to the battle in the public mindset. His order of the day often functioned as a shorthand reference to the day's events and their meaning. Eisenhower's book, his participation in documentaries, and some of his speeches helped cement these themes, even as he turned attention elsewhere. D-Day for Eisenhower always held a mixture of positive meanings. Eisenhower felt it was the defining moment of his military career and indeed of his entire life.[57] The religious terminology and the moral assurance he repeated at the time and ever after were not mere posturing. Eisenhower firmly believed that D-Day saved Western civilization and that the noble sacrifices of the brave American men therefore demanded respect. One thing he feared was that people would forget the noble cause and the reason for the crusade, and lapse back into a self-centered unwillingness to conduct the difficult task of stabilizing the world. When finally opting to run for president in 1952, Eisenhower largely did so to combat the isolationist wing in the Republican Party and the Democratic leadership that had enmeshed the United States in a dangerous and unwinnable war in Asia.[58]

One striking element of Eisenhower's campaigning and his early presidency was the rather sly way that D-Day crept into conversations.

Eisenhower did not find it necessary to make repeated overt references to that battle. He did frequently employ some of the key phrases that evoked D-Day, most notably the "crusade" terminology evident in his presidential campaigning efforts. A typical example came from a speech given in Philadelphia on September 4, 1952, in which Eisenhower proclaimed, "Seven years ago, Freedom had just won its greatest Crusade. Today, Freedom cringes and Communism crusades."[59] Naturally, few people needed explicit reminders of Eisenhower's war record at this stage in his life: they knew he had been the Supreme Allied Commander, the one who led the march to victory in Europe. His staff found little need to bog down the presidential campaign in specific details of that record. Nevertheless, the underlying link between the previous and current wars remained close to the surface. With the war in Korea avowedly fought to combat unwarranted aggression, the mantra of liberating Europe proved an irresistible framing device—one that reminded audiences of Eisenhower's obvious wartime leadership abilities.

Taken altogether, this array of points may create a misleading sense of D-Day's prominence throughout American society in the first decade that followed the Second World War. The breadth of examples serve more to show the variety of commemorative approaches that spanned the cultural horizon. Diversity should not indicate, however, an overwhelming presence, as Americans largely lived their lives with, at most, an occasional reminder of the battle. Even as a speech or a movie showed something of D-Day's popular depiction, it is still worth remembering that a host of other matters occupied people's attention at the time. Significantly, as Omar Bradley or Dwight Eisenhower showed, a reminder of the battle and an honorific ascription of its meaning could appear rather infrequently. With the Korean conflict reenergizing discussions of the Second World War, D-Day began reappearing with significant connections to the then present. The striking aspect of this memory work stemmed not from sheer numbers but rather from the ways people characterized and used D-Day.

Planting Seeds for Future Growth

Americans got on with life in the period following the end of the Second World War. As they faced new problems as well as new opportunities, they did not look back that much to the earlier conflict. Regardless, there were individuals and organizations that began discussing the battle in these early years. The themes and stylistic presentation of D-Day they offered for wider consumption formed early seeds for the future. Remarkably, little debate emerged over what the battle signified. Instead, the few disputes in this period stemmed more from authority, medium of commemoration, and deciding which point to emphasize.

The themes that materialized in this period expanded upon some of those evident at the time of battle. This process of borrowing from the past, then adapting and changing to suit present needs, fit models of historical memory covered earlier. For a brief period, as America faced a new Cold War with an implacable foe, the significance of the past seemed less acute in light of terrible new realities. Therefore, D-Day discussions receded into more generalized coverage of the war as a whole, which again seemed less a guide to future action. America was good because it was great, and great because it was good, as the mainstream consensus on the Second World War affirmed at this point. D-Day fit comfortably into this worldview as demonstrated by the themes of honorable service for world civilization carried out by gallant yet nonmilitaristic men. Still, the battle tended to fade away from mainstream consideration as the war and its key events seemed less meaningful for the early Cold War era.

The individuals connected to the battle, lower-ranking veterans as well as high-level leaders, had new tasks to face in these years. Those out of military service returned home to a tense environment that did not automatically promise rewards for their wartime efforts. Some remained in the military or had to rejoin when the Korean conflict broke out. The leadership figures from the previous conflict illustrated the impact of new roles and responsibilities even more pointedly. Bradley and Eisenhower traveled around the country making speeches on pertinent issues of the day. D-Day appeared less often as a direct reference while these men mentioned the successful Second World War effort in more generalized terms. They would then quickly move on to one of many major issues facing the country. Discussions on veteran readjustment, proposed universal military service, new military alliances, and interservice competition as the Department of Defense came into being all occupied far more public space in this initial postwar moment.

Interestingly, President Eisenhower did not choose to go to Normandy for D-Day's tenth anniversary in 1954. With Korea still smoldering and the recent French defeat at Dien Bien Phu in Vietnam, Cold War tensions had strained Franco-American relations nearly to the breaking point.[60]

Eisenhower was content to release a statement while a delegation of other American officials attended ceremonies in France. His State Department seized on the president's statement as a chance to emphasize yet again the moral authority of the Western Allies in a war for liberation while reminding the French of the ties that bind these countries together. The department officials also wanted to probe the new Soviet leadership, which was still sorting out policies a year after Stalin's death. The proposed draft exuded a far more truculent tone than the final statement. Still, throughout the working document and final version, the Normandy campaign stood as a symbol of strength and determination to right wrongs in the world. Those who sought to continue down tyrannical paths could expect the same determined opposition. Eisenhower's released statement ended by avowing, "The courage, devotion and faith which brought us through the perils of war will inevitably bring us success in our unremitting search for peace, security and freedom." Challenging Cold War enemies on moral terms led Americans to rely on past examples of rectitude to assert America's benign intentions in the world. Rhetorically casting D-Day as an indicator of American benevolence, as a battle fought primarily to liberate others from tyranny, fed into this Cold War propaganda campaign.[61]

The first decade following the Second World War witnessed certain fluctuations in the coverage of D-Day. At times, newspapers would carry an article on some aspect of the invasion, usually presenting a local person's experience on June 6, 1944. Aside from celebration and the occasional movie, however, there was no constant hammering home of D-Day's importance in American public conversations. Despite its oscillating presence, the themes attributed to the day were firming up in this period, laying the foundation for later remembrances of the battle. There were disputes over the authority to depict the battle, as the squabbling between the ABMC and the Society of the First Division attest. Yet these quarrels did not encompass the interpretation of the battle so much as they sorted out who had the authority to shape commemorative processes. The disputants concurred on the moral superiority of the victors, their combined skills, and the world-saving importance of the battle.

D-Day served as one way to extol America's democratic ethos. Unavoidably, this message was rather militant in nature. American fighting men got the job done, even in the most adverse of circumstances. These soldiers were not lifelong militarists but citizen-soldiers, as one speaker reassured audiences at the 1954 Bedford memorial dedication.[62] They left their normal lives and banded together for a necessary, though unpleasant task. With the job done, and civilization saved, they returned home, married, pursued civilian careers, raised families, and made America great. Many of these odes to the fighting forces first arose during the war years as part of the propagandistic effort to maintain Allied morale while attacking that of the enemy. Significantly, these characterizations remained long after the war finished. Americans served as the liberators, the guarantors of freedom and democracy, the preservers of justice and fair play. The D-Day battlefields constituted the "portal of liberation," the beginning of this quest to restore freedom, as the ABMC reminded visitors to the Normandy American Cemetery. Divine sanction for this role stood assured, and was often mentioned, as God's chosen people beat back the darker impulses of savage humanity. The crusade paradigm first evoked by Eisenhower, and repeated frequently in discussions of D-Day, implicitly cast the invasion as an act in accordance with divine will. That a new enemy, albeit a former ally, fit so well into the old mold fashioned for the Germans only served to perpetuate and strengthen such claims. D-Day's role as exemplar of all that was right about America, therefore, assured its place of primacy as the Cold War confrontation with the Soviet Union intensified in the 1950s and 1960s.

Sometimes a word is just a word, one chosen among many others to convey an idea. Here, however, the prevalence of religious terminology and allusions did signify important perceptions of self and enemy. As the Cold War intensified, Americans pledged allegiance to the flag while also acknowledging that their nation stood "under God," as the 1954 addition to the pledge reminded them. In the late 1940s, federal agencies and private organizations came together to develop a "Freedom Train," which displayed the foundational documents of the country to the public in stops across the continental United States. Nearly 50 million Americans visited the train, took a "Freedom Pledge," or signed a "Freedom Scroll" while repeatedly evoking liberty as America's traditional hallmark.[63] Yet just as freedom often stood as the stark counter to Soviet oppression at this time, the religious terminology reflected another way to differentiate the Promised Land from the den of "godless Communism."[64] D-Day fit so easily into these developing images that it regained its former stature as a result. The day's outcome allegedly showed divine favor for a moral America, a land that even championed the freedoms of others. It became also a point of rhetorical distancing from the totalitarian opponent that was increasingly likened to the hated enemy of the Second World War. D-Day as a day of liberation additionally worked as the memories of the prior war gradually phased out the Soviet contribution to victory. Sleeping with the devil may have been a wartime necessity. By casting D-Day as *the* turning point in a war against evil, the uncomfortable marriage of convenience faded away. Americans, and to a lesser degree their Western allies, arose as the shining knights restoring decency to the world. In a mutually influential process, D-Day and the Cold War shaped one another even at this early stage. D-Day assumed greater importance as evidence of the Western love for freedom, especially in comparison to the continued occupation of Eastern Europe by Soviet forces. Americans liberated while the Soviets conquered. Then again, the growing emphasis on D-Day's role in liberation, while downplaying other aspects of the battle, became more prominent, due partially to the rhetorical confrontations of the Cold War.

One portent of the future, however, forecast that even as D-Day came to resonate with increased force in American public discussions, it would also fade back into relative obscurity. The next decade would produce several important cultural works that imprinted D-Day on America's public consciousness. The themes of freedom, divine support, and democratic ethos solidified as standard points during this period. Yet Robert Capa's death in 1954 ominously suggested that the situation in Vietnam remained far from stable. One thing to bear in mind here is that all the displays of mutual amity between France and America, such as with the Bedford memorial, occurred at a time when France depended on American assistance. With the outbreak of the Korean conflict, the United States began funding France's recolonization effort in Indochina. Four years later, with nothing more to show than death, destruction, dissent at home, and problems brewing in Algeria, the French backed ungracefully out of Vietnam.[65] That this settlement took place over the tenth anniversary of D-Day only strengthened the need for rhetorical bonds between France and the United States. D-Day in the Cold War thus became a means of reaffirming America's sense of greatness but also served as a blanket for the many struggles during superpower confrontation and proxy warfare. For the immediate future, these tendencies would lead to an increased American predilection for the battle. In the longer term, however, an undercurrent of unease was also forming about the platitudinous usage of a prior war to justify an array of current policies.

CHAPTER 3
THE DAWN OF *THE LONGEST DAY*

Dedicating the Cemetery

Typical for summer months, rain soaked Normandy on July 18, 1956. Despite the inclement weather, up to 2,000 people gathered for a ceremony. This group included approximately 150 Americans who came to witness the opening of the Normandy American Cemetery. The hour-long observances included a military escort and salute, a wreath laying, and several speeches. The French president, René Coty, indicated in a statement read on his behalf, "Twelve years have passed since that Spring daybreak when the soldiers of the young and free America landed on our shores to deliver our old Europe from oppression." Coty asserted, "We do not forget, we shall never forget, the infinite debt of gratitude that we owe to those who have given all for our freedom."[1] Coty stressed the liberating role of Americans, foremost of the Allies, who began their acclaimed work on D-Day at the site of the new cemetery.

Stirring thoughts indeed, but indicators suggested that Americans were ambivalent about D-Day and their martial past even into the mid-1950s. Just the previous year, one veteran had visited the Normandy area and decried the state of disrepair blemishing the 1st Division monument in Colleville. This individual complained that nobody paid for upkeep of any sort.[2] The cemetery's dedication demonstrated a mixture of attraction and neglect by American society. The ABMC sought to use such occasions to honor the men lost and reaffirm the ties binding together western societies. Despite such grand intentions, the cemetery's official opening was a decidedly lackluster affair. The French president failed to attend, having his statement read by a representative. President Eisenhower likewise skipped the function, as did the U.S. ambassador to France. The sitting chair of the ABMC, General of the Army George C. Marshall, absented himself even though his name adorned the invitations. The ABMC, in fact, prepared for the 1956 ceremony in a sluggish fashion. Funding for the event remained uncertain until a few months out, which delayed the selection of speakers. The French had only just ceded the grounds in perpetuity to thus mark the site as hallowed *American* territory.[3]

Notwithstanding the apparent official neglect, certain thematic emphases ensured that D-Day retained a positive connotation when considered in public settings. The liberation paradigm presented in these observances both demonstrated and reinforced popular understandings of the battle. Eisenhower sent his American delegation off to Europe with ringing words. The president claimed that "the American soldiers who rest forever near the beach-head they won, and in the land they helped free, will never be forgotten." He added, "Their memory will always help strengthen the bonds of friendship between our countries, historic allies for the cause of human freedom."[4] In the late 1950s and early 1960s, American D-Day stories narrowed to a few central themes that highlighted America's apparent moral rectitude in past and present. Yet this approving take on the past did not emerge all at once.

As an official effort to shape public appreciation of D-Day (and U.S. society), the Normandy American Cemetery provided a suitable site for those seeking to mourn American losses. The large sculpture situated in the center of the memorial area, *The Spirit of American Youth,* honored the young men killed in battle. The bronze statue of a male figure, standing on a cresting wave with hands raised to the sky, conveyed an uplifting impression for visitors. Sculptor Donald De Lue surrounded his statue with an inscription bearing multivalent significance for Americans. Borrowing from the "Battle Hymn of the Republic," the famous Civil War rallying song, De Lue chiseled "Mine Eyes Have Seen the Glory of the Coming of the Lord" on the stone base surrounding his construction. One critic claimed that this sculpture "transformed the legacy of the slaughter at Omaha Beach . . . transcending the idea of tragedy completely."[5] Yet that argument elides the palpable feeling of loss communicated by the sheer number of remains interred in the cemetery. Pamphlets, books, speeches, and ceremonies focusing on the cemetery have often borne witness to the specific number of deceased buried in its grounds. The final number of graves there amounted to 9,386. The backdrop to the eastern section of the cemetery listed the names of an additional 1,557 missing persons. The cemetery has served as a commemorative site, albeit a sanitized one, for nearly 11,000 killed or missing Americans.[6]

Visitors have often commented on the sense of reverent awe evoked by this cemetery dedicated to so many lives. An abundance of documentaries, films, books, tours, speeches, and ceremonies dwelt on this patch of ground sanctified by the dead laid there. These memorializations consistently fixated upon the specific numbers of lives lost. That tendency reinforced the democratizing trend in popular memory that stressed the suffering of common soldiers.[7] The numbers involved, however, must give us pause. Any count of D-Day losses remains an estimate. The most authoritative account for the day is that the American forces suffered slightly less than 2,500 combat deaths.[8] No sources used in this research ever claimed that the numbers represented by this memorial site stood solely for D-Day. Nevertheless, over time the commemorative activities connected to the cemetery did risk a conflation. The cemetery acquired an aura as a place for *D-Day* commemoration rather than as a site marking those lost in the overall Normandy *campaign.* The cemetery, after all, stood on the ground of major D-Day combat. The 11,000 lives represented by the cemetery make the American contributions to D-Day seem even more significant.[9]

The cemetery's dedication was linked to certain events in 1956 that ensured D-Day commemoration remained tied to contemporary concerns. Proclaiming France and America as "historic allies for the cause of human freedom" held important implications that year. Just a few months after the Normandy dedication, the French, British, and Israelis attempted to gain control of Egypt's Suez Canal. The outcome there divided the allies with Franco-American relations becoming particularly strained because of Eisenhower's effort to halt the armed intervention.[10] The Soviet occupation of Hungary late that year, on the other hand, reminded people that Americans liberated while the Eastern Bloc oppressed. "In God We Trust" became America's national motto in 1956, which further stressed the religious difference between the two main Cold War competitors.

All these events took place in a presidential election year. Previously, D-Day crept into the campaign rhetoric of 1952. In 1956, Eisenhower's campaign committee moved away from the earlier "I Like Ike" slogan and opted for the "Fourmore Crusade."[11] Eisenhower accentuated familiar themes throughout the election cycle. In a televised speech on the anniversary of D-Day, Eisenhower indicated that the major lesson of the battle was that peace only obtained through strength.[12] Speaking at the American Legion Convention held that August in New York City, Eisenhower continued the chant of liberation. He insisted, "We must tell the Kremlin that never shall we desist in our aid to . . . any man who keeps burning among his own people the flame of freedom or who is dedicated to the liberation of his fellows."[13] Eisenhower hammered on the distance between Soviet oppression and American freedom. In the 1950s, freedom became a mantra, "an inescapable theme," as historian Eric Foner put it, "of academic research, popular journalism, mass culture, and official pronouncements."[14] D-Day fit into this trend as an example of American love for liberty.

With D-Day signifying past and present rectitude, it seems that by the mid-1950s the battle had assumed a firm place in American public consciousness. The speeches, books, films, ceremonies, and monuments attesting to the importance of this day proliferated. For years, the public on both sides of the Atlantic had traveled to Normandy to visit the battlefields and the still-forming cemetery. The inscriptions along the southern doors of the chapel there proudly reminded visitors of America's "sons who gave their lives in the landings on the Normandy Beaches and in the liberation of Northern France."[15] The pilgrimage trope that attended American visitation to Normandy proved revealing. People came out of a dutiful sense of devotion, hailing the grounds as sacred because of the selfless sacrifices commemorated there.[16]

These examples demonstrated D-Day's draw on the American public by the mid-1950s. There nevertheless remained some ambivalence over the usage of the day's ascribed meanings. After all, monuments could go up, but without numerous visitors they served as little more than unappreciated signifiers of past actions. Ceremonies furnished brief honorific events. Then again, the lack of high-level attendance and media attention also indicated the limited appeal of D-Day celebration. During this period the Gold Star Mothers, those who had lost sons in battle, visited the Normandy area. Their presence visibly testified "that it was American mothers, American women, who had offered their *sons* for Europe's freedom." Yet, unlike the post-First World War period, no official Gold Star pilgrimage campaign materialized, which left each mother to her own devices for such a trip.[17]

Americans did not focus steadily on D-Day until the 1960s. By that time, the Cold War added a layer of militant bellicosity to the American Civil War centennial anniversaries.[18] The same held true as superpower conflict shaped the ways Americans employed D-Day. The Cold War tendency to emphasize American righteousness ensured the spread of morality tales linked to D-Day. This melding of past and present created the atmosphere that made D-Day seem relevant. Just as some people used D-Day to indicate American moral strength in a time of crisis, the Civil War centennial helped intensify the freedom rhetoric flowing throughout society. Despite current-day strife, particularly over race-related matters, the celebration of both Union and Confederate troops fed into a larger narrative of America's unique regard for freedom.[19] The concept of "freedom," however, offered various interpretations.[20] The favorable reading of the past emphasized certain aspects of America's quest for freedom while overlooking countervailing proclivities from the historical record.

People advanced these interpretations of the past. D-Day returned to the forefront of the American cultural landscape owing to the work of veterans' groups, authors, filmmakers, government officials, and interested citizens. As D-Day assumed a greater prominence, those who felt excluded began questioning the stories circulating in the public sphere.[21] Contests over exclusion or authority aside, the overall direction of the decade running from the mid-1950s to the mid-1960s witnessed a dramatic expansion of D-Day commemoration. The variety of remembrance activities in this period shows a striking conformity in overall interpretation of the battle. That degree of correspondence indicated the common acceptance of these themes while also furthering their diffusion through repetition.

The Longest (-Lasting) Metaphor: D-Day to the End of the 1950s

By the mid-1950s, Americans generally viewed D-Day in a favorable light. While the Cold War expanded, this battle from the past came to stand as an example of American values. The ability to exclude the Soviet Union when commemorating this battle for freedom helped explain why one component of the vast Second World War gained prominence over so many others. The D-Day battle area stood as the "portal of liberation," where American soldiers laid down their lives for the freedom of others.

Many actors and actions contributed to the spread of D-Day commemoration in this period, including even fictional treatments of the battle.

William Bradford Huie released his D-Day novel, *The Americanization of Emily,* in 1959. Lieutenant (JG) Huie had served as an aide for a high-ranking American naval officer during the war. In the process, he saw the workings of power at the top echelons, which inspired the irreverent tone of his novel. Like Huie, the main character of *The Americanization of Emily,* James Monroe Madison, belongs to an admiral's staff. While thus occupied in pre-D-Day England, Madison falls in love with Emily, an English girl. Huie's work is complex and critical, taking aim at the Allied high command. At one point, the main character derides Ike's famous order of the day as overly pompous and verbose. One of the sailors accompanying Madison explodes, "Great Crusade, my ass. Who the hell writes such crud?" Although affording only brief coverage to the battle, the story contains a horrific moment involving the death of one of Madison's men. Madison's guilt over the loss undermines any sense of accomplishment attending Allied success on D-Day. Huie also interjected an encounter that demonstrated French sullenness over the destructive form of their liberation.[22]

Huie's short book indicated a nascent rejection of the triumphal themes ascribed to D-Day. He sharply criticized military leaders. Instead of a harmoniously joint effort, Normandy becomes an interservice scramble for glory. As Madison's admiral complains, "It's an Army show. The Navy makes the invasion possible, but the Navy will be forgotten in a day."[23] Huie's treatment of these rivalries suited a period that witnessed American military reorganizations, strategic disputes, and squabbling over resources. Huie rejected the glamorization of battle, instead depicting combat as a confused, terrifying action resulting in death or, at the least, psychological trauma. The author had a record of criticizing flaws in society, as demonstrated by his other works that denounced sexism, the abuse of power during war periods, and violent racism.[24] In this work, Huie attempted to challenge the increasingly sentimentalized views of D-Day combat circulating in the public sphere.

Huie, however, was fighting an uphill battle. Official histories at this time offered depictions of a more forgiving nature. The U.S. Army published its official history of the Normandy campaign in 1951. The U.S. Navy responded with the semiofficial 1957 book, *The Invasion of France and Germany, 1944–1945*. The latter came as the ninth in Samuel Eliot Morison's sixteen-volume treatment of the navy's war. Morison emphasized the naval role in the invasion, a side of the story he felt Americans underappreciated. The book presented more than a dry analysis of the invasion's naval component.

Morison indulged in grandiose moralizing, noting at one point, "There were indeed things so remarkable in this [channel] crossing as to suggest divine guidance." Morison focused on moments of intense danger, like the destroyer USS *Corry*'s destruction or the close-to-shore action of other ships on D-Day. He pontificated, "Omaha Beach—there's a name that will live, like Tarawa and Guadalcanal, as long as men prize valor and feel for suffering."[25] Morison's smug sense of satisfaction in his treatment of D-Day validated popular American perceptions of the battle.

Rather than reject popular accolades as Huie suggested, veterans too by this period began publicly telling their stories in ways that demonstrated their acceptance of more approving interpretations of D-Day's meaning. Bruce Bliven, an enlisted man with the 111th Artillery Battalion who landed on Omaha Beach on June 7, 1944, released *The Story of D-Day* in 1956. "The end of the Second World War began on June 6, 1944," Bliven argued, while equating D-Day with such legendary battles as Bunker Hill and Gettysburg. Bliven boiled down the story to an American effort conducted by heroes. In his view, the courage and initiative of individual Americans overcame all challenges. As Bliven put it, "In the crisis, a handful of heroes came forward."[26] Bliven's simplistic take on D-Day has proven popular enough to keep his book continuously in print since its initial publication.

The growing popular acceptance of D-Day inspired many others to enter into the discussion of the battle and its significance. Cornelius Ryan published his honorific account, *The Longest Day,* on June 6, 1959. Ryan proclaimed, "What follows is not a military history. It is the story of people: the men of the Allied forces, the enemy they fought and the civilians who were caught up in the bloody confusion of D Day—the day the battle began that ended Hitler's insane gamble to dominate the world."[27] He focused on this single day as the key turning point in the war, and indeed in Western civilization. Ryan's work grabbed attention because of his superlative ability to convey the drama of battle in accordance with popular perceptions of D-Day. He perpetuated the moral assessment of the fighting forces that resonated with Americans.

Ryan characterized the eleven years he put into *The Longest Day* in a letter to his editor, "So much tripe has appeared on the subject of D-Day that all along I have been ruthless in sticking to what actually happened *rather than what generals or others thought happened.* Something else: you'll find no mention here of 'Mama's blueberry pie' or the term 'GI.' I'm doing my best to abide by a single rule of thumb: accuracy."[28] Following his journalistic instincts, Ryan focused on the tension and excitement of the fighting. Ryan confined the narrative to those units and individuals that most typified the drama of the day.[29] He reduced the story to the intense combat occurring in the most hotly contested areas. In a work hailed as the definitive word on the subject, Ryan's circumscribed narrative directed public attention to some aspects of the battle at the expense of others.

Ryan sought to provide a ground-level view on the battle. The narrative remained devoid of soaring paeans to godlike leadership. Ryan instead emphasized the heroism of common men struggling for a worthy cause. He assured his readers, "The great crusade's unalterable purpose was not only to win the war, but to destroy Nazism and bring to an end an era of savagery which had never been surpassed in the world's history." His story highlighted the gallantry of soldiers in hazardous situations, such as the U.S. Army Ranger units that had scaled the cliffs at Pointe du Hoc on a mission to neutralize a German artillery battery. Even as Ryan insisted that "there were no heroes in these boats—just cold, miserable, anxious men," he also remarked, "Never had there been a dawn like this. In the murky, gray light, in majestic, fearful grandeur, the great Allied fleet lay off Normandy's five invasion beaches." The Allies "had history on their side," as Ryan linked this battle to the American tradition of fighting for freedom.[30]

The Longest Day became an immediate best seller and generated widespread admiration. Book reviews, newspaper articles, letters, and word of mouth all hailed it as the new standard on the subject. From scholars through war correspondents to D-Day veterans, people acclaimed the author's accuracy and thanked him.[31] Ryan's writing compelled one Texas oilman to write a congratulatory note: "Your forthright and sensitive treatment of D-Day is going to be crammed down the throats of each of my four boys as soon as they are old enough to digest the importance of this fine book." This effusive fan signed his name—George H. W. Bush.[32]

These authors were not alone as D-Day appeared in other venues, such as television productions and Hollywood films. The popular television program *You Are There* highlighted D-Day in 1955 while focusing on one of the American assault regiments, the 116th Infantry, which landed on the western portion of Omaha Beach. The host, Walter Cronkite, concluded this tale of a divinely sanctioned American effort by reading Roosevelt's D-Day prayer.[33]

Hollywood entered the fray with the 1956 film *D-Day, the Sixth of June.* This production opens with the invasion armada advancing toward the Norman shore. The primary focus, however, lingers on a convoluted and maudlin backstory that goes on for almost ninety minutes. The film returns to the D-Day assault during its final eighteen minutes.[34] Based on Canadian war correspondent Lionel Shapiro's 1955 tearjerker *The Sixth of June,* the film employs D-Day as a background plot element. In the final landing sequence, two of the main characters work out their differences, thus restoring unity to the alliance. Both men earn glory in Normandy. The American Captain Parker (Robert Taylor) and British Colonel Winter (Richard Todd, a British D-Day veteran) survive the landing and the fighting afterwards. In a departure from the original book, Winter dies moments after the action halts by stepping on a mine. In this manner, world responsibility symbolically passes from the established orders to the rising American power.[35] Overall, the film follows the book in its melodramatic nature. The author had frankly acknowledged that his "memories of 1942, '43, and '44 [held] an incredibly romantic aura which is the vital element of the historical novel."[36]

Film historian Jeanine Basinger noted that the "film illustrates how [a] basic combat situation and familiarity with historical fact can provide [the] setting for a romantic story."[37] Her dismissal of the movie seems justifiable to a degree. Some problems with the production include the romantic treacle and poorly executed special effects. Yet the testament to the military capability of America fighting alongside allies fit Cold War priorities by demonstrating the effectiveness of coalition warfare.[38] The primary characters all acquit themselves well. Nobody shirks their duty, questions the need for them to be there, or cowers in the face of danger. Story aside, the producer explained that studio executives demanded placement of *D-Day* at the beginning of the film's title to attract a larger audience. D-Day seemed salable. Unfortunately, scanty box-office returns reflected audience disinterest in this particular story.[39]

By 1959, however, publishers, authors, veterans' groups, and some political leaders felt that more Americans would pay attention to D-Day, if only in better constructed stories. Several authors, most notably Ryan, sought to capitalize on the anniversary. The tremendous success of his book helped boost public interest in D-Day.[40] The 116th Regiment Association used the occasion to erect a monument in the Omaha Beach area of Normandy. The association faced the obstruction of Thomas North and the ABMC.

The group overcame this resistance in time to have a monument ready for the fifteenth anniversary. Once again, a veterans' group refused to defer to the ABMC's desire for an uncluttered landscape.[41] During that summer, American newspapers carried stories about local men who had assaulted the beaches on June 6, 1944. Reenacted airborne landings, dedication ceremonies for new monuments, and celebrations at liberated French towns marked the anniversary in France.[42]

By the fifteenth anniversary, D-Day had come into its own in American society. The battle served as an indicator of past alliance strength and as a potential precedent for any Cold War military venture. The shibboleth of liberation fit contemporary concerns in the United States. The year 1959, after all, saw the Senate Judiciary Committee hold hearings on the creation of a "Freedom Academy" to combat the international Communist conspiracy.[43] Yet, a plaintive note appeared at this time. D-Day, although reassuring, represented an obsolete form of warfare. The existence of nuclear weaponry may have precluded the repetition of large-scale amphibious operations in any future war. As evident in one *Los Angeles Times* news article, wistful invocations of the "great crusade" offered opportunities to wax nostalgically over D-Day.[44]

Stability in Tumultuous Times? D-Day at the Outset of the Sixties

During the next five years, from the end of 1959 to mid-1964, acknowledgments of D-Day regularly surfaced in American society. People began overtly using D-Day as an instructional tool to guide younger generations. It functioned as a prop to promote unity between the United States and its allies. D-Day also served as a marketing device to attract audiences.

The growing temporal distance from the battle pushed some to worry that a forgetful public might consign D-Day to oblivion. In a Cold War climate fostering fears for liberty, D-Day could instruct American youth to fight for national values. With the dedication in Abilene, Kansas, of the Eisenhower Museum in 1954 and Presidential Library in 1962, the man who had led the crusade reminded Americans that freedom demanded enduring vigilance.[45]

Another museum demonstrated the conflation of D-Day's celebratory and educational utility. Robert McCormick had served in the 1st Infantry Division during the First World War. McCormick owned and published the *Chicago Tribune* for years, increasing his immense family fortune. When

McCormick died in 1955, his estate's executors established a charitable trust. This group, which included McCormick's friend and business associate Arthur Schmon, decided to erect a museum dedicated to the 1st Infantry Division on the McCormick estate near Chicago. The division's D-Day commander, Clarence Huebner, had lobbied them concerning the need for a museum devoted to its history. Under Secretary of the Army Charles Ficuane designated the Cantigny War Memorial Museum as the official display site for artifacts related to McCormick's old unit.[46] Cantigny referred to the division's first sizeable combat action during the First World War.[47] Ironically, the historical narrative that Schmon and the other trustees approved contrasted sharply with McCormick's views. Robert McCormick was an old-school, isolationist Republican who had vexed Eisenhower.[48] The Cantigny War Memorial Museum, which opened on August 20, 1960, however, presented a morality tale of the need for American intervention in a dangerous world.[49]

Although Cantigny honored the entire 1st Infantry Division and its auspicious history since 1917, D-Day occupied center stage in the museum's layout. In advertisements, the museum's staff singled out D-Day for specific mention.[50] Upon entering the site, visitors faced a replica of the Normandy American Cemetery's *Spirit of American Youth* statue. A mural of D-Day combat action stood behind this sculpture. The D-Day exhibit consisted of a dramatic diorama accompanied by an audiotape narration. The script focused on Eisenhower's leadership and the heroism Americans displayed on Omaha Beach. It extolled the significance of the day "that meant victory for the Allies and death to Hitler." In accordance with the McCormick Foundation's intent to promote citizenship, the exhibit extolled 1st Infantry Division personnel as "men of more than ordinary moral strength," words calculated to highlight the worth of military service.[51] The museum presented D-Day as one of America's finest moments. That message reached over 500,000 visitors in the first three years following Cantigny's opening.[52] Connecting the different D-Day commemorations, Captain Henry J. "Mike" Kelty, the museum's first director, wrote Cornelius Ryan in 1960 requesting for display an autographed copy of *The Longest Day*.[53] Ryan's book had passed a million copies sold by the early 1960s, and its popularity no doubt brought the museum many of its visitors.[54]

American history textbooks adopted the habit of using D-Day as a morality lesson for the nation's youth. With the release of the first edition of *The*

Making of Modern America in 1954, historians Leon Canfield and Howard Wilder argued that aggressor countries had disturbed the peace, started the Second World War, and forced America to act. In "a fundamental struggle between two opposing ways of life," America acquired power because of unity at home, an immense productive effort, and battlefield successes. Of course, "On June 6 (D-Day), the final phase of the war began," through the "greatest amphibious (water and land) force in history."[55] The popular textbook series started by Thomas Bailey, *The American Pageant,* came out two years later. Bailey stressed a unique regard for democratic ways as the central theme in his discussion of American history. Thus, the Second World War stood as a test of democracy and its vindication once Americans led the way to victory. D-Day ranked as a key battle in this analysis.[56] The didactic employment of D-Day and its supposed lessons in this manner ensured that countless American youth engaged with these concepts.

In an era of the "best and the brightest," with a new frontier on the horizon, D-Day reaffirmed and drew strength from these larger currents. The silver screen once again prominently displayed such predilections. Films portraying the Second World War had grown commonplace and profitable by the early 1960s. The stories of valor, manliness proven in combat, and success confirmed American self-images. They also offered guides for emulation in times of national or personal strife. One movie loomed larger than the rest.

Cornelius Ryan sold the screen rights for his book, *The Longest Day,* to French producer Raoul Levy. Little money changed hands. American producer Darryl F. Zanuck read Ryan's book late in 1960 and saw it as the basis for a successful movie. He bought the rights from Levy. As Mel Gussow, a charitable biographer of Zanuck, observed, this movie "changed his life, *saved* his life, and saved the life of Twentieth Century-Fox as well." Gussow added, "Before *The Longest Day,* [Zanuck] was a washed-up, played-out producer. After *The Longest Day,* he was one of the most powerful men in the movies."[57] As an advanced promotional sheet on the movie proclaimed, Zanuck "fully expect[ed] it to be the most important war film ever made."[58] The impact of this film was so immediate, and turned out to be so long lasting, that it became the main historical primer on D-Day for millions of people. *The Longest Day* served as the initial introduction to D-Day for many Americans then (and since). It also reaped enormous financial rewards for Zanuck and his studio.

Cornelius Ryan served as scriptwriter for both the stalled French project and the comeback Zanuck epic. Ryan and Zanuck possessed oversized egos, however, and that virtually guaranteed a clash of personalities.[59] Feeling that all the material from the book remained vital, Ryan's working scripts extended into several hundred pages before even getting to the combat action on D-Day.[60] Disputes over content flared up frequently. Ryan left the project in anger while Zanuck claimed to have helped write the script and direct 60 percent of the film.[61] Zanuck assembled an international cast and production team, which lent an air of authenticity to the film. Yet the product unmistakably bore the stamp of Zanuck himself.

Even with factual inaccuracies, Ryan admitted that Zanuck's film was a brilliant piece of work.[62] Zanuck's proclaimed intentions give some hint of the movie's appeal. He stated, "The Allies made every conceivable blunder and error. . . . But the Germans were even more stupid." Zanuck continued by asserting, "From all of this, we can only come to the conclusion that God was on our side."[63] The film captured the chaos of battle. Audiences viewed an epic movie that depicted a grand event—one that many knew would end happily for the "right" side. As one historian would later indicate, the "film reinforces one patriotic theme: the triumph of democracy over dictatorship."[64] The defeat of evil was certainly one of the film's undertones.

Zanuck meshed skillful storytelling with an immense production effort. As reported by *Time* magazine, Zanuck led the ninth largest military force in the world during the filming.[65] The production's black-and-white footage re-created the look of wartime documentaries or news briefs.[66] Zanuck went to extreme lengths to ensure a "realistic" depiction of the fighting and the drama of soldiers interacting with one another, even if some of the plot elements were distortions.[67] Focusing on partners and enemies, all in a somewhat balanced light, helped bolster confidence in America's current allies, which now included West Germany as a NATO partner.[68]

Before the title, the movie opens with rousing drum music while displaying an upended helmet resting alone on the beach. The camera shifts to German occupiers pursuing and gunning down in cold blood a French resistance agent. With the moral stakes firmly established, the plot develops as the German leadership prepares for battle and Allied troops fret over the impending action. The difference here is instructive: the film perpetuates the Prussian militarist image while humanizing the Allies. The story begins on June 5, just one day before the "longest day." This abrupt introduction to the war affords no chance for strategic discussion or an explanation of how the conflict had developed to that point. The storyline combines a focus on high-ranking leaders with depictions of stirring action involving all ranks. All the landing beaches receive some treatment, although Canadian forces do not figure in the story. By exclusion, then, the American contribution to D-Day seems more significant. Although the film seeks a realistic depiction of warfare, a jaunty musical score and stirring combat scenes carry a glamorized tint. This is essentially an adventure tale of one glorious day. Even at Omaha Beach, the Allies surge forward to victory.

Audiences flocked to see *The Longest Day,* which earned over $17 million in its first year. Reviewers quibbled about points of accuracy and drawn-out action sequences, but overall the reception proved favorable.[69] As author Lawrence Suid contended, "*The Longest Day* became [the] quintessential war film because of the authenticity of the battle scenes" as well as its focus "on men on both sides before, during, and after the battle."[70] Further, in letters, memoranda, publicity releases, and interviews, Darryl Zanuck insisted that his film had a purpose. That cause transcended mere dramatic artistry and fed into Cold War requirements. Zanuck claimed that his was a patriotic film that inspired love for America. He also argued that it fostered alliance unity in opposition to totalitarian government.[71] The producer sometimes took this publicity campaign to extremes. Zanuck even mustered the gall to insist that he had a harder time filming D-Day than Eisenhower had with the actual assault.[72] Such hubris aside, American audiences enjoyed the film. Only a select few, such as Norman Cota, the 29th Infantry Division's assistant commander on D-Day, refused to condone any movie that profited from the carnage of battle.[73]

The Longest Day resonated with millions on both sides of the Atlantic. Despite the smattering of television shows and books, this movie appeared a year after one newspaper found that most local children did not "have the faintest idea what D-Day stood for."[74] After the film's release, people once again talked a lot about D-Day, and, in Suid's words, "*The Longest Day* served as the model for all subsequent combat spectaculars."[75] The D-Day story did not just influence some higher cultural circles. In one indication of the film's power, John Steele sought to attend the French premiere despite suffering through the last stages of terminal cancer. Steele was the private in the 82nd Airborne Division whose parachute snarled on the church steeple at Sainte-Mère-Église—one of the film's most memorable vignettes.[76] *The*

Longest Day also served educational purposes to teach American youth about core national values. One teacher in New York City developed a packet for students centered on the movie. The booklet described D-Day as an "action which liberated an imprisoned Europe and doomed forever Hitler's insane dream of enslaving the world."[77]

This movie's stunning visual display was in some respects overpowering. In fact, it quickly overshadowed the more nuanced analysis presented in Ryan's book. Although similar, a few discrepancies between the two productions have led to several controversies. One dispute concerned the assault at Pointe du Hoc. Ryan noted in his text that the Rangers struggled to climb the cliffs in the face of determined German resistance. This costly assault seemed particularly heartbreaking when the soldiers failed to locate the targeted German artillery battery. Nevertheless, Ryan mentioned in a footnote that several Rangers continued inland, found the guns, and put them out of commission, thus completing their mission.[78] The film does not continue the story with the eventual discovery of the battery. The assault seems pointless as one man laments, "You mean we climbed up here for nothing?" This editorial decision bruised the sensibilities of veterans who felt pride in what they accomplished on D-Day.

"D-Day Plus Twenty Years"

With the growing hype over D-Day, the twentieth anniversary was destined to attract a great deal of attention. Books, movies, monuments, and ceremonies raised awareness of D-Day's significance. Contemporary concerns increased the fixation on the past for morality lessons, reassurance, and guidance.

In preparation for the anniversary, CBS anchorman Walter Cronkite interviewed Eisenhower on location in southern England and Normandy for the documentary *D-Day Plus 20 Years.* The program's depiction of the battle highlighted a number of problems that disrupted the assault plan. Success here came from the individual initiative and heroism of the junior soldiers, a theme Eisenhower had repeated often before. At the outset, the narration intoned that on D-Day, "a battle was joined between the world of freedom and the world of tyranny." Eisenhower claimed that American soldiers were there "not to gain anything for ourselves, not to fulfill any ambitions that America had for conquest, but just to preserve freedom." The production followed Eisenhower in areas relating to the invasion. On the way, Cronkite posed questions that allowed Ike to pontificate on the moral authority of allies fighting for liberty. Contrasting the chaos of D-Day to a placid Normandy in the present, sunbathing families displayed the benefit of freedoms purchased at such steep cost. The concluding thoughts focused upon the sacrifices soldiers had made to create a better world. Cronkite and Eisenhower urged a continued willingness to preserve freedom. Yet they also cautioned against rashly committing young men to similar scenes of devastation.[79]

Early planning conferences for the filmmaking trip demonstrated Eisenhower's acute desire to remain inclusive: this was not "to appear an 'All American' show." The planning took place just on the heels of the Cuban Missile Crisis that came at the end of 1962, and Eisenhower understandably sought to promote allied unity in response. Then again, as the producer for the show also made clear, D-Day "was the greatest day in American history and we have never quite recovered its grandeur since."[80] This sense of eclipse foreshadowed developments more clearly evident decades later.

At the moment, however, the documentary's focus on Eisenhower's leadership in 1944 highlighted the American contributions on D-Day. Coming in an era of increasing racial turmoil at home, the return to D-Day sites offered a chance to highlight the collective achievements of the nation in a way that shifted the discussion away from domestic discord. This message received wide distribution at the time. Eisenhower later indicated his approval that the documentary "had achieved rare 'perfect clearance' status by airing on every CBS TV affiliate (even in Alaska, Hawaii, and Guam)."[81]

Many commemorations marked D-Day's twentieth anniversary. Anniversary events included airborne and Ranger cliff-scaling reenactments. An estimated ten thousand American veterans traveled to France for yet another rainy anniversary day.[82] Historian Martin Blumenson capitalized on the fervor by publishing his celebratory article "D-Day in Retrospect." Blumenson noted the unlikelihood of Allied defeat but predicted a harsh Soviet-dominated peace for Western Europe had that happened.[83]

As with the tenth anniversary, however, undercurrents of dissent emerged amid this gala celebration. At this time, U.S. senators remained in heated debate over a civil rights bill. With no evident sense of irony, the fracas over rights continued at home while Americans celebrated preservation of rights abroad.[84] Growing Gaullist nationalism strained Franco-American relations.

Ceremony officials remained uncertain over how to treat Germany's involvement in any observances. Crises in Cuba, Vietnam, and Cyprus exacerbated international tensions.[85] Even as the D-Day anniversary afforded a chance to acknowledge alliance bonds, divisions splintered friendships. At the local level and in interpersonal terms, the twentieth anniversary saw a great deal of goodwill. Nevertheless, at the interstate level, words and reminiscences only went so far. Just two years later, Charles De Gaulle would announce French withdrawal from NATO oversight and demand the removal of allied headquarters from France. Betraying the building tensions, De Gaulle refused to attend the D-Day ceremonies in 1964, which President Lyndon Johnson also avoided.

Johnson sent an official delegation to France, much as Eisenhower had done ten years earlier. Before their departure, Johnson read a message to the group that emphasized the liberating intent of the Allied forces on D-Day. "The beachheads of Normandy have been opened into beachheads of hope for us all," the president intoned. Then he linked the commemoration of the battle to present-day concerns: "Where we have commitments to the cause of freedom, we shall honor them—today, tomorrow, and always. Freedom is not the cause of America alone, however, nor the hope of Western man alone."[86] The public pronouncement read on Johnson's behalf at Normandy reminded the mixed European and American audience, "On June 6, 1944, the Armed Forces of the United States joined with the forces of your nations to fight and die for the liberation of your lands and the freedom of all lands." Other comments of the day stressed the liberating impact of the battle, the need for unity to confront oppression, and the obligation to remember the costs exacted in the quest for freedom. The Veterans of Foreign Wars subsequently published a commemorative pamphlet that contained many of these speeches. The U.S. government likewise issued a report notably titled *D-Day Plus 20 Years* a few months after the anniversary. In both publications, statements by Americans dominated, and British or Canadian comments leavened the mix, but French remarks remained relatively absent.[87]

While the ceremonies presented a flurry of activity from June 5 through 7, other indicators emerged in 1964 that demonstrated American attention devoted to D-Day. The Cantigny War Memorial Museum experienced a surge in attendance that exploded around the mid-year anniversary. This spike came after advertising and news articles acclaimed the D-Day role of the 1st Infantry Division.[88] The continuing struggle between the ABMC and proponents of additional monuments in Normandy led to the increase of honorific markings in the region. In March 1964, the ABMC approved a request by the National Guard Association for a marker near Omaha Beach, the site of the "National Guard" 29th Infantry Division's fight on D-Day. Picking up steam that year, discussions on additional markers for the Utah Beach area also occupied the ABMC's time.[89] The mayor of Sainte-Mère-Église, after working with James Lawton Collins, dedicated a plaque honoring the city's liberation by American airborne forces on D-Day.[90] The ABMC tried to retain control over the commemorative landscape. As D-Day became a potent symbol in American public memory, however, more groups acted to commemorate their role in the battle.

Ominous Clouds on the Horizon

Critical assessments of the battle did begin raising concerns at this time. By the mid-1960s, D-Day signified many laudable aspects of American society. Some people, however, looked with dismay at ignoble characteristics of that same society. These individuals saw an opportunity to provoke discussion by questioning mainstream views. The glowing paeans to D-Day heroism provided a fitting target for one such effort. Seeking a large potential audience, one critical film entered into conversations of the Second World War and this battle.

Arthur Hiller's 1964 film *The Americanization of Emily* conveyed a more critical assessment of D-Day heroics. Director Hiller said, "One thing we can do toward eliminating war from our world is to get rid of the goodness and virtue we attribute to war."[91] Employing the self-professed cowardice of the protagonist, Lieutenant Commander Charles Madison (James Garner), the primary message of the movie contains a biting critique of the glorification of war.[92] "Charlie" avers that we "perpetuate war by exulting its sacrifices."[93]

Charlie is a coward trying to find an easy way through the Second World War. His commander, Admiral Jessup, decides to bolster the navy's reputation by claiming one of their own as the first dead man on Omaha Beach.[94] Despite Charlie's efforts to avoid participation in that scheme, he lands at the head of the Allied invasion on June 6, 1944. Refuting the prevailing imagery of the invasion, Charlie does not land with a group of fellow sailors and soldiers. He storms the beach on his own. One American sailor who follows behind him captures Charlie's "heroic" death in a photograph that gains international adulation. Jessup realizes his mistake and proclaims in self-admonishment, "You don't send a man to die if you want a hero." Fortunately for Charlie, an explosion had only knocked him unconscious. Instead of delighting over Charlie's survival, however, his friend laments, "We had a nice dead hero; now we have a damn live coward!"

The film cynically rejects themes evocative of D-Day, including honorable service, military glory, and nobility of sacrifice. Film critics were divided in condemning the imputed slur on the military services or praising the antiwar critique.[95] Hiller and scriptwriter Paddy Chayefsky set out to shift the public perception of warfare in general by assaulting the cherished ideal of D-Day heroism and honor. Because of limited audience turnout that greeted the film's release, however, that message did not seem to reverberate with much force.[96] Perhaps the questioning of D-Day heroism proved too disorienting for the moment.

While Hiller and Chayefsky's avowed intentions remain central to reading this film, it is important to remember the many influences on film production in America. Importantly, the Hays Code of Hollywood self-censorship remained in effect until the late 1960s. Historian Leonard Leff argued that it took the Warner Brothers film version of *Who's Afraid of Virginia Woolf?* (1966) to break this system. By the mid-1960s, the code seemed out of date. Yet American studios continued to bow to its demands for limited violence, no bloodshed, and delicate treatment of sexual themes.[97]

Latter-day critics of this era's war films miss the point when they compare bloody "realism" to the more stoic deaths caught on film of earlier decades.[98] Zanuck, for instance, confronted severe constraints in just how gruesome he could make combat appear when filming *The Longest Day*.[99] On the other hand, audiences who recently lived through major wars realized that men collapsing gently to the ground symbolized far harsher realities. When it came to *The Americanization of Emily*, however, the head of the Code Administration fretted less over the depiction of battle and more over the sexual liaisons shown or hinted at on screen.[100]

Despite *The Americanization of Emily*'s critique of glorified militarism, the earlier scripts omitted any portrayal of combat action. Huie, the author of the book and the writer of the first working script, insisted that the movie required no combat scenes. Instead, viewers would "see" events through Emily's perspective, meaning they would wait to hear of the battle's outcome.[101] Paddy Chayefsky, Huie's replacement as scriptwriter, inserted a combat scene. Yet, with the Code Administration leery of the film and the military smarting from fallout that arose with *The Longest Day* production mishaps, official support did not prove forthcoming.[102] Hiller had to rely on stock-film shots of D-Day preparations or ships firing at shore.

The film's characters denounced the evils of militarism in statements that moved well beyond the original book. William Bradford Huie had offered a whimsical romp through a wartime setting, one in which his main character sensibly feared death but still did his duty. Chayefsky turned the protagonist into an outright coward to deglamorize war. He felt that "to maim and kill and destroy in the pursuit of peace was the most immoral and absurd act that man was capable of."[103] Chayefsky presented a battle scene that stood in another dimension when compared to war films of the time. Genre conventions included dramatic tension, honorable service, and the achievement of manhood through military action.[104] Chayefsky's D-Day scene offered the opposite: zaniness, dishonor, and effacing of manhood.

The Longest Day celebrated D-Day whereas *The Americanization of Emily* used D-Day to confront the militarization of society. Audiences flocked to see the glorified presentation of D-Day in *The Longest Day. The Americanization of Emily,* on the other hand, enjoyed limited box-office success. Although initially greeted with ambivalence, the latter film found a wider audience as the decade wore on. By the mid-1960s, the United States was stepping into the Vietnam imbroglio. The mounting critique of political and military institutions stemming from that war caused rather significant shifts in the commemoration of military affairs. Ironically, *The Americanization of Emily* gained a wider audience by the end of the decade while it became the last major D-Day film to appear until after the Vietnam War concluded.[105]

At the time of its release, the film failed to overcome widespread support for approving interpretations of D-Day and American society. Just two weeks before D-Day's 1964 anniversary, President Johnson spoke at the dedication of the George C. Marshall Research Library. Johnson used the occasion to emphasize the imperative to continue ensuring freedoms worldwide.[106] The D-Day anniversary enabled him to deplore threats to liberty caused by oppressive governments. Since Johnson was secretly considering a more overt American role in the Vietnamese conflict, such rhetorical constructions deserve close attention. Johnson used one June 1964 press conference to describe "Vietnam as 'not just a jungle war, but a struggle for freedom on every front of human activity.'"[107] With the allure of D-Day's moralistic message still palpably in the air during the twentieth anniversary period, linking Vietnam to struggles for freedom formed one way to borrow legitimacy from the widely supported Second World War. Tellingly, there was nothing comparable in the more recent Korean War experience that offered political leaders rhetorical support when selling this new intervention.

D-Day had provided a means for politicians, writers, and filmmakers to tell a story palatable to Americans: America and its allies had triumphed over evil on the beaches of Normandy. Significantly, popular common renderings placed America in the forefront with the rest of the usually unnamed "Allies" following in its wake. Such a complacent portrayal of the nation's history, however, became less sustainable in the midst of Sixties Era tensions and divisions. "It was a bare two decades from the beaches of Normandy to the beachfronts of Danang, from Overlord to Operation Hades, from GIs as liberators to grunts as perpetrators, from home front mobilization to anti-war demonstrations organized by the 'Mobe,'" noted author Tom Engelhardt.[108]

Historians disparage simplified "lessons" of the past. The Munich analogy, which instructs societies to confront would-be aggressors rather than appease them, as was done at the 1938 Munich Conference, is one such deplored lesson.[109] The particular depiction of D-Day prevalent in American remembrance constitutes a potential accompaniment to the Munich analogy. While Munich pushes societies to confront aggression, D-Day tales suggest that a resultant war fought for such purpose will lead to honor, glory, and worldwide admiration. Wars of liberation carried out against aggressors, according to this reading of history, will prove popular at home and abroad. The basic point that policy makers such as President Johnson were making by June 1964 held that, as a land of liberty, the United States could, indeed should, engage in liberating missions when oppressors strike.

By the mid-1960s, Americans had faced a virtual bombardment of cultural constructions depicting D-Day. The battle signified American military strength and the benefits of alliances in times of war. Yet the stories told by Americans often focused primarily on America's contributions to the battle. D-Day stood as a day of liberation, as the beginning of the end of the war, and as evidence of American benevolence in a dangerous world. America's cultural landscape took shape from such characterizations of the battle. A good fight waged by brave patriots to liberate others created a paradigm that made subsequent wars seem more acceptable.

Two decades after 1944, D-Day remained somewhat mutable in the American popular mind. D-Day reverberated through a mounting wave of articles, books, monuments, movies, and commemorations. The recurrent themes that extolled American martial prowess in a quest for liberty indicated the widespread acceptance of this version of the past. These commemorative works reflected prevailing notions of D-Day, the Second World War, and America while they also strengthened those popular understandings. Several disputes over authority to commemorate the battle indicated that contests could erupt even over this venerated event. Because of the politicized use of the past, the potential for a far more serious backlash surfaced. The D-Day stories circulating in American society often reaffirmed cherished notions of America's nature and role in the world. These mostly benign interpretations of the past, however, would face an enormous challenge from events taking place in the jungles of Southeast Asia.

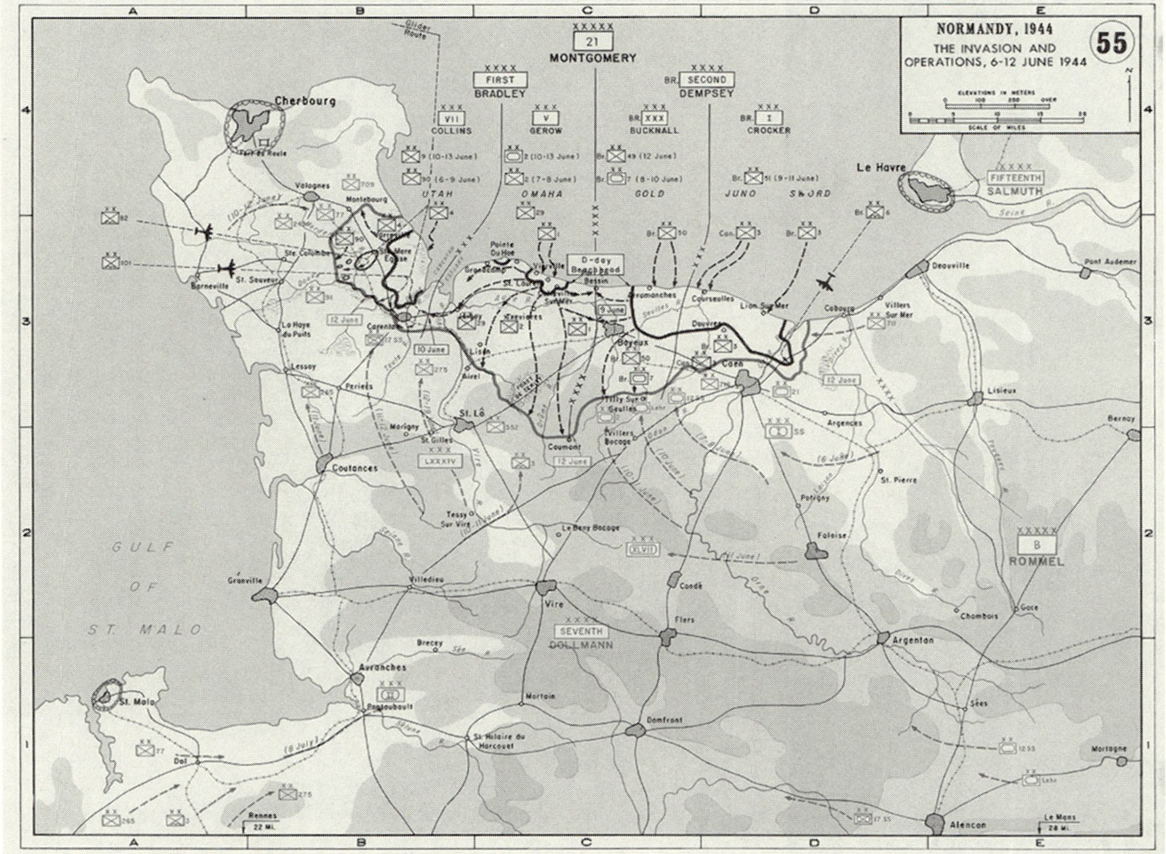

Map of the Normandy invasion area. The Cotentin Peninsula is to the left. The beaches, running west to east, include Utah (U.S.), Omaha (U.S.), Gold (U.K.), Juno (Canada), and Sword (U.K.). The American airborne forces landed behind Utah beach on the Cotentin (approximate areas denoted). The British air landings, of Pegasus Bridge fame, occurred on the eastern flank of the invasion zone shown on the right here. Map courtesy of David Stephens, "Making Sense of Maps," *History Matters: The U.S. Survey Course on the Web,* February 2002, http://historymatters.gmu.edu/mse/maps/ (accessed 11 October 2014).

American soldiers wade ashore on Omaha Beach, June 6, 1944. This shot represents one of the iconic and most often reproduced images associated with the invasion. Courtesy of U.S. Coast Guard Collection at the U.S. National Archives and Records Administration.

Low tide on Omaha Beach looking toward the bluffs, 2010. This picture covers the western portion of Omaha, Dog Green sector, with the Vierville draw located to the right. On June 6, 1944, anti-landing obstacles littered the beach. Author's collection.

Eastward view over Omaha Beach, Charlie and Dog Green sectors, at low tide. This shot looks out from the remains of one German defensive position. *Wiederstandsnest* 72 provided murderous enfilading fire on the landing forces while obscuring its own location from naval bombarding units. The invading forces had to confront beach obstacles while moving from left to right in front of this position. This section of the beach witnessed the destruction of A Company, 116th Infantry, 29th Infantry Division—the so-called Bedford Boys. The Vierville draw appears on the right of the picture where the National Guard Monument stands today. Author's collection.

Bird's-eye view of landing craft, barrage balloons, and allied troops landing in Normandy, France on D-Day." June 6, 1944. *New York World-Telegram and Sun* Collection. Library of Congress.

SUPREME HEADQUARTERS
ALLIED EXPEDITIONARY FORCE

Soldiers, Sailors and Airmen of the Allied Expeditionary Force!

You are about to embark upon the Great Crusade, toward which we have striven these many months. The eyes of the world are upon you. The hopes and prayers of liberty-loving people everywhere march with you. In company with our brave Allies and brothers-in-arms on other Fronts, you will bring about the destruction of the German war machine, the elimination of Nazi tyranny over the oppressed peoples of Europe, and security for ourselves in a free world.

Your task will not be an easy one. Your enemy is well trained, well equipped and battle-hardened. He will fight savagely.

But this is the year 1944 ! Much has happened since the Nazi triumphs of 1940-41. The United Nations have inflicted upon the Germans great defeats, in open battle, man-to-man. Our air offensive has seriously reduced their strength in the air and their capacity to wage war on the ground. Our Home Fronts have given us an overwhelming superiority in weapons and munitions of war, and placed at our disposal great reserves of trained fighting men. The tide has turned ! The free men of the world are marching together to Victory !

I have full confidence in your courage, devotion to duty and skill in battle. We will accept nothing less than full Victory !

Good Luck ! And let us all beseech the blessing of Almighty God upon this great and noble undertaking.

The Order of the Day issued by General Dwight D. Eisenhower to the "Soldiers, Sailors and Airmen of the Allied Expeditionary Force" prior to the invasion. With it, Eisenhower assured his fighting forces that they were engaged in a "Great Crusade" to liberate the oppressed and restore morality to the world. Courtesy of U.S. National Archives and Records Administration.

The Normandy American Cemetery in St. Laurent in 1947. The temporary grave markers were still in place at this time. Courtesy of U.S. National Archives and Records Administration.

Bird's-eye view of the Normandy American Cemetery in St. Laurent. Courtesy of the American Battle Monuments Commission.

Mourning the loss. The 1st Infantry Division monument in Normandy. The small column, erected in the late 1940s, stands along Omaha Beach at St. Laurent.

"The Spirit of American Youth" (above) by Donald de Lue stands at the eastern end of the Normandy American Cemetery. Riding atop a cresting wave, a young American looks skyward in an allegorical depiction of those lost in the quest for liberty ascending to heaven. Another photo (below) appeared in 1956 to document the cemetery's July 18 dedication. It looks east at the statue. The image on the bottom shows the cemetery today, looking westward towards the graves area. Above photo from author's collection; below photo courtesy of American Battle Monuments Commission.

Church steeple at Sainte-Mère-Église (above) in 2010. Residents of the town continue to drape there a re-creation of an American airborne infantryman caught by his parachute. The reference of this scene is to one of the harrowing vignettes immortalized by Cornelius Ryan in his book *The Longest Day* (1959) and in the film adaptation several years later (1962). The town presents many similar actions that convey the "experience" of D-Day to the thousands of visitors who flock there every year, such as the veterans of the battle and active-duty soldiers shown below. As the caption for that photo indicates, "Zane Schlemmer, a veteran U.S. Army paratrooper who jumped into northern France as a sergeant with the 82nd Airborne Division, walks in his jump boots down the main street of Sainte Mere Eglise with other World War II veterans during the sixty-seventh anniversary of the Allied invasion of France, June 5, 2011." Above photo from author's collection; below photo courtesy of U.S. Army, taken by Sergeant Michael J. MacLeod.

One section of the D-Day mural unveiled in 1967 at the museum for the U.S. Army Military Academy, West Point, New York. The artist, William Linzee Prescott, was a D-Day veteran. The mural was a gift of the Class of 1944, which graduated on the day of the invasion. Photo courtesy of Eric Klinek.

By the late 1970s and early 1980s, D-Day toys and games became increasingly popular. The box for the popular 1977 rerelease of *D-Day* by the Avalon Hill company. This game featured detailed rules, well-researched background notes on the invasion that included period newspapers (Allied only), and an intricate combat system to let gamers determine the outcome of "the greatest invasion in modern-day history." Photo from author's collection.

CHAPTER 4
THE NIGHTMARE ECLIPSES THE LONGEST DAY

The Quagmire

The steel prows of the landing craft crashed through a stormy, troubled sea. An overcast sky in the early morning hours threw an ominous pallor over the day. Men in the craft grunted and jostled about in nervous anticipation as the shore grew ever closer. Amphibious assaults are never cakewalks, and the sheer uncertainty of what was soon to unfold added to the tensions. The rough seas wreaked havoc with the landing plans, disorienting the incoming forces and producing the first casualties of the day. Despite such challenges, landing craft began crunching into the beach just a few minutes later than the intended assault hour. The men inside lurched forward upon landing, crossed the lowered ramps of the craft, and came out onto the beach. Rather than hostile fire, the men encountered a gaggle of smiling children and university students. Signs welcomed the landing force as local residents handed out colorful leis to the Americans of the 3rd Marine Division. It was March 8, 1965, and the many incongruities in this scene at Da Nang, South Vietnam, foreshadowed the ironic war that followed.[1]

That day most Americans did not worry about distant war.[2] One did not even have to look overseas for violent conflict. The prospect of racially motivated violence in Selma prompted the NAACP to call for U.S. military intervention in Alabama.[3] Public apathy concerning Southeast Asia enabled Johnson administration officials to disguise the move towards war in the crucial period of 1964–65.[4] President Johnson's shift from election campaigning on a non-war stance in 1964 to authorizing military action in Vietnam the following year dashed any hopes to avoid outright war.[5]

Some people compared the Korean War's 1950 Inchon landings to D-Day. Following the Marines' arrival at Da Nang, however, the American government employed a different paradigm to explain events. This approach is understandable because of the differences between D-Day and the almost festive Da Nang landings. In March 1965, American officials claimed that the 3rd Marine Division constituted a "defensive" force.[6] The peaceful insertion of Marines to defend an embattled ally stood a world apart from D-Day's bloody assaults. Over the following decade, popular war stories that had trumpeted American successes like D-Day while evading ambiguous military ventures, such as Korea, seemed increasingly different from the Vietnam experience. Tales of Second World War heroism shifted from helping sell a new war for liberty and freedom to undermining popular support for a conflict that failed to live up to expectations.

Literary scholar and Second World War veteran Paul Fussell developed an analytical framework useful for explaining the American perception of the Vietnam War. Fussell stressed the role of irony in shaping understandings of war. He insisted, "Every war is ironic because every war is worse than expected."[7] The dissonance between a naively optimistic outset and the nightmarish realities of the Vietnam War struck a powerful blow to the American psyche.

Americans came to discern two overwhelming and related ironies regarding Vietnam. The American people assumed that their military forces would win after confronting some difficulties, and they expected the South Vietnamese to appreciate American efforts to forestall a Communist takeover. The American public and their military forces would face tremendous chasms between what they expected and what they found out in Asia. In this new war of eight, nine, ten, or eleven years—depending on the starting and ending dates selected—America would follow with faltering steps its French ally's doomed path in Vietnam.[8]

The irony lay in American expectations of easy success and warm thanks. Instead, Americans endured hardship, defeat, and growing doubts concerning their country's moralistic worldview. In early 1965, America's allies remained unsure regarding the chances for success in Vietnam.[9] The South Vietnamese government only reluctantly accepted increased foreign intervention, while the American public stood more confused than reassured.

Americans had often turned to history for guidance. Tales of D-Day glory helped sell an uncertain public on the feasibility of new military adventures abroad. Vietnam, however, seemed so different from the outset that the past appeared to offer few indicators for America's future course.[10] As the gulf between expectation and outcome became more obvious, cynicism took hold, and fewer Americans deemed as relevant a vision of war based on battlefield heroics. D-Day stories, as a result, lost the degree of mainstream attention evident in the earlier 1960s. Some people attempted to cling to laudable elements of the nation's past even in the depths of doubt engendered by the Vietnam War. The prevalent interpretations of D-Day fit an effort to focus public attention on an ennobled past rather than a divisive present. Their rear-guard popularizing activities showed stability in the ascribed meaning of D-Day, only with fewer reverberations as American society attended to other matters.

When the Past Muddles the Present

Commemorations of D-Day and the Second World War did not create the impetus for war in Southeast Asia. These interpretations of the past, nevertheless, did factor into the American march to war in Vietnam. D-Day stories of glorious combat, honor earned, and morality reaffirmed validated military action as a justifiable response to provocation. Rhetorical constructions emphasizing freedom and liberty influenced American foreign policy formation in the twentieth century.[11] The Johnson administration's decision to cast its Vietnamese gambit as a struggle for freedom ensured public support for the growing American commitment. By the mid-1960s, Americans had absorbed two decades' worth of stories celebrating their country's strength, moral superiority, and benign leadership. These conceptions of the past drew largely on the Second World War, and on key battles like D-Day, to strengthen America's positive self-perception. Stories of D-Day facilitated the militarization of American society. Americans increasingly favored militaristic approaches as policy solutions.[12]

Militarism, following one definition, includes romanticized views of soldiers, the feeling that national greatness depends on military strength, and belief in the efficacy of military force.[13] The prevailing D-Day accounts in circulation when the United States plunged into Vietnam as an active belligerent fit all three of these characteristics. These stories hailed American troops as democratic heroes, emphasized military success as a hallmark of American greatness, and argued that military force proved a better way to deal with aggressors than Munich-like concessions. Public memories of D-Day characterized combat as a bloody trial but one elevated by nobility and honor. This paradigm touted wars of liberation as the proper duty of powerful, free nations. D-Day stories by the 1960s evoked the moral and military power of freedom-fighting allies in a quest to defeat totalitarian enemies—a characterization shaded by Cold War priorities.

President Johnson explained the reason for American involvement in Vietnam during a July 28, 1965, news conference. Johnson invoked lessons from the past, liberally drawing on examples from the Second World War. "Three times in my lifetime," the president pointed out, "in two World Wars and in Korea, Americans have gone to far lands to fight for freedom." Johnson continued by indicating that the Second World War taught that weakness in the face of aggression only invites continued assaults. While employing the Munich analogy, the president's repeated references to freedom, liberty, and the commitment to preserve peace—through war—evoked common understandings of D-Day.[14] Two months to the day after U.S. Marines began the American occupation of the Dominican Republic, Johnson alleged that American forces occupied the Caribbean country for a justifiable purpose—to quell a military revolt. Quite in contrast, as he saw it, North Vietnamese aggressors sought to subvert democratic freedoms in South Vietnam.[15] These characterizations of the Dominican occupation and intervention in Vietnam hid murkier realities from the American public. Tropes of liberty, freedom, and America's benign use of power echoed the popular D-Day story in circulation over the preceding two decades. D-Day showed America using military force to liberate, not conquer, and that morality tale connected to the president's foreign-policy salesmanship.

Praising the liberty-preserving intent of the mission served as Washington's standard approach in the early years of America's overt involvement in Vietnam. At the same time, though, the Johnson administration and the Pentagon allowed a defensive tone to creep into their public pronouncements on the war. Johnson invoked repeatedly the moral justification for American intervention as a rallying cry to gain popular support for the war. Yet a clash between government rhetoric and reality defined much of the Vietnam imbroglio. Drawing on historical memories to legitimize America's attempt to preserve an independent South Vietnam, pro-war advocates found plenty of ammunition in the notion of D-Day's liberating mission—at first. Over time, the Vietnam War appeared increasingly distant from the honorable, justified, and decisive Second World War most Americans remembered.[16] The Vietnam War years witnessed a decline in the frequency and scope of D-Day commemorations. It seemed as though that much-celebrated event no longer spoke to America's present concerns.

Yet people still commemorated D-Day. Dwight Eisenhower remained an active D-Day advocate during these final years of his life.[17] He participated in the 1967 dedication of the D-Day mural at the U.S. Military Academy at West Point, New York. June 6, 1944, not only launched the Normandy invasion, but it was also graduation day that year at West Point. Eisenhower's son, John, belonged to that graduating class. The Class of 1944 decided to commemorate D-Day with a mural unveiled in the West Point Museum on June 2, 1967. The mural's artist, William Linzee Prescott, had jumped as a private with the 82nd Airborne Division on D-Day.[18] The mural's dedication highlighted D-Day's pedagogic value and link to the present. Colonel Winfield S. Scott, another member of the Class of 1944, organized the dedication ceremony and corresponded with the elder Eisenhower concerning the event. Scott also stressed the need for future officers to study operations like Overlord in "these days wherein non-nuclear hostilities can break out any place in the world."[19] In an article covering the mural's dedication, one journalist conveyed Eisenhower's explanation that military victory would come to American forces in South Vietnam as they fought once more for the liberation of a country.[20] Linking the two wars lent some initial legitimacy to the fighting in Southeast Asia.

Compared to the attention Americans had devoted to D-Day in the early 1960s, the following decade produced relatively few major commemorative activities focusing on the battle. Nevertheless, it did arise in some interesting areas. Cornelius Ryan's book *The Longest Day* continued to reach an ever-expanding circle of readers, selling more than five million copies worldwide by June 1965.[21] In the winter of 1966, members of the 1st Infantry Division collected and distributed toys for children. This charitable effort took place in parts of South Vietnam, the division's current deployment area, and an older battlefield in Colleville, France. Colleville stands at the end of one beach exit where the division had fought on D-Day. Of all locations on the division's long battle rolls, only a site connected to D-Day warranted such consideration.

Monument building activities in Normandy gathered steam in the late 1960s. The ABMC approved the National Guard Association's plans for a monument in 1964. By 1966, the commission noted that the town of Vierville, located at the end of another Omaha Beach exit, had allocated land for a monument marking the landings of the 29th Division.[22] These memorial projects indicate that in the early stages of the Vietnam War, the public and government remained generally supportive regarding D-Day commemoration.

While this construction proceeded, discord surfaced regarding the relatively neglected Utah Beach area. For years, veterans of the battle, such as then Major General James Lawton Collins, complained about the dearth of commemorative works in the area. The French had built a museum interpreting the battle at Utah Beach, but no American entity had placed its mark on this sector of the D-Day landings. While the ABMC moved toward approving the National Guard Association's project at Vierville, the commissioners also considered their own attempt to commemorate fighting on Utah Beach.[23] One project originated in the months leading to D-Day's twentieth anniversary. Two years later, with an architect selected, a plan in place, and $300,000 secured to fund this project, a monument consisting of two enormous pylons seemed well set for completion. Franco-American relations, however, had undergone a radical change between 1964 and 1966. French president Charles de Gaulle had ordered NATO forces, including American units, removed from France by March 1966. The chill in French attitudes also turned the projected American monument on Utah Beach into a bone of international contention. The monument lost local support in Normandy after word spread that the construction plan envisioned the destruction of several beachfront homes. In the face of expanding cost estimates, the ABMC halted this project in 1970.[24]

Even in the midst of international and domestic turbulence inspired in large part by the Vietnam crisis, D-Day still appeared in various guises. The battle remained a part of the national story of which mainstream society approved. Nevertheless, with the rising storm of dissent, elements of that national story came under increasingly sharp criticism or even outright rejection. America's benevolence, military competence, nonmilitaristic nature, and divine sanction all seemed less sustainable as the Vietnam quagmire led to greater destruction without appreciable gain. As one historian argued, "Between 1945 and 1975, the U.S. military reduced first Japan, then Korea, and finally Indochina to ruin. In each case, however, the end result proved disconcertingly unlike the one that the war story assured Americans would come." As a result, he noted that during this period "victory culture ended in America."[25] For those eager to retain the national morality tale, D-Day heroics offered a way to burnish American credentials as a powerful yet benevolent power. Yet D-Day, ebbing with this victory culture, received less consistent public attention over the next decade.

Ambivalence in a Time of War

The Tet Offensive in early 1968 often serves as a major turning point in narratives of the Vietnam War much as D-Day does in Second World War histories. The turn in this case, however, went for the worse as America's Vietnam venture supposedly slipped away. Enemy forces surprised Americans and their allies through a series of shocking attacks that began in late January. Blaming a hostile American press and weak-willed home front, however, many Americans preferred to overlook the strategic, tactical, and diplomatic problems that contributed to defeat.[26] Yet, by 1968 it was rather evident that Vietnam would not lead America to anything resembling a Second World War-style victory. As the country seemed on the brink of chaos with race riots, political assassinations, and widespread clashes among antiwar forces, pro-war forces, military, and law enforcement, this one year exhibited the darker sides of American society. Lyndon Johnson's withdrawal from the presidential election in March added to the sense of uncertainty wracking the country. Richard Nixon won the presidency in 1968 by promising a return to "law and order," while intimating that he had a secret plan for success in Vietnam.[27] Once Nixon took office, however, his plan proved nonexistent. The war lasted four more years for America, ending in early 1973, and went on two years more for the Vietnamese people.

Amid this turmoil, the twenty-fifth anniversary of D-Day in 1969 provided an opportunity for some to focus on positive aspects of America. With the looming anniversary, finishing preparations went into place to mark the dedication of three new monuments in the Normandy region. Instead of a project directed and financed by the ABMC, these monuments stemmed from the efforts of private organizations representing the 90th Infantry Division, 4th Infantry Division, and the National Guard. Smaller in scale than the ABMC's Utah Beach project, each of these monuments benefited from the more directed focus of their respective constituencies and the lower costs of less ambitious intentions. The National Guard Monument, commemorating the 29th Infantry Division's landing on Omaha Beach, indicated the political utility of these memorializing activities. At the dedication ceremony, Major General James Cantwell, president of the National Guard Association of the United States, insisted that this particular memorial would help to "maintain and to strengthen relationships between Allies that predate the founding of our Country."[28] Even as Franco-American relations fractured over Vietnam, European defense plans, or economic competition, Cantwell and others tried to fill in those fissures by emphasizing the historic ties between the countries.

Darryl Zanuck commemorated the twenty-fifth anniversary with an hour-long television special ostensibly honoring the men of D-Day. *D-Day Revisited* aired on May 30. Zanuck served as narrator, speaking to the camera as he walked through Normandy. The program featured clips from Zanuck's famed movie, *The Longest Day.* Zanuck claimed to salute the men of D-Day by discussing this film. At the end, Zanuck feigned dismay that his stark portrayal of the costs of D-Day failed to deter humanity from rushing into subsequent wars.[29] Such a claim revealed the difficulty of questioning war through visceral displays of combat since audiences might delight in thrilling action just as much as they may shrink from horrific carnage. The reception of the documentary tended towards the negative.[30] Notwithstanding such controversy, Zanuck's production did help publicize D-Day. Adding to the exposure, Cornelius Ryan's book had also exceeded 2.5 million volumes sold in the United States by late 1968 (less than half of the worldwide sales total but still a striking level of interest).[31]

Ryan returned to Normandy in June 1969 with a group of war correspondents. This group buried a time capsule and installed a plaque honoring General Eisenhower, who had died a few months earlier on March 28, 1969.[32] Eisenhower's death gave Americans an opportunity to pause and reflect on their country's recent past. The conjunction between his passing and D-Day's twenty-fifth anniversary inspired a joint celebration of the man and his most famous act as a leader. He had come to personify the positive D-Day story popular in America while serving as a representative of the wartime "heroes." As Omar Bradley confided to a reporter shortly after Ike's death, "I think the decision he made to go on D Day . . . was one of the greatest decisions in history."[33]

Eisenhower had previously worked with staff at his presidential library in Abilene, Kansas, to organize the 1969 D-Day commemorations. The museum adjacent to the library displayed a combat art exhibit created by veterans.[34] The library hosted a conference on D-Day. What the participants had to say shows that the positive characteristics ascribed to D-Day remained even as American society fragmented. War correspondent Don Whitehead insisted, "The history of the world changed on D-Day," and that with a reversal of the battle's outcome the "horizons of free men would have shrunk." Whitehead asserted that the Normandy American Cemetery enshrined "the spirit of free men fighting for the cause of freedom."[35] As America faced crises at home and abroad, some people clung to the sense of affirmation and assurance that the D-Day morality tale seemed to offer. Nevertheless, a sparsely attended conference hardly indicated that D-Day commemoration remained a pressing concern for the American public.

This conference took place in an atmosphere of extreme tension in American society. A majority of Americans no longer supported the war effort, which presented President Richard Nixon with the difficult task of steering the ship of state through the rocky shoals that an unpopular war had created.[36] His 1969 anniversary statements marking D-Day represented one official attempt to diffuse public dissent by idolizing the past. He asserted, "The Sixth of June was transformed on that day from a date on the calendar to a historical landmark in the history of freedom," a day that saved Western civilization. Nixon chose rhetoric that honored veterans, soothed those harboring doubts concerning America's benign intentions, and indirectly attacked his critics. Nixon could hope to quiet dissent against the ongoing war in Vietnam by linking it to D-Day's quest for freedom. Reminding Americans that the valorous actions of D-Day contributed to the "salvation of Western civilization," Nixon distanced American combat actions from those of others. Americans fought for freedom. "Our Nation and nations of free men everywhere," Nixon asserted, "are forever grateful for the sacrifices made in Normandy."[37] Nixon's avowals here suggested that freedom for the oppressed lay ahead, if only the Americans stayed the course.

Nixon avoided the Normandy ceremonies in 1969, as did many high-ranking officials from America's former wartime allies. The officials and veterans in attendance, however, attempted to reaffirm the honorific interpretation of D-Day even at this divisive juncture. The ceremonies in Normandy, therefore, constituted another venue to air these readings of the past, albeit with smaller audiences than had attended the twentieth-anniversary events. The twentieth anniversary brought nearly ten thousand American D-Day veterans to Normandy. In 1969, a little more than a thousand of these men came to France.[38] The media coverage of the anniversary also displayed a less intense fixation on D-Day. News articles or television programming appeared but quickly lapsed in the following day or two, again unlike the twentieth anniversary.

The messages conveyed at the D-Day observances in Normandy that year stressed the need for alliance unity. They also extolled an Allied military triumph against enormous odds while highlighting America's sacrifices to free people from oppression. Former president Johnson issued a statement that declared, "Many brave soldiers laid down their lives on that occasion—and no man ever died in a higher cause. For this was an invasion, not to enslave people, but to free them, not to oppress, but to liberate." The American ambassador to France, Sargent Shriver, argued that the "cause of freedom has always demanded a fearsome price" but the "6th of June was the birth of a new day on the Continent of Europe." A recycled proclamation from 1964 carried the views of the late President Eisenhower. Eisenhower had insisted that "we are impelled to thank a kindly Providence for the success of the entire venture."[39] By 1969, many of these points had long pedigrees in American commemorations of D-Day.

Yet even as these familiar views surfaced, other sentiments joined them. Some American newspaper stories connected the D-Day commemorations with the ongoing war in Vietnam. Several U.S. Army units that had fought on D-Day, such as the 1st and 4th Infantry Divisions, were then deployed in Vietnam and articles noted the connection of past and present service.[40] Norman locals gratefully enthused over returning veterans, and the multiday festivities included bands, marching troops, reenactments, and souvenir sales. The celebratory mood that gripped Normandy, however, stood in stark contrast against a background of tense international relations.

Individuals still found ways to keep memories of D-Day and the Second World War alive in American remembrance. Veteran and historian Charles MacDonald, for instance, published the popular book *The Mighty Endeavor* in 1969. MacDonald took his title from a line in President Roosevelt's D-Day prayer. The book devoted a chapter to the invasion that presented the standard narrative of vast Allied preparations for and skillful execution on D-Day.[41]

Demonstrating the allure of the Second World War, the Academy Award-winning 1970 movie *Patton* set box-office records with a riveting portrait of one of the most famous and controversial American generals of that conflict. George C. Scott's masterful performance permitted varied readings on Patton, which suited politically divided audiences. Delivering a monologue alone in front of a huge American flag, Patton started the movie by instructing his (unseen) soldiers: "I want you to remember that no bastard ever won a war by dying for his country. He won it by making the other poor dumb bastard die for his country." Striking a chord during the divisive Vietnam era, Patton assured that "all this stuff you've heard about America not wanting to fight, wanting to stay out of the war, is a lot of horse dung." He confidently asserted, "All real Americans love the sting of battle." According to Patton, "That's why Americans have never lost and will never lose a war. Because the very thought of losing is hateful to Americans."[42] Americans had grown ambivalent about military affairs—wanting to win in war yet leery of gung-ho militarism, hoping for a Second World War victory yet uncertain of outcome in Vietnam.[43] Patton fascinated Americans because he was a winning military leader, and this production highlighted a war quite at odds with the grueling conflagration in Vietnam.[44]

Just one month after *Patton*'s April 1970 premiere, President Nixon authorized an invasion of Cambodia that expanded the conflict zone while sparking massive protests in the United States. The Cambodian invasion reflected the fluid nature of the Vietnam War, a conflict that superseded the niceties of international borders. Vietnamese Communist forces traversed ostensibly neutral countries, such as Cambodia, when funneling personnel and matériel to South Vietnam. In tandem with the Vietnamization policy of turning combat over to the Army of the Republic of Vietnam (ARVN), Nixon hoped that major strikes like the Cambodian incursion would help place South Vietnam on stable footing to continue its anti-Communist fight. While the mid-1970 thrust into Cambodia did disrupt significant logistic infrastructure, it failed to destroy the Communist forces. Furthermore, after drawing down the American presence in Vietnam, the new attack—although reflective of realities on the ground that included all sides freely crossing borders—appeared to be an escalation when most Americans simply wanted an end. Massive protests flared up in the United States, leading to the Kent State University shootings of American youth by an Ohio National Guard unit and a similar shocking event at Jackson State College in Mississippi.[45]

It took more than two years before American and North Vietnamese negotiators could come to an agreement in their stuttered talks. A cease-fire went into effect in January 1973. This settlement facilitated the final withdrawal of American combat forces from South Vietnam. The North Vietnamese army and the Viet Cong remained in place throughout the South. Although Nixon proclaimed "peace with honor," the United States had actually pulled out of a war it could not win and was no longer willing to fight.[46] Two years after this settlement, the North Vietnamese consummated victory in a major offensive that reunited the country under their control. The iconic photo of the hasty American retreat from Saigon via a helicopter evacuation displayed none of the triumphalism attendant with the prevalent D-Day imagery.

While this calamity played out, a new British documentary series, *The World at War,* debuted in the United Kingdom and the United States in 1973–74. Thames Television had committed four years and an unprecedentedly large budget to complete this twenty-six-episode production. Immediately hailed for its unflinchingly realistic view of the Second World War's horrors, the series has rerun almost continuously ever since.[47] Sir Laurence Olivier graced the production with an appropriately somber narration. In 1944, he directed and starred in a jaunty film version of Shakespeare's *Henry V,* which depicted a historic English invasion of France that played in theaters during the period of Operation Overlord. Olivier's lyrical rendition of Shakespeare influenced the wartime documentary *The True Glory.* With *The World at War,* Olivier mesmerized audiences once more with his verbal incantations as scenes of devastation flashed across the screen. Unlike the dash and adventurism in a Shakespearian paean to English might, *The World at War* portrayed the Second World War as a horrifically destructive tragedy.[48]

The seventeenth episode in the series, "Morning: June–August 1944," covers the Normandy invasion. As a British production, the script lingers more on transatlantic cooperation than standard American versions of D-Day had done. Winston Churchill functions here as the moral backbone, predicting the new dawn for Allied fortunes. D-Day constitutes the realization of that prediction, the new "morning" of the title. Stock shots accompany a familiar rendition of the enormous planning and preparation for the invasion. Once again, Ike's decision to launch despite the dangers appear as almost divinely inspired because of the fortuitous results. Through the grim depiction of costly battle, the Allies advance despite staunch German resistance. After approximately thirty-seven minutes of coverage, Olivier pays homage to the more than nine thousand casualties the Allies sustained on June 6, 1944.

While depictions of war's barbarous nature added to the somber atmosphere of the early 1970s, some of the personalities who had dominated D-Day commemorative activities and the stories circulated about the battle stood down or passed away. Thomas North, the long-serving secretary of the ABMC that had shaped so much of the Normandy commemorative landscape, retired against his wishes in late 1968.[49] In March of the following year, Eisenhower died. Brigadier General Willard G. Wyman, assistant commander for the 1st Infantry Division on D-Day, also passed away in 1969.[50] Major General Clarence Huebner, Wyman's chief, followed him three years later.[51] James Earl Rudder, the lieutenant colonel commanding the 2nd Ranger Battalion at Pointe du Hoc, died in 1970.[52] Mike Kelty, the original director of the Cantigny War Memorial Museum, passed on in 1973.[53] Cornelius Ryan, whose book and the movie it inspired did so much to popularize D-Day, lost his battle with cancer late in 1974.[54] This group's collective voice was no longer available as America turned to a trying post-Vietnam era.

An American Crisis of Confidence

The mid-1970s seemed vastly changed from the mid-1960s, a mere decade before. With the convivial celebrations commemorating D-Day's twentieth anniversary, Americans heard stories of past greatness that reaffirmed present power and righteousness. By 1974, after withdrawing from Vietnam and experiencing years of massive domestic unrest, anecdotes of former glory no longer seemed quite so alluring. Adding to the shifting priorities of society, economic crises ended the long period of abundant growth that had been the apparent norm since the Second World War. Guns and butter with Vietnam and the Great Society proved too much for even the doughty American economy and, by the early 1970s, major cracks appeared in the system.[55] Energy crises and oil embargoes, increased global economic competition, and rising prices combined with stagnant American growth into the miserable era of "stagflation."

Amid all this tumult, the thirtieth anniversary of D-Day came and went with relatively little fanfare. In 1974, American veteran tour groups either canceled their trips to Normandy or witnessed drastic drops in attendance. The National Guard Association brought fifteen hundred attendees for a Normandy reunion tour in 1969, but that figure declined to a mere twenty-four in 1974. A poor exchange rate hampered travel plans. Frosty Franco-American relations and Vietnam-induced weariness played important roles as well.[56] With the Watergate crisis building to its traumatic conclusion in America that summer, understandably few high-ranking officials journeyed to France for commemorative events.

Official Franco-American ceremonies nevertheless marked the anniversary. Despite decreased attendance, people still traveled to France to commemorate D-Day. June 6, 1974, like many other Norman summer days, opened with overcast skies and rain. The D-Day anniversary attracted approximately fifteen hundred American veterans and nearly one thousand French citizens.[57] A few of the remaining high-ranking figures from D-Day, such as Omar Bradley, James Lawton Collins, and Matthew Ridgway, came to the fetes that trumpeted well-established themes. The French duly thanked the Americans for restoring their liberty. American speakers noted the bonds of friendship uniting the two republics in their mutual quest for freedom.

The Veterans of Foreign Wars produced a publication in 1974 describing the thirtieth anniversary ceremonies in France. This booklet printed the remarks read at the day's various ceremonies. John N. Irwin II, the American ambassador to France, honored the D-Day combatants by proclaiming, "They were willing to fight, suffer and die to gain peace and freedom. We must match the resolve they had if we are to preserve the peace they won." That latter sentiment echoed throughout many of the day's statements. An almost plaintive insistence emanated from many of the claims, such as Omar Bradley's urging, "Our veterans kept the faith. It is now up to us to keep the faith."[58] Freedom, liberty, and unity in the face of danger all proved familiar topics for D-Day commemorations. The undercurrent of criticism in these remarks, however, distinguishes the mid-1970s commemorative approach from years past, when the "keeping the faith" sentiment failed to appear.

For the moment, few seemed to pay attention to these assertions. Sagas of past glory faded in relevance as one hammer blow after another fell on American society. One major film production on the battle was not even released in the United States at this time. The 1975 British film *Overlord* presented a frenetic, gruesome, and rather somber depiction of war's costs and consequences. The production portrayed the enlistment, training, and D-Day experience of Tom Beddoes, played by Brian Stirner. Beddoes's

D-Day experience was incredibly short as he died from a bullet shot to the head while still aboard his landing craft on the run into the beach. *Overlord* did not appear in American theaters for thirty years.[59] The film's director, Stuart Cooper, explained what delayed its American debut: "It was at the back end of the Vietnam War at the time, and it was not the most salient time to bring out a war picture."[60]

Some people wrote letters to the ABMC proposing plans for new monuments in Normandy. The commission often turned down such suggestions because of the budget cuts that dogged it in the 1970s. In fact, the ABMC found it difficult to maintain its extant structures. In 1976, a campaign arose to transfer the Pointe du Hoc commemorative area to American control from its French owners. One report noted the area's unkempt nature and the lack of safety or public-access features. Pointe du Hoc stood in the forefront of America's D-Day memories, symbolizing Allied troops as underdogs transformed by heroism into liberators. Through sheer grit and determination, U.S. Army Rangers climbed the cliffs in the face of heavy fire, seized their objective, and then held it for several days without support from the main Allied forces. Despite the thrilling stories associated with this action, Americans had neglected this part of the battlefield in their commemorative activities since the war. French residents and some Americans sought ABMC oversight of this area in a quest to secure the funds necessary to establish a suitable memorial. Despite such a link, officials remained hesitant to act because of fiscal concerns, which likely would not have factored so heavily into considerations a decade before.[61]

While sporadic discussions ensued over commemorations of a battle thirty years in the past, Americans at this time avoided memorializing the more recent war in Vietnam. Access to commemorative space shapes public remembrance, and a hostile Vietnam prevented any American memorialization efforts on its soil. Mainstream American society felt closer ties to Western Europe anyway, a more accessible region in geographic, financial, and cultural terms. After the Second World War, organizations like the ABMC—an independent government agency—made a concerted effort to retain control of battle sites in Europe, not in Asia.[62]

As with Korea and Vietnam, the disinclination to implant permanent American markers outside of Europe continued. Of course, one other obvious point is that commemorating the Second World War did not take America out of its comfort zone; the war was a success, after all. American stories about Vietnam have tended to focus on America's experience in

Vietnam.[63] Rather than a holistic appraisal of the causes, conduct, or consequences of this conflict, the stories boil down to accounts of Americans in Vietnam or the effects the war had on America. If American war stories have tended to dwell on America's experiences, the Second World War stood in a more appealing light than Vietnam. The prior conflict, and key battles like D-Day, offered *better* stories of success and salvation. Still, relatively few people celebrated warfare in the late 1970s in national conversations.

Celebration was not quite the order of the day in 1979. Early that year, President Jimmy Carter decided to reorient Americans by issuing a hard-nosed consideration of the country's problems. Carter acted on this impulse with his "malaise" speech of July 15, 1979, which referred to a general crisis gripping the country. He claimed that it struck "at the very heart and soul and spirit of our national will." Carter continued, "We can see this crisis in the growing doubt about the meaning of our own lives and in the loss of a unity of purpose for our nation."[64] Adding to a sense of uncertainty at home, the Iranian Revolution of 1978–79 overthrew the ill-fated Shah Mohammad Reza Pahlavi from power, which resulted in the storming of the American embassy. American hostages seized there remained in Iranian hands for 444 days. Americans could not believe that such a small country had succeeded in defying the United States with impunity.[65]

In this atmosphere of doubt, the thirty-fifth anniversary of D-Day witnessed limited overt celebration. When Carter met with West Germany's chancellor Helmut Schmidt on June 6, 1979, he failed to mention D-Day in their press conference.[66] Carter knew of the battle. Indeed, he had visited the Normandy battlefields in 1978, the first sitting president to do so.[67] Carter's apparent disregard perhaps stemmed from the many pressing issues he faced in the period preceding the "malaise" speech. Panegyrics to D-Day, perhaps, did not fit his mood in mid-1979. The celebration of warfare, even to ease American despair, simply did not complement Carter's three main themes while in office: "peace, human rights, and the environment."[68]

In 1979, nevertheless, Frenchmen and Americans gathered on Pointe du Hoc to dedicate the new Ranger Dagger monument. The monument symbolized the distinctive weapon issued to the U.S. Army Rangers who climbed the cliffs there on D-Day. French citizens paid for the monument's construction. Upon its completion and dedication, the local French government ceded the monument and surrounding area to the ABMC. The French wished to pass on the onerous maintenance costs demanded by such an enhanced site.

Omar Bradley traveled to this place that epitomized American D-Day heroics to offer a poignant dedicatory speech. While too frail to stand without assistance, Bradley's evocation of the extraordinary courage required to scale those cliffs proved a stirring testament to the Rangers. "Let us pay honor to those men," he urged, "and pray that there will always be people prepared to do the impossible."[69] Drawing five thousand total attendees, mostly locals, the 1979 anniversary attracted half the number of American veterans who had flocked to the 1964 ceremonies.[70]

Attendance rates at commemorative ceremonies only partially demonstrated the relative decline of D-Day's prominence at this time. It is worth stressing that for some people the battle remained an important event. Even during a period of general torpor that limited widespread D-Day celebration, ceremonies, monument constructions, tourism, and writing related to the battle continued, albeit in diminished forms. Participation in overseas honorific ceremonies declined noticeably. Poor exchange rates, declining discretionary income, and international tensions likely dissuaded some Americans from traveling abroad.

Decreased historical tourism does not imply that Americans had forgotten about D-Day. One indicator of a more personalized engagement with the past comes from individualized consumption of remembrance activities. The desire to own an object connected to D-Day—even something smacking of the vulgar or kitsch—shaped a tourist-based economy in France's Calvados coast, site of the Normandy landings. Shops there sold an array of memorabilia linked to the battle or items merely with the name, date, or commemorative year emblazoned in a sort of brand-name fashion. Tourists could purchase Zippo lighters, hats, maps, bottles of sand, buttons, and scraps of metal throughout the beach zone, especially on any D-Day anniversary.[71]

Beyond owning a piece of history, other ways of connecting to D-Day flourished. A war-gaming culture emerged in America during the 1970s.[72] These war games enabled a performance-based interaction with the past. For instance, the Avalon Hill company produced a number of popular board games in the 1970s, including the popular 1977 rerelease of *D-Day.* This game featured detailed rules, well-researched background notes on the invasion that included period newspapers (Allied only), and an intricate combat system to let gamers determine the outcome of battle. The game, however, pushed players in certain directions. The scenarios only permitted a combined amphibious and airborne invasion in a few different locations, and seriously hampered a "German" player's ability to thwart even a mediocre opponent's attempted operation. Labeling the enemy as the "Nazi forces" also reminded players which side in the end stood for morality.[73] Board games of this nature depicted a particular kind of history, one of aggression, warfare, militant solutions to problems of all sort, and a world of clear linearity.[74] The Avalon Hill game ensured that the Western Allies would, most of the time, win in the "greatest invasion" that "determines the outcome of World War II." Guidance for a "correct" perception of the events appeared in abundance here.

The publishing and the film industries also afforded opportunities for individuals to interact with the past. The late 1970s, however, contained relatively few examples of D-Day-specific content in any of these areas. Perhaps a mixture of market saturation and general war weariness combined to deter companies from producing more works in this vein. A dearth of new film or television programming on D-Day did not mean the event no longer mattered to many Americans. For instance, filmmaker Sam Fuller, a Second World War veteran, finally returned to his long-postponed project of paying homage to his beloved 1st Infantry Division. Fuller had kept his 1st Infantry Division friends informed of his plans and setbacks with updates sent to their association's newsletter, *Bridgehead Sentinel,* throughout the 1970s. He reassured his fellow veterans that his film would offer due regard to the unit and its wartime members.[75]

Fuller's film, *The Big Red One,* finally hit the big screen in 1980. It followed a small group of men in the starred 1st Infantry Division through their hard fighting all over the Mediterranean and Northwestern Europe.[76] The film marked the end of one long dream for Fuller, as he had sought to make this cinematic ode to his beloved division for over two decades. The beginning of the movie displayed the disclaimer, "This is a fictional story based on factual death," which set an appropriately somber tone.[77] Audiences came to identify with a group of affable young men enduring an arduous ordeal.[78] People could more easily empathize with these lifelike characters than with the flurry of individuals portrayed in *The Longest Day,* which reflected a "difference between the personal and the epic."[79] Owing to Fuller's own combat experiences, which formed the basis of his book and movie, *The Big Red One*'s depiction of battle contrasted with war films of the late 1970s. Productions about the Vietnam War that began appearing in the late 1970s often portrayed combat as pointless terror, brutalizing those on both sides of the fighting. These productions usually offered their characters minimal hope for self-preservation and few chances to achieve victory or glory.[80] Fuller's main characters, on the other hand, survived the war and acted nobly in the process.

Fuller's *The Big Red One,* filmed in the post-Production Code period, included scenes that would not have passed in earlier films, such as some graphic bloodshed. The violence and brutality of conflict shifted in their presentation from allusion to ghastly special effects–produced gore. Yet Fuller's film is also a rejection of Vietnam-era movie tendencies in that there is an ultimate purpose to the violence, and that purpose is just. The enemy forces are moral inferiors, and the small group of Americans followed, despite errors and excesses, are "good" guys.

One notable undercurrent in *The Big Red One* is a tense cynicism regarding the abilities of high-level leadership. In the buildup to D-Day, the men are constantly reassured that the action will be a cakewalk over second-rate forces. Quite abruptly, though, the camera shifts to chaotic battle, massive explosions, and gory deaths. It serves as a telling indictment of high command, especially as all the results come from the small groupings of disconnected men performing on their own initiative. The cynical rejection of high-level leadership certainly seemed au currant with the 1980s.[81] Nevertheless, in *The Big Red One* there was a point to the violence: defeating evil. Although that theme had appeared in many other movies, its reemergence in a film portraying the D-Day invasion is noteworthy.

Fuller indicated that his production entered into conversation with other depictions of the war, such as *The Longest Day.*[82] In a 1980 interview, Fuller explained that he opted to focus on the raw emotions of combatants in war rather than provide strategic overview, show high-level commanders, or rely upon a cavalcade of stars.[83] Fuller claimed to avoid sentimentalizing the war and wallowing in unrealistic plot lines. He rejected the stylistic conventions that defined American war films, particularly those related to the Second World War. Instead, Fuller sought to focus upon the infantryman's struggle to survive, devoid of higher moralizations. Nevertheless, in his hands, GIs appeared as cynical yet moral champions of order. The Americans ceased fighting briefly to help deliver a baby, cared deeply for one another, and stood as defenders of democratic ways. Germans, on the other hand, slaughtered innocents and used foul tricks. The final major combat scene conveyed their bestial nature. After Fuller's GIs have fought their way through an abandoned concentration camp, the camera lingers on a still-smoking section of ovens. The few surviving emaciated prisoners symbolized Nazi atrocities.[84]

The Big Red One failed at the box office. Despite Fuller's usual cost-conscious filming, his production budget ballooned, as did post-production costs, especially for advertising. For a film that required $9.5 million to make and market, it returned only $2.5 million in the initial theater run. Lorimar Pictures, *The Big Red One*'s production company, shortly thereafter went out of business.[85] War films like Fuller's seemed to be a risky investment in a war-weary America.

Fuller's attempt to refurbish American honor, however, fit with a new development in society. The concentration camp scene highlighted Nazi atrocities in the war, which not only reflected history but also a shift in how Americans chose to remember the Second World War. American society had not paid much attention to the Holocaust until the 1970s. Clearly, some communities focused more on the Holocaust than others. Interpretations of the Holocaust that cast Jews as the main victims of a uniquely evil deed had appeared sporadically before the late 1970s. The Holocaust surfaced in books, plays, movies, or in all three, as with *The Diary of Anne Frank*.[86] It even appeared referentially in such untoward places as an episode of the popular series *Star Trek*.[87] The point is not that the Holocaust failed to appear, but rather that it only became an archetypal event in American popular consciousness by the late 1970s.[88]

The Holocaust emerged as a striking aspect of the past at that time for a variety of reasons.[89] For Americans, it was a "safe" memory. In a period that witnessed a rash of criticism highlighting American racism or social ills, stories of the Holocaust safely located evil overseas. The Holocaust helped restore American honor because of the country's significant role in ending Nazi atrocities. As with D-Day, a combination of prior history, current pressures, and the concerted efforts of memory activists helped imprint particular versions of the Holocaust on the American mind. This increase in attention drew on many sources, like the 1978 broadcast of the popular NBC miniseries, *The Holocaust.* Interestingly, the newfound American interest in Nazi genocide helped stimulate D-Day's resumed prevalence in American society. The Holocaust conveyed, in the starkest terms possible, what the Allies had fought to defeat. D-Day, as the beginning of the end, regained relevance in conjunction with this rise of Holocaust memories. In a sense, D-Day heroics and Second World War stories in general could once more serve as reminders of the positive side of America's past—even its military past.

Darkness before Dawn: The Low Point in D-Day Awareness

America's national story went askew in the late 1960s and 1970s. With a divisive and unsuccessful war, economic decline, social divisions, and political crises, a dark cloud had settled over the country. This period was not one of pure misery or absent progress.[90] Nevertheless, a perceptual change from relative confidence and abundance at the outset and the cynical, doubt-ridden society by the end of this era showed a noteworthy transformation. Jimmy Carter was more right than wrong with his crisis-of-confidence speech. People just did not want to hear such blunt assessments of their travails. A focus on previous world-saving exploits, like the liberation of France, could have helped American society work through the negative period of the late 1960s and 1970s. Yet the role that D-Day and Second World War veneration had played in the too-easy march to war in Vietnam likely made both memories victims of the palpable antimilitarism that crept into national conversations. Antimilitarism, however, was surface deep and transitory in the mainstream. The striking descent of D-Day's prominence from 1964 to 1974 indicates the rapid withdrawal from Second World War-related celebrationism in American society. D-Day had shown America at its greatest, as the stories went; dulled by the pain of defeat abroad and dissent at home, that tale just seemed less relevant. D-Day did not lead to Vietnam, but a growing sense of unease with former self-assurance pushed it into the background.

Whether the end came with a delusional peace with honor in 1973 or the implosion of South Vietnam through military defeat in early 1975, American ambitions had faltered in Southeast Asia. In the process, American self-conceptions came under intensive scrutiny. Was America truly the land of liberty when its own government fought a brutal war in support of an oppressive regime? Were Americans the beneficent liberators they appeared to be in Second World War stories? Old stories lost their luster, for the moment at least. With a crisis of confidence, an economy in tatters, and a hostile world obstructing the American dream at home and abroad, a litany of woes beset America. Naturally, these points are selective in nature; yet they represent the dark mood evident by the end of the 1970s.

As Americans faced these challenges, celebrations of certain former glories contracted in comparison to previous years. The national bicentennial celebration in 1976 afforded one opportunity to celebrate the laudable past. The bicentennial events had commemorated the nation's foundation in liberty and stressed the positive achievements of the ensuing two centuries. The intentions of event organizers to promote unity and depoliticize the revolutionary nature of the past showed the strains of post-Vietnam America. Even here, however, fears of current social divisions and sensitivity to charges of national racism propagated concerns about disrupted celebratory events, which mostly proved unfounded.[91] With this national commemorative fish to fry, by the late 1970s memorialization activities centered on the Second World War passed once again into the nether region of relative silence.

Quite obviously, some Americans kept D-Day at the forefront of their personal lives and historical imagination. Some still wrote books, made films, erected monuments, organized ceremonies, and engaged with the D-Day past in a variety of personally meaningful ways. As before, the commonality in ascribed themes or interpretations demonstrated the staying power of these constructions even in times of relative doubt. Compared to the early 1960s, however, this activity appeared far less frequently and demonstrated a more constrained scope. Significantly, the terminology and meanings linked to D-Day did not produce sustained or vocal critiques. Rather, D-Day commemoration just faded from mainstream attention as the battle seemed less relevant in the post-Vietnam confusion. It would require the next decade for D-Day and the Second World War as a whole to return with force to mainstream conversations and national attention. D-Day would serve once again as a prime exemplar of cherished American traits—in the past as well as the present. The resultant restoration of national pride marked a turnaround in public spirits that bordered on the revolutionary, a remarkably conservative revolution.

CHAPTER 5
REDEMPTION

D-Day Upstaged

It rained gently in Normandy on June 6, 1982, the thirty-eighth anniversary of D-Day. The U.S. president, Ronald Reagan, did not attend the ceremonies held on the Norman beaches. He instead participated in a summit with NATO allies in Versailles, France. Rather than visit Normandy, Reagan remained near Paris seeking support for his confrontational approach to the Soviet Union.[1] In a May 29 radio address discussing the trip to Europe, Reagan stressed the importance of preserving alliance bonds in a time of multiple dangers to freedom. He neglected, however, to mention the upcoming anniversary of D-Day, observed during his trip to France.[2]

The president's wife, Nancy, did make an appearance in Normandy that June. Mrs. Reagan's staff made three visits to prepare for her role in the anniversary observance.[3] Planning documents indicate that Reagan administration officials, such as staff on the National Security Council (NSC), wanted nothing more than a brief statement from the first lady stressing American alliance commitments. Yet the Normandy ceremonies afforded her a chance to show Americans what they should celebrate. Mrs. Reagan and her staff honed her commemorative speech to emphasize the need to honor those who had sacrificed their lives to liberate others.[4]

On June 6, 1982, the first lady flew from Paris to Normandy. She attended the official ceremonies at the Normandy American Cemetery, gave her speech, laid a wreath, lunched with the mayor of Vierville, and departed in just over three hours. Mrs. Reagan sought to "honor these [D-Day veterans] heroes by speaking of what their courage accomplished for freedom." American soldiers had preserved liberty and, therefore, demanded the utmost reverence from those who followed in their wake. Nancy also spoke for her absent husband at this ceremony: "If my husband were here today, he would tell you how deeply he feels the responsibilities of peace and freedom. He would tell you how we can best ensure that other young men on other beaches and other fields will not have to die. And I think he would tell you of his ideas for nuclear peace. Certainly he would speak of Normandy's message to all who love liberty."[5] According to Mrs. Reagan's view, D-Day instructed Americans to combat threats to liberty. Yet the carnage invariably accompanying battle warned against a foolhardy waste of lives. Her speech tacitly acknowledged the strains of post-Vietnam America. Celebrating past glories now came with the painful recognition that military ventures do not always produce victory.

A limited amount of publicity attended the D-Day anniversary in 1982. The news media provided sparse coverage of the events, though the assessment was typically positive. The press depicted Mrs. Reagan in starkly gendered terms. One journalist, for instance, felt compelled to describe her attire while in Normandy, calling her a "pinpoint of color." He devoted as much space to describing the first lady's lunch as he did to her speech.[6] Nevertheless, her visit forced the American media to focus at least some attention on the Normandy ceremonies.

President Reagan did not ignore D-Day even if he lacked the inclination to participate in the commemorative activities. On June 5, he released another radio message to the American people and taped a brief television broadcast for French audiences. Reagan explained in the radio transmission that D-Day showed that "only strength can deter tyranny and aggression." His efforts at this time displayed a prevailing tendency to draw on previous depictions of D-Day. Reagan invoked Roosevelt's D-Day prayer and Eisenhower's order of the day, drawing on the approving portraits of the day's meaning drawn by these two strong leaders. He described D-Day as "a mighty endeavor, an endeavor of liberty, sacrifice, and valor." Reagan concluded by informing the American people that the quest for liberty defined his foreign policies.[7]

The Reagan team campaigned for the presidency in 1980 using a mixture of messages pertaining to law and order, anti-Communism, and restoring pride in America. In the early years of his administration, the saber-rattling approach to relations with the Soviet Union ratcheted up international tensions ever higher. The trip to Europe in mid-1982 served, in part, to reassure America's allies that Reagan did not seek outright war even as he strove to challenge the Eastern Bloc. His D-Day statements served a multitude of purposes, which had become the usual practice whenever national political figures alluded to the battle: to bolster alliance unity, deliver rhetorical attacks on Cold War enemies, and promote positive views of America. Reagan employed the Second World War as an example of American greatness while evading the more recent Vietnam War. Reagan's heartening optimism helped him succeed in such delicate tasks. "At the beginning of the decade, when a majority of Americans feared that the country's greatest days were a thing of the past, Reagan promised them economic recovery and global leadership in the war on communism," historian David Farber wrote.[8]

The Reagan administration intended to use this 1982 European summit to reaffirm America's leadership and ensure that the country's allies supported his policies. The D-Day anniversary presented a chance to issue a reminder of America's congenial use of power. America had sacrificed to guarantee humanity a moral world order. Unfortunately for Reagan, his messages receded into the background as several crises broke on the global stage. The Falklands War between the United Kingdom and Argentina intensified in the weeks before the D-Day anniversary. The culmination of that brief conflict, coming in early June, pushed the Normandy ceremonies to the sideline in media coverage. On June 6, 1982, Israeli forces invaded Lebanon after a year of mounting regional tensions. Several journalists described the NATO summit as simply "upstaged."[9] That characterization fit the D-Day commemorations as well.

Reagan gamely continued to tout the messages he and his wife had presented in their D-Day releases. Two days after the anniversary, he spoke to the British Parliament and linked the climaxing effort in the Falklands to a longer Western struggle for freedom. On June 17, Reagan delivered a speech at the United Nations in New York City. "The United States has fought four wars in my lifetime," the president stated in a manner reminiscent of Lyndon Johnson's July 1965 press statement on the Vietnam crisis. "In each," Reagan continued, "we struggled to defend freedom and democracy." Then he added, "We were never the aggressors. America's strength, and yes, her military power, have been a force for peace, not conquest; for democracy, not despotism; for freedom, not tyranny."[10] This interpretation of American actions would define Reagan's viewpoint throughout his presidency.

From the late 1970s to the outset of the 1980s, D-Day subsided somewhat in American remembrance. Reagan did not even go to Normandy in 1982, despite evoking D-Day "lessons." D-Day appeared and then just as quickly receded into the background for Reagan. Although Reagan's attempt to use D-Day glory to promote alliance solidarity, pride at home, and world acceptance of American leadership fit into his overall agenda in these early years, D-Day constituted but one of many potential props, one the president picked up or dropped with ease.[11] D-Day never disappeared entirely from the public sphere, as news stories, books, speeches, and ceremonies covered the battle. Yet it did not occupy a central position in national conversations.

D-Day commemoration would retake the national stage by the mid-1980s. That reemergence reflected a prevalent American desire to see redeeming value in the country's military actions. This inclination required some memory work to overcome the less inspiring Vietnam War experience. President Reagan struggled to place that conflict within a celebratory metanarrative of the American past. Reagan proclaimed in his 1980 campaign that the Vietnam War represented a "noble cause."[12] He faced an uphill battle when attempting to spin Vietnam as a positive interlude of American history. The Second World War offered a more convincing sell to the American people.

With the D-Day anniversary in 1982, Reagan took some tentative steps towards restoring national pride by tapping past heroics. D-Day served as a simple icon of American greatness, one that Reagan employed with ease in a trying period. Confronted by a bevy of crises at the time, he did not devote an overwhelming amount of attention to the D-Day ceremonies. Compared to later years, his 1982 addresses only functioned as brief and underwhelming spotlights on the battle. While national attention remained fixated on other concerns, some people commemorated the battle in their own ways, which paved the way for a major change in course by mid-decade. Reagan's actions constituted only the most prominent of memorial efforts that countless other memory activists conducted during the early 1980s.

D-Day Commemoration in the Early 1980s

America in the early 1980s experienced a number of ups and downs. January 20, 1981, witnessed Ronald Reagan's inauguration and Iran's release of American hostages held over the past 444 days. It was a new beginning. Carteresque negativity (or perhaps honest appraisals of national problems) faded before the optimistic radiance generated by a far more sanguine president. Reagan promised a change for a nation that thought itself in decline. Yet the challenges confronting the country did not evaporate overnight. Americans faced an uncertain future with a dismal economy, staggering inflation, terrorist threats, a reinvigorated Cold War, and crime, poverty, and social unrest at home.[13] Celebration of the present was certainly not the order of the day.

At the dawn of the Reagan era, the Second World War generation approached retirement age.[14] With the coming of old age, veterans found the time, means, and inclination to reminisce about their wartime experiences. Veterans' organizations surged in membership and activities during the late 1970s and early 1980s. At a time of economic and social dislocation, the return to the past offered a way to recall one's youthful years while forgetting problems of the moment. Remembering the trials of war could act as an outlet, a way to discuss a traumatic period in a person's life after time had dulled the sharpest pains. Finally, an American public waxing nostalgic over a successful and righteous war encouraged veteran reunions and activities.[15]

Individuals who had previously avoided veterans' organizations began joining these groups, participating in events, and sharing their memories. The 8th Air Force Historical Society, for instance, came together in 1975 and rapidly expanded in the early 1980s. Starting with 390 members in its first year, this organization jumped to a membership of 8,000 by 1981 and added over 6,000 more people in the next three years.[16] John "Bob" Slaughter, a native of Bedford County, Virginia, first organized local veteran reunion activities in 1982. Slaughter, a sergeant with D Company, 116th Infantry, 29th Infantry Division, landed on Omaha Beach early on D-Day morning. After the war, he remained ambivalent toward commemorative activities. In 1982, however, Slaughter arranged a D Company reunion in his small city of Roanoke. Slaughter then became heavily involved with the 29th Infantry Division Association.[17] First Lieutenant Richard Winters jumped into Normandy on D-Day with E Company, 506th Parachute Infantry Regiment, 101st Airborne Division. Winters did not regularly attend veteran association functions until the 1980s, although he had maintained sporadic contact with his former subordinates. By the late 1970s, however, he began collecting detailed information, particularly testimony of wartime experiences, from those still in touch. Winters accelerated his data gathering efforts in the first few years of the 1980s.[18]

Visitation rates at major commemorative sites expanded dramatically at this time, showing that it was not just veterans who were renewing interest in the events of this war. The ABMC tracked the annual visitation at the Normandy American Cemetery. Between fiscal years 1979 and 1980, the number of Americans visiting the cemetery doubled from 91,435 to 180,700 persons. The following year, that number more than doubled once again to 410,200 American visitors. Over that same period, the non-American visitation remained stable at approximately 1.1 million people per year. By 1983, the inflow of visitors overwhelmed cemetery officials, who then gave up tracking visitors.[19] Those who identified themselves as next of kin to someone buried in the cemetery numbered in the few hundred at most. Several possible factors explaining this rise in visitation include warming transatlantic relationships, the increase in history-related tourism, an intent to honor a passing generation, and an aging veteran population wishing to return to the places of their past. Newsletters, such as the *Bridgehead Sentinel* for the Society of the First Division or the *Ivy Leaves* for the 4th Infantry Division Association, continuously advertised annual pilgrimages to Normandy that attracted numerous visitors.

The Second World War was not the only conflict attracting commemorative attention in these years. Vietnam veteran Jan Scruggs led a forceful, connected, and media-savvy group. They emplaced a black granite slab on the National Mall in Washington, D.C., that listed the names of American soldiers killed in the Vietnam War. Known simply as "the Wall," this monument bore witness to the casualties of war. Rather than commemorate the war, this monument honored its American dead as implied by its official name, the "Vietnam Veterans Memorial." The design provoked heated controversy at first, eliciting a vituperative characterization as the "black gash of shame and sorrow" from one irate veteran. Nevertheless, the Wall ultimately offered an open-ended memorialization that has attracted throngs of visitors continuously ever since its unveiling in 1982.[20] The multiple readings of this site seemed fitting for a war that remained hotly debated.

The National Mall serves as a stage to display America's story to the capital's visitors. The Wall operated as a cathartic release mechanism for a society still wracked by doubt and pain over those lost in the war. This monument shifted the story of Vietnam from one of confused intent or problematic conduct to a fixation on American suffering and sacrifice. Unlike the assortment of American monuments erected after the Second World War, the Wall did not connect to a victorious crusade, nor did it evoke a sense of American power or social unity.[21] Vietnam remained a source of national contention in the early 1980s. Yet of the three twentieth-century wars commemorated with a major monument on the Mall, the Vietnam memorial came first.[22]

Unlike Vietnam, there remained little apparent debate on the national stage concerning Second World War commemoration. Even as lower-key commemorative activities emerged, no major monument had to function as an externalization piece for leftover emotions tied to D-Day. No heated debates on the battle raged through society. Reagan did not yet feel the need or the ability to extol America's virtues through D-Day stories. Still, those connected to D-Day by personal experience, familial relation, or individual interest marked the battle and its meaning in ways similar to years past. Smaller groups or individuals could, and did, commemorate D-Day even as American society failed to zero in on this one event. In 1981, a few hundred Americans traveled to Normandy for the anniversary ceremonies, which one journalist described as "quiet." Relatively quiet, perhaps, yet one hundred American and French paratroopers still honored the occasion by parachuting into Sainte-Mère-Église , site of American airborne landings on D-Day.[23]

Several influential books on D-Day also appeared in the early 1980s. American military historian Russell F. Weigley published his comprehensive *Eisenhower's Lieutenants: The Campaign of France and Germany, 1944–1945* in 1981. In it, Weigley criticized American planning, preparation, and performance on D-Day.[24] Following suit, renowned British military historian John Keegan released his well-received *Six Armies in Normandy* in 1982. Evoking the monumentally influential *The Face of Battle* (1976), Keegan's latest combined a treatment of the common soldiers' perspective with just enough operational and strategic detail to provide context.[25] The book described each of the Allied armies and their German opponents in the Normandy campaign in a more inclusive manner than found in most American-authored works. A best seller on both sides of the Atlantic, Keegan's book offered an engaging yet critical assessment of the Normandy campaign that echoed the conclusions of Weigley. In the end, Keegan depicted D-Day as a key turning point since it unhinged the Germans in the West, commenced the final phase of the war, and determined the postwar order.[26]

Almost challenging the critical stance of Keegan, Carlo D'Este, a Vietnam veteran and retired U.S. Army officer, published a 1983 book that more closely conformed to standard American perceptions of D-Day. His work, *Decision in Normandy,* described the invasion as "the most complex and daring military operation in the history of modern warfare." In a detailed discussion of the planning for Overlord, D'Este took every opportunity to fault General Montgomery for the problems Allied troops experienced in Normandy. For the majority of the book, he presented a damning assessment of British military capability, further Americanizing what was really an Allied victory.[27] D'Este echoed far more reassuring tales for American audiences that focused on their military's contributions to victory in a decisive battle against evil. Three decades after the initial publication of D'Este's book, it likely remains the most widely read single-volume account of the campaign.[28]

While it is tempting to get lost in historiographical developments, it should be noted that scholars of collective remembrance sometimes overemphasize the role of the written word. Perhaps this is a fault stemming from the scholarly minded individuals conducting such analyses. With this series of books one can see a reemergence of a niche in historical studies that has continued to this day. Obviously, publishers, scholars, and independent researchers have all identified a popular demand for D-Day stories. These books in the early 1980s ushered in a cascade of titles that more often than not provide the same generalized hero worship of selfless soldiers purportedly fighting against evil for the common good. To greater or lesser degrees, these individuals have to overcome challenges (sometimes, as described, inflicted by their own command). Yet, in the end, they win the day and, with it, restore moral order to the world. Interestingly, it is difficult to argue without fear of rebuke just how the casual relationship works. Many of these D-Day books offered stories that major segments of society sought to consume. So the question remains whether such treatments have served more as reflections of commonly held perceptions of the battle or more as sources that shape such views in the first place. The right answer surely includes some of both.

Sales of these major D-Day books accompanied, and likely fanned, a growing sense of anticipation for the fortieth anniversary celebrations. The ABMC began allocating funds in June 1983 for the following year's festivities.[29] The *Philadelphia Inquirer* printed a story on May 29, 1983, devoted to the next year's ceremonies. Gene Krzyzynski wrote that D-Day had "required more than a year of preparations—about as much lead time as necessary for those who are planning to participate fully in its 40th anniversary." He warned of scarce hotel accommodations in Normandy more than a year away.[30] *The Ranger,* the newsletter for the U.S. Army Ranger Association, devoted most of the November 1983 issue to the looming anniversary. One article hailed Len Lomell for organizing the group's pilgrimage to the celebrations. Lomell, a first sergeant on June 6, 1944, advanced inland from Pointe du Hoc along with one other soldier to locate and neutralize the German battery.[31] Charles Cawthon, a D-Day captain in the 116th Infantry, wrote an article for the October/November issue of *American Heritage.* While describing his personal experiences, Cawthon summed up D-Day as an ordeal in which "innocence was lost, trepidation surfaced, and discipline and training somehow prevailed."[32]

The moral implications of these D-Day tales remained as doughty as usual; they also fit into contemporary affairs as a fine accompaniment to belligerent Cold War rhetoric. In a speech delivered on March 8, 1983, Ronald Reagan famously denounced the Soviet Union as an "evil empire." While casting the Cold War adversary in a negative light, Reagan claimed, "The glory of [America] has been its capacity for transcending the moral evils of our past."[33] The Soviet Union typified evil, whereas America championed good in the world. If the latter committed any incidental misdeeds, it quickly rectified them.

That conceptual framework defined the early Reagan administration. While intensifying the Cold War confrontation with the Soviets, Reagan cast the challenges confronting the United States in Manichaean terms.[34] When terrorists blew up the U.S. Marine barracks in Beirut on October 23, 1983, Reagan described this act as another example of the evils with which Americans had to contend. He insisted that such evils called for correction, by suasion if possible or force if necessary. Reagan, in fact, opted for the selective use of force. Two days later, he unleashed Operation Urgent Fury, the American invasion of Grenada. In a televised address on October 27, Reagan began by noting the recent Soviet destruction of Korean Air Lines flight 007, which killed 269 civilians, depicting the Soviets as aggressors and Americans as the guardians of peace. Reagan asserted, "The events in Lebanon and Grenada, though oceans apart, are closely related." He claimed that violence, terrorism, and the evil empire formed one intertwined problem for the United States. Reagan explained that a new era had dawned in which American security demanded intervention in faraway places—to preserve freedom abroad and at home. He vowed, "Americans of today will keep freedom and maintain peace."[35]

Standard tropes provided justifications for an interventionist foreign policy that demanded sacrifices from the American people. Reagan had not quite hit the connection—yet. As demonstrated at the outset of this chapter, he did not automatically link moral refurbishment and bellicose internationalism with D-Day glories. The symmetry between his moralistic conception of America in the past and present, however, would help push D-Day to the forefront of national consciousness in the next year.

1984: A New "Morning in America"

The history of D-Day in American remembrance combines steady evolutionary development with moments of radical change. In the later part of this story, which played out after the Vietnam War, the single most important moment came with the fortieth anniversary of the invasion. Many extremely influential commemorative events took place that year, some of which powerfully shaped the ways American people thought of the past, present, and future. To be sure, some of these events stood out more notably than others. Yet the overall cultural climate of 1984 pushed D-Day to the front of national conversations. Although prior activities helped determine this outcome, the year 1984 served as the fulcrum point between scattered D-Day commemorations of the past and a fixation on D-Day afterwards.

To capitalize on the coming storm of popular interest, publishers released many books in 1984 that attracted attention to the Second World War and those who lived through it. One such work played an integral role in reshaping American perceptions of D-Day and the Second World War: Studs Terkel's *"The Good War": An Oral History of World War II.* In a collection of 118 interviews, Terkel presented a diversity of views on the wartime years. The compiler intended to combat what he called the "disremembrance of World War Two." In a section labeled "D-Day and All That," Terkel included testimony from a Red Cross nurse, an African American tanker, an artilleryman, and a neurosurgeon. Elliott Johnson, a lieutenant serving with the 4th Infantry Division's artillery, landed on Utah Beach. After crossing the open sands in a self-propelled 155mm howitzer, Johnson captured a German prisoner and assisted American infantry advancing inland. Johnson described this experience as a "lifetime in one day."[36]

Terkel explained the incongruity of merging "good" with "war" in his book's title. He rejected as mere posturing the American tendency to characterize the Second World War as a good conflict in contrast to others (for example, Vietnam). Years later, Terkel explained that his wife insisted on the title to emphasize the dissonance between the words good and war.[37] Yet the tension the Terkels sought to convey eluded many people. The phrase "good war" came into use as a frank assessment of the Second World War. Terkel, however, hardly created the "good war" paradigm cherished by Americans even if his phrase ultimately supported a view he rejected.

Milton Dank's 1984 work, *D-Day,* demonstrated another trend gaining ground in popular treatments of the invasion. Dank found nothing wrong with the Allied performance before, on, or after D-Day. He hailed D-Day as the sole turning point in the war. Failure in Normandy, Dank questionably claimed, would have allowed Hitler to "swiftly win the war" with his secret weapons or convince "Stalin [to] sign a separate peace."[38] The grandiose characterization of D-Day, the moral sense of purpose, and the hyperbolic assessment of dashing men conducting glorious work proved a popular formula. Dank's book prefigured the type of popular historical works on D-Day that would soon explode in number. While these new D-Day works were largely uncritical of American actions, the sheer sales figures they enjoyed would prove the feasibility of such an approach. "Popular history in print appeals to, and caters for, a mass audience in a way that is generally unaudited by professional historians. It is also extremely profitable," British scholar Jerome de Groot observed.[39] The point is one returned to in a later chapter. Suffice it to say now that academic historians were far from the only ones shaping public appreciation of D-Day and its perceived meaning. As the noted historian Gordon Wood posited, "Intellectual activity in a culture is not a one-way flow between the great minds and passive recipients; it is a discourse, a complex market-place-like conglomeration of intellectual exchanges involving many participants all trying to manipulate the ideas available to them."[40]

Written histories contributed to the building excitement for D-Day in 1984, but they failed to hone popular attention in quite the same way as did the actions of a few key individuals. On June 1, tapping the growing public appreciation of D-Day, President Reagan explained that his upcoming commemorative activities in Normandy would reaffirm alliance bonds: "We will mark that historic day when armies of the free nations of the West began the battle to liberate Europe." Reagan further connected the past to present by insisting that "we will be renewing our determination to keep that peace and our allied partnership intact."[41] The following day, Reagan claimed in a radio address that the Normandy invasion "set Europe on the course toward liberty, democracy, and peace." He hoped to strengthen alliance bonds while in France so that "Europe and America can continue to enjoy peace—40 more years of peace."[42] Although these words were similar to Reagan's declared intentions two years earlier, this time around he and his team astutely latched on to the power of D-Day stories to convey their messages worldwide.

Reagan did not stand alone in promoting the impending anniversary. The weeks prior to June 6 witnessed an astonishing array of people discussing D-Day.[43] In a May 28 *Philadelphia Inquirer* editorial, under a section notably titled "Memorial Day, The Last Just War," Clark DeLeon paid tribute to the American soldiers of the Second World War. DeLeon "long[ed] for the feeling of patriotism, altruism and moral certainty that carried those citizen-soldiers through the duration." Extending that wistful point, DeLeon wondered "how grand it would have been to be an American soldier during World War II," while he "thank[ed] and env[ied] the men who were part of it."[44] Another article described the D-Day commemorative activities of Pennsylvania's Royal Heritage Society of the Delaware Valley. Jack Guss, a thirty-six–year-old member of the reenacting group, described the Second World War as "a popular war," asserting, "We were liberating the oppressed people of Europe under fascism. It was right for us to go to war at the time."[45]

Studs Terkel was correct when asserting that Americans thought of the Second World War as a "good war." Romantic nostalgia defined America's approach to D-Day in 1984. A younger generation come of age honored its elders while envying the supposed clear morality and sense of purpose of the earlier war period. After experiencing the ultimately unsuccessful Vietnam War, prominent public actors in the 1980s sought to restore a veneer of morality, perhaps even righteousness, to the national mission in past and present. Working through the post-Vietnam social fragmentation and evident erosion of American power depended in part on the commemorative attention accorded to the Second World War. The shining heroism of grand events like D-Day helped cast America as a virtuous, powerful, and benevolent country—all themes that stand in almost inverse relationship with critiques of the Vietnam morass.

Resultantly, D-Day dominated the news, as seen in *Time's* May 28 issue. The front cover carried one of the invasion photos shot from an LCVP showing American soldiers struggling through the waves. The cover article, "D-Day: Every Man was a Hero," began with the Shakespearian paean to the band of brothers from *Henry V.* Journalist Otto Friedrich insisted that D-Day formed the crucial turning point in the war. Allied success there denied a German victory. D-Day instructed us "that war is cruel and wasteful but sometimes necessary. That a blundering victory is more to be valued than a heroic defeat. That might and right sometimes come to the same end."[46]

Another article in this issue of *Time* mourned the lost morality of the Second World War era. Journalist Lance Morrow claimed, "The invasion of Normandy was a thunderously heroic blow dealt to the evil empire." "Never again," he continued, "would war seem so unimpeachably right, so necessary and just. Never again, perhaps, would American power and morality so perfectly coincide." Morrow Americanized the battle by arguing, "Normandy was, of course, a joint Allied operation. But the Americans, from Eisenhower down, dominated the drama." Others could join in the glory, but D-Day represented a largely American triumph:

> There was an aspect of redemption in the drama, redemption in the Christian sense. The Old World, in centuries before, had tided westward to populate the New. Now the New World came back, out of the tide, literally, to redeem the Old. If there has sometimes been a messianic note in American foreign policy in postwar years, it derives in part from the Normandy configuration. America gave its begotten sons for the redemption of a fallen Europe, a Europe in the grip of a real Satan with a small mustache.[47]

Articles such as these epitomized the self-satisfied tone that characterized American D-Day celebrations. Walter Cronkite, serving still as the CBS anchorman and once more returning to Normandy, interviewed countless veterans and President Reagan for the Americans back home. He "asked America to start honoring every June 6, not December 7 (Pearl Harbor Day), as the formative anniversary of the Second World War." This interpretive thrust pushed Americans to celebrate a moment of military success that depended upon citizen-soldiers fighting in a moral cause.[48] Evidently, the fascination with D-Day provided a means to laud American ideals while passing over the troubling implications of the Vietnam War.

As the stories, speeches, and books that covered the fortieth D-Day anniversary noted, this uncharacteristically mild day seemed to be tailor-made for a younger generation to honor and thank the fading wartime heroes.

According to one estimate, some ten to fifteen thousand American D-Day veterans traveled to France in June 1984.[49] With so many living historical relics on hand, the homage accorded to a shrinking generation overwhelmed some journalists on site. American tourists and French residents milled about the veterans, waiting to hear their stories and often asking for autographs.

The letters, speeches, and broadcasts that Ronald Reagan generated for the fortieth anniversary of D-Day in praise of these aged veterans have received much attention. There is a danger in making too much out of the president's words. They alone were not responsible for renewing the American public's appreciation of D-Day. Nevertheless, the impact of his speeches on June 6, 1984, demands extended consideration.

Reagan had a crack team working for him that pushed a particular version of D-Day through his speeches.[50] Media guru Michael Deaver and speechwriters Peggy Noonan and Anthony Dolan set the stage and prepared the messages Reagan transmitted to American audiences. These speeches developed in a collaborative process. Organizations like the State Department and NSC sought to influence the speechwriters, who in turn consulted a variety of sources. Noonan relied on Ryan's *The Longest Day* and Keegan's *Six Armies in Normandy* for the anecdotes that added a personal touch to the Pointe du Hoc speech.[51] Reagan's optimism and belief in America's moral certitude also shaped the gratitude paid to the "boys" of D-Day.

Reagan's speeches glorified the past, but they also allowed the president to cover talking points pertinent to his reelection campaign. One White House memorandum addressed to the speechwriters listed six overall themes to stress in the D-Day messages. These included realism in international relations, strength, economic growth, shared responsibility with allies, nonaggression, and dialogue with adversaries.[52] Through these one can sense a moderation of the Cold War rhetoric of the early Reagan administration. Nonetheless, Reagan remained a committed Cold Warrior and, as result, freely drew upon cultural constructions that pitted the liberty-loving American people against the Communist foe. The fact that such interpretations so obviously connected to popular understandings of D-Day ensured that Reagan would make maximum use of the pulpit afforded to him through the anniversary events.

Driven by such grand ambitions, the stage-managed quality of the ceremonies ensured that Reagan's message reached the widest possible American audiences. The media-savvy Reagan administration scheduled the president's

Normandy appearances for the convenience of newscasts back at home. The Pointe du Hoc ceremony, in which Reagan delivered one of his most inspirational speeches, occurred at 1:30 p.m. in France just as the morning news programs aired in America.[53] Reagan then sat for an interview with Walter Cronkite, the CBS anchorman renowned for his coverage of D-Day anniversaries. Reagan also delivered a speech at Omaha Beach. Although Reagan toured Utah Beach, he did not use that setting for a major address.[54]

Reagan adroitly conveyed multiple messages in his Pointe du Hoc speech. After noting the brutality of the war and Nazi atrocities, Reagan proclaimed, "Europe was enslaved, and the world prayed for its rescue. Here in Normandy the rescue began." In Reagan's version, D-Day constituted the turning point in the American-dominated attempt to restore moral order to the world. D-Day's enormity combined here with a sentimental depiction of its participants. Reagan called them "the boys of Pointe du Hoc." "These are the men who took the cliffs," he announced, indicating the surviving U.S. Army Rangers in his audience. "These are the champions who helped free a continent. These are the heroes who helped end a war." These boys did not fight alone either. As Reagan asserted, they benefited from a "rockhard belief that Providence would have a great hand in the events that would unfold here; that God was an ally in this great cause." Divine grace, in this speech, stemmed from the morality of the Allied cause. For Reagan, the Second World War exemplified a just war because of the aggression and brutality of the Nazi foe. He opined that there is a "moral difference between the use of force for liberation and the use of force for conquest." God supported the Allies, according to Reagan, but only certain of those Allies proved worthy. In the end, America helped liberate a continent, whereas the Soviet Union perpetuated the slavery that Reagan denounced. He noted that the Soviet forces remained in Eastern Europe, "uninvited, unwanted, unyielding, almost 40 years after the war." Because of that occupation, Americans had to remain in Europe: "Today, as 40 years ago, our armies are here for only one purpose—to protect and defend democracy." Righteous Americans fought a trying battle to free a continent and that dedication to liberty persisted in the present. Reagan took time afterwards to meet the gathered "boys" who had aged into old men.[55]

Echoing Eisenhower in the Omaha Beach address a few hours later, Reagan expounded, "When these troops swept across the French countryside and into the forests of Belgium and Luxembourg, they came not to take, but to return what had been wrongly seized. When our forces marched into Germany, they came not to prey on a brave and defeated people, but to nurture the seeds of democracy among those who yearned to be free again." American soldiers spread the blessings of liberty even to the defeated. Reagan highlighted the actions of individual soldiers. He intoned, "Today, in their memory, . . . we celebrate the triumph of democracy." At the end of this speech, Reagan avowed, "We will always remember. We will always be proud. We will always be prepared, so we may always be free."[56] This sentiment linked D-Day with the justification for the Cold War. Reagan called upon Americans to sacrifice willingly for this noble cause and used the heroism of D-Day to elicit acceptance of these demands.

Running on a presidential campaign slogan of "It's Morning in America" in 1984, Reagan used D-Day to tell the American people why they should be proud of their country. He mimicked Lincoln's Gettysburg Address and Roosevelt's D-Day prayer by alluding to a sanctification of the world through bloodshed. Reagan cited the heroism of ordinary men to burnish America's credentials as a benevolent power. These messages reappeared over the following weeks on radio, television, and in newspapers.[57]

Douglas Brinkley has claimed that these messages formed a major turning point in American cultural and electoral politics. He identified this trend as the conservative "New Americanism" that boasted a restored national pride based on former glories.[58] It goes too far, however, to assert that Reagan's speeches alone determined the American perception of D-Day. They also did not revive conservatism on their own, which had been gaining political ground since at least the mid-1960s, if not earlier.[59] As important as presidential rhetoric remained for shaping public perceptions of D-Day, Reagan's words would not have proven so powerful if they failed to conform to widely accepted views. Brinkley asserted that the "D-Day baton was symbolically passed that afternoon from the battlefield legacy of Eisenhower to the presidential oratory of Reagan." Brinkley, however, claimed that no "proper" commemoration of the battle or of the "neglected" Second World War existed prior to Reagan's 1984 speeches.[60] Such an argument neglects decades of efforts by veterans, politicians, journalists, government officials, scholars, and filmmakers to stamp D-Day on American memory. Nevertheless, Brinkley did have a point. Compared to the recent lacuna in widespread public discussions of the battle, Reagan's honorific declarations combined with the surge of related commemorations to implant D-Day on the American consciousness as a new generation took the reins of power in America. A laudatory news media helped extend the impact of Reagan's Normandy speeches.[61]

As often mentioned at the time, a growing sense of the fleeting opportunity to honor the celebrated freedom fighters made imperative the successful transmission of D-Day messages throughout society. The *Philadelphia Inquirer* printed three separate articles covering the D-Day anniversary on June 7 alone. The paper's editor, Edwin Guthman, explained on June 10, "The landings in Normandy were truly an epic in the 20th century's bloody, implacable struggle of people to be free." As the men of D-Day faded away, Guthman urged that "it was propitious to focus world attention on their deeds now instead of waiting until the 50th anniversary rolls around when their ranks will be a good deal thinner."[62] Martin Blumenson reprinted a 1964 article on D-Day. The one change he made included a brief discussion of the intent behind the fortieth-anniversary celebrations. Blumenson asserted that these actions "paid tribute to those whose heroism and sacrifice had made possible the Allied landings."[63]

The broadcast media also stepped up coverage of D-Day in an array of documentaries, re-creations, and reimaginings of the battle. "D-Day Plus 20 Years," the Cronkite and Eisenhower interview that was first broadcast in 1964, appeared once again. Tom Brokaw of NBC filmed his own program on D-Day. Evoking the Cronkite special, Brokaw's "D-Day Plus 40 Years" began by proclaiming Normandy as "one of the bloodiest battlegrounds in American military history." Such hyperbole defined the program. Brokaw reminded viewers that this "greatest military assault in history" ensured defeat for the Nazis. He focused upon the sacrifices of average soldiers, usually in the amphibious units. Brokaw asserted that heroism overcame all problems of the day while he linked D-Day to a quest for freedom.[64] Brokaw later called this reporting assignment "a life-changing experience."[65]

Although the anniversary celebrations proved highly successful, they suffered some problems as well. Veterans and other tourists in Normandy criticized the overly commercialized presentation of D-Day. The kitsch and fetishistic memorabilia offered for sale throughout the region almost risked degrading the meaning of a day that, after all, cost thousands of people their lives. Some critics and scholars expressed concern over the trivialization of memory through the consumption of souvenirs such as these.[66] It is hard to dismiss the injured sensibilities of veterans resenting such a massive attempt to turn a profit over their service and sacrifices. Then again, another way to consider this phenomenon is to recognize the larger developments throughout America and Western Europe that turned history into big business by the 1980s.[67] Norman entrepreneurs provided services and products that people purchased, even while veterans and other visitors criticized the profit motive. By owning a piece of history, no matter how vulgar in form, tourists found ways to connect to the past.

One complaint aired by veterans in 1984 indicted the handling of the ceremonies. Reagan's visit coincided with that of seven other heads of state. The security precautions taken in a period of increasing international terrorism were understandably stringent. Yet in a series of ceremonies purporting to honor the soldiers of D-Day, many veterans found themselves unable to pass through the tight security cordons. As an added insult, these veterans noted the lack of seating for the men who had actually fought on D-Day. Many seats went to high-profile government officials from the array of countries involved in the ceremonies, which forced a large portion of the ten to fifteen thousand elderly veterans to stand throughout the lengthy observances.[68]

American accounts of D-Day had always suffered from selective focus. Quite naturally, in the case of such a large battle, only certain aspects appear in these stories—sometimes for simplicity's sake alone. With President Reagan shining the national spotlight on Pointe du Hoc and Omaha Beach, many other vital D-Day actions suffered neglect. John D. Bulkeley, a lieutenant commander in charge of a PT boat squadron on D-Day, attended the anniversary celebrations in 1984. He came away complaining about the lack of attention paid to the part he and his sailors played in the invasion.[69] Edward S. Evans wrote a strong rebuke to the U.S. Department of the Army after attending the Normandy ceremonies. Evans flew as a glider pilot on D-Day. He expressed his dismay over the lack of attention paid to his group's vital contribution to victory. Evans requested presidential assistance to establish a glider pilot monument at the entrance to Arlington National Cemetery outside Washington, D.C.[70]

Other Second World War veterans felt slighted by exclusion from the public fascination with D-Day. Lester Terry, a native of Toledo, Ohio, complained directly to President Reagan in July. Terry had served as an enlisted man in the 36th Infantry Division while it battled its way through Italy from 1943 to 1944. He resented the disproportionate public attention accorded to D-Day and other battles in northwestern Europe. "All we ever hear is the

Battle of the Buldge [*sic*] & Normandy," Terry carped. "They came 7 months after we landed at Salerno. If it were not for the division I was with there couldn't of been a a [*sic*] Normandy."[71]

The tenuous relationship with the former German enemy also strained public commemorations of D-Day. In 1984, French and American officials decided to respect precedent by refusing to invite West German chancellor Helmut Kohl to the Normandy ceremonies. German veterans of the battle, nevertheless, came of their own accord and often enjoyed an amicable reception from their former enemies.[72] The *Wall Street Journal* deplored the "snub" of a current ally amid a ceremony marking past events. Claiming that "the D-day anniversary has turned into an awkward episode for the Western alliance," journalist Roger Thurow described the invasion's significance for all involved. To him, D-Day formed an important moment in West German history, as it put that country on a new path towards the democratic capitalist order of the 1980s. Thurow questioned the wisdom of straining relations with a current ally for the sake of a historical ceremony.[73]

The Reagan administration also worried about unnecessarily provoking an important NATO ally while tensions between the United States and the Soviet Union heightened the importance of alliance solidarity. Unfortunately, arms control negotiations foundered because of a sense of mutual distrust.[74] The Cold War threatened to heat up once again. In an odd way, the "good war" conception of the Second World War impeded chances for meaningful reconciliation between former enemies. If the Allies fought for moral order, then that implied that the Germans fought for an immoral cause. Nevertheless, American officials seized upon opportunities to differentiate average Germans or the professional military from the real enemy, the Nazi regime. By the mid-1980s, that slippery distinction helped incorporate a former wartime enemy into the current moral-political order. The finesse required for such conceptual sleights of hand grew with the revived prominence of the Holocaust in memory. The Eastern Bloc countries were usually not impressed by this moralistic legerdemain.

Helmut Kohl did not come to Normandy in 1984. Reagan, however, visited a German cemetery the next year. He sought to pay respects to the "good" Germans who had allegedly suffered under the Hitler regime almost as much as outright victims of Nazi aggression, occupation, and murder. These alliance-dictated maneuvers landed Reagan in a bit of trouble, now known as the Bitburg controversy. Despite pointed criticism aired in the national media before the trip, Reagan visited the Bitburg cemetery, which contained the graves of forty-nine *Schutzstaffel* (SS) personnel. The SS constituted the most fanatically devoted elements of the Nazi regime and, therefore, poorly served as indicators of "victimized" Germans.[75] This brief episode demonstrated the official willingness to embrace a former enemy, even at the expense of threatening the morality tale of the war that proved so popular. After all, the "good war" was deemed such, in part, because the enemy was so "bad." It seems odd for American politicians intent upon celebrating their country's liberating role to enfold SS personnel in the blanket of celebration. Then again, Cold War rehabilitation permitted a tricky distinction between supposedly good and bad Germans, while needs of the moment compelled Reagan to be rather generous in his categorization, especially with the war dead. If anything, this provocative act (which might have been avoided by simply selecting a different cemetery to visit) shows in stark relief the political influence on collective remembrance activities. This process of reconciliation also emulates developments following the American Civil War whereby hostile sections of the country reunited at the cost of forgetting less palatable aspects of the past.[76]

These alliance maneuverings took place in the context of increasing superpower tensions. Reagan spent his first years in office decrying the "evil empire" while increasing economic, military, and moral competition with America's Cold War adversary. D-Day helped restore American pride and reaffirm America's uniquely beneficent position as a world leader. The Soviet contributions to Allied success in the Second World War often escaped mention in stories that cast D-Day as the turning point in the war. It was almost as if Americans could not bear to share military glory with the new hated enemy, or were somehow afraid that including the Soviet Union in these stories of Second World War success would sully the record. In response, official Soviet newspapers and a host of quasi-official announcements sounded off against the 1984 D-Day anniversary celebrations.[77] The Soviets returned the American snub of 1980 by boycotting the 1984 Summer Olympics held in Los Angeles. Following the D-Day celebrations, this affront added to the outburst of American patriotic sentiments that summer.[78]

In June 1984, Reagan sought to appear as a sensible, eloquent, and capable world leader. His praise for the wartime generation may have rankled some who felt excluded, such as other veterans, America's allies, and the Soviets. Yet his D-Day speeches struck a responsive chord in a public intent upon honoring its elders. Riding the cresting wave of popular enthusiasm for romantic nostalgia, Reagan easily clinched a second term in the White House. The 1984 presidential elections resulted in one of the most lopsided victories in American politics.[79] Although D-Day alone did not lead to four more years of Reagan, the obvious success of his speeches in Normandy doubtlessly enhanced his political fortunes. Douglas Brinkley claimed that Reagan's performance constituted a necessary transference of ownership. With Eisenhower's death in 1969, the one man most visibly linked to D-Day had left the scene just as America imploded from the Vietnam War. Sixteen years later, Reagan staked out a claim to D-Day glory for himself and for American society.[80] For many younger Americans, this new commemorative activity served as their first exposure to D-Day. The American people responded with an immense outpouring of support for an honorific view of the wartime generation and the meaning of the sacrifices it had made in battles like D-Day.

The Vagaries of Memory

The 1980s began as a relatively quiescent period for D-Day commemorative activity. The dismal box-office performance of *The Big Red One* and small-scale commemorations that garnered minimal media coverage seemed to indicate that D-Day was headed towards obscurity. Yet some veterans, authors, and interested persons kept D-Day memories alive. They had set the foundation for a major return to D-Day for American society. Eventually news media and political leaders mined a promising vein of public enthusiasm when they tapped into D-Day stories.

Looking at the cycles of public memory connected to D-Day, a few particular moments stand out. The year 1984 serves as an excellent dividing point when dealing with D-Day in American society. After the fortieth anniversary, mainstream society would not perceive D-Day as just another old battle. People felt obligated to mention D-Day in many different sorts of public conversations. Following Reagan's lead, D-Day became shorthand for sacrifice, liberation, or the commitment of democratic and "free" countries to ensure freedom. If it was morning in America, it was also the dawn of a new era of fixation on the Second World War, with D-Day standing at the forefront of public consciousness.

Themes lauded during the D-Day celebration in 1984 remained true to those developed over the preceding forty years. Reagan celebrated the democratic heroism of a nation's youth that supposedly went off willingly to restore morality to a world beset by evil. Reagan received assistance when trumpeting this message, as demonstrated by the array of tourists, ceremonies, news stories, books, and other commemorative activities that feted the Normandy invasion. The president's performance on June 6, 1984, however, thrilled Americans still coming off the depressing moral low of the previous decade. When Reagan argued that ordinary Americans fought evil in the past, he aimed at inspiring his people to battle the evils of the present day.

Such political messages combined with the sentimentalized honor paid to a passing generation. As the men of D-Day rapidly faded into history themselves, commemorations surged in number while society paid them its final respects. Speeches and articles called present-day Americas to emulate their noble forebears. Once more, herein lies evident the didactic employment of ascribed meanings and derived lessons from these constructed versions of the D-Day tale. Although the subject of this particular study remains fixed on remembrance practices, the other part of this story is an examination of what effect these activities have had on society. This memory work proved militarizing in that it promoted a fixation on martial solutions to world problems at the same time that it sentimentalized popular depictions of the military.

It does not stretch credibility to observe that a restored sense of pride emerged in the United States by the mid-1980s. Compared to the gloomy feeling of "malaise" evoked but five years earlier, Reagan spread a message of confident nationalism that proved appealing. Of course, this change in spirit benefited from an improving economy, the absence of a major divisive war, and a wave of nostalgia for an idealized past that cast America in a favorable light. The atmosphere of nationalist pride apparent in 1984 struck at least one commentator as a significant turn from years past.[81] D-Day alone did not create this attitude, and likely benefited from it a great deal. Yet D-Day celebrations garnered public attention by reminding Americans why they should take pride in their country. That sort of story gained in popularity during the following years.

CHAPTER 6
RESURGENCE

A New Museum

Thursday, August 27, 1992, witnessed the grand reopening of the Chicago-area museum dedicated to the 1st Infantry Division. At a cost of $12 million, the Cantigny First Division Museum replaced the old Cantigny War Memorial Museum. No longer a memorial in name to warfare, this state-of-the-art building preserved the legacy of American soldiers. The new museum recounted the history of a division that had often led the way for America's fighting forces. Historian John Votaw, director of the museum and guiding force in the new construction, assured the public that the new building would not glorify warfare. Rather, it "emphasized the basic theme of sacrifice, duty and achievement of soldiers during wartime and peacetime."[1]

This museum joined a growing chorus of individuals and organizations that have contributed to a national conversation on D-Day. The battle's prominence in American collective consciousness persisted and intensified throughout the period from the mid-1980s to the mid-1990s. D-Day served as a means to instruct Americans on the past and guide them towards the future. Yet as the 1990s witnessed society splintering over a bevy of domestic and international issues, a tone of needling criticism also emerged in D-Day stories. The battle evoked glory days of yore when Americans, supposedly united, had fought the good fight, and came home as celebrated heroes and world saviors. The many implied critiques of the present domestic and international order kept D-Day a topic of continual discussion. D-Day indicated all that was good in America—that is, before the Sixties, Vietnam, economic travails, and less worthy youngsters had appeared. Historian Michael Kammen described an "American inclination to depoliticize the past in order to minimize memories (and causes) of conflict."[2] That depoliticization, however, remained superficial as the past formed a means to instruct or berate present generations for an array of quite political purposes.

D-Day served multiple American constituencies during the last decades of the twentieth century. Remembrances of the battle honored a passing generation, a point of concern to veterans and their families. Veterans, politicians, journalists, and average Americans extolled America's unique regard for liberty, as exemplified by D-Day's sacrifices, which success in the Cold War had seemingly reaffirmed. Their arguments also hammered at distressing trends in an American society that appeared less willing to emulate past heroics. D-Day resonated in America because of the number of commemorative activities and political uses of the battle.

The Cantigny War Memorial Museum functioned admirably since opening in 1960. Advances in museum technology and another war involving the 1st Infantry Division caused the board of directors of the Robert R. McCormick Charitable Trust to favor the erection of a new facility. Votaw explained in May 1986 that the aging site required exorbitant maintenance funds and offered limited display or storage areas.[3] The following month, the board members approved plans to construct a new museum, hire additional staff, and expand the archival holdings. In subsequent years, the designs for the new museum developed alongside studies charting a modernized display strategy and plans for reaching the future installation's target audience.[4]

The board of directors understandably sought assurance of sufficient interest before allotting funds for the new construction. After conducting a survey of the local Chicago area, specifically targeting senior citizens, veterans, and children, the research found that "one-third of the general population is aware of Cantigny." Those previously unaware of Cantigny expressed an interest in visiting the museum, and significantly, teachers supported the its educational mission.[5] The attendance figures in 1974, the last statistical information available, indicated that roughly 60 percent of visitors came from the six-to-twelve-year-old age group. With continuous outreach efforts aimed at area schools, this trend likely remained steady. Votaw explained that the "Cantigny First Division museum personnel have a unique opportunity to tell the Army's story to young Americans in this, the nations [*sic*] third largest metropolitan area."[6] As another historian argued, "Museums and heritage projects have become increasingly important to a political agenda of lifelong learning, diversity, access and education." He continued by explaining that museums often intend to promote citizen ideals by emphasizing the duty to understand (and emulate aspects of) the past, a point readily conceded by Cantigny leadership.[7]

The decision to construct this building constituted only the first step. Votaw and his associates had to consider how to depict the 1st Infantry Division's history. They worried "that our new museum might be inappropriately judged as a celebration of war and destruction." Votaw pointed instead to "the powerful themes of sacrifice and duty by soldiers doing their best in trying circumstances." These themes would promote patriotism without glorifying the brutality of warfare.[8]

The story presented at Cantigny dwelt on key moments of the division's history, such as D-Day, while using the costs of battle to highlight the importance of civic duty. Rather than revel in carnage, the presentation honored those who served and fostered a mature consideration of warfare. D-Day testified to the division's contributions to maintaining American ideals of freedom, fair play, and moral order. Employing a mix of artifacts, audio and textual information, and representational scenes, the D-Day section portrayed the division's fight on Omaha Beach.

To begin the D-Day section, museum staff placed visitors inside a re-created version of an LCVP. A short film described the strategic situation in the Second World War that led to D-Day while veterans testified about their feelings going into battle. Original plans mimicked an LCVP with the wall behind the film screen descending like the prow/ramp of the landing craft, opening onto a mockup of Omaha Beach. Safety concerns forestalled the deployment of that mechanism. Instead, a door behind the screen opened upward. Nevertheless, visitors moved from a facsimile of an LCVP through a portal and "landed" on Omaha Beach. This area displayed the equipment used by both sides on D-Day. While sounds of battle echoed through the air, visitors stopped at stations to hear audio clips of veterans describing their D-Day experiences. After walking through a re-created German bunker, museumgoers encountered wall panels bearing statistics on the battle. They also saw examples of heroism demonstrated by citations and medals that 1st Infantry Division soldiers had earned on D-Day. The lessons distilled from that D-Day coverage focused on the duty of honorable soldiers fighting and winning amid tremendous adversity. With outreach programs to the news media, local educational institutions (eventually drawing in close to twenty thousand students every year), and researchers, Cantigny has presented this version of D-Day to countless Americans.[9]

Cantigny's mission of instilling civic virtue found expression in a message of duty, sacrifice, and honorable service. That these points related to martial experience necessarily promoted a militarized sense of civic-minded action. One major change in stylistic presentation between the old and the new museum reflected altered currents in popular memory and historical scholarship. The old building largely filtered the division's exploits through accounts about the leadership and higher-ranking officers. In the new building, stories of junior officers and enlisted men imparted the division's history. Shifting away from "great man" history, like that which focused on Eisenhower in the 1950s, common Americans here served as more fitting models for an average visitor to emulate. In a museum dedicated to the 1st Infantry Division, basing the narrative on the actions of soldiers in that division seemed understandable. That focus, however, perpetuated the Americanization of D-Day. Here D-Day remained a story of American soldiers saving the world from itself. Cantigny joined with American scholars, politicians, and veterans by advancing this moral reading of D-Day's meaning. Other viewpoints, however, began to emerge and criticize the Americanized version of the Second World War, prompted in part by a new armed conflict.

The Growing Presence of D-Day: The Late 1980s

After the orgy of D-Day celebrations in 1984, the battle gained a prominent place in American public conversations. It did not fade away, even as the battle's veterans did so. As these subjects of veneration passed on, many Americans seemed intent to distill lessons from the past for use in the present. As a result, a mounting wave of D-Day commemorative activities inundated American society. Television specials, news commentary, ceremonies, speeches, and books focused public attention on D-Day.

Veterans of the Second World War died at an increasing pace throughout the 1980s, which created a sense of the fleeting opportunity to learn from them. From a startling average of one thousand daily deaths during the 1980s, veteran mortality rates would grow to nearly two thousand people dying every day two decades later.[10] The veterans did not vanish without a parting burst of enthusiasm. The National World War II Glider Pilots

Association, for example, established a Texas museum in the midst of the 1984 D-Day mania. Aside from collecting Second World War artifacts for public display, this organization also emphasized the need to foster patriotic virtue in the public.[11] Bob Slaughter, a resident of Bedford County, Virginia, retired in 1987 and devoted his time to D-Day memorialization.[12]

The precipitate disappearance of these veterans prompted an outburst of actions honoring the passing generation while assuring consistent public attention devoted to the Second World War. The late 1980s witnessed the increased diffusion of historical subject matter across the American media. The popular magazines *Military History* and *World War II,* with lively articles and eye-catching graphics, hit the newsstands in August 1984 and May 1986, respectively. *Military History Quarterly,* an *American Heritage*–style journal, released its inaugural issue in August 1988. D-Day received sporadic treatment during the first several years in all of these publications. In fact, the first issue of *Military History* featured a cover-article interview with Brigadier General James Gavin recounting his D-Day jump with the 82nd Airborne Division.[13]

In the late 1980s, D-Day appeared in a number of venues because of individual attempts to enshrine or profit from the battle's memory. In 1985, for instance, boxing promoter Don King hosted two fights that each involved a former U.S. Marine. King labeled the June 6 event, held in Las Vegas, as "D-Day in the Desert."[14] That same year, the Battle of Normandy Foundation incorporated as a nonprofit organization. The foundation, led by business executive Anthony Stout, sought to honor the Normandy campaign and educate American youth about D-Day. It helped create a Normandy Scholars program in conjunction with several universities. That program sent groups of college students to visit the battle sites in Normandy.[15]

A mixture of personal motivations also pushed some authors to write on D-Day, an increasingly popular topic. Historian Stephen Ambrose made the first of what would become a series of notable entries into the D-Day field with his 1985 book, *Pegasus Bridge.* Ambrose, a well-established historian, had studied and published history for over twenty years at that point. As a child during the Second World War, he avidly followed events across the globe. Ambrose focused his early career on the Civil War but by the 1980s had written on a variety of subjects that included work on, and purportedly with, Dwight Eisenhower.[16] Although controversies arose later in life, at this time Ambrose had a stable of well-received and generally engaging works.[17] Yet the mid-1980s marked a profound shift in his career.

In some respects, Ambrose's personal/professional change reflects shifting currents in American society regarding warfare and commemoration. In the Vietnam era, Ambrose was a self-proclaimed dove. Ardently opposed to the war, Ambrose at one point even snubbed President Nixon when the latter was delivering a speech at Kansas State University, where Ambrose was teaching. Late in life, however, Ambrose indicated that at the same time he was working closely with Eisenhower. Questions would later surface about the extent of this interaction, but the point is that Ambrose attributed a moderating influence on his own views to Eisenhower. In the academic year of 1969–70, Ambrose served as the Ernest J. King Professor of Maritime History at the Naval War College. It was then and there that he would later suggest a changing perspective began taking hold. Through this transformation, Ambrose began to accept the more forgiving assessments of America's actions past and present that held it as the main country championing freedom both at home and abroad. Unfortunately, he still felt profoundly ill at ease with the Vietnam War still raging on around him— especially as it impacted his students and portended to affect his own children. Seeds were planted at this time. Ambrose felt a personal desire to tout the positive aspects of an American society he so dearly loved. Yet he also refused to believe that there was much of an approving nature to take out of the Vietnam experience. Those thoughts combined with the steady interaction Ambrose had with Second World War veterans (Eisenhower or not). In the end, Ambrose came to slight the more relatively recent military past in preference for the "better" Second World War. He likened the American war effort in that conflict to spreading light in a benighted world, to restoring hope for human progress via the salvation America's military offered freely, proclaiming, "The generation who fought World War II has done more to spread freedom and prosperity around the globe than any preceding generation."[18] Ambrose's personal changes serve as an apt indicator of remembrance patterns in American society from the 1970s onward. He wanted to celebrate American greatness, felt the recent past provided little for that effort, and instead turned to the heroes of the Second World War for morality lessons and reassurance in the present.

Although the Second World War became a staple for Ambrose (he published eleven books pertaining to that conflict in a twenty-year period), he would most clearly stake out personal ground around D-Day. He enjoyed success with popular, nonacademic work, such as *Crazy Horse and Custer*

(1975).[19] Now, however, Ambrose would focus his talents on the Second World War generation that he so greatly admired. Work and life in New Orleans led him to focus on D-Day because of local connections with the shipbuilding industry that produced many of the iconic landing craft employed in the amphibious assault. Ambrose began collecting interviews from D-Day veterans in 1983, depositing them at the University of New Orleans. Oral history provided a new outlet for Ambrose's interests and this turn also demonstrated his changing focus from the more distant past of the nineteenth century to topics of more recent concern.

Despite this long buildup, Ambrose's initial foray into D-Day would focus on a British action. Ambrose described a chance encounter while leading a 1981 tour group in Normandy. He stumbled upon former major John Howard of the Oxfordshire and Buckinghamshire Light Infantry, the British airborne unit that had seized that span across the Caen Canal and the nearby Ranville Bridge over the Orne River. That feat secured the eastern flank of the Allied invasion zone. Listening to Howard captivate audiences with tales of D-Day heroism pushed Ambrose to undertake a new project.[20] In *Pegasus Bridge,* Ambrose described an action that exemplified courage and boldness. A nighttime glider drop by the Ox and Bucks, the nickname of Howard's unit, administered a *coup de main* that proved essential to the success of the Normandy invasion. Ambrose wrote that a repulse here would have at least magnified the costs of D-Day for the Allies. "At a maximum," he added, "failure at Pegasus Bridge might have meant failure for the invasion as a whole, with consequences for world history too staggering to contemplate."[21] After completing this project, Ambrose returned to conclude several other ongoing efforts. His appetite for D-Day, however, had only been whetted.

Other historians also cued in on the popular interest devoted to D-Day. Historian Joseph Balkoski heaped praise on the performance of the American 29th Infantry Division and its Omaha Beach experience. In *Beyond the Beachhead* (1989), Balkoski stated, "I consider it important that later generations of Americans understand exactly how this job was accomplished, and that its fulfillment was achieved at great cost." Balkoski presented an unvarnished account of the horrors that characterize industrialized warfare. Yet he repeatedly pulled from that inferno several heroic individuals who did whatever it took to accomplish their mission. Balkoski likened D-Day to Gettysburg, describing both as battles for liberty. Nevertheless, he noted that the soldiers had fought to survive and go home rather than out of patriotic sentiment. Balkoski purportedly rejected a glorified view of warfare. His point, however, further reinforced the glamorization settling upon a generation that had sacrificed and made a better world simply because of loyalty to one another and a sense of duty.[22]

By the late 1980s, Americans celebrated an era that had produced the men of D-Day. Yet one book constituted a thorough refutation of this self-satisfied assessment of the past and present. In 1987, historian Paul Kennedy published his Pulitzer Prize–winning history, *The Rise and Fall of the Great Powers*. This book struck a responsive chord with over 225,000 copies sold in the first year alone.[23] Kennedy wrote a grand metanarrative history that covered, as the title implied, the causes behind the rise and fall of great powers in the international arena. He focused on the modern era, from the Renaissance to the present day, and intertwined economics, politics, and military affairs in an insightful discussion of state power. Some of Kennedy's points assaulted the already tender collective American psyche:

> It was as clear to a Renaissance prince as it is to the Pentagon today that military power rests upon adequate supplies of wealth, which in turn derive from a flourishing productive base, from healthy finances, and from superior technology. . . . The fact remains that all of the major shifts in the world's *military-power* balances have followed alterations in the *productive* balances; and further, that the rising and falling of the various empires and states in the international system has been confirmed by the outcomes of the major Great Power wars, where victory has always gone to the side with the greatest material resources.[24]

This comment originated in a decade of unsteady American economic performance and increasing global competition. The embrace of Kennedy's work revealed the dark underside of the American proclivity to laud the warriors of the Second World War. Paying homage to the wartime generation signaled a mixture of respect and longing for the supposedly simpler times of national unity, untrammeled power, and bright days looming ahead.

The perennial optimist Ronald Reagan rejected such dour sentiments, as evident in a 1987 address commemorating, of all things, D-Day. In a recorded television address, Reagan offered a contrast between suitable and perhaps harmful memories of the past. "President [Franklin] Roosevelt said December 7th will live as a day of infamy. And so it is remembered," Reagan asserted, "yet June 6th, in contrast, lives on as a day of triumph." Reagan preferred that Americans focus on the positive elements of their country's past. He assured the veterans of D-Day, "The service you rendered to the cause of freedom at that pivotal moment is not forgotten," and indicated that "it is etched deeply into the hearts of all your fellow countrymen and applauded by those in Europe who you helped liberate from the oppressor's boot." Reagan claimed, "One of the memories I will cherish most from my years as President is the ceremony at Normandy marking the 40th anniversary of D-Day." He further insisted that "we look back, and we are proud of all those who fought. We look forward, and we pledge that they will not have died in vain, because we will keep the torch of freedom burning." Americans typified goodness in the world because they had fought for freedom. According to Reagan, they would remain good if that willingness to sacrifice for the betterment of humanity endured.[25]

Reagan captured public attention by tugging at the heartstrings. In 1979, President Carter had pointed to an uncertain future that demanded a tightening of the belts and a lowering of expectations. Reagan, in 1980 and 1984, as well as in 1987, celebrated the past, present, and future of America. Significantly, he felt that D-Day stories in particular proved especially useful for transmitting this message. Reagan viewed past glories as precursors to present greatness and promised a continuation of that status into the future. This tendency assured him a special place in American memory. Of course, some of his contemporaries vilified him for certain controversial decisions, such as those leading to the Iran-Contra Affair. Then again, plenty of others shrugged off the less endearing aspects of the man and his presidency.[26]

Reagan's evocation of the "boys of Pointe du Hoc" and other D-Day speeches won the hearts of surviving Second World War veterans. Following those 1984 anniversary speeches, veterans deluged Reagan with requests for assistance. They asked for help with fundraising, wanted him to speak at ceremonies, and sought presidential influence to back proposed monuments.[27] Chaplain James Eric Pierce wrote a 1987 letter to Reagan requesting, unsuccessfully, his attendance at an honorific ceremony for D-Day veterans in the Philadelphia area. Pierce noted that the annual gathering began in 1984 with a few hundred attendees. Three years later, the festivities moved to nearby Fort Dix, New Jersey, to accommodate the expected five thousand people.[28] Reagan had transformed himself into a champion for veterans despite his inability to deliver on all their requests.[29]

These calls for assistance revealed the broad field of actors working to imprint D-Day and the Second World War onto the American collective consciousness. Albert H. Smith, a captain with the 16th Infantry on D-Day, rose to the rank of major general and served as the assistant division commander for the 1st Infantry Division during the Vietnam War. In the 1980s, Smith engaged in a one-man D-Day educational campaign. In one of these efforts, Smith lectured at the U.S. Army's Armor School in Fort Knox, Kentucky, in 1985. He acknowledged Reagan's stirring speeches in Normandy the year before, but Smith asserted that he spoke with the special credibility of a D-Day "survivor." "During the first 5 years of World War II, Hitler and the Axis Forces were almost completely successful," Smith argued. "However, Operation Overlord and D-Day signaled the beginning of the end for the Nazi regime." Smith heightened the importance of a battle in which he participated while writing the Red Army and other contributors to Allied victory in the war out of the story.[30]

Smith was far from the only 1st Infantry Division memory activist working at this time. Lieutenant General Orwin C. Talbott served as president of the Society of the First Division in the late 1980s. Talbott did not fight with the 1st Infantry Division on D-Day, yet he commanded the division for part of the Vietnam War. The society had erected monuments honoring the division in places such as Washington, D.C., and Normandy. This society helped maintain the monuments it had constructed as well as those established by the ABMC. From February through April 1988, Talbott corresponded with D-Day veterans and the ABMC officer in Europe. The veterans had noted an obtrusive fence surrounding one monument when they attended the 1984 anniversary events in Normandy. Captain Joseph G. Dawson wrote, "For years I have felt that Omaha Beach is and will always be one of histories [*sic*] singular localities and *nothing* can diminish its significance." Dawson, the D-Day commander of G Company, 16th Infantry, exclaimed, "I believe all members of the Division share my view that this was *our beach* and would welcome the opportunity to share in ensuring it in perpetuity."[31]

Veterans also asserted their special prerogative to review D-Day-related programming on television in the late 1980s. *The Longest Day* aired sporadically during this period. Although the movie ranked as a perennial television favorite that exposed millions to the D-Day story, some veterans felt compelled to set the record straight by picking out its inaccuracies. In 1988, Lieutenant (JG) William M. Harvin argued, "The Navy was given the short end of it in a way, because everything seems to start after the beach." He regretted that with *The Longest Day* "you start out [with] a few boats hitting the beach and a few airplanes going over, and from there on it was all Army."[32] Other televised works elicited attention. In October 1988, the new Turner Network Television channel presented a colorized version of *The Americanization of Emily.*[33] Joining in, ABC broadcast the made-for-television miniseries *War and Remembrance,* an adaptation of Herman Wouk's popular novel, in two bursts in November 1988 and May 1989.[34]

Tellingly, not all aspects of America's Second World War experience enjoyed such widespread support. In 1988, for instance, Congress settled upon compensation for Japanese-Americans interned in domestic concentration camps during the war. D-Day celebrations and the liberation paradigm led Americans to focus on the "good" side of their Second World War effort while evading other aspects of the conflict, such as the Japanese-American internment.[35]

Following on the heels of the stunning fortieth anniversary celebrations, D-Day appeared in a number of American conversations by the late 1980s. Books, television specials, news articles, speeches, and museums all sought to tap into the growing public demand for D-Day. These memorializations fostered a wider awareness of D-Day in a society increasingly populated with people who had not lived through the Second World War. Commemorations often constituted the primary exposure to the past for these people. The honor, glory, and moral clarity of purpose linked to the battle in such efforts not only described an element of America's past, but they also formed a guide for emulation in the future.

Tearing Down the Wall: The End of the Cold War

The year 1989 ushered in many transitions. President Ronald Reagan transferred power to his successor, George H. W. Bush, in January. The Soviet war in Afghanistan finally ended in February, nine years after breaking out. This latter development signaled new directions in Soviet international politics, which produced a wave of revolutionary upheavals throughout Eastern Europe that year. The world seemed a heady place as the Iron Curtain fell inward upon its rusted core. Despite trials and tribulations, the United States and its NATO allies surged ahead even as Cold War competitors pulled out of the race. The 1989 D-Day anniversary promised festive celebrations and sweeping rhetorical flourishes. The celebratory zeal tied to American observances of D-Day over the past five years mixed with the self-congratulatory atmosphere of the time.

Some American veterans used the coming anniversary as a reason to reunite. One group of these men from E Company, 506th Parachute Infantry Regiment, 101st Airborne Division, gathered in New Orleans in May 1989. Aside from rekindling bonds of friendship, the Easy Company veterans came together for historians Stephen Ambrose and Ronald Drez to conduct interviews. Ambrose decided that after the success of his previous work, *Pegasus Bridge,* to write once more on an elite unit that had participated in D-Day. The interviews with these men formed a large part of his research. Ambrose had yet to meet with the unofficial Easy Company historian, Richard Winters. The two got together, along with three other veterans, the following February. Winters felt that historians such as S. L. A. Marshall and the American public overlooked Easy Company's D-Day actions. Ambrose, for his part, found an interesting topic, a willing group of interviewees, and a bountiful collection of notes compiled by Winters and his compatriots. Building on this strong foundation, Ambrose predicted he would finish the book within a year.[36]

Ambrose understood popular demand for D-Day tales, as evidenced by the crowds who flocked to D-Day anniversary ceremonies in Normandy on June 6, 1989. Prior to the 1980s, the largest celebrations coincided with major anniversaries, like the tenth or the twentieth. One journalist estimated that at least one thousand visitors came to the Normandy American Cemetery observance in 1989.[37] On a warm and sunny day, bands played the American and French national anthems, U.S. military jets flew overhead, and speeches paid tribute to the past. President Bush did not attend, but a representative read his statement. Bush made the usual link between D-Day and liberation. The president connected the past to the present by heralding the tide of freedom sweeping through Eastern Europe. Bush proclaimed that "the ultimate victory of freedom and democracy is inevitable," even as he acknowledged a setback in China with the Tiananmen Square massacre.[38]

Veterans, naturally, arrogated to themselves the special ability to interpret these events. D-Day veteran Joseph Dawson conveyed his approval of the anniversary celebration in a brief write-up. Attending the ceremonies, he felt that "one could sense the strength, and power of our great country." Dawson thought the ceremonies duly honored the service and sacrifice of the D-Day soldiers. To him, these sacrifices demonstrated America's greatness.[39] The July 1989 issue of the *Twenty-Niner,* the newsletter of the 29th Infantry Division Association, carried multiple D-Day stories. In this issue, one article described the trip that thirty veterans made to Normandy for the celebrations. John Schildt contributed an essay with a question for a title, "Was God's Hand Involved in the D-Day Invasion?" Schildt answered in the affirmative. The November issue printed an article by Meredith L. Butterton, an enlisted man in the 126th Ordnance Company, which landed on Utah Beach a week after D-Day. "Normandy reflected a unique cause whose outcome was vital to world freedom," Butterton claimed.[40]

Veterans seemed intent upon protecting the legacy of D-Day, lest its significance fade with their passing. Orwin Talbott wrote on June 6, 1989, to instruct people in the year 2044 on the meaning of D-Day. Talbott informed these future readers of the 1st Infantry Division's exploits. He explained, "At no time in its illustrious career, however, did the Big Red One perform more valiantly, at no time in its illustrious career did it perform a more critical mission than it did on Omaha Beach on 6 June 1944." Talbott felt that "by getting off the beaches this one outfit insured . . . the invasion would be a success and insured eventual victory and the restoration of democracy in Europe."[41]

During the 1980s, the act of honoring the Second World War generation had served to heal American social fissures. Reagan's 1984 D-Day speeches employed rhetorical constructions that emphasized the glory of common Americans defeating tyranny. He sought to reinvigorate America's confidence and sense of moral worth. These framing devices advanced Cold War agendas by depicting the West, and primarily America, as the champion of liberty and freedom in opposition to the tyrannical Soviet Union.

The call upon D-Day in American remembrance did not decrease in the final stages of the Cold War. D-Day persisted in national histories and commemorations as an example of the sacrifices America had made and must keep making, in pursuit of freedom. The popular college history textbook *The American Pageant* retained nearly the same coverage of the Second World War and the Normandy invasion from its initial edition in 1956 through the eighth edition in 1987. The new coauthor, David Kennedy, changed little in that part of the book after the 1983 death of the original author, Thomas Bailey. Kennedy preserved the "enormous operation" of the Allies on D-Day against "stiff resistance" as a major turning point in the European war. In earlier editions, the final "outcome was another vindication of the American democratic system—a system founded on faith in the power and courage of free men." Kennedy's main shift in this section altered that line to argue, "Democracy had given its answer, as the dictators, despite long preparation, were overthrown and discredited."[42]

Contentious conflicts erupted over national history standards in the late 1980s and early 1990s. Professional historian organizations, like the Organization of American Historians, sought to develop a more complex, critical, and inclusive version of history education. The political-public side of the debate, espoused by people like Lynne Cheney in her role as head of the National Endowment for the Humanities, rejected these tendencies as so much intellectual sophistry. Instead, following their line of argument, history should instill patriotic love for country by employing established facts in the classroom. The Second World War remained a topic that supported the concerns of either side. The war served as a prime example of American morality, and as a "grand event," it corresponded to the fact-based history sought by educational conservatives. Yet the stories told about average Americans in the war period met the standards for inclusion sought by professional historians.[43] Thus, the popular understandings of the Second World War presented a common point of reference for people on either side of this growing cultural divide.

America, in the views most found acceptable, guaranteed liberty in the past and sought to remake the world in its own benign image. President Bush connected these sentiments to the collapse of the Cold War in his 1989 D-Day statement. He assured Americans and the world, "The new breeze of democratic change will bring mankind to better, more tranquil times."[44] Unfortunately, such a heartening global order did not materialize.

An Old War in the New World Order

Historian James T. Patterson wrote regarding the early 1990s: "Perplexed, some Americans seemed to be almost nostalgic for the Cold War era, when a simpler bipolar world had confronted them." He also argued, "Jeremiads about 'American decline' . . . seemed to hit a larger cultural nerve in the early and mid-1990s."[45] With the collapse of the Eastern European Communist regimes in 1989 and the dissolution of the Soviet Union in 1991, the Cold War ended with a whimper rather than the feared bang of global nuclear incineration. An eye on the past helped Americans navigate the unfamiliar terrain in the post-Cold War years by using what came before to indicate what should continue into the future. Out of the entirety of American history, the Second World War loomed large as an event that had pushed the United States into the foremost rank of world powers. It helped that many Americans believed that conflict had ended the Great Depression and produced several decades of relative economic abundance. Avoiding destructive combat at home, prevailing American memories of the war often contained a hint of fondness lacking in societies devastated by the fighting.

A half century after this event, nostalgic renderings of the Second World War further sanitized events. To be sure, industrialized warfare often devolved into mass carnage, and conceptions of D-Day did not entirely efface this horrid reality. Nevertheless, the linkage of the horrors of combat with the noble goals sought by venerated soldiers produced a uniquely American viewpoint on the Second World War in the 1990s and beyond.[46] Stories of the war tended to revolve around American success, morality, and military power. That D-Day so conveniently fit these themes ensured its widespread appeal throughout the decade. Jeremiads of decline during an uncertain present came at the same time that people looked back on America's former glories. As sometimes mentioned, a return to greatness seemed possible by emulating the courage of those who fought through D-Day.[47]

President George H. W. Bush came to office essentially as a continuation of the Reagan administration. Americans had elected him president based largely on the belief that much of the Reagan era would continue as before. Unfortunately for Bush, Reagan had earned far more popularity and actually possessed an insightful big-picture vision that his successor seemed to lack. Bush only slowly recognized the sea change ushered in by developments in the Soviet Union, shifts that would transform the entire world. Therefore, his first few years in office presented perhaps too much of the same, with the president even relying upon dated Cold War rhetoric while the Cold War system disintegrated. Bush announced a "New World Order" once he caught the speeding train of world transformation. Interestingly, some of the rhetorical devices used to advance Cold War priorities proved useful in this new order.[48]

For instance, as noted several years after leaving the presidency, Bush demonstrated that global quests for freedom had continued to enchant American foreign policy elites. "We have the political and economic influence and strength to pursue our own goals," he wrote. Yet Bush proceeded to assert that "as the leading democracy and the beacon of liberty, and given our blessings of freedom, of resources, and of geography, we have a disproportionate responsibility to use that power in pursuit of a common good."[49] The Second World War and its key moments like D-Day fed into a larger narrative of American commitment to liberty, at home and abroad. Americans, particularly as cast in the D-Day framework, used great power honorably to vanquish a threat to common liberty. According to this line of thought, such willing use of power must continue.

D-Day commemorations, stoked by these positive associations, expanded in the early 1990s. Sizeable crowds came to the June 6, 1990, Normandy ceremonies for the forty-sixth D-Day observance, an anniversary not originally anticipated as a large draw for attendance. The U.S. Navy sent an aircraft carrier group built around the USS *Dwight D. Eisenhower* to symbolize the invasion armada. The 1990 D-Day anniversary came in the centennial year of Eisenhower's birth, and the events in Normandy constituted a celebration of the battle and the American leader.[50]

Nearly two hundred veterans of the Second World War gathered that June in a New Jersey chapel to honor those killed on D-Day. These men had planned to hold a D-Day reunion in 1994 but advanced the schedule to 1990 because of their rapidly thinning ranks. One veteran informed a journalist, "I'm glad I had a part in [D-Day]. But I wouldn't like to do it again." That journalist described the veterans as "gray-haired men, white-haired men, balding men who spent one day of their youth in the fiercest fight of an age." "They looked like an ordinary bunch, for heroes," he suggested.[51] Throughout the 1990s and early 2000s, ceremonies dedicated to D-Day carried the sad reminder that ever fewer veterans could attend them. An urgency to honor their service while enough men remained able to participate in the venerations ensured that D-Day celebrations proliferated throughout the decade.

With the precipitous decline of the veteran population, a number of oral history projects started up or increased in tempo as if attempting to make up for lost time. As mentioned previously, Stephen Ambrose began collecting oral histories pertaining to D-Day in the early 1980s. By the turn of the decade, many other oral history projects kicked off or expanded in scope. The Eisenhower Presidential Library and Museum established an oral history collection program in the late 1980s. Aside from attempting to preserve the memories of the rapidly depleting ranks of veterans, this collection project formed one component of the institution's D-Day fiftieth anniversary preparations.

The effort to save this piece of the past revealed the influence of oral history on historical memory. The impetus to expend time, effort, and resources on these projects displayed the "tyranny of the witness." By the end of the century, popular historians and the public tended to accept witness memories without critical analysis "despite their being biased and sometimes false."[52] Witness authority and the immediacy of veteran experiences ensured that for many people this testimony equated to "real" history, plain and simple. With the accelerating disappearance of Second World War veterans, oral history programs expanded over the next two decades in a last-gasp collection measure.

The oral histories of these veterans demonstrated a degree of interaction with other commemorative activities. Recurrent themes in oral histories showed the impact of previous developments—the memory work influenced what the veterans recalled—while these themes confirmed and lent strength to those other memory currents. For instance, the "longest day" trope appeared regularly in veteran accounts of D-Day. Private Eldon Wiehe, 1st Infantry Division, asserted that D-Day "was the longest day of my life and I'll never forget."[53]

By the late twentieth century, a veteran counter-memory had faded that once rejected positive interpretations of the Second World War by emphasizing the horrors of combat. As the veteran ranks thinned out, those who remained tended to hail the more positive results of the war in an almost eulogistic effort.[54] Enlisted men John Ellery, Buddy Mazzara, and Ralph Burnett validated the common American reading of D-Day as a morality tale. Ellery, with the 16th Infantry on D-Day, asserted decades later, "There are those who will tell you today that patriotism is an eroded word. When I hear such talk, I think of Normandy, and I know that it's not true."[55] Buddy Mazzara, also with the 16th Infantry, argued that America endured as "the greatest country in the world and I'd like to see D-Day remembered so people will remember that what we fought for in the past is still an important thing and that the principles a lot of men died for that day are still important."[56] Ralph Burnett, in the 18th Infantry, hoped that younger generations would "remember that the reason we have the freedom we have today is because of D-Day," as well as "many days before and many days after."[57] The positive results came with a heavy price, though. Sergeant Joe Pilck, 16th Infantry, described the carnage and confusion on Omaha Beach as "one hell of a mess."[58] The chaotic terror of battle even appeared in accounts of the less contested Utah Beach landings. Private Bruce Bradley, 29th Field Artillery Battalion, attached to the 4th Infantry Division, stressed the hectic nature of his D-Day experiences.[59]

American D-Day veterans often emphasized similar themes in their oral histories. D-Day consisted of a trying and gruesome day of battle, often the "longest day" for its participants. What they ascribed to that experience also proved remarkably homogeneous. D-Day showed U.S. military effectiveness, but it also demonstrated America's allegedly unique resolve to preserve liberty even in foreign lands. The detailed recounting of the carnage and suffering exacted in the quest for liberty sanctified the day's fighting. These oral histories, therefore, reflected the prevalent American understandings of D-Day in place by the 1990s. They also added fuel to that interpretive fire as others, such as authors, politicians, filmmakers, and educators, tapped into such testimony to support their claims about D-Day's meaning.

Contemporary events on the world scene also influenced D-Day remembrance activities. Iraqi dictator Saddam Hussein ordered his troops to occupy bordering Kuwait, an oil-rich country, to boost economic recovery following the Iran-Iraq War. Unleashed on August 2, 1990, this aggression provoked international outcries. American leaders first sought to contain Saddam's expansionist move and then ultimately prepared to push Iraqi forces out of Kuwait. U.S. president George H. W. Bush likened Hussein to Adolf Hitler in a rhetorical effort to build a case for intervention.[60] Painting with such broad brushstrokes, however, limited the options available to deal with this situation. Drawing on the tropes of evil, despotism, and aggression, all evocative of the Second World War fight against Hitler, helped garner support for military action in the Gulf. Yet Bush had, in journalist Rick Atkinson's words, "drawn the terrible swift sword without knowing when or how to sheathe it again."[61] This rhetoric heightened expectations: grand crusades demand decisive results. D-Day memories factored into the atmosphere: if Saddam equaled Hitler, and Hitler's demise began on D-Day, then decisive clashes of arms in battle promised success once more.

The Persian Gulf War lasted six weeks in its aerial-bombardment phase (January 15–February 28, 1991) with approximately one hundred hours of ground-level combat (February 24–28). In fact, a visible link emerged between the Second World War and the new conflict. In the wake of the 1984 D-Day celebrations, the U.S. Navy secured congressional authorization to construct a new guided-missile cruiser named the USS *Normandy.* In 1989,

D-Day veterans attended the commissioning ceremony. The *Normandy*'s first combat service came in the Persian Gulf War.[62]

Evocations of the Second World War suffused the American political atmosphere in the early 1990s. Simplified allusions to the Second World War promoted public acceptance of this new military action. "In 1990–91 we [Americans] came close to believing that we could wish upon a war," and felt that "if we applied the magic formula of an allied war effort against an aggressive dictator, we could again have national unanimity of purpose, renewed world prestige, and a return of the leaping prosperity that was a hallmark of American life during the best war ever," wrote one historian.[63] The Second World War served as a standard of comparison. When the Persian Gulf War did not lead to a repeat of post-Second World War prosperity, mythologized unity, or increase in international power, the rhetorical framing device lingered anyway. Rather than rethink the reliance on stock Second World War analogies, Americans intensified their fixation on the prior conflict as a hallmark of American power, morality, and capability. Writing several years later, President Bush and his National Security advisor, Brent Scowcroft, deplored the absence of a Second World War–style victory in 1991. They lamented that the Persian Gulf War lacked "a clean end—there [was] no battleship *Missouri* surrender. This is what [was] missing to make this akin to WWII, to separate Kuwait from Korea and Vietnam." Apparently, an elaborate, media-friendly, surrender ceremony would have transformed a limited war in the Middle East to the former glory of the Second World War.[64] Similar to America's persisting Vietnam syndrome, the clash between rhetoric and reality here led the nation down dark corridors. Promised a moral crusade equivalent to the Second World War, a mere year later in 1992 Americans remained sullen about the limited outcome obtained in the Persian Gulf War.[65]

With debates on warfare and historical allegories, the Second World War had acquired a new life in America. The common American framing of the Second World War as a morality tale that chronicled America's benevolent use of power proved appealing and politically useful, as seen with Bush's allusions. Such views evaded complicated episodes from the nation's past, including the more recent wars in Korea and Vietnam. The positive reading of American history depended upon selective emphases. D-Day commemorations gained wider public attention since they provided stories of a glorious quest for liberty.

As part of this selective reading of the past, the fifty-year commemorative activities for various features of the Second World War often enjoyed wide support. Lou Lisko served as a corporal with the 2nd Ranger Battalion when it assaulted Pointe du Hoc on D-Day. Decades later, he acted as the historian for the Ranger Association. Lisko wrote to the members in 1992 regarding the upcoming "Operation Rangers Lead the Way." This project commemorated the June 19, 1942, activation date for the U.S. Army Rangers. Lisko confidently asserted that the "eyes of the nation will be focused" on the ceremonies taking place in Fort Benning, Georgia, from June 17 to 19.[66] Although the nation did not come to a stop for these ceremonies, the expected deference in the golden anniversary years for Second World War commemorations often did arise, as evident with the 1994 D-Day mania.

A growing wave of veteran-authored books on the war demonstrated the assumed interest in their personal stories. Charles Cawthon, a captain at the time, landed with the 2nd Battalion, 116th Infantry, on D-Day. In 1990, he published *Other Clay: A Remembrance of the World War II Infantry.* Cawthon wrote of his initiation to war on D-Day and described the little quirks of fate that had determined who lived or died. After slogging two hundred yards through the surf, heavily laden with gear, Cawthon made it to the shore only to discover a hellish scene: "The first assault wave, already on the beach, did not resemble a battle line as much as it did heaps of refuse, deposited there to burn and smolder unattended." The trauma of the landing burned vividly into his memory in contrast to the confused action later that same day. Survival in combat often went to the lucky, and high-minded idealism vanished amid the carnage.[67]

Stephen Ambrose completed his next D-Day book in time for a 1992 release. In *Band of Brothers,* Ambrose described a small group of an elite fighting force that had melded together through intensive training and gut-wrenching combat. D-Day figured largely in this book as the baptism of fire for the "band of brothers," the soldiers of E Company, 506th Parachute Infantry Regiment, 101st Airborne Division. Indeed, the subtitle indicated that the book followed the company "from Normandy to Hitler's Eagle's Nest," even though the narrative within covered several prior years with recruitment and training. Normandy, however, acted as a marketable selling point in the title. As well written as any of Ambrose's other popular books, *Band of Brothers* presented a stirring saga of heroism, duty, and sacrifice in an unambiguously just war. For Ambrose, those paratroopers epitomized America's democratic ethos. He disclosed that these men had suffered through the Great Depression; yet, "Whatever their legitimate complaints about how life had treated them, they had not soured on it or on their country." They were "self-reliant, accustomed to hard work and to taking orders," which served Ambrose's dual purpose of lauding these soldiers while implicitly criticizing the generations that followed.[68]

Band of Brothers served up a rousing "good war" story. Ambrose rejected assertions of dismal American combat performance in the European Theater, arguing instead that encounters between German and American elite units had usually favored the latter. Beyond the clear-cut moralizations throughout the work, Ambrose romanticized the Second World War. He never shied away from depicting the tremendous destructiveness of the fighting. Nevertheless, the goal of protecting democracy, as Ambrose characterized the American purpose, vindicated the bloodletting. The suffering exacted in such a quest ennobled the actions of America's fighting sons. This war had constituted Eisenhower's "great crusade," which Ambrose quoted without reservation. That interpretation withstood the dissenting views presented by veterans, like Cawthon, who had questioned such grandiose rhetorical flourishes. Ambrose, instead, employed a Shakespearian cant in which this band of brothers had joined in adversity, fought the good fight, and returned home as heroes, with those left standing remaining lifelong friends.[69]

Ambrose did more than write about D-Day during the 1990s. The *Band of Brothers* project coincided with his endeavor to create a national D-Day museum. Ambrose taught at the University of New Orleans and resided in the greater New Orleans area. Eisenhower had allegedly assured him that Andrew Jackson Higgins won the Second World War for the Allies.[70] Higgins was a boat designer and manufacturer who lived and worked in New Orleans. He designed an array of naval craft, including the famed LCVP, or "Higgins boat." Ambrose had tucked away those details and returned to them with force in the explosion of D-Day interest during the late 1980s and early 1990s. In 1991, he helped organize the National D-Day Memorial Foundation with the goal of establishing a museum in New Orleans dedicated to the battle. The following year witnessed congressional authorization for the building—designating it as *the* National D-Day Museum. Ambrose realized that many d-days occurred in the Second World War. Because of the local connection and the national stature of "the" D-Day, the museum focused primarily on the battle of June 6, 1944. Later additions planned from the outset would expand the coverage and lead to a name change for the museum as well. D-Day, however, has lingered as the focal point in this New Orleans facility. Ambrose drove financial collection activities, publicized the museum, and determined its portrayal of D-Day.[71]

Part of that promotional activity led him to publish articles in newspapers and popular journals. In a 1993 piece in *Military History Quarterly,* "D-Day Revisited," Ambrose emphasized two themes while publicizing yet another upcoming book on D-Day. He described his return to Normandy for the research of this impending book. While covering the visit to the invasion area, Ambrose wrote vignettes on the battle extolling the heroism of American forces. Ambrose's other theme emphasized the originality of his work. All authors profess to offer original ideas. Yet in this article Ambrose launched a far more forthright assault on previous depictions of D-Day. The film *The Longest Day* served as the particular target of his disdain. Ambrose harped on the movie's fanciful depiction of the final stages of combat on Omaha Beach. The production had American forces blasting apart a huge cement wall with minimal explosives before Brigadier General Norman Cota (Robert Mitchum) rode up the now-exposed beach exit. In reality, Ambrose argued, the breakout from the beaches depended upon small groups bypassing such obstacles and advancing up the bluffs to outflank German positions. A lone historian applying correctives to Hollywood did not seem a singular occurrence. Here, however, Ambrose advanced his personal vendetta against a thirty-year-old movie, a crusade that culminated with a 1998 blockbuster film rebuttal inspired by the historian.[72]

Ambrose's romantic take on D-Day fed a climate of Second World War enthusiasm sweeping the nation in the early 1990s. He became the preeminent public authority on D-Day; yet others jumped into the national discussion of the battle, the war, and the implications for American identity. On November 14, 1991, Representative Gus Yatron (D-PA) introduced a bill titled the "D-Day 50th Anniversary Commemorative Coin Act" to have the secretary of the treasury mint a D-Day commemorative coin. Instead of this bill, Congress passed the "World War II 50th Anniversary Commemorative Coins Act" the following October. Rather than fixate solely upon D-Day, a series of coins honored major battles in the war. Nevertheless, the prominent coin in this commemorative set remained the one depicting D-Day.

The law stipulated that the first $3 million in proceeds should go to the Battle of Normandy Foundation. This money paid for a plot near a French museum in Caen and a memorial garden there dedicated to D-Day. The foundation's Wall of Honor, on the other hand, proved far less fortunate. For a $40 fee, a charge many people gladly paid, the foundation would inscribe an individual's name on the wall. The intent with the Wall of Honor to celebrate veterans of a glorious battle stood in marked contrast to the mournful Vietnam Veterans Memorial wall that listed the casualties of war. Unfortunately, by early 1994, allegations of financial misconduct by its president, Anthony Stout, accompanied a series of board-member shake-ups. The foundation reaped nearly $15 million in contributions from coin sales alone by June 1994, which demonstrates the widespread desire to support this honorific celebration. Yet the Wall of Honor never materialized. While malicious intent did not seem to be the primary factor in this adverse turn, numerous veterans or their family members had doled out money they never saw again.[73]

A Growing Storm

The rush to commemorate D-Day involved many people with varied agendas. Some sought recognition for their own prior service or that of a loved one. Others wanted to honor a monumental battle. The desire for profit and glory motivated people as well. Whatever the impetus, through the combined actions of all these memory activists D-Day once again enjoyed a prominent niche in American popular culture.

The predominant American understandings of D-Day had not varied much in the intervening years. As popular conceptions Americanized the operation's events, the significance drawn from D-Day reflected cherished American values. D-Day stood for the willing sacrifice of Americans, foremost of the Allies, in the pursuit of liberty and justice for all. Vietnam echoed through these new takes on an old battle, as the stories told of D-Day now tended to emphasize the chaotic bloodiness of battle. That carnage, however, only further sanctified the American quest for liberty. The drastic decline in numbers of veterans from America's "best war ever" intensified the romantic nostalgia attached to the battle and the war. D-Day remembrance developed in a Cold War framework. The themes that had gained prominence, owing in part to the rhetorical confrontation between Cold War competitors, proved alluring and useful even in the post-Cold War years.

That durability may not have been readily apparent to those living in Bush's New World Order. Political scientist Francis Fukuyama famously postulated that the collapse of the Cold War had resulted in the "end of history" because of the triumph of democratic liberalism.[74] It remained debatable what baggage Americans should cast off in turning away from the past. Then again, the wide audience and interest in D-Day provided clues about the battle's staying power in American public memory. D-Day told something appealing about America, assuring the battle a special place in public attention at the outset of, during, and after the Cold War.

The growing impetus to celebrate D-Day steadily increased as people anticipated its fiftieth anniversary. In June 1993, the nation's newspapers discussed the impending celebrations. The *Philadelphia Inquirer* carried one article on June 6 that described the gala celebrations likely to come in the succeeding year. "Several thousand veterans, soldiers, tourists and world leaders—including President Clinton—are expected next year," and as a result, the hotels throughout the Normandy area already had full reservations. The 1994 D-Day observance, the article noted, "likely will be the biggest of the World War II anniversaries celebrated around the world over the last few years." Once more, the feeling surfaced that this anniversary would mark the last occasion that D-Day veterans could attend in significant numbers. Also once more, German leaders did not appear on the official invitation list.[75] In October, the *Atlanta Daily World* carried a notification that the following June would mark the fiftieth anniversary of D-Day, "a highlight of America's finest hour." The looming celebrations in Normandy seemed all the more important as they formed "perhaps the last big commemoration" relating to the war.[76] As the 1984 celebrations proved of central importance for a return to D-Day, those of 1994 would succeed in embedding D-Day in the American public consciousness for the (immediate) future.

CHAPTER 7
D-DAY VICTORIOUS

The Storm Gathers Strength

Cold War politics and social divisions exacerbated by Vietnam had influenced D-Day commemorations in the 1980s. The end of the Cold War and the rebirth of American confidence, in part because of the Persian Gulf War, betokened a new period of cautious optimism in the 1990s. Ceremonies, reenactments, and film depictions promulgated familiar themes ascribed to D-Day with a renewed fervor. If 1984 had brought D-Day back into national conversations, then 1994 cemented its place in the American collective consciousness for the time being.

As an example of the recognized interest in D-Day, the year 1994 witnessed an explosion of D-Day literature. Several publishers rereleased popular D-Day books—a testament to that battle's sales potential.[1] New titles also appeared in abundance. Robert Kershaw published a campaign narrative, *D-Day: Piercing the Atlantic Wall.* Paul Stillwell's compilation of naval veteran testimony, *Assault on Normandy: First-Person Accounts from the Sea Services,* and Richard Goldstein's pop-history treatment in *America at D-Day: A Book of Remembrance* are typical, romanticized treatments of the events. Donald Goldstein, Katherine Dillon, and Michael Wenger collaborated on *D-Day Normandy,* a book published under the auspices of the Battle of Normandy Foundation. "Instinctively everyone in the free world, from the highest to the humblest, realized that this operation had nothing to do with such forces as politics, economics, or the balance of power," these three claimed.

"It was the start of a crusade—the war's last great campaign against the forces of evil." This grandiose characterization of D-Day as not just a mere military action but as a moment that defined American morality echoed through many discussions of the battle by the mid-1990s.[2] Also crowding bookshelves were memoirs like *Eyewitness on Omaha Beach,* a book by 29th Infantry Division veteran Private Harold Baumgarten.

Several historians have provided useful suggestions about the cultural climate during the 1990s and its fixation on the past, which engendered what one of them termed a "memory boom."[3] A passing generation, current social divisions, veteran determination to transmit their experiences, growing news media interest, and the expansion of historical consumption pushed this reverence of things past. D-Day remembrance fed off and contributed to this nostalgic turn in the late 1990s. The D-Day framework also helped sanitize public understandings of warfare.

1994: A D-Day Imprimatur

Feeding the frenzy of public interest in D-Day, Stephen Ambrose released his next installment on the battle, aptly titling it *D-Day, June 6, 1944.* Ambrose called this popular book, with 320,000 copies printed in a few years, his "love song to democracy." He declared that D-Day was a "triumph of democracy over totalitarianism" for which Americans "owe our freedom" to the soldiers of liberty. Allied success on D-Day rested largely on the cooperative, selfless spirit that democratic systems allegedly had inspired in their citizens. The faults and problems of the wartime years did not appear in Ambrose's presentation. Ambrose discussed all the Allies, but he focused mostly on the Americans in this nostalgia trip. As Ambrose would have it, America was unblemished morally, its people great, and the world's fate turned on the actions of a few heroes. He did not avoid describing the carnage of battle, but acknowledging the sacrifices of the heroic soldiers made them seem nobler. Ambrose spotlighted participants who ascribed the Allied victory to divine intervention, men like Admiral Bertram Ramsay, Eisenhower's chief naval commander on D-Day. Ambrose linked deity and democracy to the American soldiers whom he saw engaged in a "trial of systems" on the sands of Normandy.[4]

By conjuring up engaging tales of heroism that vindicated America's democratic ethos, Ambrose touched a nerve that led to skyrocketing book sales and growing media appearances for an increasingly popular historian. At a professional conference held in March 1994, Ambrose reaffirmed his moralistic interpretation of D-Day. "The lesson of Normandy is that there is nothing a democracy cannot do once it agrees on what needs to be done," Ambrose argued. "No power in the world can match that of an aroused democracy." He held firm to that viewpoint regardless of challenges that faulted his thesis as overly celebratory, chauvinistic, and even a false portrait of battlefield realities that depend more on clashing arms than on ideas.[5]

As one historian recognized, "Americans certainly want and perhaps need heroes." Ambrose provided feel-good history for American society. He told stories that assured audiences of American rectitude during the world's most cataclysmic war. The good Americans, democracy-loving and divinely sanctioned heroes, saved civilization through selfless sacrifices like those willingly offered on the Norman beaches. Yet by dropping the critical stance of academic scholarship, Ambrose strayed into dangerous territory. D-Day boiled down to beguilingly simplified "lessons" of democracy vindicated and heroism reaffirmed. As a "superb storytelle[r] who catered to the general audience," Ambrose sold many books, which ensured a continuous flow of material from him.[6] These popular stories furthered and benefited from a growing American disconnect with (critical and dry) academic history.[7]

Ambrose's role as D-Day's chief advocate ensured him a growing public stature, but this popularity also depended somewhat upon the attention accorded to the impending anniversary. In April 1994, journalist Tom Infield noted that officials expected twenty-five thousand American veterans to attend the Normandy celebrations. He described a frenzied environment there, which led American officials and some veterans' groups to warn away from attendance those in questionable health. Infield felt the D-Day ceremonies were "shaping up as the biggest event in six years of big events recalling 50-year milestones of the Second World War."[8] On May 23, journalist Alan Riding argued that the impending ceremonies presented the last opportunity to honor the veterans in person. Classifying them as liberators, Riding noted that many D-Day veterans regarded the battle "as the most important day in their lives."[9]

Several journals released special D-Day issues in 1994 to contribute to and benefit from the general atmosphere of expectant remembrance. *Military History Quarterly* crammed five D-Day articles into its first ever soft-cover edition. *American Heritage* put out a D-Day issue with double the normal print run, which quickly sold out.[10] *Army* devoted its entire June edition to D-Day. Martin Blumenson reviewed Ambrose's *D-Day* in the latter journal, calling this book "the last word" on the invasion. Ambrose's work "*celebrates as nothing like it before* . . . that fateful day." General Gordon R. Sullivan, chief of staff of the U.S. Army, welded D-Day to the Persian Gulf War to recast the latter in a more glorious mold. He argued, "You can draw a straight line across the decades from the heroism on the sands of Normandy to the heroism on the sands of Southwest Asia."[11]

Television networks broadcast a large amount of D-Day programming before the anniversary. Specials Ted Koppel and Tom Brokaw had created in 1984 played on televisions again in 1994. Excerpts from Ronald Reagan's two major speeches of June 6, 1984, also appeared frequently. This regurgitation proved revealing. Replaying these programs served, in a sense, to commemorate past commemorations. The festivities of 1984 had created new standards. Some journalists explicitly forecast a less-inspiring performance by President Bill Clinton than Reagan's superb oratory in 1984.[12]

New D-Day content also crowded the airwaves. Dan Rather and General H. Norman Schwarzkopf, coalition commander in Operation Desert Storm, hosted a two-hour documentary on D-Day. The Discovery Channel also presented a two-hour special on the battle. ABC sent Peter Jennings to Normandy to shoot a ninety-minute special. CNN ran a one-hour documentary for the anniversary. NBC devoted five hours of coverage to the ceremonies on June 6 alone.[13] C-SPAN allocated almost an entire day's programming to D-Day. One South Carolina CBS affiliate televised a special on hometown D-Day heroes.[14]

These commemorative acts evinced the public fixation on D-Day, which stood reaffirmed by the immense attention devoted to the 1994 Normandy ceremonies. President Clinton, as a primary speaker at the events, sought to sell a mythic image of America to the public. Caught in the early stages of a scandal over sexual infidelity, and facing vituperative partisanship, Clinton also had to sell himself once more to the American people. International developments likewise shaped the president's D-Day messages. Although Germany still missed an official invitation to participate, American officials felt that the demise of the Cold War left room for new themes to intermingle with the traditional D-Day message. American orations in 1994, for instance, paid increased tribute to the Red Army's contribution to Allied victory in the Second World War.

Considering the importance of these media-hyped ceremonies, Clinton spent the final few weeks beforehand ingesting information on D-Day. He read widely, interviewed veterans, and brainstormed within his administration. Clinton met with historians Paul Fussell, John Keegan, and Stephen Ambrose to discuss D-Day. Ambrose's latest D-Day book had topped Clinton's reading list, and echoes of that work sounded throughout his speeches.[15] The professional historian's unique place in shaping public remembrance becomes apparent through such interactions. These historians drew upon their credentials and their access to researched, reasoned, and articulated understandings of the past. Through this process, these historians staked claims as empowered advocates for particularized views on D-Day. Historians, naturally, as thinking individuals in society reflect contemporary concerns and biases.[16] Yet they also act as influences on public discussions and uses of the past, sometimes in hidden ways such as talking to politicians as they prepare major speeches.

President Clinton frequently repeated themes advanced by scholars like Ambrose. He remarked in a May 28 radio address that D-Day "was the turning point of World War II and in many respects a turning point of the 20th century." Clinton asserted, "It was the beginning of the end of Nazi tyranny and a downpayment on all the years of freedom the rest of us have enjoyed ever since." D-Day, as an act of liberation, presaged America's new role in the post-Cold War era. The president defined America's national mission as expanding "freedom's reach."[17] In a Memorial Day speech at Arlington National Cemetery, Clinton cited D-Day as an example of America's love of freedom—a freedom that should spread throughout the world.[18]

Clinton held interviews in succession with CNN, CBS, ABC, and NBC on the evening of June 5. For nearly an hour starting at 8:00 p.m., Clinton spoke with journalists about D-Day. The interviews occurred aboard the aircraft carrier USS *George Washington,* as if to connect his nation's present military power with the defining moment of the twentieth century. Three common lines of thought emerged in the interviews. The journalists probed Clinton on tensions with North Korea, wondering whether America could conduct another D-Day to take care of that troublesome state. The reporters also asked Clinton how a president who had avoided service and protested the Vietnam War could honor the soldiers of the Second World War. ABC's Sam Donaldson questioned whether the president could "follow" Reagan's performance in 1984.[19] Finally, Clinton hailed D-Day as indicative of America's unique desire to promote global freedom. He argued that America had to continue advancing liberty throughout the world.[20]

With all the hype and expectation, the fiftieth anniversary events promised to be spectacular. At 7:00 a.m. on June 6, Clinton kicked off his hectic day by applauding members of the U.S. armed forces. Speaking to the sailors aboard the *George Washington,* Clinton asserted that divine assistance had led to Allied success on D-Day. "It was faith in their Maker's mercy and their own ability that helped to carry the day," he claimed. "It was also raw courage and love of freedom and country." Clinton exhorted, "As we begin this new day of remembrance, let us also ask God's blessing for all those who died for freedom 50 years ago and for the Americans who carry on their noble work today."[21]

An hour later, Clinton rose to speak in the official ceremonies at Pointe du Hoc. Addressing the theme of the day, Clinton argued, "Most of them [U.S. Army Rangers] were new to war, but all were armed with the ingenuity of free citizens and the confidence that they fought for a good cause under the gaze of a loving God." God's democracy had bested an evil enemy even in the most pressing of situations. Emphasizing the democratic ethos of America also afforded Clinton the chance to wrap the entire nation with a mantle of honor: "The mission of freedom goes on; the battle continues. The 'longest day' is not yet over."[22] Americans should celebrate and even emulate the world-saving conduct of the D-Day soldiers.

Two hours later, shortly after 11:00 a.m., Clinton spoke at a Utah Beach ceremony. Reagan's main speeches in 1984 had taken place at Pointe du Hoc and the Normandy American Cemetery. Clinton went to Utah to assuage veterans of the 4th Infantry Division who felt neglected during Reagan's Normandy visit. Clinton's speech at this event, however, reflected the relatively minor place the Utah Beach landings have occupied in American collective memory. Although Clinton repeated the freedom mantra and noted the debt of gratitude owed to the veterans, his speech here treated D-Day in general terms. On the *George Washington,* Clinton tailored his speech to his audience. At Pointe du Hoc, he honored the Rangers and reviewed their actions in depth. In the final speech of the day at the Normandy American Cemetery, Clinton talked about Omaha Beach. At Utah Beach, however, he offered a generalized eulogy to the D-Day forces.[23] The landings there on June 6, 1944, did not capture the public imagination with the same magnetic force as "Bloody Omaha." Casting D-Day as an act of selfless American sacrifice demanded both a high level of suspense and a substantial death toll. Evidently, the 197 men killed at Utah did not constitute a large enough oblation.

President Clinton echoed Reagan in his 6:00 p.m. speech at the cemetery. Clinton stressed the youth of American soldiers who stepped reluctantly into the role of liberators, a role they nonetheless brilliantly filled. He made the standard references to the horrors of the battle and the individual heroism that had surmounted fierce German opposition. Clinton characterized D-Day's outcome as an example of democratic power. American soldiers sacrificed and acted together "to free a continent," not for national aggrandizement: "They had all come to stop one of the greatest forces of evil the world has ever known," the president intoed. "At that exact moment on these beaches, the forces of freedom turned the tide of the 20th century." Clinton exhorted Americans to guarantee freedom across the world in the present as well.[24]

Clinton's remarks demonstrated the continuities in American conceptions of D-Day that had settled in by the last quarter of the twentieth century. D-Day, not the Eastern Front, had started the end of Nazi tyranny. The heroism of American soldiers had saved the day and deserved veneration. The example of this battle should embolden Americans to continue the fight against other tyrannies such as Communist or dictatorial regimes.[25] D-Day served as a guide that kept the pursuit of freedom at the center of a narrative of American international leadership.

The anniversary events attracted hundreds of thousands of visitors, which ensured an enormous audience for these messages.[26] On June 5, continuing a well-established tradition by this point, individuals parachuted into the Sainte-Mère-Église area. One group of veterans refurbished and sailed a Liberty ship from California to Normandy to symbolize the invasion armada.[27] D-Day veterans also participated in the official ceremonies, often escorting or introducing Clinton before he made his rhapsodic remarks. Staff Sergeant Walter Ehlers assaulted Omaha Beach with L Company, 18th Infantry. He had fought bravely on D-Day and in the campaign that followed, receiving a Congressional Medal of Honor for exhibiting "conspicuous gallantry" a few days after the landing. Ehlers stood with Clinton during a wreath laying on June 6, 1994. Ehlers briefly spoke and linked D-Day to an American quest for freedom. "The world changed on June 6, 1944, the day the good guys took charge again," Ehlers indicated. "It did not mean peace, but it marked the stand for freedom that would continue through the Korean War, the Vietnam Conflict, the fall of the Berlin Wall, and the Allied Containment of Iraq." He concluded, "We picked up our guns to protect our faith, to preserve our liberty."[28] Captain Joe Dawson introduced President Clinton at the Normandy American Cemetery. Dawson applauded attendees who came "to recognize and pay homage to those who shaped the course of history."[29]

These veterans introducing or standing with Clinton served as a more suitable torch passing than the ceremonies of 1984. President Reagan belonged to the "greatest generation," while Clinton was a child of the Sixties and the first Baby Boomer president. The 1994 observances presented an opportunity to praise a fading generation while symbolically passing responsibility for world leadership to younger Americans. Clinton employed D-Day as an example of American efforts to preserve democracy in foreign lands. He sought to use that message to inspire a new American generation to continue expanding democracy abroad. In a sense, Clinton was reassuring the older generation that younger Americans were up to the task of following suit when required to protect freedom at home and abroad. Walter Cronkite once more came to Normandy to cover the events, interview the sitting president, and reassure Americans that the older generation approved of the acclaim accorded to a shining moment from its past. His coverage helped enable the smooth handoff of responsibility between the generations.[30]

The press adulation that attended all these commemorative activities helped maintain the public focus on D-Day. On June 7, the *Philadelphia Inquirer*'s Terril Jones printed an article full of the stock phrases on D-Day. The "heroes" of Normandy returned on a "pilgrimage" to the site where they had corrected the world's misdeeds. Jones also mentioned the generational torch passing.[31] A *Time* article on June 20 applauded the veterans and the ceremonies that constituted, once more, a torch passing between generations. Lauding the "audacity and the spirits of young servicemen sustained by the singular strength that comes from freedom," journalist Hugh Sidey emphasized D-Day's affirmation of American democratic values. He approvingly quoted Ambrose's characterization of the battle as "the greatest event of this century." Sidey hoped that "the D-day anniversary may evolve into a continuous celebration of liberty."[32]

D-Day represented a combination of emotive and evocative concepts that proved particularly revealing of America in the late twentieth century. When Americans commemorated the Second World War, they tended to dwell on the surprise attack at Pearl Harbor that had vindicated their war effort, the retributive atomic bombings that had capped the war against Japan, and the D-Day invasion that had inaugurated the end of the war with Germany. Of the three, D-Day represented the "safest" memory. Pearl Harbor had dented American pride. The atomic bombings helped end the war but ushered in a new era of mass terror. Indeed, the controversy surrounding a projected Smithsonian Museum exhibit on the *Enola Gay,* the B-29 that had dropped the first atomic bomb, indicated the complexities surrounding public memories of the Pacific Theater. Public outcries and high-profile pressure in 1994–95 derailed a plan to display the plane along with an exhibit that acknowledged Japanese suffering.[33]

D-Day, on the other hand, inspired no moral ambiguity, at least as commonly viewed in the United States. Americans, assisted by effaced "Allies," had confronted the German army in a bold operation that altered the course of the war in Europe. The liberation mantra reinforced this point. Americans had liberated Europe and, as Clinton intoned, "turned the tide of the twentieth century" as a result. The public enjoyed these tales of D-Day glory, which made the underlying message of world responsibility—even in the face of military action—easier to consume.

"The Bloody, Heartfelt Cultural Salve"

By the 1990s, an intense fervor suffused American society regarding the Second World War. D-Day fit into mainstream understandings of what America symbolized. After the fiftieth anniversary, D-Day remained a topic of conversation throughout the remainder of the decade.

The public interest in D-Day benefitted from an outpouring of written work that described the battle. The Cantigny First Division Foundation, for instance, published transcripts from the 1994 D-Day conference at which Ambrose had defended his assertion about the democratic implications of the battle.[34] Historian Peter Mansoor's 1999 book, *The GI Offensive in Europe,* rejected aspersions cast on the military effectiveness of U.S. Army divisions in the Second World War. Tellingly, Mansoor opened the book with a vignette of the D-Day invasion. Mansoor returned to D-Day several chapters later. He stressed the enormity of the undertaking while offering positive assessments of America's military forces. Mansoor explained that the "invasion succeeded primarily due to the skill and bravery of the soldiers." D-Day indicated "that an army of democracy, citizens turned into soldiers in a short period of time, could improvise and prevail against the supposedly superior military system of the Wehrmacht."[35]

Professional historians did not stand alone in the desire to write about D-Day. Journalist Tom Brokaw claimed that he had a "life-changing experience" while reporting the 1984 D-Day anniversary. Those ceremonies further impressed upon him the heroic nature of America's people. Brokaw's hagiographic and reductionist interpretation of America's wartime populace suffused his best-selling 1998 book, *The Greatest Generation.* Much like Studs Terkel, Brokaw coined a new term with this title. Brokaw, however, did not hint at irony. Offering examples of stoic resolve and moral clarity as inherent characteristics of the Americans who fought the Second World War, Brokaw dismissed any problematic traits as ephemeral excesses of the moment. The entire generation, he averred, had united to confront evil, successfully bested it, and then made America great in the years that followed the Second World War. The "greatest generation" earned its greatness through religious faith, marital fidelity, self-reliance, and, of course, military success—traits that Brokaw found lacking in succeeding generations. His book offered younger Americans an opportunity to indulge in sentimental filial devotion. Brokaw, mimicking Ambrose, told stories about the greatest generation's heroism.[36]

Yet some veterans became uncomfortable with the intense celebration of the Second World War. The cantankerous Andy Rooney took repeated swipes at the "good war" tinting to these stories. Rooney refuted Brokaw's designation of the "greatest generation," yet he undercut the force of his argument by having Brokaw write the foreword to his book *My War* (2000). Therein, Brokaw insisted on the validity of the "greatest generation" cognomen.[37]

Rooney rejected simplified notions of heroism. He noted that wars tend to elicit challenging questions about dissent, patriotism, and the legitimate use of violence. Rooney nevertheless perpetuated popular notions of the war. He characterized D-Day as the turning point in the war against Germany, one of the most decisive days in all world history. The liberating intent of the Allies had made the invasion "one of the most monumentally unselfish things one group of people ever did for another." Selflessness had characterized the invasion, yet Rooney denounced the French for staking a claim to what was supposedly an American day. "The French call D-Day 'J-Jour' and I don't have a lot of complaints with the French but it was our day and I think they ought to call it by our name, D-Day." Apparently, the recipients of American largess ought to remain in the background lest they detract from

American glory. Rooney carped on the financial exploitation of battlefield tourism. He also rejected war movies as glamorizing tales of carnage while cashing in on the suffering of others.[38]

Rooney's critique of those profiting from the war may seem to be the usual ranting of a media personality who reveled in his curmudgeonly image. Yet his claims had merit, at least concerning the D-Day hype prevalent in America during the late 1990s. Documentaries abounded, kitsch proliferated, and even toymakers capitalized on the new D-Day interest. Hasbro, Inc., the manufacturer of GI Joe action figures, issued two separate D-Day varieties in 1997, including the D-Day Salute figure and the Omaha Beach soldier. Volumes on D-Day swarmed bookshelves across the country. From tales of bravado to collections of wartime pictures, many authors exploited D-Day.[39] D-Day historians appeared on countless television programs. No author surpassed Ambrose in this capacity. His popularity, smooth performance, (sometimes audacious) claims to originality, and D-Day public history projects kept him in the limelight.

Media fixation on D-Day persisted throughout the decade. Not all of these accounts conveyed the heartwarming tales of heroism, glory, or sacrifice for a good cause. Indeed, as the Battle of Normandy Foundation's travails played out through the latter half of the 1990s, repeated news articles detailed the decline of the organization. Public outrage greeted revelations that financial mismanagement had derailed an opportunity to honor the veterans.[40]

Nevertheless, the growing public fascination with all things related to D-Day produced an upsurge in television programs depicting the battle. The History Channel, which began broadcasting in 1995, stoked this interest in its early years by focusing intently on Second World War topics. Interestingly, D-Day's small-screen presence did not translate immediately into big-screen coverage. In fact, Sam Fuller's 1980 film, *The Big Red One,* had been the last major D-Day re-creation witnessed by American theatergoers. Fuller's attempt to honor his 1st Infantry Division comrades flopped at the box office. The rejection of Fuller's film coincided with shifts in American society that seemingly led to the demise of the standard war film by the 1980s. Although Second World War nostalgia had swept the country since at least the mid-1980s, Hollywood production companies lagged behind television attention devoted to this subject.

Hollywood eventually jumped on board. In a 1999 episode of the series *Inside the Actor's Studio,* host James Lipton indulged in the usual embellished statements about his guest, Tom Hanks. Lipton asserted that Hanks represented the quintessential American screen hero of the 1990s. Hanks argued that the variety and impact of his films depended upon their essential ability to project "the truth" of a situation to audiences.[41] His truth earned tremendous box-office success and critical acclaim. From comedic fare like *A League of Their Own* (1992, partly filmed at the Cantigny estate) to probing social commentary like *Philadelphia* (1993), Hanks seemed to do no wrong. Interestingly, this actor born nearly a week before the dedication of the Normandy American Cemetery in 1956 had recently turned his attention to D-Day. His 1998 blockbuster movie, *Saving Private Ryan,* in fact, rejuvenated the entire war film genre.[42]

Saving Private Ryan broke new grounds in terms of box-office success, cinematic skill in telling a complex story, and unbounded hyperbole. Most discussions of the movie center on the second scene, which is the graphic, twenty-five-minute-long D-Day assault that slaps viewers in the face early in the film. At the time of release, there was an outpouring of concern over the intense realism of the film, as many felt the viewing would spark new pains and horrors in combat veterans.[43] Part of this concern came from the media campaign enacted prior to the film's release. The director, Steven Spielberg, the main star, Tom Hanks, and their consulting historian, Stephen Ambrose, all extolled the realism and graphically violent accuracy of the film. Ambrose, in fact, asserted, "There's no other World War II movie like this. The only things missing are the smell of battle and the smoke of battle." Spielberg claimed, "I wanted the audience to realize what it was like to be in a real war rather than a Hollywood war."[44]

Ambrose's viewpoint is imprinted on this film. Scriptwriter Robert Rodat was considering possible film projects after reading Ambrose's vivid new work *D-Day* in the summer of 1994. Rodat focused on the Second World War and the D-Day landings. His story presented a reimagining of Sergeant Fritz Niland's experience. Here the small slips in Ambrose's version of history came to have a profound impact. In the attempt to convey the toll of war on one American family, Ambrose wrote poignantly about Sergeant Niland of the 101st Airborne Division. As it turned out, however, Ambrose garbled the details. Four Niland boys fought in the Second World War. Two died on D-Day, one with the 82nd Airborne Division and the other with the 4th Infantry Division. The third brother went missing in Burma. Ambrose erroneously recounted the effort to remove Fritz from combat because of these other losses by writing that the U.S. Army "snatched [him] out of the front line." The army did send Fritz home, but in a less dramatic fashion. Father Francis Sampson, a U.S. Army chaplain, arranged for Fritz's trip home from England after the 101st returned there later in 1944. The fallacious version of this story formed the starting point for Rodat's script.[45]

This fabricated tale of a rescue under fire offered a thrilling plot device. Rodat pitched the project, and Paramount signed him to write a script in June 1995. Production notes indicated Rodat's thrust. "The film is about decency, and how patriotism ultimately has to do with one's responsibility to family, to neighbors and to those one fights alongside in the military," he explained.[46] By 1996, Steven Spielberg joined the project. Following his critically acclaimed production on the Holocaust, *Schindler's List* (1993), Spielberg sought to show another side of the Second World War. He claimed that the Holocaust project honored his mother; the war film would honor his father and all American soldiers.[47] Spielberg lured his friend Tom Hanks to help him shape and then star in the production. Those two extended and also intensified the violent display of Rodat's D-Day scene.[48]

Hanks had suggested a special company to Spielberg, one that would help ensure an accurate depiction of the American soldiers at the heart of this story. Captain Dale Dye, a retired U.S. Marine, formed Warriors Incorporated in 1985. Dye intended to correct what he saw as the overwhelmingly negative portrayal of the American military that had circulated on television and in Hollywood movies. He wanted "to correct misperceptions about the military and celebrate the courage, devotion, and sacrifice of the men and women who've worn our uniform."[49] Dye ensured a verisimilitude in *Saving Private Ryan* that led some historians and enthusiasts to rave over its production techniques. He also ran a mini–boot camp for the main actors. The ten-day immersive experience fostered an appreciation in the actors, none of whom had prior military service, for the rough life of combat soldiers. Dye had run them so ragged that a mutiny surfaced in a few days. The faux training proved too demanding, that is, for all except the oldest actor—Tom Hanks. Hanks's resolve convinced the rest to return to duty.[50]

This level of commitment pervaded the entire production process. Spielberg employed a cast of thousands to convey the enormity of the Allied military effort in Europe. In the quest for authenticity, he made risky choices, like filming without camera lens filters. The grainy footage evoked film stock taken during the war, in striking contrast to the polished imagery audiences expected to see in blockbuster movies. The loving attention to detail devoted to the Omaha Beach scenes had demanded twenty-four days of shooting out of the fifty-nine days expended on the entire movie.[51] Spielberg scoured multiple places looking for the right landscape on which to re-create the D-Day landings and ultimately settled on a beach in Ireland. Explaining that decision, Spielberg stated that he dared not profane the actual D-Day beaches with a movie's production activities.[52]

The publicity effort displayed an equally intense approach. In the months leading up to the July 1998 release of *Saving Private Ryan,* Spielberg, Hanks, and Ambrose conducted a media blitz to promote the movie. Spielberg claimed that he was "not making another 'movie,' but rather *the* American war movie."[53] He argued that the film celebrated the simpler times of national unity, innocence, and world-saving actions by the greatest of generations.[54] Ambrose declared that Spielberg had pulled off the best and most realistic film depiction of D-Day.[55] The historian wrote a 1998 article for *American Heritage* that labeled D-Day the "pivot of the twentieth century." Ambrose insisted, "What had gone before that day led up to the invasion of France, and what followed was the consequence." He dramatically argued, "At stake was the future of democracy."[56] D-Day programming on television heightened public awareness and interest in the subject. The History Channel, for instance, broadcast several programs on D-Day in the weeks surrounding *Saving Private Ryan*'s theatrical debut.[57]

Saving Private Ryan attained major commercial success, grossing almost \$500 million in domestic and international markets. Spielberg's claim to make the movie to honor his father and the "greatest generation" resonated at a time when many of these individuals were passing away. The shocking violence of the opening and closing scenes was not senseless, as in many Vietnam movies. The nobility of soldiers engaging in deadly work for a clear, justifiable goal (securing a fellow citizen) appealed to American audiences. Moreover, the rescue of one man seemed to counter the Vietnam story, at least the version of that war that focused on the missing in action, prisoners of war, and those left unaccounted for by a corrupt government and fickle society. The film, in a sense, redeemed the country from its Vietnam nightmare scenario.[58] As one scholar argued, in the movie "Spielberg reunifies white, masculine identity. He (re)imagines a time before the social dislocations of mid-century movements for gender and racial equality. He restores moral authority to the modern American nation-state. Perhaps most important, he confronts and engages cultural cynicism about the legitimacy of blood sacrifice to the nation."[59]

Saving Private Ryan told a story about America that Americans wanted to hear. The older generation had come together in a time of intense danger and, through collective effort, pulled through to success. Spielberg, Hanks, Ambrose, and Brokaw all sang the same tune in 1998, one that the American public absorbed in rapt awe. The gore depicted in the movie served to sanctify the characters' sacrifice. *Saving Private Ryan* also challenged the "'me' generation sitting in the audience" by asking what it was doing for America.[60]

Without a doubt, the D-Day scene is tremendously affecting. An ominously overcast sky hovers over the American forces making their way towards Omaha Beach. The overburdened landing craft advances with loads of nervous men, many vomiting, praying, or both. Soldiers shift about as they listen to last-minute instructions. The men had trained for this moment for years. Some had even experienced combat before this day. Yet none fully anticipates the ferocity of the reception looming ahead. In the distance, the shoreline breaks through the early morning gloom. The landing craft approaches the beaches as small arms fire and thunderous explosions confirm that the enemy stands alert and ready. When the ramps on the Higgins boats go down, the debarking American troops meet a hail of withering fire. Chaos ensues amid a technologically induced frenzy of destruction. Agonizing deaths erode cohesion as well as collective morale. A few dazed survivors gather for cover behind the German anti-landing obstacles. They rally under the direction of junior leaders, who remind the men that remaining on the beach means certain death. A mad dash leads to relative safety along a seawall midway up the beach. Limited cover affords the chance to gather forces there for a determined assault. The Americans force a break in the defenses through sheer tenacity and the heroic action of several individuals. Captain John Miller (Hanks), one source of inspiration, leads the remnants of his Ranger company through such a breach. Once the Americans make this breakthrough, the local front dissolves. The youthful sacrifices enable victory.

The grandiose claims of *Saving Private Ryan*'s promoters mixed with the movie's inspirational message. The film reaffirmed popular conceptions of the war and this battle—drawing liberally on prior depictions in some points.[61] Yet it is important to note that *Saving Private Ryan* decontextualizes

D-Day from the war. Audiences join Hank and his costars as they hit the beach. The film comes with no prologue—no explanation of what preceded the invasion or what made it necessary. Highlighting Omaha Beach, it also depicts the operation as an all-American affair. The blinkered view of D-Day as uniquely America's day stemmed from such constrained depictions. *Saving Private Ryan* made more people aware of D-Day but kept them ignorant of the strategic context and diverse experiences of the battle.[62]

Regardless of such issues, people flocked to see *Saving Private Ryan* and then enthused over its depiction of war. Journalist Andrew Hindes cited Stephen Ambrose to explain the moralistic component of the film that gave meaning to the extreme carnage portrayed on screen: "Ambrose and others say the dramatic appeal of WWII is its clear-cut heroes and villains, a refreshing escape from the murky morality of Vietnam and other more recent regional conflicts."[63] *Saving Private Ryan* offered a story about a "good war" with American heroes defeating German enemies. Because audiences felt that just watching this production paid homage to the "greatest generation," the movie itself became a cultural event. Spielberg asserted, "This isn't the kind of movie you see and then go to a bistro and break bread talking about it—you have to go home and deal with it privately."[64] Some veterans publicly lent *Saving Private Ryan* their approval by acknowledging its bloody "realism."[65] Discussions of *Saving Private Ryan* have often asserted that civic duty demanded viewing a movie that reminded Americans that "freedom isn't free."[66]

This thought coexisted along with claims, as succinctly expressed by Tom Hanks, that in *Saving Private Ryan* "there's no overt sort of patriotic statement or even curve."[67] The assertion of American honor and morality in the Second World War, of militant civic duty in restoring moral order to the world, seemed so obvious by the late 1990s that these arguments transcended "politics." Journalist Neal Gabler, however, identified the cultural and generational politics that had suffused the film and the public reaction to its portrayal of warfare: "In effect, 'Saving Private Ryan' has become the bloody, heartfelt cultural salve to the divisions and tumult that have riven this country throughout the postwar period." Gabler insightfully argued, "The text of the film may be warfare 1944, the subtext is unity 1998." "In short, it is not Private Ryan who gets saved; it is the lost vision of America," he concluded. That vision included unity in trying times that had enabled America to defeat evil and rise to global prominence.[68] Veterans, scholars, politicians, the public, and the U.S. military celebrated this version of the past.[69]

Not every reaction to *Saving Private Ryan* proved favorable.[70] Historian John Votaw, at the Cantigny First Division Museum, acknowledged the movie's realism. However, he urged interested persons to check out History Channel programming for its greater depth and accuracy.[71] An *Atlanta Daily World* editorialist rebuked Spielberg for excluding African Americans from this tale of glory when some had indeed served that day.[72] Second World War veteran and cultural historian Paul Fussell argued that this film had presented nothing new to audiences conversant with American war films.[73] Reviewing *Saving Private Ryan* for *American Heritage,* historian Roger Spiller noted that the film perpetuated "one of the great myths of war . . . that fighting in one somehow makes one a better person." Spiller also rejected the tendency of cultural critics to use "the film to wag reproving fingers at effete Baby Boomers who were filling up theater seats." He lampooned "commentators [who] have actually expressed regret they did not fight in World War II (a regret, it should be noted, that is easy to express half a century later)."[74]

Part of the problem with *Saving Private Ryan* stemmed from promotional activities tied to the film. The claims of individuals like Spielberg or Ambrose that this movie excelled all previous war films, that it somehow transcended mere entertainment and connected with higher reality, struck commentators like Spiller as absurd. No matter how artful a film, the reminder by Second World War veteran and director Sam Fuller remained valid: a movie is *not* actual war.[75]

These reservations found few listeners amid the positive buzz that surrounded *Saving Private Ryan;* Americans enjoyed the new burst of D-Day-related war romanticism. Rereleased in December, *Saving Private Ryan* earned eleven Academy Award nominations and won in five categories. After the success of 1962's *The Longest Day,* a "longest day" paradigm had emerged in conversations on D-Day and warfare in general. Following *Saving Private Ryan*'s success, a new framing point appeared with the carnage of the D-Day scene standing as a ready reference for war's gruesome nature. The film's popularity had long coattails. It boosted financial collection efforts for D-Day and Second World War commemorative projects. Hanks became a national spokesman for American veterans. He and Spielberg agreed to team up on another Ambrose-generated Second World War story. In December 1998, they announced an HBO miniseries adaptation of *Band of Brothers.* Spielberg and Hanks also helped raise funds and awareness for Ambrose's D-Day museum project taking shape in New Orleans.[76] The two granted many interviews to publicize the film or promote D-Day commemorative activities.

Saving Private Ryan even had a profound impact on video game development. Home video game consoles enjoyed explosive sales during the 1990s. Americans of all ages and types played these games, but one genre tended to attract young, male audiences. First Person Shooters (FPS) are games of violence that employ a first-person perspective while pitting the player against computer or human opponents.[77] Prior to the late 1990s, many FPS games had borrowed heavily from science fiction tropes, casting players as space marines of some sort battling aliens or demons. Game developers recognized the allure of the Second World War with *Saving Private Ryan*'s success. Spielberg assisted in the development of historically themed games, particularly those centering on the Second World War. The *Medal of Honor* suite of games that explored this new direction has often used D-Day as a major component of the played activity, as typified in the original installment.[78]

These games pushed historical awareness in particular directions. They tended, in the words of one historian, to construct "a sense of linearity and historical direction through . . . landscape and gameplay," while emphasizing the heroic action of individuals. Players vicariously "lived" the trial of war. *Medal of Honor* and the games that followed have relied heavily on *Saving Private Ryan*'s "*verité* documentary style." Employing shocking visuals and the semblance of individual control, these games have presented a specific version of the past for consumption by young audiences.[79] *Saving Private Ryan* attracted game developers to historical content. This new round of history-shooters has often targeted D-Day. For the millions of Americans who have purchased and played each of these installments, D-Day appeared as a shocking, carnage-filled, albeit thrilling day of action. Nobody had shirked duty or "refused" to participate. Individual heroes liberally peppered the American forces—heroes that allegedly had changed the course of world history by preserving freedom in faraway lands. "The firmly established traditions of this genre," noted one pair of scholars, "presume that your finger must always be on the trigger, that you must be ready to kill easily defined enemies, and that you will hesitate only for tactical reasons. . . . In such a world, the idea of judicial restraint on violence becomes laughable."[80] The *Medal of Honor* series included fourteen original titles. This successful run of games spawned many imitators like the *Call of Duty* series that has tapped into D-Day repeatedly.

Video games, books, Hollywood movies, documentary films—these presented just some of the many venues for an outburst of D-Day fascination in the late 1990s. An informal competition actually emerged among several of the major groups seeking to commemorate D-Day. With a major museum planned in New Orleans, a large-scale monument planned in Bedford, Virginia, and the imploding Battle of Normandy Foundation in its last gasps, an array of projects called attention to D-Day. The National World War II Memorial, the commemorative project on the National Mall in Washington, D.C., also further divided public attention while competing for limited financial support. Tom Hanks helped organize fundraising for the latter project while the success of his movie, *Saving Private Ryan,* had boosted contributions to the assortment of D-Day projects. Bedford residents, for instance, eagerly anticipated that film's Academy Awards triumphs in the hope that such exposure would increase contributions to their memorial project.[81]

Ambrose attracted public attention in the 1990s and used the opportunity to advance his personal agendas. He repeated stirring tales of the Normandy invasion and drummed up support for opening his D-Day museum in New Orleans. In 1996, Ambrose publicized the museum in one installment of the A&E network series *Save Our History.* The episode, "The Making of the National D-Day Museum," showcased some of the artifacts intended for the museum while affording Ambrose a pulpit to advance his D-Day interpretations. Ambrose claimed that "D-Day was the decisive point of the century. It turned world history." Americans had united and fought a good war for democratic principles. D-Day reaffirmed the moral worth of America, which had employed power benevolently for a just purpose. Emphasizing the event's carnage, Ambrose proclaimed every Allied participant a heroic fighter for democracy. Finally, Ambrose assured viewers that innovative and interactive displays would bring this history to life, offering lessons about citizenship, heroism, and democracy for future generations.[82]

The enduring public fanfare that began with the grand opening on June 6, 2000, vindicated the $25 million spent on the National D-Day Museum. The exhibits combined a mixture of artifacts, painstaking re-creations, audio-visual access points, and traditional information panes. The museum portrayed America's Depression years, lack of military preparedness, thrust into war, and eventual redemption through D-Day combat. The overall gist of the museum's presentation celebrated honorable service by (primarily)

American troops in a glorious battle. The moral stakes remained unquestionably clear—this was a "good war"—and the democratic ethos of the American forces had contributed to battlefield success and ensured a just peace after the war. Local Second World War veterans volunteered in droves to work as museum docents. D-Day vets even helped build some of the re-created pieces, like a Higgins boat. The opening events alone attracted an estimated ten thousand Second World War veterans.[83]

In a 2000 *American Heritage* article, Ambrose noted that the fifteen-year campaign to create the museum had demanded much of his time and energy. Fundraising was consistently strong, but it had received a major boost because of *Saving Private Ryan*'s success. Ambrose grandiosely opined that in the (many) years to come, the museum "will teach billions of young Americans that freedom doesn't come free, that nothing can beat the fury of an aroused democracy, that teamwork always prevails, and that the virtues of dedication, patriotism, loyalty, and doing one's duty will prevail forever."[84] An ambitious vision, to be sure, but Ambrose's points were not so much groundbreaking ideas as encapsulations of the traditional American understandings of D-Day. Telling a story that audiences wanted to hear ensured that all of Ambrose's D-Day canon—including his appearances in documentaries and his museum—garnered the highest accolades and considerable success. In a way, the National D-Day Museum stood as a monument to Ambrose the historian just as much as it promoted his particular interpretation of the battle.

A Time for Everything

The 1990s witnessed a great deal of commemorative activity surrounding D-Day. Part of this process undoubtedly stemmed from the fact that half a century had passed since the day of battle. D-Day attracted increasing American attention as part of a general surge of interest in the Second World War. With the "greatest generation" growing smaller by the day, the tendency to celebrate its achievements loomed larger than ever.

The entire decade of the 1990s produced examples of commemoration tied to the battle. D-Day has served as a glorified moment in the last war that most Americans regarded as "good." Americans dwelt on the Second World War as a mythologized time of supposed unity, national power, and moral clarity. One author, citing Ambrose's work in particular, called the tales told in this vein "the wartime equivalent of big fish stories." She condemned this stylistic presentation as a "genre [that] encourages hubris and includes a boisterous excitement about war, the sense that life was never quite as rich again in action or comradeship for those who fought."[85] Such a pointed critique may be correct, but for mainstream American society in the 1990s, it was largely irrelevant. People enjoyed these stories, as evidenced in their eager consumption, which cast America as the powerful country preserving morality in a benighted world. These tropes tapped into long-standing components of America's self-perception as the city on a hill holding evil at bay. That the Korean and Vietnam Wars had failed to fit into such a mold helped explain why the Second World War, and D-Day in particular, returned with such force. The "good times" of the war era served as reaffirmation of America's greatness, something Americans wanted to hear following the murky decades of the Cold War, social fragmentation, and the divisive Vietnam War. Facing an uncertain post-Cold War era, America's leaders and memory activists turned to the past for guidance. This use of history served initiatives as diverse as Bill Clinton's agenda of promoting democracy and the wider public intent to honor the war generation.

These constructed versions of the past provoked real-world reactions. Some critics decried the commercialization of D-Day.[86] Others deplored the Battle of Normandy Foundation's failures.[87] Even sharper rebukes faulted the sentimentalized conceptions of warfare that these readings of the past have encouraged in the American public. Historian Michael Adams condemned the American sentiment that the Second World War had constituted "the best war ever." The sense of a war fought to save the world, which had pulled America out of the Depression while fostering national unity, reflected present-day concerns more than accurate descriptions of the past. This mythologized version of the Second World War stimulated a desire to emulate past glories through new military adventures, such as Vietnam and Desert Storm.[88] That similar scholarly rebukes of Second World War celebrationism kept emerging, however, revealed their limited purchase in American society.

An air of unease emerged in the 1990s as Second World War mania swept the country. In the background, some people raised objections to the glorification of warfare and the romanticized stories told to honor a past generation. These versions of the past polemicized current maladies. That the D-Day celebrations served as the most publicized, most grandiose, and most romanticized elements of the fiftieth Second World War anniversary wave indicated the particular tinting of that conflict in American collective memory. For most Americans, D-Day reigned unchallenged as the turning point in the war, a day of liberation, a triumphal event that had demonstrated America's love of freedom and rightful leadership in world affairs. When faced with different challenges in a new millennium, these popular constructions would help shape public reactions to startling developments.

Above, President Ronald Reagan delivered one of his most stirring addresses in front of the "boys of Pointe du Hoc" on June 6, 1984. Venerating the war generation helped Reagan push Americans to focus on the positive aspects of their country's history and helped bring D-Day back into national conversations. Below, Reagan shaking hands with several of the veterans who fought at Pointe du Hoc. After this anniversary, men such as these would repeatedly call upon Reagan for support and assistance. Top photo courtesy of U.S. Department of Defense, taken by Specialist Vincent R. Kritts; bottom photo courtesy of U.S. Department of Defense.

Right, the recently dedicated (1979) Ranger Dagger monument that appears behind Reagan in the image above. Below, the grounds of Pointe du Hoc (2010), one of the major sites of combat on D-Day. The heavy shelling here by the Allied forces left the terrain pockmarked, as evident to this day. The Pointe du Hoc scene in the film *The Longest Day* would prove controversial to veterans. The site itself remains a popular tourist attraction. Right photo courtesy of American Battle Monuments Commission, taken by Warrick Page; bottom photo from author's collection.

The innovative diorama of the D-Day landings occupied a central place in the original Cantigny War Memorial Museum in Wheaton, Illinois. This exhibit highlighted the 1st Infantry Division's action on Omaha Beach. Parts of the diorama moved as an audiotape narration played nearby. Courtesy of Cantigny First Division Foundation.

Thirty years after the museum first opened in 1960, the Cantigny First Division Museum replaced it with expanded space and new displays that touted a more immersive experience. D-Day remained a central feature, as visitors sit in a mock landing craft and then walk into a re-created beach area littered with defensive obstacles and the detritus of battle. Author's collection.

Stephen Ambrose escorting U.S. Secretary of Defense William Cohen and his wife while visiting what was then called the National D-Day Museum in New Orleans, June 6, 2000. Courtesy of U.S. Department of Defense.

Hasbro, Inc., released two D-Day figures in 1997, including the "D-Day Salute" and the Omaha Beach army infantryman. Photo courtesy of Cantigny First Division Museum.

Ambrose's public history activities bore fruit in 2000 with the dedication of the National D-Day Museum in New Orleans. Although since renamed the National World War II Museum, this facility continues to focus on "the" D-Day. In the main entrance hall, visitors encounter a re-created LCVP that local D-Day veterans had helped build. Author's collection.

The Bedford, Virginia, National D-Day Memorial symbolically re-creates the Omaha Beach landing with bronze figures struggling to the shore. The towering Overlord Arch captures the epic nature of the invasion. President George W. Bush dedicated the memorial on June 6, 2001, to an estimated crowd of twenty thousand. Author's collection.

Monument at the Brecourt Manner site made famous by the 2001 HBO miniseries *Band of Brothers*. The monument was erected adjacent to the primary battle scene in the D-Day episode of that series. The names of the Easy Company soldiers killed on D-Day adorn the monument. Author's collection (2010).

U.S. president George W. Bush and French president Jacques Chirac (above, standing center right) commemorate the D-Day invasion in a June 6, 2004, observance. Amid an Iraq war that divided Americans and splintered alliance relationships, Bush attempted to exploit D-Day as a unifying moment in the nation's history. Reenactors (below) have crowded the Norman countryside, especially during any D-Day anniversary period. Many of the "American" soldiers are British or French citizens. This photo shows one reenactor camp set up for the sixty-sixth anniversary on June 6, 2010. Above photo courtesy of WhiteHouse.gov; below photo from author's collection.

The Cantigny First Division Museum secured and restored a Higgins boat that had participated in the Normandy invasion. It is pictured here prior to the official unveiling on June 6, 2009, for the sixty-fifth anniversary. Author's collection.

President Barack Obama in Normandy during the seventieth D-Day Anniversary Celebrations in 2014. He is shown greeting veterans of the invasion who continue to come for the annual fetes despite dwindling numbers as age claims more of them. These celebrations often acknowledge the debts younger generations owe to their elders, specifically those who fought to liberate the oppressed and make the world a better place, as framed in the official and unofficial coverage of these events. Courtesy of U.S. Navy, taken by Petty Officer 1st Class Arif Patani.

The Normandy American Cemetery (2010). Visitors from Europe and the United States continue to flock to the cemetery, particularly during anniversary periods. The pathos of lives sacrificed at the "portal of liberation," as characterized by one inscription here, highlights the nobility of the American cause in the Normandy invasion. Courtesy of American Battle Monuments Commission, taken by Warrick Page.

CHAPTER 8
AN EXCESS OF D-DAY?

The National D-Day Memorial

George W. Bush, the son of George H. W. Bush, assumed the presidency on January 20, 2001. The new Republican leader sustained certain foreign policies from his Democratic predecessor that by this point transcended partisan divides. Bush had campaigned on the seemingly incongruous aims of promoting democracy abroad while avoiding the dismal prospect of "nation-building." Moral suasion and economic pressure constituted his preferred means for extending democratic government.[1] American divisions, covered under the broad cloak of the "culture wars," also persisted. These problems challenged a new leader who had squeaked into office because of a Supreme Court ruling rather than a popular electoral mandate.

One mainstay of American society that survived the turn of the millennium was the widespread attention devoted to the Second World War. D-Day endured as a prominent point in the public appreciation of that conflict. A new monument specifically devoted to D-Day took center stage in 2001. Following the 1994 D-Day extravaganza, veterans in southwestern Virginia, like the ubiquitous Bob Slaughter, received wider support for a regional D-Day commemoration project. This undertaking would lead to the creation of the National D-Day Memorial in Bedford. Slaughter had faced a series of difficulties with fundraising. Because of these problems, the memorial moved from Slaughter's intended site in Roanoke to Bedford. Bedford claimed the rights because of the nineteen local men killed on June 6, 1944. Benefitting from the increased public attention generated by *Saving Private Ryan*'s success, the memorialization project gathered steam in the late 1990s. Famed cartoonist Charles Schulz also focused the national spotlight on Bedford. Schulz, a Second World War veteran, helped commemorate D-Day by contributing time, energy, and even several productions featuring his popular "Peanuts" characters. Schulz also chaired the fundraising efforts for Bedford's D-Day memorial. His wife, Jeannie, took over this role when Schulz died on February 12, 2000. Mrs. Schulz urged those wishing to honor her husband to donate money to the D-Day memorial. An allotment by the State of Virginia facilitated the dedication of the new facility on June 6, 2001.[2]

Stressing themes of "valor, fidelity, and sacrifice," the eighty-eight-acre memorial site in Bedford contains many symbolic, figurative, and educational components. The memorial is divided into four sections representing the preparations for the Normandy invasion, D-Day combat, the end of the war, and the postwar development of the free world. The preparation section consists of a replica English garden with statuary busts of the major Allied commanders. A life-size statue of Eisenhower dominates this area. A large adjacent plaza evokes the English Channel crossing. At one end, a symbolic re-creation of a Higgins boat opens onto a pool containing several bronze figures of American soldiers struggling through the surf and onto the beach. Off to one side, several re-created pieces symbolize the role of airborne forces on D-Day. The names of nearly forty-five hundred Allied soldiers killed on D-Day appear around the plaza. Bronze plaques inform visitors about Allied units. Throughout the site, deference to the coalitional nature of the invasion clashes with the emphasis on American soldiers and their D-Day exploits.[3] After navigating the amphibious assault area, visitors behold the pièce de résistance, the Overlord Arch. Impressively emblazoned with "OVERLORD," the arch towers an emblematic forty-four and a half feet (June 1*944* representing the *half*way point of the year). After marveling over this impressive construction, visitors end up in a small plaza with the flags of twelve Allied nations acknowledging wartime unity and postwar amity.[4]

The National D-Day Memorial Foundation has also touted an educational mission. Foundation employees have sought to instill a respect for the American citizen-soldier tradition that has preserved freedom at home and abroad.[5] The foundation has linked success on D-Day to the liberation of Europe, victory in the Cold War, and post-Cold War efforts by NATO in the Balkans.[6] This memorial has helped connect the trials of Bedford, Virginia, to a key event in national history. By the turn of the century, this small community's D-Day-related suffering captured the attention of national audiences already in a mood to commemorate the heroism of American soldiers and the stoicism of the wartime home front.[7]

President Bush dedicated the memorial in person on June 6, 2001. He honored the fallen soldiers and hailed their efforts to protect global freedom. Bush asserted that D-Day had revealed America in all its grandeur. The New World liberated the Old, and, as he suggested, "Free societies in Europe can be traced to the first footprints on the first beach on June 6, 1944." Bush dutifully acknowledged the painful losses that this liberating quest exacted. Nevertheless, he assured the twenty thousand people joining him that day in Bedford that these sacrifices had established lasting peace and promoted the spread of democracy. After noting that American interests demanded vigilance abroad, Bush concluded his speech by praying "that our country will always be worthy of the courage that delivered us from evil and saved the free world."[8] While Bush's words echoed former commemorations, his chauvinistic claims took on an added resonance in that fateful year of 2001. The National D-Day Memorial tapped into the popular conceptions that stressed the enduring story of American sacrifice in a just cause. Although the National D-Day Memorial Foundation would soon suffer a litany of financial woes, for the moment it—and the nation—could bask in the outpouring of public approval for the memorial.[9]

The memorial ultimately presents the standard view of D-Day as an event dominated by American heroes who selflessly fought to liberate others. Although public treatments of D-Day admitted the gruesome nature of combat, in the end the horrors of industrialized warfare added to the claims of American nobility in a quest to free the world from evil. D-Day stories formed a point of mutual agreement in an American society wracked by divisions in the early 2000s. These stories would shape American reactions to a new time of crises, threats, and warfare.

"One of Those Moments in Which History Splits"

The positive public reception of Bedford's National D-Day Memorial reflected the national mood in early 2001. Although social, cultural, and political rifts fragmented the country, Second World War commemoration seemed above the fray. The combined imperatives to honor a passing generation, reaffirm America's morality, and guide the youth based on the past ensured that the Second World War has remained a continuous topic of public conversation. D-Day served as a central turning point in a war that had thrust America to global prominence.

The battle, as before, appeared in a variety of venues. In 2001, historian Adrian Lewis published *Omaha Beach: A Flawed Victory.* He described the failures in doctrine, planning, preparations, and execution that had marred American performance on "bloody Omaha."[10] More prevalently, though, D-Day programming once more appeared on television. With the success of *Saving Private Ryan,* Steven Spielberg and Tom Hanks decided to produce an HBO miniseries based on Stephen Ambrose's *Band of Brothers.* The book and this 2001 series focus on the men of E company, 506th Parachute Infantry Regiment, 101st Airborne Division. The portrayal of the airborne jump on D-Day in the second of ten episodes re-creates the sense of confusion, carnage, and heroism that has often characterized depictions of the battle on film. The paratroopers find themselves in a challenging situation because of the darkness, misdrops, and committed German opposition. As epitomized by Lieutenant Richard Winters (Damian Lewis), the men heroically step up to the occasion, win the day, and ultimately the war as a result.

This series sought to tap into a growing American interest in D-Day and the Second World War while emulating the cinematic style of *Saving Private Ryan.* With a $125 million price tag, the miniseries required ten months of shooting and "involved eight directors, seven writers, 500 speaking roles, some 10,000 extras and a huge investment in uniforms, boots, weapons and World War II tanks."[11] This series' depiction of combat and the lesson of selfless sacrifice to improve the world remained true to popular understandings of D-Day. The Normandy episode aired on September 9, two days before terrorist attacks rocked the United States.

September 11, 2001, or 9/11, formed a breakpoint akin to Pearl Harbor's announcement of an earlier war. As historian James T. Patterson put it, the day constituted "one of those moments in which history splits, and we define the world as before and after."[12] A series of attacks then dealt devastating blows to America, shattered symbolic buildings, and took thousands of lives. Close to three thousand people died. In addition to the horrid losses, these attacks cracked American prestige and self-confidence. A few men, using simple box-cutters, changed the focus of a nation. Americans no longer blithely assumed that their country remained insulated from global events and fanatical hatreds. As one author asserted, "After a breathtaking eighty-two minutes of terror, America's mission was abruptly redefined, its resources reallocated, its troops redeployed."[13]

In her study of another crisis, historian Emily Rosenberg investigated American public memory of Pearl Harbor. She identified patterns similar to D-Day remembrance. Beginning with key orations and formative efforts at the time of attack, especially President Roosevelt's widely repeated phrase "a date which will live in infamy," the collective memory of Pearl Harbor has developed in varied ways over the subsequent seven decades. Again, as with D-Day memories, Pearl Harbor stories fluctuated in prevalence over the years. Interpretations of Pearl Harbor returned to the American public consciousness in the 1990s owing in part to disputes over fiftieth-anniversary commemorations. In 2001, a major blockbuster movie, *Pearl Harbor,* tapped into the popular fascination with America's last "good war." Rosenberg described the construction of public memories related to a major traumatic event: "Pearl Harbor 'lives' less as a specific occurrence in the past than as a highly emotive and spectacularized icon in an ongoing present—always in interaction with the mediated representations that constitute memory/history." Following the 9/11 terrorist attacks, Pearl Harbor's "infamy" trope came into prevalent use as people drew parallels between the bolt-from-the-blue surprise attacks. Pearl Harbor evoked treachery, lack of preparedness, the need for national unity, a righteous pretext for vengeance, and the assurance of eventual American victory.[14]

Ronald Reagan once argued, "President Roosevelt said December 7th will live as a day of infamy. And so it is remembered, yet June 6th, in contrast, lives on as a day of triumph."[15] While Pearl Harbor memories helped Americans come to grips with 9/11, D-Day and other "good war" constructions reassured people of their nation's rectitude and martial prowess. These formed two sides of the same narrative coin. Pearl Harbor validated Americans' anger over 9/11 while D-Day told them what to do about it: fight evil and liberate the oppressed.

Journalist William Safire, countering the national mood of the moment, cautioned in the *New York Times* against several loaded words fraught with danger. Highlighting Eisenhower's "great crusade," Safire described the implications of that concept when pressed into service by Bush for the fight against terrorism. Such terminology evoked the medieval crusades and implied a clash of civilizations or religions.[16] This phrase, though alluring because of its positive association with D-Day and the Second World War, threatened to disrupt the tenuous balance that Bush had to create in a war targeting Islamist terrorists and not the entire Muslim world.[17]

As the crusade terminology readily demonstrated, however, D-Day stories possessed lasting power and shaped American perceptions at the dawn of this unsettling new era. With the recent broadcast of the *Band of Brothers* D-Day episode, a reminder lingered in the air of what the nation could or should do when faced with seemingly implacable foes. ABC televised *Saving Private Ryan* for Veterans' Day in 2001, drawing 18 million viewers.[18] The network aired the movie without cuts. ABC had intended to edit about thirty minutes of graphic scenes from its broadcast. Executives decided to keep the full version after the terrorist attacks.[19] Several news articles argued that *Saving Private Ryan* showed Americans what the terrorists sought to destroy: democracy, fair play, and moral order.[20]

At the dawn of this new war period, D-Day remained a prominent part of the national collective consciousness. This argument is sustained by a number of new books that described the battle. Carlo D'Este published the hagiographic 2002 book *Eisenhower: A Soldier's Life,* which opened by noting D-Day's importance for Eisenhower and the world.[21] Paul Fussell's 2003 book, *The Boys' Crusade,* challenged film versions of D-Day.[22] In 2004, Joseph Balkoski attempted to close a purported gap in public D-Day knowledge with *Omaha Beach.* Flint Whitlock, with *The Fighting First,* and John McManus, with *The Americans at D-Day,* claimed a similar intent.[23] Popular histories of D-Day proliferated. Mark Bando's 2003 book covered the American airborne effort in *Vanguard of the Crusade.* Released the same year, Alex Kershaw's *The Bedford Boys* eulogized the ill-fated Virginians who had assaulted Omaha Beach in his 2003 book of that title. D-Day veterans and civilian eyewitnesses dived into the publication effort, as seen with Albert Smith's 2003 work on the 1st Infantry Division.[24] Rereleases appeared in force, including a 2003 compilation of journalist Don Whitehead's war-related articles and a 2004 update to Charles Cawthon's *Other Clay.*[25] In these works, D-Day often amounted to Americans liberating others from evil, a claim with particular significance in light of America's ongoing war on terror.

D-Day still repeatedly appeared in the news media. Stories circulated of veteran reunions, ceremonies, and celebrations. Laudatory articles venerated these men as world saviors. Even just grasping onto D-Day through commemorative activities ensured some popular acclaim. Stephen Ambrose died on October 13, 2002. His passing elicited an outpouring of releases, statements, editorials, and commentaries that honored the historian. These pieces often cast Ambrose's D-Day work as his most significant historical contribution.[26]

Although the one storyteller most directly linked in the public mind to D-Day was gone, the battle continued to appear across the media spectrum. The small screen, for instance, contained a welter of D-Day material during the early 2000s. The HBO miniseries *Band of Brothers* aired from late 2001 to early 2002 and enjoyed a special DVD-collection release a few months later. Twentieth Century Fox offered a "Fox War Classics" series of rereleased movies for home entertainment, which added *D-Day, The Sixth of June* to its list in 2002.[27] Documentary films and television specials on D-Day abounded. The Cambridge Educational company produced videos on major American museums for classroom use, including one 2003 spotlight on the National D-Day Museum. Tom Czekanski, the museum's collections manager, cast D-Day as the "story of how America saved the world for democracy."[28]

Saving the world for democracy once more took on added connotations as the United States stepped into another era of conflict. Beginning in late 2001, U.S. assistance provided to the Northern Alliance helped drive the Taliban regime from power in Afghanistan. The Taliban harbored the al-Qaeda terrorists who had perpetrated 9/11. This assault kicked off what the Bush administration labeled the Global War on Terror. Declaring war on a technique rather than a specific group left an open-ended state of war without distinct goals or standards of evaluation.[29] During the Korean War, government officials had alluded to the Second World War to validate the current conflict.[30] To build support for this new season of war, President Bush frequently tapped into popular views of D-Day and the Second World War.

As an example, Bush joined a Memorial Day prayer service at Sainte-Mère-Église on May 27, 2002. He commented upon the connections forged between France and the United States through shared experience in war. Bush claimed that an American desire to fight for liberty, as on D-Day, persisted as "we defend our freedoms against people who can't stand freedom."[31] Shortly afterward, President Bush delivered an address at the Normandy American Cemetery. A fixation on freedom dominated his speech. Bush evoked a long tradition of American love for liberty and argued that the Allied militaries on D-Day had constituted a "liberating force." He acknowledged the grief caused by losses in war—both in the past and present. Yet the president offered the consolation that lives lost in the quest for freedom earned national reverence. Bush stated, "Here where we stand today, the new world came back to liberate the old."[32]

In a continuation of this theme, on June 1, 2002, President Bush delivered an address to the graduating class at the United States Military Academy at West Point. "You walk in the tradition of Eisenhower and MacArthur, Patton and Bradley—the commanders who saved a civilization," Bush argued. "America has no empire to extend or utopia to establish." The president explained, "We wish for others only what we wish for ourselves, safety from violence, the rewards of liberty, and the hope for a better life." Yet he suggested that a better life depended on America's preferences: "The 20th century ended with a single surviving model of human progress, based on nonnegotiable demands of human dignity, the rule of law, limits on the power of the state, respect for women, and private property and free speech and equal justice and religious tolerance. America cannot impose this vision, yet we can support and reward governments that make the *right* choices for their own people." Those making the "wrong" choices deserved more than reproof. In the post-9/11 era, Bush argued, "If we wait for threats to fully materialize, we will have waited too long." Bush insisted, "Our security will require all Americans to be forward-looking and resolute, to be ready for *preemptive* action when necessary to defend our liberty and to defend our lives."[33] As he later explained, "9/11 hit, and we had to take a fresh look at *every* threat in the world."[34]

After the Second World War, Americans had merged the "lessons" learned from Pearl Harbor with the atomic bombings of Japan. Dangers could strike suddenly and, with atomic weapons added to the mix, a culture of fear pervaded America.[35] Following 9/11, a new climate of fear emerged, fanned in part by the Bush administration's efforts to link terrorists to "rogue states" holding weapons of mass destruction. The conjunction of Munich (oppose aggressors with force), Pearl Harbor and the atomic bombings (lest they devastate you while unprepared), and D-Day (and concerted military effort leads to liberty and peace), shaped American proclivities in the early twenty-first century.

Mixing morality with American foreign policy was certainly nothing new. From colonial times, British settlers in North America had cast theirs as a Promised Land, a New England, which would serve as a moral exemplar to the world as if it formed a shining city on a hill. Neoconservatism and an expanded religious evangelicalism in the late twentieth century pushed the moral reading of American foreign affairs to new extremes. Historian David Farber argued, "The United States, [Bush] believed, was inherently a moral nation that only sought to safeguard its people and its principles against evil. As a result, its use of exceptional measures was moral, because a moral nation had used them under threat from immoral people." Farber explained that this view contained a retaliatory aspect: "Those who opposed [the United States] opposed the world-historical virtues for which it stood, and thus America's enemies were enemies of freedom, democracy, and liberty."[36] Historian Richard Immerman argued that the "dichotomy between the good America and the evil 'other' leaves little space for compromise" and "is a temperament that favors pugnacity." The United States led a wayward world, which meant that American leaders must use the power at their disposal to remake the world anew in the service of liberty.[37] D-Day, to be sure, did not create these impulses in American political culture. (Although one is tempted to wonder whether George H. W. Bush ever made good on his vow in 1960 to "cram" D-Day via Cornelius Ryan's book down the throat of his son George—and what lessons the younger Bush took from that experience.)[38] Nevertheless, the freewheeling use of D-Day in political rhetoric helped reaffirm these favorable assertions about American power and morality.

In March 2003, following a new doctrine that called for preemptive wars against threats, the United States and a "coalition of the willing" invaded Iraq before Saddam Hussein could use a purported stock of weapons of mass destruction.[39] Bush later explained, "Before 9/11, Saddam was a problem America might have been able to manage. Through the lens of the post-9/11 world, my view changed." *Any* potential threat warranted a massive use of force *before* that threat could strike at America. Bush also cast the Iraq invasion as an opportunity. Stressing a "transformation," he claimed, "Once liberty took root in one society, it could spread to others." This domino theory of spreading democracy undercut his earlier disavowal of nation building.[40] The task would be relatively easy, according to Vice President Dick Cheney, who claimed on March 16, 2003, that "we will, in fact, be greeted [in Iraq] as liberators."[41]

The progress of the American-dominated invading force, aside from some mistakes and one lull, did prove breathtaking in speed. In short order, the

Iraqi military and Saddam's regime collapsed. Major combat halted in April, President Bush reveled in apparent victory, and Saddam hid until captured that December. The problem is that in the rush to go to war against Iraq many inconvenient factors had escaped planners and politicians. The purported weapons of mass destruction that formed the linchpin of justification for the war never materialized.[42]

In the haste to fight a war for regime change and the spread of democracy, little concerted thought went into what would happen in the post-Saddam moment. Journalist Thomas Ricks argued, "Because the Pentagon assumed that U.S. troops would be greeted as liberators and that an Iraqi government would be stood up quickly, it didn't plan seriously for less rosy scenarios." He further explained, "The war plan had called for the Iraqi population to cheerfully greet the American liberators, quickly establish a new government, and wave farewell to the departing American troops." Ricks noted the debilitating impact of this a priori assumption on the military's response to an insurgency that broke out in Iraq after major combat had ended.[43] Another historian argued that the liberation chant had paved the way for wars in the Middle East to liberate peoples from oppressive regimes. He expostulated, "By invading Iraq, the United States reaffirmed and reinvigorated the nation's 'great liberating tradition,' as the president put it."[44]

Colonel Peter Mansoor (U.S. Army, retired), who holds a PhD in history, served as an American brigade commander during the first year of Operation Iraqi Freedom. He published a combat diary titled *Baghdad at Sunrise* in 2008. Mansoor, while proud of his soldiers, condemned the disorganized American political-military hierarchy that had hampered the effectiveness of his brigade: "The grand assumption [in the prewar planning stages], however, was that Operation Iraqi Freedom would be a war of liberation that could be waged quickly and decisively by a small but agile force." That assumption fostered problematic expectations: "The Iraqi people on the whole would welcome coalition forces with open arms once Saddam Hussein fell from power, civil servants would remain at their posts, ethnic and religious differences would not fracture the country, and the large majority of U.S. forces would redeploy to their home stations within a matter of weeks, or at most months—as was the case after the first Gulf War."[45] None of this happened, unfortunately. Americans confronted a profound irony when the rhetoric of liberation did not lead to decisive victory, a stable Iraq, and a grateful world. Their leaders had failed to consider the turbulence that regime change would unleash. They also demonstrated a naïve understanding of democracy—assuming that it could magically bloom in an area that lacked civic identity, infrastructure, stability, and security.[46]

D-Day remembrance did not create the impetus for the Second Gulf War, and it alone did not produce a problematic strategy that failed to preempt a destructive insurgency in Iraq. The prevailing understandings and use of D-Day in the American political-military environment, however, did help sell the invasion of Iraq as just, necessary, and a potentially easy venture.

A Celebration of America

In a nation struck by economic problems, an ongoing war, and major social divisions, the sixtieth-anniversary D-Day celebration in 2004 seemed destined for minimal fanfare. Instead of fading into obscurity, however, the observances in Normandy attracted global attention and throngs of visitors. D-Day celebration in 2004 remained a surprisingly nonpartisan (for Americans) and even internationally supported breather from bitter disputes of the moment.

A variety of commemorative actions presaged the gala D-Day ceremonies. San Francisco residents dedicated as a floating museum the SS *Jeremiah O'Brien,* the Liberty Ship that had sailed to Normandy for the fiftieth anniversary.[47] The spring issue of the *Bridgehead Sentinel* printed an article describing one veteran's planned return to Normandy. A Public Broadcasting Service film crew tagged along with him to create a documentary record of the celebration. This issue also described a D-Day photographic display at the Cantigny First Division Museum.[48] *Military History Quarterly* again devoted its summer issue to D-Day articles.[49] Martin Blumenson hit once more with a reprinting in *Army* of his article, "D-Day: Launching the Great Crusade."[50] In all this coverage, D-Day remained a battle that had saved humanity, one in which Americans had fought for morality and justice.

In 2004, director, writer, and producer Richard Schickel released an expanded DVD version of Sam Fuller's 1980 movie, *The Big Red One.*[51] Fuller's initial cut had run to four and a half hours. Angered by postproduction studio interference with his masterwork, Fuller left the production. Lorimar Pictures demanded excisions that resulted in a two-hour theatrical release. Corporal Sam Fuller had landed on Omaha Beach and, according to his Silver Star commendation, "displayed magnificent courage and outstanding devotion to duty, in saving the lives of wounded comrades, and then playing a vital part in the control and organization of the drive inland."[52] The scene depicting Fuller's heroism, however, had fallen on the chopping block. Two decades later, Schickel's version of the film included Fuller's longer D-Day scene in an effort to honor the director and his wartime generation.

In the May/June 2004 issue of *Film Comment,* journalist Kent Jones wrote an article about *The Big Red One*'s rerelease. Jones asserted that Fuller "knows that war, real war, can never be encapsulated or reduced to its essence, that you can't try to 'balance' the insanity of the enterprise with firelit discussions of Emerson or interior monologues about the duality of human nature." The reference to Emerson was a swipe at *Saving Private Ryan,* which had featured such a conversation. Fuller, hampered by a far smaller budget, did not try to re-create battle à la Spielberg. The combat veteran/film director insisted that such an approach guaranteed artificiality—no film could realistically reproduce war. Instead, Fuller provided slices of soldiers' experience. Jones claimed, "If you want to quake in your boots, watch the first 20 minutes of *Saving Private Ryan*—but remember, it only works once." He argued, "If you want the full measure of the experience of war, *The Big Red One* is the movie."[53]

Taking advantage of the general atmosphere, the A&E Television network broadcast a made-for-television film on May 31, 2004, that treated the events leading up to D-Day. *Ike: Countdown to D-Day* was not a blockbuster spectacular, but it showed the willingness of television networks to delve into the potential profits that D-Day movies offered. *Ike* also continued the effacing of non-American roles in the day of days. The program focused on Eisenhower's leadership and the unique stresses he had suffered in the preinvasion period. The makers of this film took arguments between Montgomery and Eisenhower that actually came up later as the Allies swept across France (the broad-front versus narrow-front plan to reach Germany) and pasted them into the pre-D-Day preparations. The British, therefore, appeared totally opposed to D-Day, and the United States seemed to be the only country insisting on the invasion.[54]

These articles and movies kept D-Day alive in public conversations in 2004. Providing additional fuel for that interest, the sixtieth anniversary included elaborate ceremonies and grand moralistic rhetoric. Wartime distractions and national crises did not seriously hamper the celebratory zeal. In fact, D-Day observance could serve as a distraction from the painful present, a point worth considering as June 2004 witnessed "the height of the Abu

Ghraib scandal," according to one journalist. The torture and humiliation of Iraqi prisoners in that installation by American military personnel belied their country's pretentions to benevolent liberation from tyranny.[55] The D-Day anniversary, in contrast, afforded an opportunity to refocus domestic and international attention on a more positive record.

President Bush made several addresses in the period leading up to the anniversary that connected the commemorative past with present political needs. On May 29, Memorial Day, Bush officially dedicated the National World War II Memorial in Washington, D.C. He argued, "When it mattered most, an entire generation of Americans showed the finest qualities of our Nation and of humanity."[56] Later that day in a radio address, Bush declared, "Because of their [U.S. soldiers'] sacrifice, tyrants fell; fascism and Nazism were vanquished; and freedom prevailed." The freedom rhetoric appeared frequently in this communiqué and in the many Bush statements made to justify the nation's new wars. In the next line he indicated, "Today, freedom faces new enemies, and a new generation of Americans have stepped forward to defeat them." Bush reassured all that victory would come in Iraq, permitting the new generation of freedom fighters to "hold this hard-won ground for the realm of liberty."[57]

A week later, President Bush argued in another radio statement, "Iraq is on the path to democracy and freedom." Repeatedly invoking the two words "freedom" and "democracy," he cast the Iraq war in terms designed to attract American support despite continuous costs. Bush linked this effort to the Global War on Terror: securing a bastion for Middle Eastern democracy would undermine, in his view, support for and the capabilities of terrorists. Simply stated, "It is our work to win this struggle."[58] He repeatedly invoked the moral power of allies, in the Second World War or the present, fighting for just causes. Bush evidently felt that the D-Day paradigm—of America liberating others at great cost because it was right to do so—would ease his salesmanship efforts in 2004. He urged Americans to stay the course in Iraq, which implicitly would lead to another world-saving victory akin to D-Day.

President Bush eagerly attended the D-Day observances in Normandy that year. At 10:27 a.m. on June 6, 2004, a pleasant sunny morning, Bush began to speak. He sought to provide a brief history lesson, honor veterans, and reaffirm alliance partnerships. The president duly acknowledged the few veterans of the battle in attendance, some of whom mingled in the VIP section with Tom Hanks and Steven Spielberg.[59] After grimly reminding the audience of the costs of war, Bush highlighted the heroism of the soldiers. Turning to the results of their sacrifices, he argued, "The nations that battled across the Continent would become trusted partners in the cause of peace. And our great Alliance of freedom is strong, and it is still needed today." He suggested that "America honors all the liberators who fought here in the noblest of causes, and America would do it again for our friends."[60]

Continuing the pattern established in anniversaries over the previous two decades, the 2004 commemorations attracted large crowds and media attention. Since it was a Sunday, the morning talk-show programs in the United States covered the festivities to a degree, providing excerpts of Bush's speech. Major news publications, such as the *New York Times,* released stories immediately before, on, and after the anniversary. These articles presented a generally critical assessment of the stage-managed quality of the official ceremonies, yet repeated the themes of "the terrible sacrifice of war, but also its nobility."[61] The messages stressed in this coverage included the honor of liberating Europe, the passing of the generation responsible for such heroic deeds, and the use of the commemoration to heal rifts in the Atlantic community.

The sixtieth anniversary of D-Day took place the day after former President Ronald Reagan passed away at ninety-three years of age. The timing of Reagan's death assured the resultant coverage could connect him to D-Day and its commemoration. His iconic speeches on D-Day's fortieth anniversary in 1984 furnished a natural framing device for many of the stories the national media ran on him twenty years later. Unfortunately for the sitting president, Bush's commemorative activities suffered in comparison to Reagan's telegenic and polished performance. Much of the day's commentary also emphasized the strained Franco-American relations and Bush's heavy-handed attempts to patch up a rift of his own creation.[62]

In 1984, Reagan had traveled to France to honor a generation, to reunify a post-Vietnam divided America, and to advance his late Cold War confrontation with the Soviet Union. Twenty years later, Bush faced a war in Iraq that divided Americans and poisoned the international environment. While stressing the previous act of American beneficence, Bush's 2004 D-Day anniversary speech acted as one attempt to emphasize the unities rather than the points of friction between France and the United States. Furthermore, Bush's speechwriting team composed this statement with a U.S. presidential campaign season in mind.[63]

Some new elements emerged in this familiar tale of American D-Day glory. An official Russian delegation attended the D-Day anniversary in Normandy for the first time, as did the Germans.[64] Russia and Germany played significant roles in setting international opinion, an important point during a global war against terrorism. Admitting these two newcomers to the ceremonies displayed the political utility of commemorative functions as the past could promote unity in the present. Nevertheless, dissent appeared in 2004 regarding Bush's overtly politicized usage of D-Day. One journalist noted that President Eisenhower, with personal ties to D-Day, had avoided the self-satisfied ceremonies that now served as American foreign diplomacy.[65]

Nancy Gibbs, a writer for *Time,* criticized Bush's use of D-Day and Second World War analogies even as she repeated many of the stock platitudes attached to the war's "greatest day." Gibbs astutely recognized the appeal of D-Day memories, where "Americans are the ones who ride to the rescue, vanquish the enemy, get hailed as liberators, set everything right and then come home having left a place better than we found it." She applauded the "valor of a few men [who] altered history's course" on this day. "God smiled" and confounded the German defenders with deceptive weather that ultimately assisted the Allied surprise invasion. Gibbs's stress here on martial ardor, the democratic ethos, and divine sanction reflected the staying power of the basic themes Americans associated with D-Day. Yet Gibbs sought to criticize Bush when she admitted these D-Day memories "set a trap." Perhaps the trap was too great for even this sharp journalist to escape, as she argued, "World War II remains the model Good War, and D-day, its greatest day." Nevertheless, Gibbs insisted that Bush had erred in drawing so liberally on D-Day and the Second World War. In questioning the reliance on loose analogies, though, Gibbs also claimed, "Nothing that followed [D-Day] surpassed in difficulty or cost the demands of that one day, when luck and fate and genius and nerve worked to give Freedom her victory." It is conceivable that Bush slipped when putting his present war in the same light. Then again, the criticism offered by Gibbs ended up reinforcing just as much as it tore away such hackneyed employment of a mythologized past.[66]

Significantly, the limited criticism evident in popular media targeted official employment of a sacred past—there were few notable contests over the meaning of D-Day. For a brief moment, many Americans took solace in the celebration of a passing generation (as frequently mentioned). Some more blatantly attempted to link a previously successful battle and war with current military ventures abroad. A few went to extremes in this regard. *USA Today* printed a controversial cartoon on June 1, 2004. Scott Stantis depicted a longhaired man, evoking Vietnam-era antiwar protestors, aboard a Higgins boat. This disparaging representative of "The Left" implored the soldiers of D-Day to "Turn Back! Turn Back! It's too Hard!!!" Stantis captioned the cartoon, "If D-Day were today . . . ," implying that liberals of 2004 would have undermined American willingness and ability to fight even on D-Day. Three days later, the generally conservative newspaper printed several letters to the editor deploring Stantis's conflation of the Second World War with the Iraq War. Harry Lee of Kentucky described the cartoon as "flawed, disingenuous and insulting." Bob Faulkner of Kansas explained that "there is one important difference between the Normandy invasion and the Iraq invasion: We were wanted in Normandy."[67] Despite such claims, the lambasting of a fickle society by lampooning its supposed response to D-Day proved a remarkably durable approach throughout the 2000s.[68]

The "Story of Normandy, but Also the Story of America"

Political exploitation of D-Day had existed in American society since June 6, 1944. Backlash against President Bush's attempted linkage of D-Day to an increasingly unpopular war, however, challenged the acceptance of this past. The politicized use of D-Day by American leadership formed a point of comment, concern, and sporadic debate. Interestingly, the employment of D-Day by wide segments of the population—often in ways similar to those of politicians—remained supported, even hailed. In a sense, this dynamic demonstrated that the themes evocative of American honor, unity, morality, and sense of purpose in the Second World War have moved into a realm above politics. These assumptions, although simplistic, distortive, and quite political in nature, became the base point for American discussions of the Second World War. The stories of D-Day retained basic features similar to those told in years past. Yet people divided over whether or not the fight for liberty aptly described current American wars. D-Day became a benchmark in several ways. Either wars measured up to its glory and morality, or they did not. Either American society emulated the "D-Day generation," as previously labeled by author and Reagan speechwriter Peggy Noonan, or it suffered in comparison.[69]

D-Day surfaced as a standard of success that Americans expected in warfare. In the recent movie *Home of the Brave* (2006), two veterans of Operation

Iraqi Freedom meet back at home. One plaintively wonders whether future generations will venerate them like the soldiers of the Second World War. This character notes that D-Day's heroism, morality lesson, and contribution to victory starkly contrasts with the lingering uncertainty of Iraq.[70]

Even as *Home of the Brave* was released in theaters, the 1975 British film *Overlord,* directed by Stuart Cooper, became a staple at American film festivals. The latter film's producers delayed its release in America because of weariness with the Vietnam War. By 2007, Americans could purchase a DVD version of *Overlord.*[71] In fact, an explosion of D-Day home entertainment options appeared in the 2000s. Commemorative editions of older films combined with a spate of new documentary productions. The History Channel generated at least a half-dozen D-Day programs in a few years.[72]

The Public Broadcasting Service entered the market with the 2007 documentary series *The War* by famed documentarian Ken Burns. Burns took six years to make this program. In a *Newsweek* article covering Burns's work, journalist David Gates demonstrated the received wisdom about the supposed apolitical nature of American Second World War stories. "Burns simply shows, spin-free, both the heroics and the atrocities," Gates contended, and allegedly employed "studious neutrality" in his depiction of events. The production combined an array of photographs and film stock from the National Archives. The only on-screen personalities shown in the series were veterans or participants in the events discussed. Gates suggested, "Burns's film . . . belongs to a newer way of looking at the war: the deadpan realism exemplified by Tom Hanks's 1998 movie 'Saving Private Ryan,' which presents straight-on the brutality and absurdity from the soldier's viewpoint." Conventions extolling the "greatest generation" and its honorable fight to save the world figured even in this supposedly spin-free rendition.[73]

The fourth of seven episodes borrowed from FDR's D-Day prayer for its title, "Pride of Our Nation." The off-screen narrator, Keith David, reminds viewers of D-Day's magnitude by stating, "Everything that had happened so far in the war had been a mere preliminary." D-Day was *the* turning point of the war. Burns re-creates several iconic moments in his program, including a full reading of Eisenhower's order of the day and FDR's prayer. Tom Hanks chimes in, reading a dispatch by the Minnesota newsman Al McIntosh. Scholar Paul Fussell, a Second World War veteran, contributes a disparaging comment about real war versus sanitized memories of warfare. In this program, the fighting is bloody and gruesome, but not a single bit less noble for all that. Fixating on "Bloody Omaha," which receives nearly twenty-two minutes of coverage compared to the less than three minutes devoted to Utah Beach, Burns harps on the enormity of American losses in a fight to free France. Walter Ehlers, the 1st Infantry Division sergeant who had accompanied President Clinton in 1994, describes his horrifying D-Day fight, insisting, "Probably the biggest thing I've ever did [*sic*] in my life is get those 12 men [in his squad] off the beach." The losses stand vindicated in this program as the landing had enabled the eventual liberation of Europe. At the conclusion of this episode, the camera jumps to the present-day Normandy American Cemetery and lingers on the numerous gravestones.[74]

Burns does in fact put a spin on his D-Day episode. His portrayal is not necessarily wrong, but it presents just one way of relating the D-Day experience. Burns's series casts Americans as reluctant but formidable warriors, with their country united in the quest to right the world's wrongs and save civilization. This episode reinforces the popular view of D-Day as an example of America's unique commitment to liberty. Following repeat broadcasts, *The War* soon appeared in stores with a companion book and a special DVD release.[75]

These programs displayed the common American acceptance of dominant themes attached to D-Day, an acceptance furthered by an explosion of D-Day literature. Scholarly histories appeared with D-Day as part of the narrative, such as Norman Davies's 2006 *No Simple Victory.*[76] Works focused solely on D-Day also continued to hit bookstores, such as John Buckley's 2006 compilation *The Normandy Campaign 1944: Sixty Years On.* Bookshelves sagged with popular histories that offered plentiful pictures, oral testimony, and celebration in lieu of rigorous analysis. Ed Ruggero's *The First Men In* (2006) shone another spotlight on the American airborne forces in Normandy. The popular Osprey campaign series offered four separate volumes on Overlord, and one 2009 compilation of them all.[77] Jeff Shaara revived romantic novelization of D-Day with *The Steel Wave* in 2008.[78]

One trend that emerged in D-Day literature of this period was a tendency to treat some D-Day soldiers as celebrities. Cole Kingseed edited the combat diary of Captain Joe Dawson, which appeared in 2005 as *From Omaha Beach to Dawson's Ridge: The Combat Journal of Captain Joe Dawson.* Although Dawson's diary opened well before he landed at Omaha Beach, the title of Kingseed's version tapped into D-Day's popularity.[79] Kingseed returned with another book in 2006 that he coauthored with Dick Winters. *Beyond Band of Brothers: The War Memoirs of Major Dick Winters* covered Winters's war experiences and the public prominence he accrued from Ambrose's 1992 book and its

2001 HBO miniseries adaptation.[80] According to historian John Bodnar, this Winters-Kingseed book "became a primer for managers of all kinds in American society, conveying the need for them to exhibit 'character' and 'courage, honesty, selflessness, and respect for our fellow man.'"[81]

The extremely popular HBO miniseries produced a "band of brothers" mania, which emanated from an outpouring of books by or about this group of celebrated individuals. Marcus Brotherton authored or co-authored four separate band of brothers works from 2006 to 2011. In a typical hagiographic gesture, Brotherton used *We Who Are Alive and Remain* (2010) to extol the heroism of American soldiers. He provided snippets of veteran testimony that reinforced the notion of valorous men fighting reluctantly, but tenaciously, for global freedom.[82] Larry Alexander contributed two similar books. *Biggest Brother* (2005) focused on Dick Winters in war and afterwards. Alexander's *In the Footsteps of the Band of Brothers* (2010) described a battlefield tour he had taken with Forrest Guth, an Easy Company veteran, before the latter's death.[83] The romantic lure of the band of brothers paradigm threw American publishers into a regular feeding frenzy as they competed for the dollars of Second World War buffs.[84]

Some authors attempted to arrest the rampant celebration of war. Thomas Childers aimed his 2009 book, *Soldier from the War Returning*, at injecting a sense of variety, complexity, and moral ambiguity into popular understandings of the Second World War. He rejected Tom Brokaw's "greatest generation" as reductio ad absurdum, a "reassuring, uncomplicated portrait [that] has been repeated so often in public commemorations and memorial addresses that it has become almost an incantation, more liturgical than historical."[85] Historian Norman Davies faulted "the patriotic vision of the war associated with Ambrose and Spielberg" for ethnocentrically lauding virtues and ignoring vices.[86] Yet popular frameworks for the past, as historian Gordon Wood had explained, proved resistant to these types of frontal assaults: "Distorted heritages are precisely what many people want and perhaps need in order to keep the past alive and meaningful." He warned that "myths of national identity are not so easily shed or manipulated if they bear some accurate relation to the social reality."[87] By the 2000s, the social reality in America included a pronounced desire to laud Second World War heroics as typified in popular D-Day stories.

The sheer amount and variety of material available for any American interested in D-Day multiplied out of all bounds by the 2000s. The desire to honor those who fought valiantly in the past provided a starting point, a seemingly apolitical act of gratitude.[88] By the end of this decade, however, the continuous celebrations of the "greatest generation" increasingly underlined the perceived shortcomings of the generations that followed. D-Day became a rhetorical bludgeon commentators could use to strike at the allegedly fickle, self-centered, and unpatriotic Americans born after the Second World War.[89]

The undeniable allure of D-Day evident in news stories and Internet posts has demonstrated the ready use and a broad, if not quite deep, public familiarity with the battle. Internet sites have revealed the multivalent use of and relationship with the past. Enormous audiences have sought out, consumed, and added to knowledge available on matters from the supremely important to the arcane and bizarre.[90] Reflecting the national interest, D-Day has abounded in cyberspace. Veterans' groups, such as the Society of the First Division, created websites to both connect with one another and educate the public on their past actions. General history sites, such as History.com, or public knowledge storehouses like Wikipedia, have played host to plentiful and sometimes rather expansive pages on D-Day. Museums and memorials, like the Cantigny First Division Museum and the National D-Day Memorial, have generated sites full of educational detail on D-Day while simultaneously promoting visits to their physical premises. The tourism industry connected to D-Day also has appeared in force on the Web. Stephen Ambrose Tours, for instance, has provided itineraries, photographs, and background historical information on its two most popular packages: Operation Overlord and the Band of Brothers tours. Personal opinion blogs and discussion sites, academic or otherwise, often have conveyed the drama and world-saving significance of D-Day to wide audiences. Owning a piece of D-Day history has also grown easier with the advent of consumption-oriented Internet engines. Ebay.com recently listed 4,229 items for sale under the search term "D-Day."[91]

The conference circuit has not missed out either. The National D-Day Memorial Foundation cohosted a 2009 D-Day Conference with Liberty University in Lynchburg, Virginia. The conference brought together scholars, veterans, and the public to discuss the battle. On the June 6 anniversary, an audience in the thousands gathered in observance at the National D-Day Memorial in nearby Bedford.[92] The Eisenhower Presidential Library and Museum also celebrated D-Day in 2009. Previously, one veteran had written the library's director, Karl Weissenbach, to inveigh against the lack of due pomp and circumstance for nondecennial anniversaries. In response, Weissenbach made the library's D-Day observance one of its key events for 2009. Nearly fourteen thousand people attended dances, concerts, speeches, and solemn observances commemorating D-Day's fallen.[93]

Active members of the 1st Infantry Division helped coordinate the D-Day celebration at the Eisenhower Library and at another event hosted by the Cantigny First Division Museum. Cantigny acquired the remains of a Higgins boat that had participated in the D-Day landings. The museum officially unveiled the restored craft during the sixty-fifth-anniversary ceremonies. This celebration, with six thousand people in attendance, honored the nearly one hundred D-Day veterans gathered that day. Paul Herbert, executive director of the Cantigny First Division Foundation, indicated the intent to highlight the veterans themselves: "Their sacrifices helped free us from the terrible dangers of that time and shaped the world we live in today. We want them to know that their legacy will not be forgotten." Soldier demonstrations and helicopter flybys linked this past to the current service abroad of the 1st Infantry Division.[94]

In 2009, Normandy attracted large numbers of commemorative tourists making their historical pilgrimages to the sanctified battle zone. U.S. president Barack Obama and French president Nicolas Sarkozy sought to use the D-Day observance to heal wounds in the transatlantic relationship. In a news conference held before the ceremonies, Sarkozy pointedly began by stating "in the strongest, most sincere terms that never in the history, perhaps, of our two countries, the United States and France have been so close to one another on major issues, major questions." Maintaining the air of comity, Obama explained that the D-Day observance "marks not only the triumph of freedom, but it also marks how the transatlantic alliance has allowed for extraordinary prosperity and security on both sides of the Atlantic." That alliance stood reaffirmed, incidentally, with French reintegration into NATO, announced earlier in the year.[95]

Obama delivered a speech at the Normandy American Cemetery a few hours later. He offered stirring words that honored the few attending veterans, celebrated D-Day as a moment of American triumph, and encapsulated many of the conceptions of the battle prevalent in American society. Obama noted the enormity of D-Day, which had brought countless people from across the world together in commemoration of the battle ever since it had occurred. Asking himself why the "liberated and their liberators" so frequently came together, the answer stemmed from the enormity of a triumph against the odds and the obvious morality of Allied intentions: "The sheer improbability of this victory is part of what makes D-Day so memorable. It also arises from the clarity of purpose with which this war was waged." While acknowledging some faults in the Allied nations, Obama claimed that "whatever God we prayed to, whatever our differences, we knew that the evil we faced had to be stopped." The evil of Nazism had allegedly unified Americans, assuring them of the righteousness of their cause. Moral clarity pushed those at home to work more and those in battle to fight harder on D-Day. In Obama's view, "Had the Allies failed here, Hitler's occupation of this continent might have continued indefinitely. . . . What we must not forget is that D-Day was a time and a place where the bravery and selflessness of a few was able to change the course of an entire century. . . . That is the story of Normandy, but also the story of America." It was, Obama asserted, "a story that has never come easy, but one that always gives us hope."[96]

D-Day celebration offered Obama the opportunity to stress honorable aspects of the American past, features that provoked minimal dissent or criticism at home. The brief celebratory interlude to the contentious debates raging throughout America offered nothing more than a lull before returning, with renewed intensity, to clashes of the moment. The night of Obama's speech in Normandy, he turned to one of those confrontations in a radio statement addressing the upcoming fight over health care reform.[97]

D-Day commemoration presented a unifying theme, one that inspired respect in America. D-Day, in addition, came to acquire a sort of brand identity, with mass marketing of goods or products tied in name to a battle that became a common point of reference in American society by the new millennium. D-Day suffused American culture. Although far from ever present, the battle and its ascribed meanings remained readily available for a variety of uses. In the past, D-Day had cloaked actions of all sorts, including new military ventures, in a veil of moralistic legitimacy. President George W. Bush, for instance, attempted to tap into D-Day's popularity and affirmation of American rectitude to support his new military and foreign policy initiatives. Rather than solely imposing his views on a compliant public, he was engaging in a conversation that had Americans defining their present and future based on common understandings of the past. Yet, whether such pronounced public acceptance and political employment of the D-Day morality tale will continue remains debatable.

CONCLUSION

Periclean Oratory and Honoring the War Dead

In the winter of 431–430 B.C., the famed leader Pericles delivered a moving funeral oration for the Athenian dead stemming from the initial clashes with their Spartan-led enemies. Pericles sought to boost the morale of his fellow citizens in the wake of Athens's early setbacks in the Peloponnesian War. This oration also included several messages that demonstrated the political utility of testaments to those killed in war. Pericles announced, "Comfort, . . . not condolence, is what I have to offer to the parents of the dead." Although such a bold statement may seem hardhearted, Pericles had a point. Rather than weep over the dead, his fellow citizens should revel in the glorious and selfless sacrifice of those lost for the greater good. Boasting of Athenian "freedom," Pericles felt that liberty had pushed Athens to greatness, a greatness that others—out of jealousy and fear—now threatened. "Choosing to die resisting, rather than to live submitting," the Athenian dead "fled only from dishonor, but met danger face-to-face, and after one brief moment, while at the summit of their fortune, left behind them not their fear, but their glory." They would enjoy a "renown which never grows old."[1]

Pericles attempted to soothe the emotional wounds wrought by warfare. Seeking to bolster morale served political-military ends: he wanted to keep his people in the fight. While this oration confronted the mournful deaths of loved ones, Pericles inspired listeners by ennobling loss through the proclaimed morality of the cause. He importuned Athenians: "Take these as your model, and judging happiness to be the fruit of freedom and freedom of valor, never decline the dangers of war."[2] Rather than lament those consumed by war's voracious appetite, this oratory urged Athenians to focus on the glory of battle, the nobility of sacrifice, and the morality of a society that had produced people willing to die for the preservation of freedom.

The Athenian historian Thucydides captured Pericles's oration for future generations. The speeches that dominated Thucydides's *The Peloponnesian War* warrant caution on our part, standing more as the historian's depictions of what these people *ought* to have said. Yet this passage, Pericles's Funeral Oration, has reverberated through the ages. As should be rather evident at this point, many of the D-Day commemorative activities described in this book have mirrored Pericles's messages. Glorifying war-related deaths for political purposes—in the broadest sense of that concept—has a long pedigree in recorded history.

Political leaders, however, do not operate in a vacuum. The past they draw upon, the present purposes for which they exploit these historical constructions, and the reactions to their rhetoric all keep such reveries mutable, contested, and fraught with social meaning. In the end, remembrance of the past is "unstable, plastic, synthetic, and repeatedly reshaped."[3] Rather than a purely elite-driven process, historical remembrance affords a stage for multiple constituencies to stake claims on the past with implications for the present and future. We can look at the interplay between political employment and popular culture regarding one iconic battle, D-Day, to glimpse the workings of American culture in a time of upheaval and change. Commemorations of this battle have developed notable iterations.

At no point did any single actor dominate the stage alone. Nevertheless, some actors and their actions carried more weight and influence. From the day of battle, political and military leaders, news media personalities, historians or other scholars, and the D-Day combatants shaped wider understandings of not only what this battle was like but also what it meant. Rather than acting as mere spectators, the American public joined in a collective effort to celebrate the battle and mourn its losses. Over the years since that day in June 1944, public memories of D-Day have narrowed to specific points that echoed through the many platforms of remembrance.

This narrowing process reflected the currents of an America undergoing vast changes first in the uncertain postwar moment, then in the Cold War confrontation that followed, and finally in the post-Cold War and post-9/11 periods. Powerful politicians and ordinary citizens advanced similar characterizations of D-Day. Certain themes gained ground in different periods, reacting to prior versions, and served as guideposts at key moments of need. These D-Day stories drew on select mythic images embraced by popular American culture and reaffirmed them at the same time. According to this narrative, D-Day demonstrated the military competence of a free republic that put its faith in citizen-soldiers. Through violent action, America had redeemed the world, reshaping it into a new, improved, quasi-American version of its old self. The redemptive power of D-Day violence enjoyed divine blessing, and even, as was sometimes claimed, outright assistance. America fought on D-Day to further benevolent goals—defeat an evil foe and restore moral order to the world—not for territorial aggrandizement.

These claims emerged on June 6, 1944, from many directions all at once and did not represent solely the political leadership's point of view. Indeed, without widespread support for such a positive slant, it seems highly unlikely that these instant moralizations would have gained such a wide and long-lasting presence in American society. Admittedly, D-Day celebrationism receded to the background in certain periods of national confusion or strife, like the postwar moment or Vietnam. Yet it is also equally important to remember that over seven decades, from D-Day to the present, positive depictions of the battle have remained intact even during the relative dark days of neglect. D-Day memories, collectively and over the long term, have exerted a powerful influence on American conceptions of patriotism, civic duty, martial action, and the efficacious use of warfare. These collective constructions shaped national and individual identity.[4] In the most commonly circulated stories, D-Day attested to positive aspects of American character.

Admittedly, "memory" is a vague analytical tool and simply slapping "collective" or "public" in front of it only increases the potential problems with its usage. As elucidated in the preceding chapters, however, a construction process set in immediately after D-Day. Indeed, in some respects, that process existed beforehand as a preparatory framing for the event. This process highlighted certain themes, excluded various aspects of the battle, and steadily shaped American perceptions of D-Day, the Second World War, the United States, and warfare in general. Many constituencies contributed to this shaping process. Although I have traced the dominant themes and uses of D-Day, the "collective" memory even in just the American national context actually involved multiple agglomerations of sometimes distinctive, sometimes overlapping groups. Some veterans or their family members may have reacted to D-Day memories in ways that took issue with these dominant themes; here, consider the mournful approach in Bedford, Virginia, for the first ten years after the battle. Yet in the end, the overall course of public, national conversations flowed in certain directions. Countercurrents emerged, but they tended to remain background noise limited to small constituencies, faded over time, or became co-opted into the prevailing stories circulating across America. Taking the sorrowful reaction to those killed on D-Day again as an example: over time, the sharp pangs of grief and anger over death blended into the more generalized sense of honor and hero worship for the soldiers who had sanctified D-Day with their sacrifice. Pericles would have been proud indeed.

These particular constructions were not necessarily wrong. They offered readings of the battle that more or less accorded with veteran testimony, the documentary record, or other forms of evidence. Nevertheless, these honorific constructions also represented just one way to read the past—and that version tended to relate to present-day needs. Thus D-Day and the Second World War reemerged in American national conversations with the advent of the Korean War after a brief, atomic fear–fueled hiatus. Now, the old war seemed to offer practical lessons for a new conflict involving another implacable foe. The linkage between old-new adversaries visibly surfaced in the whole "totalitarianism" line of study that we are only just now beginning to probe more critically.[5]

With the new signposts provided by a selective focus on Second World War heroics, as exemplified by D-Day in particular, a mounting crescendo of commemorative activities built up in the 1950s and early 1960s. D-Day specifically peppered a variety of conversations on warfare, national identity, civic duty, and the like. The event popped up in a startling number of places, from the Normandy American Cemetery to museums, news stories, books, speeches, documentary films, and Hollywood movies. Perhaps even more astounding, the recurring themes that appeared across the media demonstrated the salability of D-Day's purported morality lesson. Cornelius Ryan enshrined more than created de novo a new paradigm with his enormously popular book *The Longest Day.* From that work sprang one of the last great epic war films—one that has resonated through repeated airings over the decades since, shaping understandings of D-Day and America. The tempo of D-Day commemoration increased rapidly from the late 1950s to the early 1960s.

Then came the fall. It is important to consider the ways that new war experiences have shaped common understandings of old conflicts. Just as important, however, is the imperative to explore the ways in which common perceptions of previous armed conflicts factored into the discussions of and preparations for new military ventures. Frankly, few smoking guns explicitly link public memory to real-world events. Nevertheless, by teasing out similarities in stories and initial justifications for the Vietnam War, it becomes rather evident that *something* was afoot. Political and military leaders felt sure in drawing on Second World War morality—and what was more moral than liberating the oppressed through selfless sacrifice? D-Day stories shaped the American cultural environment in the 1960s. They did not cause Vietnam, but they certainly helped the Johnson administration's efforts to sell armed intervention to the American people. Of course, connecting the past to the present created its own problems. Sometimes, as explained earlier, the past had muddied the present. Vietnam was not France, and Ho Chi Minh was not Hitler. When Vietnam did not turn out like the Second World War, a backlash set in that derailed the growing embrace of the former war's glories and (avowed) morality lessons.

Backlash did not mean a total rejection as many Americans kept D-Day memories alive. New monuments, annual ceremonies, some books, and even sporadic speeches all tapped into D-Day even in the depths of national despair during the 1970s. D-Day and the Second World War did fade from mainstream national conversations. Americans in groups and as individuals kept the torch burning, ready to pass it on to followers when the time came due.

That time emerged in the 1980s. No single actor determined this change in course. The moment had arrived for a return to D-Day. What fostered this moment? Aging veterans began to push their stories more forcibly into the public sphere. A new generation nearing its grasp of power also started a sort of national reevaluation concerning Vietnam.[6] With a conservative political leadership in place, the time seemed ripe to advance a version of the past that glorified the United States and restored pride in American hearts. As historian Sam Edwards explained, "If Reagan led America back to its World War II past . . . he did so because . . . others had helped prepare the way and, secondly, because people were ready to follow."[7] Reagan's 1984 D-Day speeches captured and defined this new sentiment even if they did not create the impetus to honor the D-Day generation entirely on their own. The stories he told of D-Day glory would prove extremely popular. The American people at the time and since enjoyed hearing such positive interpretations of the past—of America selflessly saving the world—that held significant implications for the present. America had liberated the oppressed in the past and remained ever-vigilant regarding threats to liberty, whether they arose from the Soviet Union, the North Vietnamese (per this renewed line of argument), or Caribbean dictatorships and Middle Eastern rogue states.

After 1984, D-Day gained an increasing presence in the American collective consciousness—defined as the memories kept accessible and in use in the public sphere. Another wave of D-Day commemorations appeared in new museums, television documentaries, print news articles, books, and games. The venues and advocates may have varied, but the messages and characterizations did not differ all that much. The stories told of D-Day acquired a bloody sheen, in part a reflection of Vietnam's desensitizing impact on America; yet the noble tinting emanating from the world-saving glory of this battle's results sanctified the carnage.

The D-Day surge also accompanied a fresh American war. Interestingly, with each new bout of D-Day mania since the 1960s, another American military venture appeared soon afterwards. Maybe film director Arthur Hiller's antimilitarist critique proved prescient as the protagonist in his *The Americanization of Emily* (1964) insisted, "We perpetuate war by exalting its sacrifices."[8] Casting Hiller aside in preference for Periclean utterances, the Persian Gulf War in 1991 also displayed politicians, military leaders, public opinion makers, and common Americans advancing themes evocative of D-Day: crusade, liberation, and defeating evil incarnate. The short war seemed, for the moment, to confirm American confidence and self-worth in a new, post-Cold War era. With the Soviet foe fading from the scene, America could turn to propagating its version of a moral order throughout the world. The Wilsonian imperative leapt back to the forefront of American politics in a surprisingly bipartisan manner. From the Republican George H. W. Bush to the Democrat William J. Clinton, and back to the Republican George W. Bush, liberating the oppressed and extending freedom abroad formed major foreign policy initiatives.[9]

Did D-Day create such an inclination? That assertion would be hard to validate as clear forebears to this imperative existed prior to June 6, 1944. Indeed, the desire to remake the world into a better place likely shaped the perception of D-Day in the first place. A mixture of deeper tendencies in the dominant American culture and specific needs of the moment focused attention here. D-Day reaffirmed cherished American notions of democracy, fair play, moral order, and the militant (yet nonmilitaristic) use of power for divinely sanctioned and benevolent purposes. This reading of the past has proven so popular, so salable, that D-Day commemorations intensified out of all bounds in the 1990s, assuming a life of their own. By the late 1990s, new standards of commemoration and comparative evaluation emerged with Stephen Ambrose's romantic historical commentary standing out in particular relief across the media. The blockbuster 1998 movie *Saving Private Ryan* likewise transmitted the horrors and allure of D-Day combat to yet a new generation. This movie inspired widespread emulation in movies, games, and books that has yet to run its course more than a decade later.

Once more, a new burst of fixation on D-Day's morality tale accompanied a march to the latest round of military ventures abroad. There arose an instant public comparison between Pearl Harbor and the terrorist attacks of September 11, 2001.[10] Yet with D-Day ringing through the air while the dust was settling from the assault, plenty of cues stood in place ready to help Americans understand and interpret this new development. A D-Day paradigm of bold action, selfless sacrifice, defeating evil, liberating the oppressed, and restoring moral order to the world and military security to America, helped move Americans from mourning those lost that fatal day to acting concertedly in response. The D-Day framework helped validate the Bush administration's proposed response. America as a moral nation was in the right, and its opponents were just wrong. Military action aimed at eradicating evil would win this new war, garner international approbation, and return America to the glories of yore.

To be sure, with such politicized renderings of the past and present, dissenting voices emerged. As one scholar cautioned, "Precisely because the past is, except in the mundane details of *l'histoire événementielle,* not some fixed and immutable entity, but rather what we choose to make of it, the same events or historical figures can sometimes be used to support causes that are diametrically opposed to one another."[11] Those who questioned the applicability of the Second World War's morality tales, however, rarely rejected the tales in and of themselves. They only debated the linkage of these stories to affairs in the new millennium. Nevertheless, such arguments remained a minority position in the years that witnessed Americans leading a NATO force to free Afghans from their Taliban oppressors and a supposed "coalition of the willing" to liberate Iraqis from Saddam's (or Hitler's?) tyranny.

D-Day has come to transcend dusty "history" and assume the status of a popular icon, something for politicians or common Americans alike to employ with startling regularity. D-Day did not always mean the same thing to all people. D-Day and D-Day's commemoration offered many potential stories. Nevertheless, this book has presented a few consistent themes about D-Day's perceived moral lessons—those that have dominated national conversations.

Commemorative works have led to D-Day's ubiquitous presence in American society. No single locus of control or main actor dominates this activity, which showed the scale and support for these versions of the past. D-Day as a term, as a reference point, as a brand icon has almost advanced into the superstrata of symbols ingrained in American culture. In March 2010, CBS news reported the "D-Day" launch for a new Apple handheld computer tablet.[12] That report came one day after a joint press conference between French president Nicolas Sarkozy and U.S. president Barack Obama in Washington, D.C. Barely a minute into the briefing, Obama mentioned the "enduring ties" between sister republics that has lasted "from Yorktown to Normandy to Afghanistan."[13] On November 20, 2010, the United States Military Academy football team played against Notre Dame. One announcer pointed out that the 101st Airborne Division soldiers who had parachuted onto the field beforehand came from a unit with a long pedigree. The only specific battle honor that he deigned to mention, however, was—predictably—D-Day. The 101st Airborne Division's current deployment to Afghanistan went unmentioned.

D-Day could also contribute to needling critiques. The 60 Plus Association, self-described as the "conservative alternative to the liberal AARP," began an advertising campaign in late 2010 targeting President Obama's proposed health care reform. In one televised ad, the narrator compared the D-Day fight against tyranny to the association's current effort to cut government spending. D-Day veteran Philip Storer argued, "We fought to protect something we all hold very dear, our freedoms. Today, our freedoms are threatened by a very different kind of enemy." His enemy was "big government, wasteful spending, and crushing debt."[14]

Remembering War the American Way

American culture, politics, social dynamics, and national experience have heavily affected the pattern of D-Day remembrance explained herein. Americans have developed a distinctive form of collective remembrance over the past century and a half, as displayed in four ways: the role of the federal government, public disputes, a singular emphasis placed on democratic ethos, and the dialectic between tradition and progress. In each of these categories, Americans have remembered their past in ways at odds with other societies.[15] The federal government has shaped D-Day remembrance in many venues, such as the Normandy American Cemetery, presidential speeches, and even with military assistance to filmmakers.[16] This direct influence over national memory gained in strength following the Second World War even as official memories never became the sole arbiters of the past. These accounts had to compete for acceptance in the chaotic marketplace of ideas. Public contests over D-Day emerged over time. Yet as seen earlier, most of these disputes concerned the use of D-Day more than the interpretation of the battle. One prevalent feature in American interpretations of the battle has remained the emphasis on democratic themes: the democratic ethos of the soldiers, the liberty-preserving results of the battle, and the transitional moment of D-Day in the war and in the narrative of European or even global democracy. D-Day stories also sustain the argument about an American dialectic between tradition and progress. Americans hailed the day as one of transcendence for national power and world affairs. It also appeared in nostalgic reveries of a mythologized past.

Historian Kurt Piehler described a "distinctive American pattern of remembering war." He pointed to the limited ability of the federal government to propagate an authoritative version of the past via public commemorations. Despite the actions of organizations like the American Battle Monuments Commission, the federal government's portrayals competed with those presented by groups representing veterans, concerned citizens, academics, and popular media figures. Piehler additionally stressed the tension between the sanctity of an individual and the needs of the nation in public understandings of warfare.[17] The reactions D-Day evoked in the small community of Bedford, Virginia, highlighted the conflicting pulls of this particular dynamic. At first, the pain of loss overwhelmed any effort to place the battle and the wider war in a celebratory narrative. Over time, however, veterans and family members patched up the holes left in the community. They erected monuments to those lost in war and developed a special local connection to one clash that had defined the nation's recent past. By the 1990s, as the sharpest pain of loss had dulled to a degree, a renewed impetus emerged to celebrate those killed in action on D-Day as a sort of communal sacrifice for a better world order.[18]

The American experience in the Second World War was unique in many ways. America suffered the least of major belligerents in terms of a devastated homeland and proportionate loss of population. Yet D-Day provided a story that emphasized the sacrifice of American lives on the altar of freedom. Stories have dwelled on the costly airborne drop and "Bloody Omaha," where America—emphasized over all other Allies—gladly paid to liberate the world from tyranny.

The interplay between official and other group or individual memories in the years since shaped the D-Day story in a dynamic, iterative process. Older strains in American culture fed into this development. The notion of a city on a hill fending off darkness in the world, lighting the path for mankind's salvation, helped shape America's D-Day story. This cultural imperative, likewise, drew strength from America's Second World War experience. The advent of the Cold War intensified these priorities. The past helped combat an inveterate foe, firm up global support, and convince the American people of their country's rectitude.

A winnowing process developed whereby a complex history boiled down to simplified versions of the past that offered reassuring lessons. Those narrative choices revealed American perceptions of this conflict, warfare in general, and America itself. Take, for instance, the relative distancing of the Pacific Theater from wider conversations or commemorations of the war that developed in the 1980s and has continued since. The "good war" version of this horrendous conflict depended in large part on glamorizing combat through an ennoblement of purpose. Racial hatreds and atomic destruction of the Japanese enemy did not seem all that "good." Common American characterizations of the war in Western Europe as an honorable fight that ended in the liberation of the Old World better fit an endearing take on the past. Cold War priorities pulled public attention to the European war as a seminal event, one that had set up the postwar order and inaugurated a new struggle for freedom. D-Day purportedly exemplified America in the same way that the Revolutionary War experience was reduced to a few key moments that "revealed" something about the country it established. American reveries casting the battles of Lexington and Concord as the start of a quest for liberty, as the acts of democratic heroes in the face of overwhelming power, were compared to popular D-Day tales.[19] Multiple voices pushed versions of the past that smoothed out the rough edges by denying complexity, extolling the morality of American patriots, and inflating the importance of one moment in the past.

When Americans confronted the stark challenge to their pietistic sense of nation in the jungles of Vietnam, a backlash against military affairs and freewheeling moralisms ensued. For a brief moment, D-Day faded from the national public scene. Significantly, D-Day played a major role in moving beyond this lamentable past. Through a process of selective focus and unique readings of the past, Americans once more found much to celebrate in their past-present-future national course by the mid-1980s. Sidestepping the murkier Cold War era, American Second World War remembrance lauded the liberation of Europe, the salvation of the world, and the country's martial-moral strength in times of dire crises. By the new millennium, the mixture of needs and desires that had prompted the development of this version of the past helped ensure its continuance in light of new, profound challenges to American pieties. D-Day stories have existed in a liminal space between identities of the individual, community, nation, and world. The presentation here has argued that most of these identities fed into a specific national framework to produce a story about *America* on D-Day and in the years that followed.[20]

The Vagaries of Historical Remembrance

In 1997, historian Walter McDougall identified lingering strains in American culture and diplomacy. A focus on liberty, unilateralism, and expansion had guided (to varying degrees) the United States since its founding. McDougall argued that significant changes altered the politico-cultural landscape during the twentieth century. These new impulses included Progressive imperialism, Wilsonianism, Containment, and Global Meliorism. All these, save perhaps meliorism, seem familiar schemata for analyzing the American approach to the twentieth century. McDougall defined meliorism as the "belief that America has a responsibility to nurture democracy and economic growth around the world." Following his analysis, while drawing on the liberty imperative, acting unilaterally, and seeing an expansive notion of interests in the world, Americans in the twentieth century reacted to new challenges and possibilities in distinctive ways. Wilsonianism held "that power in the hands of righteous custodians had to be good, and that all who challenged that power were unwitting tools of Satan." Wilsonians maintained that America must use its great power for good or risk letting the world fall into self-destructive chaos. Combining impulses to force reform and contain evil, meliorism acted as a "socio-economic and politico-cultural expression of an American mission to make the world a better place." American leaders "assumed that the United States alone possesses the power, prestige, technology, wealth, and altruism needed to reform whole nations." McDougall observed that in contrast to an earlier "Promised Land [that] had held that to try to change the world was stupid (and immoral), America the Crusader State held that to *refrain* from trying to change the world was immoral (and stupid)."[21] According to this new line of thought, America, the land of liberty, struggled to right wrongs in the world. Its use of power was good, just, and divinely sanctioned.

If militarism did not constitute one of McDougall's key points, its presence appeared in all of his characteristics and the overall thrust of his twentieth-century framework. Throughout this era, Americans increasingly glorified their military forces, preferred military solutions to problems in the world, and defined national greatness based largely on martial prowess—all core aspects of militarism. Notwithstanding such tendencies, the American people continually disavowed their militaristic nature. The citizen-soldier mantra served this end: American democratic heroes only picked up arms to confront threats to the nation/world and quickly returned to civil pursuits once finished with defeating evil. As presented in this book, these framing devices fit long-standing tropes apparent as early as the day of battle. However, they also gained strength and additional legitimacy through repetition, particularly when accompanied by the authoritative status of professional historians.

A fixation on liberty, a militaristic nonmilitarism, and a sense of divine favor and of a divinely approved mission to remake the world anew became the cultural underpinnings of the American Century. They helped single out D-Day from all of America's Second World War experiences as a shining moment. These constructs pushed American mainstream understandings of D-Day towards the morality tale described in this book. They also drew renewed strength from the D-Day paradigm.

Yet it would be remiss to assume that D-Day inevitably had to appear as a turning point in the Second World War and the twentieth century. Contingency has played tremendously important roles in this story. Of course, the greatest contingency stems from the outcome of the battle itself. D-Day did not lead inevitably to an Allied victory. The tough fight to secure the beachheads and the real possibility of failure, however, have further strengthened the feeling of divine intervention in a quest for liberty fought by competent, democratic heroes.

Contingent factors have also heavily shaped the national conversations on D-Day. For instance, consider the impact of Robert R. McCormick and his charitable trust. Through their efforts, D-Day became the central focus in a museum just outside Chicago. Its academic outreach efforts and civic educational mission were tied to the 1st Infantry Division. If McCormick had served in a different unit during the First World War, would another powerful, well-funded, and similarly inclined institution like the Cantigny First Division Foundation have taken shape? What if Ronald Reagan's speechwriters had not focused on the D-Day celebration in 1984? Historian Douglas Brinkley perhaps overstated his case, but he made a compelling point about the significance of Reagan's speeches: "If it hadn't been for Reagan's two elegiac June 6, 1984, homilies . . . there may never have been Stephen Ambrose's *Band of Brothers,* Tom Brokaw's *The Greatest Generation,* Steven Spielberg's *Saving Private Ryan,* or numerous memorials—like the National D-Day Museum in New Orleans—built to exalt the citizen soldiers who liberated Europe."[22] Although many factors and personalities combined to thrust D-Day back into the national limelight in 1984, without Reagan's lead, would the D-Day story have returned to prominence in quite the way that it did over the ensuing two decades? Without Ambrose's steady drumbeat hailing D-Day as a glorious tale of American heroes fighting evil, would the American public have retained such an intense and specific devotion to this one battle?

The contingent impact of personalities also merged with contemporary developments. With the Cold War, several hot wars, post-Cold War turbulence, and then an age of mass terrorism, the D-Day story has remained a steady reminder of national verities, moral rectitude, military skill, and world mission. Admittedly, the reach of this story has fluctuated at times. The mainstream presence of that story also does not mean that other possible readings or remembrances of D-Day have failed to appear. Veterans of the bloody battle have displayed diverging views: sometimes rejecting the glorification of any combat as profane and dangerous but at other times exulting in the honor accorded to them for partaking in grand events like D-Day. What remains important here is that counter-memories and conflicting group memories aside, the overall development in the national mainstream consciousness has led to a rather specific, particular, and problematic take on D-Day, the Second World War, and America.

The contingency involved in narrative choices warrants consideration as well. For instance, consider the extreme plaudits advanced for the logistic skill that had enabled this grand quest for freedom. Logistics definitely proved decisive in the Normandy operation. Yet the American mania for self-approval in even this regard has overlooked the startling impact of Operation Overlord's logistical preparations on the overall Allied war effort. Giving priority to Northwestern Europe hampered Allied operations in other theaters. For example, the D-Day buildup diverted much-needed shipping from carrying food to India in the midst of a devastating famine during 1944.[23]

Selection of content, evidence, and narrative approach has shaped understandings of D-Day. Recent trends in military history have shifted attention to the lower ranks. D-Day stories have altered their focus as well, but they still tend to dwell on a few higher commanders like Eisenhower, Bradley, or such heroicized men as Brigadier Generals Theodore Roosevelt Jr. and Norman "Dutch" Cota. Roosevelt and Cota, assistant commanders of the 4th and 29th Infantry Divisions respectively, had landed on June 6 and profoundly shaped the battle—earning lasting renown in the process. The third American amphibious assault unit, the 1st Infantry Division, had Brigadier General Willard G. Wyman. Wyman was an equally important assistant commander who helped organize men for effective action in the most chaotic sector of Omaha Beach. America's D-Day stories, however, have largely excluded Wyman. Clarence Huebner, the 1st Infantry Division commander on June 6, 1944, wrote to Cornelius Ryan in 1958 to urge the author to interview Wyman. Though Wyman proved willing to tell his tale, this request passed unfulfilled, and Ryan made heroes out of Roosevelt and Cota.[24] Subsequent D-Day books have continued to neglect Wyman and his conduct.[25] The aerial and naval components of the invasion have also attracted less public attention in America.

Overall, the dominant D-Day stories have represented a combination of choices, long-standing tendencies in American society, reactions to global events, and personal, group, and national biases. As the world has turned, the past seeped into present conversations while the present-day outlooks influenced understandings of the past. This duality led many Americans to see new challenges and new developments with a set of Second World War blinkers framing the view—blinkers heavily dependent upon a few iconic moments like D-Day. With the Cold War, D-Day interest underwent renewal as the story of American martial prowess in a quest for liberty. That liberation mantra affirmed American morality in the past and present as new battles and a twilight struggle for freedom took shape. These enduring constructions intensified during the Cold War and ultimately outlasted that confrontation. They appeared across the board, from popular to scholarly analyses, in political rhetoric and memorial services, in the form of monuments and ephemeral media productions. As the eminent historian Gerhard Weinberg remarked, "Interestingly, the passage of time makes the significance of the invasion as the basis for major postwar developments all the more, not the less, apparent."[26]

The D-Day tale remained a story of America, of Americans, and of American perceptions of themselves. Casting D-Day as a costly yet decisive battle involving white men fighting and dying in the name of liberty tells us something about the society that latched onto such constructed versions of the past. The day's service represented willing sacrifice and military strength in a great crusade to vanquish evil, save the world, and launch the American Century. These democratic heroes of D-Day then returned home, made America great, and became the "greatest generation" as a result. The striking thing is not the veracity of this tale but its staying power over the decades since it first formed. This D-Day story represented nostalgia for an era before race riots, gender upheaval, and political-social-economic-religious crises that would shake America to its core when the country was rising to the top, not precariously tottering at the brink.

Just as much as those constructions of the past responded to shifting social and political developments, American understandings of this past shaped their responses to those changes. The "good war" characterization of the Second World War, the most horrifically destructive cataclysm in human history, developed several iterations. From an earlier sanitized version the "good war" changed into a far more gruesome depiction of the conflict, a shift owing in large part to the brutal Vietnam War. An important point missed by historian John Bodnar in his recent analysis of this phenomenon, however, is that *both* versions glamorized warfare.[27] The bloodier version perhaps represented an even more disturbing tendency as it tapped into the moral justifications offered in things like D-Day stories to ennoble or further sanctify the carnage of mass, industrialized war. This particular construction has acknowledged the butchery that modern conflicts breed, but it casts such slaughter in a heroic vein. Thus, a strong military full of democratic heroes fought a horrendous battle on D-Day but overcame the foe and ensured global freedom. America had allegedly reaffirmed its greatness through a sacrifice that changed the world for the better.

In 1984, journalist Lance Morrow drew on the "redemptive" aspect of this event, arguing that "never again would war seem so unimpeachably right, so necessary and just. Never again, perhaps, would American power and morality so perfectly coincide."[28] Might making right, might confirming right—here D-Day told something of the past while offering guidance for the future. When confronted with evil, gird the national loins, prepare to use overwhelming military force, accept that losses are necessary oblations in defense of morality, and, remember, *never* appease when decisive power is readily at hand.

Explorations of D-Day have constituted a questioning of the past just as much as they formed an analysis of the present and a forecast for the future. Yet the battle now occupies an uncertain place in American society. With Vietnam, D-Day and the Second World War faded for a moment from national consciousness. The possibility of another recession has emerged with divisive military ventures and social fragmentation echoing the turbulent 1970s. Nevertheless, wide interest in D-Day, the impact of previous commemorations, and moral ascriptions that seem to relate to present struggles all suggest that D-Day and the Second World War may avoid such oblivion. Americans may continue to cling to aspects of the past that prove most reassuring. A dichotomization between "good" and "bad" wars could intensify with D-Day serving as the key standard of the former.

The D-Day story that has developed in America carried so much weight because the battle seemingly connected with cherished American values like liberty, salvation, democracy, and pride in martial strength. The obvious question to ask, then, is whether these cherished values and the particular conception of them will remain popular, accepted, and utilitarian. Previously, Americans touted their empire of liberty, with a Manifest Destiny to spread the blessings of freedom, enterprise, and Christian morality to the less fortunate—an opportunity as much as a solemn duty, a white man's burden. Nevertheless, these phrasings, if not always their underlying thoughts, ultimately lapsed from widespread usage. "The collective remembrance of old soldiers and the victims of war is, therefore, a quixotic act," wrote historian Jay Winter. "It is an effort to think publicly about painful issues in the past, an effort which is bound to fade over time." Of course, the moral reading of D-Day moved the story away from negative sentiments. A more positive take on an old battle has certainly lent some renewal and continuing strength to D-Day commemorative actions. National priorities change, individuals pass from the scene, and as "memory activists" die or lose interest, the commemorative impulse fades away. These understandings of the past stem from "groups of people come together in public to do the work of remembrance," a "process, not a product."[29] When those producers halt the activity, their arguments or interpretations risk evaporation, especially in the frenetic and ever-changing American culture.

Perhaps D-Day commemoration has passed its prime. Leaders on the day of battle, such as Eisenhower or Bradley, have long since passed from the scene. The same fate has befallen popularizers of D-Day, like Cornelius Ryan, Stephen Ambrose, and Walter Cronkite. The celebrated veterans have also faded into history. Dick Winters of Easy Company fame (January 2, 2011) and Len Lomell of the Pointe du Hoc assault (March 1, 2011) are both no longer alive as objects of public fixation. The same holds true, more recently, for Easy Company vets Edward "Babe" Heffron (December 3, 2013) and Bill Guarnere (March 11, 2014). That thought of eclipse also stems from rancorous debates on the utility and consequences of military interventions abroad, which have lessened the allure of "liberating" the oppressed. A sense of passing emerges as memorial projects like Bedford's National D-Day Memorial suffer from a lack of funding. Maybe a pronounced focus on this specific past will recede in light of new difficulties, new challenges, new potentials that—perhaps—seem to relate in minimal ways to the D-Day paradigm.

As Winter observed, "A nation obsessed with memory is one which has exhausted its sense of a historical mission," and the D-Day mania of the past two decades fed into a national obsession with the Second World War.[30] That preoccupation stemmed from the evocation of *past* glory days, a sense of national unity and purpose that had seemed lacking in the present as a doubtful future loomed on the horizon. Scholars like Stephen Ambrose trumpeted what Second World War veteran and writer Edward S. Wood Jr. deplored as "immature" and overly celebratory takes on warfare.[31] With Ambrose's death, that advocacy lost a powerful and popular voice.

Ambrose's passing, however, has not left gaps in D-Day celebrationism. For instance, his trusted cohorts Douglas Brinkley and Ronald Drez have continued the effort. They have joined a large and growing body of people writing about, popularizing, lauding, and perpetuating the standard takes on D-Day covered at length in this book. D-Day proponents include museums, memorial sites, and commemorative associations spread throughout the United States and abroad. Authors still write on D-Day and conferences focused on the battle abound.[32] Drawing on historical tourism, residents of the Normandy region certainly will strive to keep D-Day remembrance alive. Tours continue to attract thousands of Americans to the area every year. For now, political leaders feel obliged to pay homage to the remaining veterans and the societies that spurred them on their liberating mission, as evidenced by the June 6, 2014, celebrations in France.[33] Whether such activities continue to have allure, to attract attention, to educate on the past-present-future, remains to be seen.

Is it time to "master" our own past, to historicize the American tale of redemption and morality affirmed through military action in the most destructive war ever? Time will tell. Still, the lingering positive connotations of D-Day—interpretations that have now assumed a sacrosanct status in their own right—seem to indicate that America's D-Day story has not finished just yet.

NOTES

NOTE ON METHOD AND SOURCES

1. Alon Confino, "Collective Memory and Cultural History: Problems of Method," *American Historical Review* 102 (December 1997): 1387.

2. Gordon S. Wood, *The Purpose of the Past: Reflections on the Uses of History* (New York: Penguin, 2008), 8.

3. Mark Connelly, *We Can Take It! Britain and the Memory of the Second World War* (New York: Pearson, 2004), 9.

4. Pierre Nora, "Between Memory and History," trans. Marc Roudebush, *Representations* 26 (Spring 1989): 8. Compare Jacques Le Goff, *History and Memory,* trans. Steven Rendall and Elizabeth Claman (New York: Columbia University Press, 1992), 111.

5. Emily S. Rosenberg, *A Date Which Will Live: Pearl Harbor in American Memory* (Durham, NC: Duke University Press, 2003), 5. She further explained, *"History/memory, in this investigation, is about production, contestation, and circulation in diverse print, celluloid, electronic, and commemorative media,"* 7 (italics in original).

6. For more on this concept, see Eric Foner, *The Story of American Freedom* (New York: W. W. Norton, 1998), xiii–xv, and throughout.

INTRODUCTION

1. Harold J. Goldberg, *D-Day in the Pacific: The Battle of Saipan* (Bloomington: Indiana University Press, 2007), 6, portrayed the battle of Saipan (which began on September 15, 1944) as an amphibious operation more difficult than the invasion of France. Joseph Balkoski, *Omaha Beach: D-Day, June 6, 1944* (Mechanicsburg, PA: Stackpole Books, 2004), 4, argued, however, "Although many 'D-Days' occurred in World War II, history recognizes only one."

2. Charles B. MacDonald, *The Mighty Endeavor: American Armed Forces in the European Theater in World War II* (New York: Oxford University Press, 1969), 279; "Sol [Standards of Learning] Education Packet," National D-Day Memorial Foundation, 2002; "D-Day Plaque Project," National D-Day Memorial website, 2013, http://www.dday.org/component/content/article/42–the-memorial/programs/75–d-day-programs (accessed October 3, 2014).

3. This order even appeared on the original back cover of Eisenhower's book describing his World War II experiences. Dwight D. Eisenhower, *Crusade in Europe* (New York: Doubleday, 1948, 1997).

4. Carlo D'Este, *Decision in Normandy* (Old Saybrook, CT: Konecky and Konecky, 1983), 13.

5. Stephen E. Ambrose, "The Meaning of D-Day," in *The Greatest Thing We Have Ever Attempted: Historical Perspectives on the Normandy Campaign,* ed. Steven Weingartner (Wheaton, IL: Cantigny First Division Foundation, 1998), 169.

6. Dan van der Vat, *D-Day: The Greatest Invasion; A People's History* (Toronto: Black Walnut Books, 2003).

7. On the French civilian population's difficult experience of liberation, see William I. Hitchcock, *The Bitter Road to Freedom: A New History of the Liberation of Europe* (New York: Free Press, 2008), 19–59.

8. William Faulkner, *Requiem for a Nun,* in *William Faulkner: Novels 1942–1954,* ed. Joseph Blotner and Noel Polk (New York: Library of America, 1994), 535.

9. Scholars Eric Hobsbawm and Terence Ranger described what they termed "invented traditions." These two, as editors, and their fellow contributors composed an essay collection that emphasized the role of power when manipulating historical memory. Unlike some later works, though, they acknowledged the contested and sometimes antiestablishment nature of popular memory. Hobsbawm, introduction, *The Invention of Tradition,* ed. Hobsbawm and Ranger (New York: Cambridge University Press, 1983), 1.

10. Here I follow Jay Winter while emphasizing the process and not the final product of "memory." Winter, *Remembering War: The Great War between Memory and History in the Twentieth Century* (New Haven: Yale University Press, 2006), 3–4.

11. Lewis Coser, introduction, *On Collective Memory,* by Maurice Halbwachs, ed. and trans. Lewis Coser (Chicago: University of Chicago Press, 1992), 21.

12. Richard Slotkin, *Regeneration through Violence: The Mythology of the American Frontier, 1600–1860* (Middletown, CT: Wesleyan University Press, 1973), 294. See also Joseph Campbell, *The Hero with a Thousand Faces,* 3rd ed. (1949; repr., Novato, CA: New World Library, 2008); and Roland Barthes, *Mythologies,* ed. and trans. Annette Lavers (1957; repr., New York: Noonday Press, 1972). Slotkin wrote elsewhere, "Myth therefore performs its cultural function by generalizing particular and contingent experiences into the bases of universal rules of understanding and conduct; and it does this by transforming secular history into a body of sacred and sanctifying legends." Slotkin, *The Fatal Environment: The Myth of the Frontier in the Age of Industrialization, 1800–1890* (New York: Atheneum, 1985), 19.

13. Mary Louise Roberts, *What Soldiers Do: Sex and the American GI in World War II France* (Chicago: University of Chicago Press, 2013), 59; Connelly, *We Can Take It,* 49. Following Barthes, *Mythologies* (11, 129), myth constitutes a basic form of communication with familiar problems of veracity and hyperbole. One other somewhat approving conception of myth comes from an interesting work on the role of heroes in American culture; see John Shelton Lawrence and Robert Jewett, *The Myth of the American Superhero* (Grand Rapids, MI: William B. Eerdmans, 2002), 111.

14. For an example of startling diversity, see Nora, "Between Memory and History: Les Liuex de Memoire," 7–26; and Pierre Nora, ed., *Realms of Memory: Rethinking the French Past,* 3 vols., ed. Lawrence Kritzman and trans. Arthur Goldhammer (New York: Columbia University Press, 1996–98). This three-volume translation only provides a small portion of the original essays, which fill seven volumes (from 1981 to 1992).

15. Benedict Anderson, *Imagined Communities: Reflections on the Origin and Spread of Nationalism*, rev. ed. (New York: Verso, 1991), 6.

16. Geoff Eley, introduction, *War and Memory in the Twentieth Century*, ed. Martin Evans and Ken Lunn (New York: Berg, 1997), vii; Winter, *Remembering War*, 1.

17. Michael G. Kammen, *Mystic Chords of Memory: The Transformation of Tradition in American Culture* (New York: Vintage Books, 1991), 3, 13. Kammen shows an obvious mastery of detail in this lengthy book. Nevertheless, the overall impression is of an encyclopedic listing of "memories" through time rather than a sustained analysis of what those memories signify.

18. G. Kurt Piehler, *Remembering War the American Way* (1995; repr., Washington, DC: Smithsonian Books, 2004), 3.

19. Kammen's exhaustive book and Piehler's broad focus serve as ample long-view works on American memory. Memory and history studies of military affairs, however, have tended to focus on single conflicts or even lone battles. The extant list of books dealing with memory and military history continues to grow. Some of the best works on the Civil War include David W. Blight, *Race and Reunion: The Civil War in American Memory* (Cambridge, MA: Harvard University Press, 2001); Jim Weeks, *Gettysburg: Memory, Market, and an American Shrine* (Princeton: Princeton University Press, 2003); and Alice Fahs and Joan Waugh, eds., *The Memory of the Civil War in American Culture* (Chapel Hill: University of North Carolina Press, 2004). The Second World War also has a large body of memory-relevant works: Michael C. C. Adams, *The Best War Ever: America and World War II* (Baltimore: Johns Hopkins University Press, 1994); Edward Linenthal and Tom Engelhardt, eds., *History Wars: The Enola Gay and Other Battles for the American Past* (New York: Metropolitan Books, 1996); Rosenberg, *A Date Which Will Live;* Robert S. Burrell, *The Ghosts of Iwo Jima* (College Station: Texas A&M University Press, 2006); and John Bodnar, *The "Good War" in American Memory* (Baltimore: Johns Hopkins University Press, 2010). For Vietnam, see Kristin Ann Hass, *Carried to the Wall: American Memory and the Vietnam Veterans Memorial* (Berkeley: University of California Press, 1998); Patrick Hagopian, *The Vietnam War in American Memory: Veterans, Memorials, and the Politics of Healing* (Amherst: University of Massachusetts Press, 2009); and Michael J. Allen, *Until the Last Man Comes Home: POWs, MIAs, and the Unending Vietnam War* (Chapel Hill: University of North Carolina Press, 2009).

20. Studs Terkel, *"The Good War": An Oral History of World War II* (New York: New Press, 1984), 3.

21. Ronald Reagan, "Remarks of the President at U.S.-French Ceremony Commemorating D-Day," June 6, 1984, Box—D-Day Anniversary VOF Dawson Gen. Smith/Gen. Allen & Gen. Huebner, Robert R. McCormick Research Center, Cantigny First Division Museum, Wheaton, IL. Hereafter referred to as CFDM.

22. Edward Linenthal and Emily Rosenberg have both explored changing interpretations of Pearl Harbor and the conceptual linkage of this battle to the atomic destruction of Hiroshima and Nagasaki. See Edward Tabor Linenthal, *Sacred Ground: Americans and Their Battlefields* (Urbana: University of Illinois Press, 1991); Linenthal and Engelhardt, *History Wars;* and Rosenberg, *A Date Which Will Live.* Robert Burrell presented a critical operational analysis of the seizure of Iwo Jima. He also explored the sentimentalized conception of the battle that emerged afterwards, especially with the enshrinement of Joe Rosenthal's famous photograph of the flag raising on Mount Suribachi. See Burrell, *The Ghosts of Iwo Jima.* Karal Ann Marling and John Wetenhall, *Iwo Jima: Monuments, Memories, and the American Hero* (Cambridge, MA: Harvard University Press, 1991), examined the same events but without a theoretical framework or detailed consideration of the way that memories of this battle changed over time.

23. Tom Brokaw, *The Greatest Generation* (New York: Random House, 1998); *Saving Private Ryan,* dir. Steven Spielberg, 169 min., DreamWorks Pictures and Paramount Pictures, 1998. For box-office figures, see "Box office/business for *Saving Private Ryan* (1998)," Internet Movie Database (IMDB), n.d., http://www.imdb.com/title/tt0120815/business (accessed March 18, 2007). The movie grossed an estimated $216 million domestically and $224 million internationally, while winning five Academy Awards.

24. Though the popular mood was ready for reverential treatment of the fading war generation, some scholars began to challenge roseate views of what amounted to a horrendously destructive period. See Paul Fussell, *Wartime: Understanding and Behavior in the Second World War* (New York: Oxford University Press, 1989); John W. Dower, *War without Mercy: Race and Power in the Pacific War* (New York: Pantheon Books, 1986); and Michael S. Sherry, *The Rise of American Air Power: The Creation of Armageddon* (New York: Yale University Press, 1987). Moral criticism of the American war effort appeared even earlier in literary form. For a few representative examples, see Irwin Shaw, *The Young Lions* (New York: Random House, 1948); Joseph Heller, *Catch-22* (New York: Simon and Schuster, 1961); and Kurt Vonnegut, *Slaughterhouse-five; or, The Children's Crusade, a Duty-Dance with Death* (New York: Delacorte Press, 1969). Historian Michael C. C. Adams also questioned the implications of this simplistic version of the past. He rejected the overly positive image displayed in most commemorative activities relating to the war throughout the 1980s and the early 1990s. Adams asserted that such a benign view of war fostered a proclivity for future military adventurism. See Adams, *The Best War Ever,* 4–5. Compare Kenneth D. Rose, *Myth and the Greatest Generation: A Social History of Americans in World War II* (New York: Routledge, 2008).

25. Adams, *The Best War Ever,* 69–74. Adams noted that wartime propaganda and the relative isolation of the home front created sanitized, American-centric versions of the war in the public consciousness. These influences carried over into the postwar years and have continued to shape American perceptions of the conflict.

26. Paul S. Boyer, *By the Bomb's Early Light: American Thought and Culture at the Dawn of the Atomic Age* (New York: Pantheon, 1985), 334.

27. The *New York Times* front-page headline proudly announced, "Allied Armies Land in France in the Havre-Cherbourg Area; Great Invasion Is Under Way" (June 6, 1944). The *Chicago Tribune* (and, no doubt, other papers) carried an Associated Press story that promptly characterized D-Day as the "largest and most daring such undertaking in the history of warfare." Associated Press, "Allies Invade France: 'D' Day Reward of Four Years' Faith and Toil," *Chicago Tribune,* June 6, 1944.

28. Alex Kershaw, *The Bedford Boys: One American Town's Ultimate D-Day Sacrifice* (Cambridge, MA: Da Capo Press, 2003), 199–238.

29. Douglas Brinkley, *The Boys of Pointe du Hoc: Ronald Reagan, D-Day, and the U.S. Army 2nd Rangers Battalion* (New York: HarperPerennial, 2005). A great deal of ink has been spilled over the valiant actions of the Rangers and the varied measure of success accorded to their mission. The Rangers scaled the sheer cliff face at Pointe du Hoc despite a hail of machine-gun fire and grenades from defending Germans. Once over the top, these Rangers found that the Germans had held the targeted battery of 155mm artillery back, pending the construction of concrete casements to protect the guns. The Rangers did find four pieces of the six-gun battery, along with a considerable cache of ammunition, hidden among the trees a short distance from the intended cliff-side emplacements. Upon disabling those four pieces, the Rangers, in a sense, did fulfill the dictates of their mission, even if at a tremendous cost. A discussion of the controversy over this aspect of the battle appears in chapters 3 and 7.

30. Although the "good war" imagery may appeal to conservative elements in the American public, Brinkley overlooked a large body of scholarship that dated the emergence of neoconservatism back at least to the 1960s. For representative works on this subject, see William C. Berman, *America's Right Turn: From Nixon to Clinton* (Baltimore: Johns Hopkins University Press, 1998); Lisa McGirr, *Suburban Warriors: The Origins of the New American Right,* new ed. (Princeton, NJ: Princeton University Press, 2002); and Kevin M. Kruse, *White Flight: Atlanta and the Making of Modern Conservatism* (Princeton, NJ: Princeton University Press, 2005). David Farber, *The Rise and Fall of Modern American Conservatism: A Short History* (Princeton, NJ: Princeton University Press, 2010), went back ever further, dating the emergence of this conservative movement to the 1930s.

31. Roberts, *What Soldiers Do,* 15–43, 124, and throughout.

32. Anderson, *Imagined Communities,* 6.

33. For a provocative argument regarding American culture and diplomacy that follows these lines, see Walter A. McDougall, *Promised Land, Crusader State: The American Encounter with the World since 1776* (New York: Houghton Mifflin, 1997).

34. Foner, *Story of American Freedom,* xiii–xiv. Richard H. Immerman noted Americans' longstanding justification of imperial ambitions, stemming from a belief in the liberty-spreading function of their empire. Immerman, *Empire for Liberty: A History of American Imperialism from Benjamin Franklin to Paul Wolfowitz* (Princeton, NJ: Princeton University Press, 2010), 5–6.

35. Michael Sherry, *In the Shadow of War: The United States since the 1930s* (New Haven, CT: Yale University Press, 1995), ix–x.

36. Slotkin, *Regeneration through Violence.* Andrew Bacevich has held up the belief in the efficacy of violence as a central feature of what he sees as a new form of militarism in American society. Though Bacevich is perceptive in many ways, many of the developments he attributes to the post-Vietnam period had clear precedents in the decades well before that divisive war, as Sherry, Slotkin, and others aptly demonstrate. See Bacevich, *The New American Militarism: How Americans Are Seduced by War,* new ed. (New York: Oxford University Press, 2006), 2.

37. George Herring, *From Colony to Superpower: U.S. Foreign Relations since 1776* (New York: Oxford University Press, 2008), 1–4. A point recently reinforced by Christian G. Appy, *American Reckoning: The Vietnam War and our National Identity* (New York: Viking, 2015), 322-23, and throughout.

38. Michael H. Hunt, *Ideology and U.S. Foreign Policy* (New Haven, CT: Yale University Press, 1987), xii, 13–16.

39. Frank Ninkovich, *The Wilsonian Century: U.S. Foreign Policy since 1900* (Chicago: University of Chicago Press, 1999), 5, 10. For more on Wilsonianism in American foreign policy, see Lloyd E. Ambrosius, "Woodrow Wilson and George W. Bush: Historical Comparisons of Ends and Means in Their Foreign Policies," *Diplomatic History* 30 (June 2006): 509–54; and Constance G. Anthony, "American Democratic Interventionism: Romancing the Iconic Woodrow Wilson," *International Studies Perspectives* 9 (2008): 239–53.

40. Michael Hogan, introduction, *The Ambiguous Legacy: U.S. Foreign Relations in the "American Century,"* ed. Michael Hogan (New York: Cambridge University Press, 1999), 1.

41. Ninkovich, *Wilsonian Century,* 13, 48.

42. David Farber recently examined Senator Robert A. Taft's involvement in shaping modern conservatism in American political culture. Taft strenuously opposed internationalism in the 1940s and early 1950s as likely to breed an overpowered and burdensome federal government, one that was threatening to Americans' liberties. Farber, *The Rise and Fall of Modern American Conservatism,* 25–27, 37.

43. For other comprehensive works that directly address the political implications of war memory, see Evans and Lunn, *War and Memory in the Twentieth Century;* T. G. Ashplant, Graham Dawson, and Michael Roper, eds., *The Politics of War Memory and Commemoration* (New York: Routledge, 2000); and Michael Keren and Holger H. Herwig, eds., *War Memory and Popular Culture: Essays on Modes of Remembrance and Commemoration* (Jefferson, NC: McFarland, 2009). The last work has a chapter by Sam Edwards, "Commemoration and Consumption in Normandy, 1945–1994" (76–91), which covers the commemorative practices for D-Day in the Normandy region. This chapter originated from Edwards's insightful dissertation, which examined American and British efforts to commemorate both D-Day and the air war of the European Theater in Britain and France. While Edwards's writing and personal communications proved extremely valuable, this book takes a broader look at specifically the American memory of the battle. See Edwards, "War and Collective Memory: American Military Commemoration in Britain and France, 1943 to the Present" (PhD diss., Lancaster University, 2007).

44. Cornelius Ryan, *The Longest Day: June 6, 1944* (New York: Simon and Schuster, 1959); *The Longest Day,* dir. Ken Annakin, Andrew Marton, Bernhard Wicki, and Darryl F. Zanuck, 178 min., Darryl F. Zanuck Productions and Twentieth Century–Fox, 1962.

45. Sixties-era scholarship is as immense as it is divided in terms of focus and analysis. Several noteworthy general works include Terry H. Anderson, *The Movement and the Sixties: Protest in America from Greensboro to Wounded Knee* (New York: Oxford University Press, 1995); David R. Farber, *The Age of Great Dreams: America in the 1960s* (New York: Hill and Wang, 1995); and Maurice Isserman and Michael Kazin, *America Divided: The Civil War of the 1960s,* 2nd ed. (New York: Oxford University Press, 2003).

46. Stephen E. Ambrose, *Pegasus Bridge: June 6, 1944* (New York: Simon and Schuster, 1985), looked at one aspect of the British effort on D-Day. Ambrose, *Band of Brothers: E Company, 506th Regiment, 101st Airborne from Normandy to Hitler's Eagle's Nest* (New York: Simon and Schuster, 1992), covered one unit before, during, and after D-Day. Ambrose, *D-Day, June 6, 1944: The Climactic Battle of World War II* (New York: Simon and Schuster, 1994), provided his comprehensive account of the battle, while *Citizen Soldiers: The U.S. Army from the Normandy Beaches to the Bugle to the Surrender of Germany, June 7, 1944–May 7, 1945* (New York: Simon and Schuster, 1997), presented a brief recounting of D-Day. See also *Band of Brothers,* dir. David Frankel, Mikael Salomon, Tom Hanks, David Leland, Richard Loncraine, David Nutter, Phil Alden Robinson, and Tony To, 705 min., HBO in association with DreamWorks Pictures, 2001; and, on the National D-Day Museum, since renamed as the National World War II Museum, Stephen E. Ambrose, *To America: Personal Reflections of an Historian* (New York: Simon and Schuster, 2002), 201–11.

47. Elisabeth Bumiller, "How a Quiet Observance Evolved into a Day of Drama," *New York Times,* June 7, 2004.

48. For an international comparative perspective on D-Day remembrance, see Michael Dolski, "To Set Free a Suffering Humanity": D-Day in American Remembrance" (Ph.D. diss., Temple University, 2012), 388–414; and Michael Dolski, Sam Edwards, and John Buckley, eds., *D-Day in History and Memory: The Normandy Landings in International Remembrance and Commemoration* (Denton: University of North Texas Press, 2014).

49. Piehler, *Remembering War the American Way,* xiv.

50. Adams, *Best War Ever,* 4.

51. Terkel, *"The Good War."*

52. I am not trying to deny the moral implications of liberating the French countryside in a war against Nazi Germany. Americans have tended to minimize some problematic aspects of this battle, such as the suffering inflicted on civilians caught in the path of war. Nevertheless,

this invasion did help speed the end of a necessary war against horrendous aggressors. What American society has chosen to make of this war stands out in contrast to the controversies surrounding the Pacific War, both in terms of the racial overtones of the effort and in the emotions still provoked by the use of atomic bombs at the end of the conflict. D-Day, on the other hand, serves as a far "safer" moment, which offers less in the way of explosive controversy stemming from American actions. For more on the American unwillingness to confront the French people's painful experience of liberation, see Hitchcock, *Bitter Road to Freedom*, 3, 11–59; and Dominique François, *Normandy Breaching the Atlantic Wall: From D-Day to the Breakout and Liberation*, trans. Gayle Wurst (Minneapolis: Zenith Press, 2008), 11–13, 283–84.

53. The marketplace-of-ideas concept holds that free competition of ideas, as with goods in a capitalist system, will lead to the strongest (most fitting or suitable) idea winning out over all others. Foner, *Story of American Freedom,* 184.

54. Herring, *From Colony to Superpower,* 937.

CHAPTER 1

1. Franklin D. Roosevelt, "D-Day Prayer," June 6, 1944, History Place website, http://www.historyplace.com/speeches/fdr-prayer.htm (accessed November 19, 2009). Earlier on that Tuesday, June 6, 1944, Roosevelt had exhibited a slightly different air during a press conference in the White House. At that point, the president jocularly admitted, "No, I'm not so solemn, I suppose." This statement suited the sense of celebration that gripped some Americans upon hearing of the invasion. "38 Excerpts from the Press Conference on D-Day, June 6, 1944," June 6, 1944, Franklin D. Roosevelt Presidential Library and Museum website, http://docs.fdrlibrary.marist.edu/04DD009.HTML (accessed September 28, 2010).

2. Lawrence Resner, "Country in Prayer," *New York Times,* June 7, 1944.

3. Blight, *Race and Reunion,* 18–19.

4. "Draft of the D-Day Prayer, June 6, 1944," n.d., Franklin D. Roosevelt Presidential Library and Museum website, http://docs.fdrlibrary.marist.edu/04DD010.HTML (accessed September 28, 2010). According to personal communication with one archivist, little else on the prayer resides in the library's holdings aside from this copy with editorial notes and press coverage from the time.

5. Kershaw, *The Bedford Boys,* 172.

6. For an engaging treatment of the outbreak of war in both Europe and Asia, see Williamson Murray and Allan R. Millett, *A War to Be Won: Fighting the Second World War* (Cambridge, MA: Belknap Press of Harvard University Press, 2000), 1–17, 143–68. The surprise attack on Pearl Harbor helped Americans maintain a sense of outraged victimhood throughout the war, leading to a vindictive approach in the Pacific seldom seen in Europe. Themes of infamy, treachery, and villainy ascribed to the attack, and then carried over to the Japanese as a whole, persisted throughout the war. Emily Rosenberg's astute analysis of American remembrance and Pearl Harbor informed this work in valuable ways. Rosenberg, *A Date Which Will Live,* 12–14. On the racialized nature of the Pacific War, John Dower's *War without Mercy* remains the standard account.

7. Military personnel figures drawn from Allan R. Millett and Peter Maslowski, *For the Common Defense: A Military History of the United States of America,* rev. ed. (New York: Free Press, 1994), 655–56.

8. Peter Mansoor, *The GI Offensive in Europe: The Triumph of American Infantry Divisions, 1941–1945* (Lawrence: University Press of Kansas, 1999), 1.

9. One of the better known works that pushed material superiority as the sole explanation for Allied success is Martin van Creveld, *Fighting Power: German and U.S. Army Performance* (Westport, CT: Greenwood Press, 1982), 178–79, and throughout.

10. Gerhard L. Weinberg offered an authoritative account of the United States' descent to war in his book *A World at Arms: A Global History of World War II* (New York: Cambridge University Press, 1994), 238–63.

11. Richard J. Overy, *Why the Allies Won* (New York: W. W. Norton, 1995); Rick Atkinson, *An Army at Dawn: The War in North Africa, 1942–1943* (New York: Henry Holt, 2002); Douglas Porch, *The Path to Victory: The Mediterranean Theater in World War II* (New York: Farrar, Straus and Giroux, 2004).

12. Gordon A. Harrison, *Cross-Channel Attack,* U.S. Army in World War II: European Theater of Operations (1951; repr., New York: BDD, 1993), 83–126.

13. Russell F. Weigley, *Eisenhower's Lieutenants: The Campaign of France and Germany, 1944–1945* (Bloomington: Indiana University Press, 1981).

14. Flint Whitlock, *The Fighting First: The Untold Story of the Big Red One on D-Day* (Boulder, CO: Westview Press, 2004), xi.

15. Robert Kershaw, *D-Day: Piercing the Atlantic Wall* (Annapolis, MD: Naval Institute Press, 1994), 26–28, 37. Kershaw noted that even Rommel's energy was insufficient for the task before him in early 1944 and that much of the effort expended in hurried defensive preparations ultimately enervated the defending units in the region.

16. Intelligence and counterintelligence operations form largely absent features of earlier treatments of the battle because of lingering government restrictions on relevant information after the war. A great deal of insightful material on this aspect of the battle has come out in the past few decades. See Michael Howard, *Strategic Deception in the Second World War: British Intelligence Operations against the German High Command* (New York: W. W. Norton, 1995), 105–29; Mary Kathryn Barbier, "Deception and the Planning of D-Day," in *The Normandy Campaign 1944: Sixty Years On,* ed. John Buckley (New York: Routledge, 2006), 170-84; and John Ferris, "Intelligence and OVERLORD: A Snapshot from 6 June 1944," also in the Buckley volume, 185–200.

17. Rather soon after the war, authors began to focus on the high drama of inclement weather potentially wreaking the invasion itself. Eisenhower himself discussed the weather factor in his book *Crusade in Europe,* 248–52. See also Bruce Bliven, Jr., *The Story of D-Day: June 6, 1994* (1956; repr., New York: Random House, 1994), 40; and David Howarth, *Dawn of D-Day: These Men Were There, 6 June 1944* (1959; repr., Mechanicsburg, PA: Stackpole Books, 2001), 30. Howarth wrote that when pondering the decision, Eisenhower "carried as heavy a burden as has fallen to the lot of any man."

18. Howarth, *Dawn of D-Day,* 201–3.

19. Ronald J. Drez, ed., *Voices of D-Day: The Story of the Allied Invasion Told by Those Who Were There,* with a foreword by Stephen E. Ambrose (Baton Rouge: Louisiana State University Press, 1994), 63.

20. Ed Ruggero, *The First Men In: U.S. Paratroopers and the Fight to Save D-Day* (New York: HarperCollins, 2006).

21. Harrison, *Cross-Channel Attack,* 278–300, offers a straightforward account of the American airborne landings. Mark Bando, *Vanguard of the Crusade: The 101st Airborne Division in World War II* (Bedford, PA: Aberjona Press, 2003), 23–98, actually provides a wealth of detail on both American airborne divisions on D-Day. D'Este, *Decision in Normandy,* 120-50, covers the British air landings.

22. Harrison, *Cross-Channel Attack,* 300–301.

23. Howard A. Andersen, "D-Day at Normandy with USS *Corry* (DD-463)," unpublished manuscript, quoted in *Neptunus Rex: Naval Stories of the Normandy Invasion, June 6, 1944,* ed. Edward F. Prados, U.S. Navy Memorial Foundation (Novato, CA: Presidio Press, 1998), 53.

24. Omar N. Bradley, *A Soldier's Story* (New York: Henry Holt, 1951), 254.

25. Joseph Balkoski, *Utah Beach, June 6, 1944: The Amphibious Landing and Airborne Operations on D-Day* (Mechanicsburg, PA: Stackpole Books, 2005), 330.

26. John Julius Moglia Questionnaire, n.d., Folder 12, Box 12, "The Longest Day" records, Cornelius Ryan Collection of World War II Papers, Robert E. and Jean R. Mahn Center for Archives and Special Collections, Ohio University Library, Athens. Hereafter referred to as CRC.

27. There is a multitude of works on the Omaha Beach assault. Several of the better books include Whitlock, *The Fighting First;* Adrian Lewis, *Omaha Beach: A Flawed Victory* (Chapel Hill: University of North Carolina Press, 2001); and Balkoski, *Omaha Beach.*

28. John Keegan pointed out the trepidation stemming from woeful tales of the Dieppe failed landings mixed with a stern sense of duty and desire for vengeance as the Canadian 3rd Division men prepared for their own invasion. John Keegan, *Six Armies in Normandy: From D-Day to the Liberation of Paris,* with a new introduction for the 50th anniversary of D-Day (1982; repr., New York: Penguin, 1994), 120.

29. D'Este, in an approach typical of American authors, castigated Montgomery for creating an overly ambitious plan, failing to achieve his objectives, and then finessing official reports and postwar history to promote a more favorable view of his generalship. D'Este, *Decision in Normandy,* 476–80.

30. Even the joyous news releases made by Allied leaders contained the suggestion that other landing sites were potentially forthcoming. See, for instance, President Roosevelt's news conference on June 6, 1944, "38 Excerpts."

31. In a volume John Buckley edited on Normandy, he astutely argued, "Far more than any defeats on the Eastern Front, even Stalingrad, the loss of France in the summer of 1944 marked a huge and fatal psychological blow to Germany, one from which she would not recover. Defeating the Allied invasion that summer arguably had represented the Third Reich's last realistic hope of avoiding total defeat and though the struggle would continue into 1945, the crushing blow suffered in the Normandy campaign proved beyond serious doubt that the defeat of Nazi Germany had moved from a case of 'if' to 'when.'" See his introduction to *The Normandy Campaign 1944,* 1.

32. Howarth, *Dawn of D-Day,* 248.

33. James Tobin, *Ernie Pyle's War: America's Eyewitness to World War II* (Lawrence: University Press of Kansas, 1997), 170-71. Regarding the repetition of minimal detail, Tobin claimed, "In short, reading newspaper accounts of Normandy (indeed, of most military operations in World War II) was like reading an account of a football game written by a sportswriter sitting outside the stadium who derives his only knowledge of the game from the hurried accounts from one team's assistant coach who runs out after each quarter to give brief and self-serving updates. It was barely better than nothing" (172).

34. Kershaw, *The Bedford Boys,* 166; Thomas Doherty, *Projections of War: Hollywood, American Culture, and World War II,* rev. ed. (New York: Columbia University Press, 1999), 84, 242; Stephen E. Ambrose, *D-Day June 6, 1944: The Climactic Battle of World War II* (New York: Simon and Schuster, 1994), 499. From the *New York Times,* June 7, 1944, see Meyer Berger, "50,000 Pray at the Eternal Light, Led by Priest, Minister, and Rabbi," "Congress Marks Day with

Prayers," "D-Day Sees Sports Take a 'Time-Out,'" "Reno Gambling Halts for D-Day," and "Liberty Bell Sounds Tocsin of Invasion."

35. An earlier draft of the order had excluded much of this soaring rhetoric. Instead, it offered the phrase "great undertaking" in place of "crusade," while omitting mention of the "liberty-loving people" whom the combined Allied soldiery was striving to save. Text from the order is widely available. I have drawn on what appears to be the copy with Eisenhower's original signature in the holdings of the National Archives. Dwight D. Eisenhower, Order of the Day, n.d. [June 6, 1944], Folder 335.18, Supreme Headquarters Allied Expeditionary Forces (SHAEF) Special Staff Adjutant General's Division Executive Section, Record Group (RG) 331, National Archives and Records Administration in College Park, Maryland. Hereafter referred to as NACP. The earlier draft appears in a letter available in the same folder; see Colonel E. C. Boehnke to Dwight D. Eisenhower, "Promulgation of Letter Relative to Behavior," May 20, 1944.

36. As quoted in Carlo D'Este, *Eisenhower: A Soldier's Life* (New York: Henry Holt, 2002), 531.

37. Even on June 5, the day *after* Clark's forces liberated Rome and *before* people in the United States knew that D-Day was imminent, a large crowd gathered in Los Angeles to pray for the fighting men—those soon to land in France. "Divine Aid Invoked for Allied Army of Freedom," *Los Angeles Times*, June 5, 1944. Gerhard L. Weinberg rightly noted that Clark "most unwisely raced for Rome rather than trying to cut off the retreating Germans"; see Weinberg, *A World at Arms: A Global History of World War II* (New York: Cambridge University Press, 1994), 677. Clark sought the glory of liberating a major city instead of concentrating on the more important task of bringing force to bear against a still capable enemy. The Italian campaign continued grinding away until the very end of the war in Europe, almost a year later.

38. Doherty, *Projections of War*, 243.

39. Years later, one disgruntled veteran of the Italian campaign contacted Cornelius Ryan, the author of the 1959 book on D-Day, *The Longest Day*. The letter pushed Ryan to consider writing about "the longest four months" of the Anzio landing, which deserved equal if not greater recognition than D-Day, in that veteran's opinion. Letter, W. H. Ellis to Cornelius Ryan, n.d. [1963?], Folder Ryan, Cornelius, Letters and Correspondence—Fan Mail A-J 1959–63 #2, Miscellaneous Supplementary Material records, CRC.

40. Earl Browder to General Eisenhower/SHAEF, "Message from the Communist Political Association," June 6, 1944, Folder 335.18, SHAEF Special Staff Adjutant General's Division Executive Section, RG 331, NACP.

41. *News of the Day, Invasion Extra!* (vol. 15, no. 280), 10 min., Metro-Goldwyn-Mayer, 1944, VHS, accessed at the UCLA Film and Television Archive, Los Angeles, CA. Hereafter referred to as UFTA.

42. Doherty, *Projections of War*, 243–44.

43. Ambrose, *D-Day*, 504; "George Hicks and the Network Coverage of the Pool Broadcast of D-Day," Radio Days website, June 6, 2009, http://www.otr.com/hicks.html (accessed May 28, 2010).F

44. See also Douglas Brinkley, *Cronkite* (New York: HarperCollins, 2012), 110–14.

45. "Fireside Chat 30: Opening Fifth War Loan Drive (June 12, 1944)," Miller Center of Public Affairs, 2010, http://millercenter.org/scripps/archive/speeches/detail/3335 (accessed October 4, 2010).

46. Although Whitehead would complain about slow transmission of news reports, his words did eventually get out to the wider world. He lambasted officials for the foul-up in news

distribution that happened when the assault stuttered at Omaha. Don Whitehead for the Combined Press, "No News of Americans for 18-Hours with American Troops in France," June 9, 1944, Folder #2, Office of War Information, RG 208, NACP.

47. Quote from John B. Romeiser, introduction, *"Beachhead Don": Reporting the War from the European Theater, 1942–1945,* ed. John B. Romeiser (New York: Fordham University Press, 2004), xxi. The main text of this book reprints Whitehead's Second World War articles, including those covering D-Day (117–23).

48. Ernest Hemingway, "Voyage to Victory," *Collier's,* July 22, 1944. Despite claims to the contrary made by Hemingway himself and some of his supporters, two thoughtful scholars each convincingly assert that Hemingway did not land on D-Day. His article gave the distinct impression that the renowned writer saw himself "not as a mere observer, but as a participant—and leader" in the battle. See Charles Whiting, *Hemingway Goes to War* (Phoenix Mill, UK: Alan Sutton Press, 1999), 46; and Frederick S. Voss, *Reporting the War: The Journalistic Coverage of World War II* (Washington, DC: Smithsonian Institution Press for the National Portrait Gallery, 1994), 187–88.

49. Tobin, *Ernie Pyle's War,* 173–78, 265–68. Tobin's book features an excellent analysis of Pyle and his wartime experience as well as reprints of some of his major articles. Pyle wrote three columns on this initial experience, which newspapers throughout the United States reprinted and one member of Congress read into the *Congressional Record.*

50. Ernie Pyle, *Brave Men*, introduction by G. Kurt Piehler (1944; repr., Lincoln: University of Nebraska Press, 2001), 389. Pyle's columns appeared in many newspapers in the United States. Several compilations, such as this book, came out during or immediately after the war as well.

51. Robert Capa, *Slightly Out of Focus* (New York: Henry Holt, 1947), 145–51; Richard Whelan, *Robert Capa* (New York: Alfred A. Knopf, 1985), 209–14.

52. Kammen, *Mystic Chords of Memory,* 420–22.

53. Letters, Robert Huch to family, June 12, 15, and 26, 1944, Folder—Huch, William [Robert's brother], Letters June 1944, William Huch Papers, World War II Participants and Contemporaries files, Dwight D. Eisenhower Presidential Library, Abilene, KS. Hereafter referred to as DDEL.

54. "The Great Day of His Wrath," *Atlanta Daily World,* June 8, 1944.

55. Michel-Rolph Trouillot, *Silencing the Past: Power and the Production of History* (Boston: Beacon Press, 1995), 26–29. Compare Bodnar, *The "Good War" in American Memory,* 3.

56. As quoted in Kershaw, *The Bedford Boys,* 179.

57. Bliven, *Story of D-Day,* viii. Irwin Shaw's fictional account of the European war included a scene similar to what Bliven experienced. The assaulting unit of one primary character misses combat on D-Day because of mechanical failures and command confusion. Irwin Shaw, *The Young Lions,* foreword by James Salter (1948; repr., Chicago: University of Chicago Press, 2000), 443–51.

58. Murray and Millett, *A War to Be Won*, 445, 480.

59. Memorandum, F. W. Jones, Jr., "Observance of 6 June as a Holiday," June 4, 1945, Folder 001, Parades & Celebrations, SHAEF Special Staff Psychological Warfare Division Executive Section, RG 331, NACP.

60. Kershaw, *The Bedford Boys,* 214. Roger Hill also noticed a reluctance to focus on the battle in Bedford until the Second World War had ended after Japan's capitulation. Roger H. Hill, "Memorializing Community Grief: Bedford, Virginia, and the National D-Day Memorial" (DA diss., George Mason University, 2006), 84.

61. Whitehead, *"Beachhead Don,"* 363–64.

62. Hitchcock, *Bitter Road to Freedom,* 3. Compare Roberts, *What Soldiers Do,* esp. chapter 1.

63. For more on French commemoration, see Henry Rousso, *The Vichy Syndrome: History and Memory in France since 1944,* trans. Arthur Goldhammer (Cambridge, MA: Harvard University Press, 1991); Robert Gildea, "Myth, Memory and Policy in France since 1945," in *Memory and Power in Post-War Europe: Studies in the Presence of the Past,* ed. Jan-Werner Müller (New York: Cambridge University Press, 2002), 59–75; Richard J. Goslan, "The Legacy of World War II in France: Mapping the Discourses of Memory," in *The Politics of Memory in Postwar Europe,* ed. Richard Ned Lebow, Wulf Kansteiner, and Claudio Fogu (Durham, NC: Duke University Press, 2006), 73–96; Claude Quétel, *A Memorial for Peace,* foreword by Jean-Marie Girault, trans. John Lee (Caen, France: Editions du Regard, 1993); Olivier Wieviorka, *Normandy: The Landings to the Liberation of Paris,* trans. M. B. DeBevoise (Cambridge, MA: Harvard University Press, 2008); and Kate C. Lemay, "Gratitude, Trauma, and Repression: D-Day in French Memory," in Dolski, Edwards, and Buckley, *D-Day in History and Memory,* 159–88.

64. Kammen, *Mystic Chords of Memory,* 667.

65. Thomas Childers, *Soldier from the War Returning: The Greatest Generation's Troubled Homecoming from World War II* (New York: Houghton Mifflin Harcourt, 2009), 3. In another telling passage, Childers argued, "Wars are not clean or neat, and neither is their aftermath. Today's comfortable assumption that 'the boys' returned home cheerful, contented, and well-adjusted, that no one suffered from serious emotional disorders, drank too much, or abused his wife or children, would have come as a surprise to contemporaries" (5).

66. John W. Jeffries, *Wartime America: The World War II Home Front* (Chicago: Ivan R. Dee, 1996), 175. Compare Rose, *Myth and the Greatest Generation.*

CHAPTER 2

1. Kershaw, *The Bedford Boys,* 7. In reference to the differing sides that each state followed in the American Civil War, the 29th earned the nickname the "Blue and Gray" division.

2. Joseph Balkoski, *Omaha Beach,* 121; Hill, "Memorializing Community Grief," 90-91. On the 29th Infantry Division's D-Day performance, see Joseph Balkoski, *Beyond the Beachhead: The 29th Infantry Division in Normandy*, foreword by Stephen E. Ambrose (1989; repr., Mechanicsburg, PA: Stackpole Books, 1999).

3. Kershaw, *The Bedford Boys,* 207, 214. The telegrams inundated the local area beginning on July 17, 1944.

4. "Presentation of the Plans and Problems of the American Graves Registration Command to C/S of TSFET and Chiefs of his General Staff," December 27, 1945, Folder—AGRC Organizational & Operations History, June-Dec. 1945, Records of U.S. Army Operational, Tactical, and Support Organizations (World War II and Thereafter), Unit Histories, 1940–1967, Quartermaster Commands, Record Group (RG) 338, NACP; Bodnar, *The "Good War" in American Memory,* 98.

5. The linkage of the two conflicts in this plaque lends support to Piehler's assertion that little, at this time, distinguished commemorative activities between the two wars. Piehler, *Remembering War the American Way,* 129–33.

6. Hill, "Memorializing Community Grief," 85–88.

7. Kershaw, *The Bedford Boys,* 222–24.

8. See, for instance, Stanley Frank, "First Stop—Omaha Beach," *Saturday Evening Post*, March 16, 1946.

9. Dwight D. Eisenhower, "Material for NBC address," June 4, 1946, Folder—D-Day, 25th Anniversary of, Dwight D. Eisenhower Papers, DDEL.

10. Kammen, *Mystic Chords of Memory,* 531–33. Kammen, as well as Piehler, saw the Civil War as the beginning of the federal government's increased participation in memory-history work. In the twentieth century, as both scholars noted, that activity increased greatly even as local or group memories sometimes came into conflict with the official versions pushed by the federal government. For more, see Piehler, *Remembering War the American Way,* 2–6.

11. For treatment of the ABMC's activities in Normandy, see Edwards, "War and Collective Memory," especially 73–74, 137–59.

12. William Siebert, "The Gravediggers," n.d., Folder—Siebert, William—Graves Registration, William Shyrock Papers, World War II Participants and Contemporaries Collection, DDEL.

13. "Presentation of the Plans and Problems of the American Graves Registration Command to C/S of TSFET and Chiefs of his General Staff," December 27, 1945, Folder—AGRC Organizational & Operations History, June–Dec. 1945, Records of U.S. Army Operational, Tactical, and Support Organizations (World War II and Thereafter), Unit Histories, 1940–1967, Quartermaster Commands, RG 338, NACP.

14. Piehler, *Remembering War the American Way,* 132.

15. The twelve are Ardennes (Belgium), Brittany (France), Cambridge (U.K.), Epinal (France), Florence (Italy), Henri-Chappelle (Belgium), Lorraine (France), Luxembourg (Luxembourg), Netherlands (Netherlands), Normandy (France), Rhone (France), and Sicily-Rome (Italy). The other two are Manila (Philippines) and North Africa (Tunisia). Of course, one can find remains of American service personnel from this conflict in many other cemeteries. The National Memorial Cemetery of the Pacific in Honolulu and the Arlington National Cemetery, to name just two, also hold significant numbers of these remains.

16. Edwards, "War and Collective Memory," 128–50; Ron Robin, *Enclaves of America: The Rhetoric of American Political Architecture Abroad, 1900–1965* (Princeton, NJ: Princeton University Press, 1992), 109–35.

17. The transfer was a drawn-out process. The AGRC was the primary authority for constructing the cemeteries and handling the bodies. The ABMC oversaw the selection and erection of monuments. The two worked together in the years following the war with the final handover from AGRC to ABMC in Normandy taking place in 1949.

18. Lt. K. W. Lange (HQ AGRC), "Memorial Day ceremonies at St. Laurent," n.d., Folder 97-AGRC-0.3.0, U.S. Military Cemetery Reports (N-St. M)—Hq. AGRC, European Theater Area—1946–48, Records of the Adjutant General's Office, WWII Operations Reports, 1940–48, European Theater, RG 407, NACP.

19. Memorandum, Col. George C. Traver to Commander AGRC Eur, "Narrative Report of Activities, Second Zone, AGRC, Camp John B. Franks, Week Ending 9 April," April 10, 1947, Folder 7856, AGRC, Second Zone Narrative Reports, Sept. 1946–Dec. 1947 (II), Records of U.S. Army Operational, Tactical, and Support Organizations (World War II and Thereafter), Unit Histories, 1940–1967, Quartermaster Commands, RG 338, NACP.

20. Memorandum, Headquarters Army Graves Registration Command, Europe, "Five Thousand Attend 'Benediction Ceremony' Closing St. Laurent U.S. Military Cemetery at Omaha Beach, Normandy, France," September 14, 1947, Folder 97, AGRC-0.3.0, U.S. Military Cemetery Reports (N-St. M)—Hq. AGRC, European Theater Area—1946–48, Records of the Adjutant General's Office, WWII Operations Reports, 1940–48, European Theater, RG 407, NACP.

21. As quoted in Robin, *Enclaves of America,* 122.

22. Letter, Harbeson, Hough, Livingston & Larson Architects, "American Military Cemetery, Normandy, France," July 5, 1949, Folder—Others Committees, Organizations & Meetings 4 (General) (COM) 1/69–, Records of the American Battle Monuments Commission, RG 117, NACP.

23. George Mosse, *Fallen Soldiers: Reshaping the Memory of the World Wars* (New York: Oxford University Press, 1990); Kammen, *Mystic Chords of Memory,* 420–22, 700; Piehler, *Remembering War the American Way,* 5–6, 187.

24. Records of Proceedings, Forty-Seventh Meeting, American Battle Monuments Commission, April 5, 1946, Folder—Record of Proceedings, Book III Issuance Management Administration (ADM) 8–4, Records of the American Battle Monuments Commission, RG 117, NACP.

25. Advocates of the monument stated their case is a series of 1946 letters: the monument was unobtrusive, paid for, and entirely in keeping with the tendency of the ABMC to honor in a solemn manner those who had served and died in the fighting. See, in particular, Letter, William J. Talbott to Commanding General, 1st US Division, February 6, 1946, Folder Monument Sites WWII, Box 280, CFDM. Compare Edwards, "War and Collective Memory," 102–3.

26. Capa, *Slightly Out of Focus,* 139–51.

27. Eisenhower, *Crusade in Europe,* 157.

28. *D-Day: The Normandy Invasion,* dir. Frank Capra, 51 min., U.S. Coast Guard, 1944 (distributed by Madacy Entertainment Group, 1998, VHS), UFTA; *News of the Day, D-Day Tribute to Americans Overseas* (vol. 17, no. 280), 10 min., Metro-Goldwyn-Mayer, 1946 (7 June), VHS, UFTA.

29. Michael Paris, "Reconstructing D-Day: 6 June 1944 and British Documentary Films," in Buckley, *Normandy Campaign 1944,* 207–9.

30. *The True Glory,* dir. Garson Kanin, 87 min., Ministry of Information (UK) and U.S. Office of War Information, 1945 (distributed by E1 Entertainment, 2009, DVD).

31. *Crusade in Europe,* 519 min., March of Time and Twentieth Century–Fox, 1949 (New Line Home Video, 1998, DVD).

32. Lawrence Suid, *Guts & Glory: The Making of the American Military Image in Film,* rev. ed. (Lexington: University Press of Kentucky, 2002), 105–24; Jeanine Basinger, *The World War II Combat Film: Anatomy of a Genre,* with an updated filmography by Jeremy Arnold (1986; repr., Middletown, CT: Wesleyan University Press, 2003), 138–39; Doherty, *Projections of War,* 272–74.

33. *Fighter Squadron,* dir. Raoul Walsh, 96 min., Warner Bros. Pictures, 1948 (Turner Entertainment and Warner Bros. Entertainment, 2010, DVD). The over 14,000 aerial missions on D-Day that assured Allied aerial dominance dwarfed the 319 sorties mustered by the German defenders. John W. Huston, "Air Leadership and Overlord," in *The Greatest Thing We Have Ever Attempted: Historical Perspectives on the Normandy Campaign,* ed. Steven Weingartner (Wheaton, IL: Cantigny First Division Foundation, 1998), 113.

34. As one example, consider a series of parades and speeches that took place in Philadelphia during June 1945. See "Proclamation by the Philadelphia Citizens Committee in Honor of Returning Heroes," June 4, 1945, Folder—Philadelphia celebration for returning WWII heroes, Elwood R. Quesada Papers, DDEL.

35. Frank S. Adams, "Citizen Army 'Core' Urged By Bradley," *New York Times,* June 6, 1945.

36. Kammen, *Mystic Chords of Memory,* 13.

37. Piehler, *Remembering War the American Way,* 158.

38. Ibid.

39. Michael Dolski, "'Dead Man's Nothin' But a Corpse': Forgetting the Korean War," (paper presented at Society of Military History annual conference, U.S. Army Historical Foundation, Arlington, VA, May 11, 2012).

40. "We Strike: D-Day in Korea," *New York Times,* September 17, 1950.

41. As quoted in David Halberstam, *The Coldest Winter: America and the Korean War* (New York: Hyperion, 2007), 301.

42. The U.S. Armed Forces Staff College had used a D-Day case study in one course for the 1949 academic year. With the outbreak of the Korean War in June 1950, that case study appeared once again for the next academic year. U.S. Armed Forces Staff College, *The Invasion of Normandy: Operation Neptune* (N.p., 1949, 1950). Copy at U.S. Army Heritage and Education Center, Carlisle, Pennsylvania. Hereafter referred to as AHEC.

43. For an examination of some contemporary discussions on military strategy and operational matters, see Hal M. Friedman, "Reactions and Non-Reactions: Lessons of the Korean War and the Public Debate over Containment and American National Military Strategy, 1950–1955," *U.S. Military History Review* 1 (December 2014): 3–24.

44. Derrill M. Daniel, "Landings at Oran, Gela and Omaha Beaches (An Infantry Battalion Commander's Observations)," unpublished paper, 1950. Copy at AHEC.

45. Eisenhower, *Crusade in Europe,* 167–68, 194, 198. Bradley singled out Bernard L. Montgomery, damning him with faint praise while lambasting Montgomery's inability to capture Caen on D-Day as planned. Bradley, *A Soldier's Story,* 193, 208, 241.

46. Harrison, *Cross-Channel Attack*, 1, 448 (quotes); on the forgiving treatment of the battle, see 101, 174, 193–97, 274, 284, 448.

47. Jerome de Groot, *Consuming History: Historians and Heritage in Contemporary Popular Culture* (New York: Routledge, 2009), 33.

48. Samuel Fuller, with Christa Lang Fuller and Jerome Henry Rudes, *A Third Face: My Tale of Writing, Fighting, and Filmmaking* (New York: Knopf, 2002), 123.

49. Ibid., 262; Lisa Dombrowski, *The Films of Samuel Fuller: If You Die, I'll Kill You!* (Middletown, CT: Wesleyan University Press, 2008), 40–50; *The Steel Helmet,* dir. Sam Fuller, 85 min., Lippert Pictures, 1951 (Criterion Collection, 2007, DVD). Fuller and his wife, Marta, visited Normandy in 1954. Marta wrote that instead of expatiating some of the horrors with this visit, Fuller focused on making a film portrayal of D-Day, which did not come together for twenty years. Letter, Marta Fuller to Marty Weiser, July 31, 1954, Folder—Marty Weiser Papers, 22.f-670, Fuller, Samuel, 1954–1972, Marty Weiser Papers, Special Collections, Margaret Herrick Library, Academy of Motion Picture Arts and Sciences, Beverly Hills, CA. Hereafter referred to as MHL.

50. One soldier complained about the hedgerows inland from the beaches. Another soldier argued that commanders *had* considered the hedgerows but skipped preparations for them because of deception efforts to confuse the Germans.

51. *Breakthrough*, dir. Lewis Seiler, 91 min., Warner Bros. Pictures, 1950 (1994, VHS).

52. Doherty, *Projections of War,* 282. Doherty's next line holds that "Vietnam erased that image," a development that forms the central component of analysis in chapter 4 of this book.

53. "D-Day," *Victory at Sea,* dir. M. Clay Adams, 27 min., National Broadcasting Company, 1953 (distributed by A&E Home Video, DVD, 2003). The D-Day episode originally aired on February 15, 1953.

54. As quoted in Kershaw, *The Bedford Boys,* 225–29; Hill, "Memorializing Community Grief," 92–96.

55. Kershaw, *The Bedford Boys,* 228.

56. The Army-McCarthy hearings formed part of Wisconsin senator Joseph McCarthy's overzealous anti-Communist crusade. McCarthy's name came to denote rabid efforts to combat Communist influence at home. Such actions often included assaults on civil liberties, which seemed less important than the need to ferret out and crush potential enemies. McCarthy's fall came as a result of his unrestrained publicity-seeking attacks on major institutions of American society, in this case the U.S. Army. Shown on national television, McCarthy's outlandish calumnies undermined his last shred of credibility. People heard tales of the army's honorable actions on D-Day at the same time that the senator argued that Communist stooges dominated the service. For more on McCarthy, see Ellen Schrecker, *Many Are the Crimes: McCarthyism in America* (Princeton, NJ: Princeton University Press, 1999), esp. chapter 7.

57. For this point, see Walter Cronkite's interview of Eisenhower, recorded in 1963 for a documentary to celebrate the upcoming twentieth anniversary of D-Day. "D-day Plus 20 Years: Eisenhower Returns to Normandy," CBS Reports, 123 min., Columbia Broadcasting Systems, 1964 (Ambrose Video Publishing, 1990, VHS), CRC.

58. Michael Korda, *Ike: An American Hero* (New York: HarperCollins, 2007), 651–52.

59. Text of speech delivered by Dwight D. Eisenhower in Philadelphia, Pennsylvania, September 4, 1952, Folder 9-4-52, Philadelphia, Pennsylvania, Convention Hall, Stephen Benedict Papers, DDEL. The word "crusade" appeared in speeches he gave in South Bend, Indiana (September 15), New Orleans, Louisiana (October 12), and Worcester, Massachusetts (October 20), where he insisted, "The crusade in Europe was, indeed, a crusade" (emphasis in original). Copies of these speeches remain in the Stephen Benedict Papers, boxes 1–6, DDEL.

60. For the tortuous relations between France and the United States in the early 1950s, see Fredrik Logevall, *Embers of War: The Fall of an Empire and the Making of America's Vietnam* (New York: Random House, 2012). See also Appy, *American Reckoning*, 39.

61. President's Statement on the Tenth Anniversary of D-Day, June 6, 1954, Folder Speech—June 6, 1954—D-Day Statement, Bryce N. Harlow Records, DDEL. The same folder contains the proposed draft from the State Department. A memorandum included with the draft explained the four goals State sought with the speech: "To improve our relations with England and France, To make the Zhukov experiment, To give a nod toward the people of Germany and Japan, [and] To draw a distinction between the peoples of the Soviet Union and their government." Memorandum, Bryce N. Harlow to President Eisenhower, June 2, 1954. The imperatives to preserve security while avoiding warfare coexisted throughout the Eisenhower presidency. The 1953–54 period provided an opportune moment to relax tensions after Stalin died, allowing new leaders to rise to power and an armistice to take effect in Korea. Unfortunately, on neither side of the Iron Curtain did mutual suspicions decrease. Furthermore, the Soviet peace offensive in that period formed a challenge that Eisenhower felt compelled to contest. Melvyn Leffler, *For the Soul of Mankind: The United States, the Soviet Union, and the Cold War* (New York: Hill and Wang, 2007), 135.

62. Kershaw, *The Bedford Boys*, 228.

63. Kammen, *Mystic Chords of Memory*, 573–81.

64. For more on religious developments throughout America in this initial postwar decade, see Robert Wunthnow, *The Restructuring of American Religion: Society and Faith since World War II* (Princeton, NJ: Princeton University Press, 1988), esp. chapters 2 and 3.

65. For more on this period of the Franco-Vietnamese conflict, see Neil Sheehan's *A Bright Shining Lie: John Paul Vann and America in Vietnam* (New York: Vintage Books, 1988).

CHAPTER 3

1. The quoted text comes from the translated memorandum, René Coty, "Message from the President of the Republic at the Dedication of the American Military Cemeteries in France," July 18, 1956, binder titled "American Battle Monuments Commission Dedication Ceremonies 1956," n.d., Records of the American Battle Monuments Commission, Record Group (RG) 117, NACP.

2. "Headquarters 26th Infantry Regiment APO139 US Army," February 15, 1955, Folder 1994.93, CFDM.

3. American and French officials signed the treaty on March 19, 1956. Transcript of Treaty, "American Dead in World War II," Folder—Agreements—Prior Years Reference Real Property Title, Facilities and Acquisition (FAA) 2, Records of the American Battle Monuments Commission, RG 117, NACP.

4. Dwight D. Eisenhower, "To Those Who Participate In The Dedication At St. Laurent," July 7, 1956, binder titled "American Battle Monuments Commission Dedication Ceremonies 1956."

5 Bodnar, *The "Good War" in American Memory,* 86.

6. The totemic invocation of these numbers in later productions mirrored the fixation on the 620,000 Americans killed in the U.S. Civil War. See Drew Gilpin Faust, *The Republic of Suffering: Death and the American Civil War* (New York: Alfred A. Knopf, 2008), chapter 8.

7. Kammen, *Mystic Chords of Memory,* 342–43, 531, 700; Mosse, *Fallen Soldiers,* 3–16.

8. Estimates of the number of deaths have grown over time. Gordon Harrison argued in 1951 that U.S. casualties (wounded, captured, and killed) totaled about 2,500. Harrison, *Cross-Channel Attack,* 329–30. Harrison explained in a footnote that his was "frankly a guess, based on a number of estimates of various dates and various headquarters, none of which agree." By the early 2000s, the National D-Day Memorial Foundation expanded that figure to 2,500 American *dead.* "Sol [Standards of Learning] Education Packet," National D-Day Memorial Foundation, 2002; "The National D-Day Memorial: D-Day Plaque Project," 2013, http://www.dday.org/component/content/article/42-the-memorial/programs/75–d-day-programs (accessed October 3, 2014). On numbers, see also Murray and Millett, *A War to Be Won,* 422.

9. Marianna Torgovnick, *The War Complex: World War II in Our Time* (Chicago: University of Chicago Press, 2005), 41–42. Michael Kammen described an "anomalous pattern of factual ignorance despite broader familiarity with subjective and contextual historical realities." With the public discussion of D-Day and the cemetery, the specifics on losses for the day of battle often remained vaguely defined at best. Kammen, *Mystic Chords of Memory,* 655.

10. Edwards, "War and Collective Memory," 199; William I. Hitchcock, *The Struggle for Europe: The Turbulent History of a Divided Continent 1945–2002* (New York: Doubleday, 2003), 180-81.

11. Archival holdings contain a series of draft letters from the Citizens for Eisenhower Committee. The "Fourmore Crusade" figured prominently throughout these letters. See, Folder—Citizens for Eisenhower, 1956, Citizens for Eisenhower Files of Young and Rubicam, Inc., 1952–61, Young and Rubicam Papers, DDEL.

12. "The President's News Conference of June 6, 1956," *Public Papers of the Presidents of the United States: Dwight D. Eisenhower, 1956* (Washington, DC: General Services Administration, National Archives and Records Service, Federal Register Division, 1958), 553–68.

13. *Campaign Statements of Dwight D. Eisenhower: A Reference Index,* n.p., n.d. [1976?], 381, DDEL.

14. Foner, *Story of American Freedom,* 260.

15. The ABMC has published pamphlets on the cemeteries since at least 1957. Those unable to visit the cemetery could browse booklets with photos, histories, and interpretive guidance on the monuments. Pamphlet, *Normandy American Cemetery and Memorial* (Washington, DC: American Battle Monuments Commission, 1957), accessed at AHEC.

16. Edwards, "War and Collective Memory," 170; Kammen, *Mystic Chords of Memory*, 547. Examples of "pilgrimages" to Normandy appeared in U.S. news stories (1952) and *Bridgehead Sentinel* articles (1953). The CFDM holds copies of the *Bridgehead Sentinel*, the newsletter of the Society of the First Division.

17. Edwards, "War and Collective Memory," 159. Emphasis in original. Compare Piehler, *Remembering War the American Way,* 101–5; G. Kurt Piehler, "The War Dead and the Gold Star: American Commemoration of the First World War," in *Commemorations: The Politics of National Identity,* ed. John R. Gillis (Princeton, NJ: Princeton University Press), 168–85.

18. Foner, *Story of American Freedom,* xiv, 252

19. Kammen, *Mystic Chords of Memory,* 590–610; Jon Wiener, "Civil War, Cold War, Civil Rights: The Civil War Centennial in Context, 1960–1965," in Fahs and Waugh, *Memory of the Civil War in American Culture,* 237–57.

20. Foner, *Story of American Freedom,* xiv.

21. James Lawton Collins complained in 1955 after noticing that "there was no appropriate marker on Utah Beach to commemorate the landings there of the 4th Division, VII Corps, or First Army." As quoted in Memorandum 215, BG Thomas North, ABMC, "Memorandum for Members of the Commission," November 18, 1955, Folder 300.6 Memoranda for ABMC 1955, Records of the American Battle Monuments Commission, RG 117, NACP.

22. William Bradford Huie, *The Americanization of Emily* (1959; New York: Signet, 1964), 33, 101–2, 112, 122–23.

23. Ibid., 65–66.

24. William Bradford Huie, *The Revolt of Mamie Stover* (New York: Duell, Sloan and Pearce, 1951); *The Execution of Private Slovik: The Hitherto Secret Story of the Only American Soldier since 1864 to Be Shot for Desertion* (New York: Duell, Sloan and Pearce, 1954); *The Klansman* (New York: Delacorte Press, 1967). Each of these also appeared in film versions in 1956, 1974, and 1974, respectively.

25. Samuel Eliot Morison, *History of United States Naval Operations in World War II,* vol. 9, *The Invasion of France and Germany, 1944–1945* (1957; repr., Edison, NJ: Castle Books, 2001), 87, 110.

26. Bliven, *Story of D-Day,* vii, 3, 81, 127. For more on the heroic efforts of the few, see 9, 59–61, 72, 99, 120.

27. Ryan, foreword, *The Longest Day*, n.p. [9].

28. Letter, Cornelius Ryan to Peter Schwed, February 24, 1959, Folder—The Longest Day Correspondence Release Sheet etc, "The Longest Day" records, CRC. Emphasis in original.

29. Letter, Cornelius Ryan to Miss Frances Ward [his research assistant in Europe], July 1, 1958, Folder—Readers Digest Correspondence between Ryan and Ward (Europe) & Lang, "The Longest Day" records, CRC.

30. Ryan, *The Longest Day,* 54, 177, 191, 196.

31. Gordon A. Craig, review of *The Longest Day,* by Cornelius Ryan, *New York Herald Tribune,* November 22, 1959; Hanson Baldwin, "D-Day—This Is the Way It Was," *New York Times Magazine,* May 31, 1959; Letter, BG John P. Cooper, Jr., to Cornelius Ryan, November 10, 1959, Folder—Ryan, Cornelius, Letters and Correspondence—Fan Mail A–J 1959–63, Miscellaneous

Supplementary Material records, CRC. The CRC holds a variety of newspaper clippings, fan letters, and errata that Ryan collected. Aside from full boxes, the collection includes several hefty scrapbooks full of praise for *The Longest Day.* The scrapbooks and several of these boxes remain in "The Longest Day" records, while a few additional boxes appear in the Miscellaneous Supplementary Material records.

32. Letter, George H. W. Bush to Cornelius Ryan, 15 June 1960, Folder—Ryan, Cornelius, Letters and Correspondence—Fan Mail A–J 1959–63, Miscellaneous Supplementary Material records, CRC.

33. "D-Day," *You Are There,* 30 min., CB-Television Network Production, 1955 (March 6), VHS, UFTA.

34. *D-Day, the Sixth of June,* dir. Henry Koster, 106 min., Twentieth Century–Fox, 1956 (Twentieth Century–Fox Home Entertainment, 2002, DVD). Film reviewer Arthur Knight caustically argued that "for perhaps ten minutes this film lingers close enough to the events of that day to justify its title." See his "review of *D-Day, the Sixth of June,*" *Saturday Review,* June 16, 1956, Folder—D-Day, The Sixth of June, 20th Century–Fox, 1956, Former Title: The Sixth of June, Core Collection, MHL.

35. I thank Sam Edwards for offering his insightful reading on this particular film. Sam Edwards, "The Beginning of the End: D-Day in British Cultural Memory" (paper presented at Society of Military History annual conference, Virginia Military Institute, Lexington, VA, May 22, 2010).

36. Lionel Shapiro, Author's Note, *The Sixth of June: A Novel of World War II* (New York: Doubleday, 1955), n.p. The battle appears at the end of the book, from pages 298 to 347.

37. Basinger, *World War II Combat Film,* 291.

38. Some critics rejected the fanciful depiction of battle. See, for instance, Bosley Crowther, "Screen: War through a Rosy Lens," *New York Times*, May 30, 1956.

39. Letter, Charles Brackett to Robert J. Wright (veteran), 6 March 1957, Folder Charles Brackett papers 1.f-[21] D-DAY, THE SIXTH OF JUNE—correspondence, Charles Brackett papers, Special Collections, MHL. Perhaps reflecting limited interest, the 1958 film adaptation of Irwin Shaw's *The Young Lions* skipped entirely over that book's D-Day scene. *The Young Lions,* dir. Edward Dmytryk, 167 min., Twentieth Century–Fox, 1958 (Twentieth Century–Fox Home Entertainment, 2002, DVD). Shaw served as a writer on a film unit that covered D-Day.

40. In a letter Ryan wrote to a publishing house, he pushed the salability of his book in light of the upcoming anniversary. Henry Holt and Company, however, did not accept the proposal. Simon and Schuster ended up publishing Ryan's work in book form, most of which *Reader's Digest* had previously printed in a series of articles. Letter, Cornelius Ryan to William Buckley (Henry Holt & Co.), November 19, 1957, Folder—Original idea letter—Buckley, "The Longest Day" records, CRC.

41. Edwards, "War and Collective Memory," 175–78.

42. Kenneth E. Crouch, "Memorial to 116th Regiment Being Built on Omaha Beach," *Bedford Democrat,* October 23, 1958, Folder Publicity—D-Day Book, "The Longest Day" records, CRC; "D-Day Landing Re-Enacted by Paratroopers," *Chicago Daily Tribune,* June 7, 1959. Eisenhower had no official proclamation; however, he did mention the battle at a June 6 picnic in Gettysburg. "Ike Recalls D-Day, Golfs with Nevins," *Daily Boston Globe,* June 7, 1959.

43. See Folder Orlando Group (1), C. D. Jackson Papers, DDEL.

44. "The Men of 'Overlord,'" *Los Angeles Times,* June 6, 1959.

45. Dwight D. Eisenhower, "Remarks at the Dedication of the Eisenhower Museum, Abilene, Kansas," November 11, 1954, and "Eisenhower Library Dedication, Abilene, Kansas,"

May 1, 1962, Dwight D. Eisenhower Memorial Commission, http://www.eisenhowermemorial.org/speeches/index.htm (accessed December 3, 2010).

46. "First Division Museum Established," *Bridgehead Sentinel,* Winter 1957, 7.

47. The "War Memorial" designation indicated that the museum would commemorate the glory of combat. "Minutes of Meeting of Trustees of Cantigny Trust, October 27, 1958," bound file—Cantigny Trust 1958, CFDM.

48. Farber, *Rise and Fall of Modern American Conservatism,* 25–27. For more on McCormick's isolationism, see Richard Norton Smith, *The Colonel: The Life and Legend of Robert R. McCormick, 1880–1955* (Boston: Houghton Mifflin, 1997), xvii, 501, 512.

49. Memorandum, Henry J. Kelty, November 7, 1960, Folder—Cantigny First Div. 57–60, Box 104 1988.33, Foundation Minutes 51–70, CFDM.

50. Folder 86, Apr 2, 1962, Publicity: Advertisement of Cantigny Museum, Box 1988.31, CFDM.

51. Transcript of Normandy Diorama, Folder—1st Div. Museum Scripts, Exhibits Dioramas Old FDM, CFDM.

52. Ronald Kotulak, "Millionth Visitor to Cantigny Garden Park," *Chicago Tribune,* August 1, 1963.

53. Letter, Henry J. Kelty to Cornelius Ryan, January 22, 1960, Folder—Ryan, Cornelius Letters and Correspondence—Fan Mail K-Z 1959–63, Miscellaneous Supplementary Material records, CRC.

54. Letter, Cornelius Ryan to Paul Gitlin [Ryan's attorney], March 13, 1964, Folder—Ryan, Cornelius, Business Correspondence, Royalty and Commission Statements, "The Longest Day" records, CRC.

55. Leon H. Canfield and Howard B. Wilder, *The Making of Modern America* (Boston: Houghton Mifflin, 1954), 688, 698, 710. This exact same presentation (and pagination) appeared in the next two editions in 1960 and 1966.

56. Thomas A. Bailey, *The American Pageant: A History of the Republic* (Boston: D. C. Heath, 1956), vi, 881, 893–94, 902. The wording and presentation remained constant until the editions in the 1980s.

57. Mel Gussow, *Don't Say Yes Until I Finish Talking: A Biography of Darryl F. Zanuck* (1971; repr., New York: Pocket Books, 1972), 198–201. Emphasis in original.

58. "Advanced Fact Sheet on 'The Longest Day,'" n.d., Folder—Ryan, Cornelius, Printed Matter, The Last Battle #3, Miscellaneous Supplementary Material records, CRC.

59. Suid, *Guts & Glory,* 168–87.

60. See, for instance, his first-draft screenplay dated June 1960, Folder—Screenplay, TLD, 1st Draft, Rough Script, 6.6.60, "The Longest Day" records, CRC.

61. Some disputes included the timing of General Erwin Rommel's departure from France (June 4 or 5), the suitability of a love interest in this war film, and the building used in the Ouistreham assault of the movie (a smaller, recent construction or the older, imposing casino). Zanuck prevailed in each case.

62. Letter, Cornelius Ryan to Kenneth E. Crouch [*Bedford Bulletin-Democrat*], August 20, 1963, Folder—Ryan, Cornelius, Correspondence, Zanuck, Darryl F., Miscellaneous Supplementary Material records, CRC.

63. Darryl F. Zanuck, "The Longest Day Second Revised Story Outline," January 13, 1961, "The Longest Day" records, CRC.

64. Stephen Ambrose, "*The Longest Day* (U.S., 1962): 'Blockbuster' History," in *World War II, Film, and History,* ed. John Whiteclay Chambers II and David Culbert (New York: Oxford University Press, 1996), 98.

65. "Operation Overblown," *Time,* October 19, 1962, http://www.time.com/time/magazine/article/0,9171,827910,00.html (accessed May 28, 2009).

66. Working in black and white helped with incorporating stock combat footage into the movie. Interview with Elmo Williams [by Lawrence Suid], July 11, 1975, Folder—Selections from Department of Defense files relating to the making of the film "The Longest Day"—copies courtesy of Lawrence Suid (3), "The Longest Day" records, CRC.

67. Harry Brand [director of publicity, Twentieth Century–Fox], "'The Longest Day' (Fact Sheet)," n.d., Folder—The Longest Day, 20th Century–Fox 1962, Core Collection, MHL.

68. A point also made by Ambrose, "*The Longest Day,*" 105. Of course, West Germans were engaged in their own war-related remembrance activities at this same time. See Wulf Kansteiner, "Losing the War, Winning the Memory Battle: The Legacy of Nazism, World War II, and the Holocaust in the Federal Republic of Germany," in Lebow, Kansteiner, and Fogu, *The Politics of Memory in Postwar Europe,* 102–10; Jay Lockenour, *Soldiers as Citizens: Former Wehrmacht Officers in the Federal Republic of Germany, 1945–1955* (Lincoln: University of Nebraska Press, 2001), 3, 63–64. In 1949, Hans Speidel, Rommel's chief of staff on D-Day, published a book that indicated the growing German interest in the western battles. Speidel argued that "the invasion of Normandy will forever remain an event of the first order in the history of war" because it had helped to end the Second World War. See Hans Speidel, *Invasion 1944,* trans. Theo R. Crevenna, introduction by Truman Smith (1950; repr., New York: Paperback Library, 1968), 32–35, 62–74, 77–79, 111–19, 156. Compare P. A. Spayd and Gary Wilkins, eds., *Bayerlein: After Action Reports of the Panzer Lehr Division Commander; From D-Day to the Ruhr* (Atglen, PA: Schiffer, 2005), 21–22; Friedrich Ruge, "The Invasion of Normandy," in *Decisive Battles of World War II: The German View,* ed. Hans-Adolf Jacobsen and Jürgen Rohwer, trans. Edward Fitzgerald, introduction by Cyril Falls (1960; repr., New York: G. P. Putnam's Sons, 1965), 317–48. For more on German efforts to confront and/or evade this particular past, see Omer Bartov, *Hitler's Army: Soldiers, Nazis, and War in the Third Reich* (New York: Oxford University Press, 1991); Omer Bartov, Atina Grossman, and Mary Nolan, eds., *Crimes of War: Guilt and Denial in the Twentieth Century* (New York: New Press, 2002), chap. 5; Norbert Frei, *Adenauer's Germany and the Nazi Past: The Politics of Amnesty and Integration,* trans. Joel Golb (New York: Columbia University Press, 2002); Omer Bartov, *Germany's War and the Holocaust: Disputed Histories* (Ithaca, NY: Cornell University Press, 2003); Helmut Schmitz, introduction, *A Nation of Victims? Representations of German Wartime Suffering from 1945 to the Present,* ed. Helmut Schmitz (New York: Rodopi B.V., 2007), 5–13; and Günter Bischof and Michael Maier, "'Sie Kommen': From Defeat to Liberation—German and Austrian Memory of the Allied 'Invasion' of 6 June 1944," in Dolski, Edwards, and Buckley, *D-Day in History and Memory,* 189–220.

69. Gussow, *Don't Say Yes,* 232.

70. Suid, *Guts & Glory,* 185.

71. Philip K. Scheuer, "'Gen.' Darryl Zanuck Takes Normandy, Reviews Battle," *Los Angeles Times,* April 1, 1962.

72. Zanuck advanced that claim in a letter to Lord Louis Mountbatten, as indicated in Gussow, *Don't Say Yes,* 198.

73. Letter, Norman D. Cota to Omar N. Bradley, 22 July 1962, Folder Personal File Correspondence 1956–62, Norman D. Cota Papers, DDEL.

74. Letter, Fred Hift [Twentieth Century–Fox] to Darryl F. Zanuck, February 7, 1961, Folder—Ryan, Cornelius, Printed Matter, The Last Battle, #3, Miscellaneous Supplementary Material records, CRC.

75. Suid, *Guts & Glory,* 188. Compare Philip D. Beidler, *The Good War's Greatest Hits: World War II and American Remembering* (Athens: The University of Georgia Press, 1998), 161.

76. Letter, John M. Steele to James M. Gavin, 18 September 1962, Folder—Ryan, Cornelius, Letters and Correspondence—Fan Mail K–Z, 1959–63, #5, Miscellaneous Supplementary Material records, CRC.

77. John P. Cyr, Study Guide for Darryl F. Zanuck's *The Longest Day,* 1963, Folder—The Longest Day, 20th Century–Fox, 1962, Core Collections, MHL.

78. Ryan, *The Longest Day,* 212.

79. Broadcast for the anniversary in 1964, *D-Day Plus 20 Years* was filmed in August 1963.

80. Memorandum of Conference with Former President Eisenhower, CBS Productions, May 27, 1963, Folder—TR Trips—Europe, July 30–August 15, 1963 (1), Principal Files, DDEL. On January 23, 1963, CBS Reports aired an interview between Cronkite and Eisenhower that had Ike comparing the presidential reticence in the early phase of the missile crisis to deception operations prior to D-Day. See Transcript, "Eisenhower, 1963," CBS Reports, January 23, 1963, pp. 9–10, Folder—Cronkite, Walter, Interview with DDE, 1–23–63, Principal Files, DDEL.

81. Brinkley, *Cronkite,* 288, 298–300.

82. "Veterans Gather at Omaha Beach," *Atlanta Daily World,* June 6, 1964; Joseph W. Grigg, "Normandy Veterans Show Pride, Tears," *Atlanta Daily World,* June 7, 1964. Chairman of the Joint Chiefs of Staff Maxwell Taylor toured Normandy trying to identify the landing sites of the 101st Airborne Division that he had commanded on D-Day. Richard Goldstein, *America at D-Day: A Book of Remembrance,* preface by Matthew B. Ridgway (New York: Dell, 1994), 275.

83. Martin Blumenson, "D-Day in Retrospect: Could the Germans Have Won?," *Army* 14 (June 1964): 69–75, AHEC.

84. President Johnson signed the compromise Civil Rights Act of 1964 on July 2. See Isserman and Kazin, *America Divided,* 106; Farber, *Age of Great Dreams,* 103–4.

85. Edwards, "War and Collective Memory," 200-2.

86. Lyndon Johnson, "Remarks to the Delegation to the D-Day Ceremonies," 3 June 1964, *Public Papers of the Presidents of the United States, Lyndon B. Johnson, 1963–64,* 746–47, EBSCO Host (accessed June 26, 2009).

87. Veterans of Foreign Wars, *6 June 1944: Twentieth Anniversary of the Normandy Landings at Omaha and Utah Beaches* (Paris: S.P.E.I., 1964); U.S. Congress, House, Committee on Veterans' Affairs, *D-Day Plus 20 Years: June 6, 1944–June 6, 1964,* 88th Congress, 2nd session (Washington, DC: Government Printing Office, 1964).

88. Lifetime attendance reached approximately 644,000 visitors by May. That number increased to nearly 867,000 persons by December, primarily between June and August. Binder, Cantigny First Div. 63–64, Box 104, 1988.33, Foundation Minutes 51–70, CFDM. Omar Bradley emphasized the world-saving importance of D-Day in "Bradley Recalls Omaha Beach," *Chicago Tribune,* May 31, 1964, 9.

89. Records of Proceedings, Eighty-Second Meeting, American Battle Monuments Commission, ABMC, March 10, 1964, Folder—Record of Proceedings, Book III Issuance Management Administration (ADM) 8–4, Records of the American Battle Monuments Commission, RG 117, NACP. On Utah Beach, see Folder 619.3, Utah Beach Memorial, (11–4–55) to (12–31–67), Records of the American Battle Monuments Commission, RG 117, NACP.

90. See the series of letters between M. de Vallavielle and J. Lawton Collins, mostly in April–June 1964, held in Folder—Monuments—Normandy, France (1), J. Lawton Collins papers, DDEL.

91. As quoted in Suid, *Guts & Glory,* 208.

92. Huie, *The Americanization of Emily,* 97–98, had the protagonist sensibly disinclined to risk his life for a publicity stunt. The film's cowardice theme version did not come from the book.

93. *The Americanization of Emily,* dir. Arthur Hiller, 115 min., Metro-Goldwyn-Mayer, 1964 (Warner Home Video, 2006, DVD).

94. In the book, the admiral sought to influence public opinion by sending in a naval photographic unit for coverage. His plan did not center on claiming the first death in the invasion. Huie, *The Americanization of Emily,* 66–67.

95. For a scathing denunciation of the movie, see James Altieri, "A Salvo of Outrage Aimed at 'Emily,'" *Los Angeles Times,* January 10, 1965. Bosley Crowther, "'The Americanization of Emily' Arrives," *New York Times,* October 28, 1964, is more approving.

96. Hiller later remarked, "I feel happiest about *Emily* because I somehow managed to do what I had intended to do." He had intended to make an antiwar movie. See Mark Deimel, "The Americanization of Canadian Director Hiller," *Bruin Index* (UCLA), February 26, 1980, Folder—Hiller, Arthur (magazine articles), Core Collection, MHL.

97. Leonard J. Leff, "A Test of American Film Censorship: *Who's Afraid of Virginia Woolf?* (1966)," in *Hollywood as Historian: American Film in a Cultural Context,* ed. Peter C. Rollins (Lexington: University Press of Kentucky, 1983), 211–29.

98. Ambrose, "*The Longest Day,*" 102. Ambrose declared that because of the sanitized deaths, *The Longest Day* "is so far remote from reality that it seems little more than Hollywood fantasy."

99. Geoffrey Shurlock, head of the Code Administration, felt that *The Longest Day* had "an excessive amount of slaughter." Letter, Geoffrey Shurlock (Production Code Administration) to Frank McCarthy (Twentieth Century–Fox), October 6, 1961, Folder—THE LONGEST DAY, Film year: 1962 (20th Century–Fox, 1962), Production Code Administration records, Special Collections, MHL.

100. MHL holds a series of files on censorship reports. See the following: Folder—Sam Peckinpah Papers, 15.f-169, THE CINCINNATI KID—Ransohoff, Martin 1963–1964, Sam Peckinpah papers, Special Collections; Folder—Motion Picture Association of America, Production Code Administration records, THE AMERICANIZATION OF EMILY 1962–1964; and Folder—Motion Picture Association of America, Production Code Administration records THE AMERICANIZATION OF EMILY 1962–1964, papers, Production Code Administration records, Special Collections, MHL.

101. William B. Huie, *The Americanization of Emily,* Vault Copy, p. 63, February 14, 1962, Folder—Turner/MGM scripts, 9390.f-A-736.f-772, THE AMERICANIZATION OF EMILY, William B. Huie Papers, Special Collections, MHL.

102. Suid described Zanuck's requirement for official military support and the furor that arose over a few ill-chosen statements released during production. Sending military forces (at public expense) to film a movie as world crises flared up (Berlin and Cuba) did not sit well, either. After *The Longest Day,* overt military support for films necessitated strict proof that a project would benefit the service at little or no cost. Suid, *Guts & Glory,* 177–90.

103. Shaun Considine, *Mad as Hell: The Life and Work of Paddy Chayefsky* (New York: Random House, 1994), 217.

104. Basinger, *World War II Combat Film;* Doherty, *Projections of War,* 282.

105. Suid, *Guts & Glory,* 207–9.

106. Lyndon B. Johnson, "Remarks in Lexington at the Dedication of the George C. Marshall Research Library," May 23, 1964, American Presidency Project, http://www.presidency.ucsb.edu/ws/index.php?pid=26264 (accessed December 3, 2010).

107. Ninkovich, *The Wilsonian Century,* 215, 218.

108. Tom Engelhardt, *The End of Victory Culture: Cold War America and the Disillusioning of a Generation* (New York: Basic Books, 1995), 10.

109. Ibid., 222–23; Adams, *The Best War Ever,* 39, 156; Jeffrey Record, *The Specter of Munich: Reconsidering the Lessons of Appeasing Hitler* (Sterling, VA: Potomac Books, 2006); David Elliott, "Parallel Wars?: Can 'Lessons of Vietnam' Be Applied to Iraq?" in *Iraq and the Lessons of Vietnam: Or, How Not to Learn from the Past,* ed. Lloyd Gardner and Marilyn Young (New York: New Press, 2007), 18, 44.

CHAPTER 4

1. Jack Shulimson and Charles M. Johnson, *U.S. Marines in Vietnam: The Landing and the Buildup, 1965* (Washington, DC: Government Printing Office, 1978), 11–15.

2. More people likely had their minds on the first round of the NCAA basketball tournament, which pitted Penn State against Princeton that evening.

3. Farnsworth Fowle, "N.A.A.C.P. Urges Troops in Selma," *New York Times,* March 9, 1965.

4. Frederick Logevall, *Choosing War: The Lost Chance for Peace and the Escalation of War in Vietnam* (Berkeley: University of California Press, 1999), 134–35, 252–53.

5. Ibid., 375. Logevall claimed Johnson opted for war in 1964. George C. Herring, *LBJ and Vietnam: A Different Kind of War* (Austin: University of Texas Press, 1994), 1–3, focuses on the July 1965 surge of American forces.

6. Jack Langguth, "Force 'Strictly Defensive'—Arrival is Protested by Hanoi and Peking," *New York Times,* March 8, 1965.

7. Paul Fussell, *The Great War and Modern Memory* (New York: Oxford University Press, 1975), 3–8, 18.

8. George C. Herring's book, *America's Longest War: The United States and Vietnam, 1950–1975,* 4th ed. (Boston: McGraw Hill, 2002), remains required reading on this conflict.

9. See, for instance, Wilfried Mausbach, "Forlorn Superpower: European Reactions to the American Wars in Vietnam and Iraq," in Gardner and Young, *Iraq and the Lessons of Vietnam,* 59–87.

10. Of course, the similarities between the Korean War and the Vietnam War, in terms of American problems and ignorance pertaining thereto, were overlooked at the time. The purposeful official distancing from the mixed results of the Korean War helped breed a pronounced degree of public disregard for that conflict in collective remembrance, earning it the oft-repeated appellation "The Forgotten War." I treated this phenomenon in my conference presentation "'Dead Man's Nothin' But a Corpse.'"

11. Hunt, *Ideology and U.S. Foreign Policy,* 16; Foner, *Story of American Freedom,* xiii-xiv, 254–55.

12. Sherry, *In the Shadow of War,* 124.

13. Bacevich, *New American Militarism,* 2.

14. Lyndon B. Johnson, "The President's News Conference," July 28, 1965, American Presidency Project, http://www.presidency.ucsb.edu/ws/index.php?pid=27116&st=&st1 (accessed December 20, 2010).

15. Lyndon B. Johnson, "Statement by the President Upon Ordering Troops into the Dominican Republic," April 28, 1965, American Presidency Project, http://www.presidency.ucsb.edu/ws/index.php?pid=26922&st=&st1 (accessed December 20, 2010).

16. Early official proclamations about American intent to preserve freedom in South Vietnam clashed with (unstated, until later) more realpolitik motives to burnish America's reputation while hemming in China by surrounding it with hostile countries. See Lloyd Gardner and Marilyn Young, introduction, in Gardner and Young, *Iraq and the Lessons of Vietnam,* 6–7.

17. In 1965, for instance, he wrote a letter of support for the British effort to complete the nave for the St. Thomas Cathedral in Portsmouth. A major naval base located in southern England, Portsmouth had served as one of the key staging areas for D-Day. Dwight D. Eisenhower, Open Letter to Residents of Portsmouth, May 19, 1965, Folder—Messages—Speeches, Principal Files, DDEL.

18. "General Eisenhower Dedicates D-Day Mural," *Bridgehead Sentinel,* Golden Anniversary Issue, 1917–1967, 34–35, Box—Bridgehead Sentinel, 1953–1978, Smith 1996.113, CFDM. The mural measures 22.5 by 8 feet.

19. Letter, Winfield S. Scott to Dwight D. Eisenhower, June 6, 1967, Folder—TR Alumnae Day, June 2, 1967, Principal Files, DDEL.

20. "Ike Dedicates Mural at Academy," *Washington Post,* June 3, 1967.

21. Letter, Cornelius Ryan to Indro Montanelli, 16 June 1965, Folder—Ryan, Cornelius Printed Matter The Last Battle, Miscellaneous Supplementary Material records, CRC.

22. Records of Proceedings Eighty-Third Meeting, American Battle Monuments Commission, January 14, 1966, Folder—Record of Proceedings, Book III Issuance Management Administration (ADM) 8–4, Records of the American Battle Monuments Commission, Record Group (RG) 117, NACP; Edwards, "War and Collective Memory," 215–18.

23. Records of Proceedings, Eighty-Third Meeting, American Battle Monuments Commission, January 14, 1966.

24. Edwards, "War and Collective Memory," 219–42.

25. Engledhardt, *End of Victory Culture,* 10, 55.

26. Historian William Hammond demonstrated that American public opinion had already made the significant turn against the war by the end of 1967, before the much-publicized Tet attacks. Furthermore, he showed that much of the media reporting on Vietnam up to 1968 had tended to support the American cause. William M. Hammond, *Reporting Vietnam: Media and Military at War* (Lawrence: University Press of Kansas, 1998), 75, 234, 291–94. Compare Adrian Lewis, *The American Culture of War: The History of U.S. Military Force from World War II to Operation Iraqi Freedom* (New York: Routledge, 2007), 265–69.

27. Michael Flamm, *Law and Order: Street Crime, Civil Unrest, and the Crisis of Liberalism in the 1960s* (New York: Columbia University Press, 2005), 162–63.

28. As quoted in Edwards, "War and Collective Memory," 230–34. The construction costs for these monuments ranged from $20,000 to $50,000, far less than the originally planned $250,000 for the ABMC Utah Beach marker. The costs for the aborted monument actually came close to doubling, by later estimates. See also Jacob Devers, Memorandum for the Record, July 10, 1969, Folder—Priv Spons, Foreign & Other Govt., 1969–73, General File Facilities Maintenance (FAM) 5–7, Records of the American Battle Monuments Commission, RG 117, NACP.

29. *D-Day Revisited,* dir. Darryl F. Zanuck, 52 min., Twentieth Century–Fox Film Corporation, 1968 [broadcast May 30, 1969] (Twentieth Century–Fox Home Entertainment, 2006, DVD).

30. Congressman Frank Horton (R-NY) wrote a letter to *TV Guide* denouncing Zanuck's documentary as merely a promotion for the impending rerelease of *The Longest Day* in American theaters." Cornelius Ryan wrote letters denouncing Zanuck as the "last of the great vulgarians." He pointed out "the 'D' in D-Day does not stand for Darryl." Frank Horton, Letter to the Editor, *TV Guide,* Los Angeles Metro edition, n.d. [July 1969?], Folder—George Stevens papers, 308.f-3559, D-Day 1960, 1969, George Stevens Papers, Special Collections, MHL; Letter, Cornelius Ryan to Ben Wright (his attorney), April 8, 1969, Folder—Ryan, Cornelius, Letters

and Correspondence, Bradley, Mrs. Omar, Miscellaneous Supplementary Material records, CRC; Letter, Cornelius Ryan to Amanda Macintosh, June 17, 1969, Folder—Ryan, Cornelius, Letters and Correspondence, Zanuck, Darryl F., Miscellaneous Supplementary Material records, CRC.

31. Letter, Paul Gitlin to Cornelius Ryan, October 3, 1968, Folder—Ryan, Cornelius, Business Correspondence, Royalty and Commission Statements, Miscellaneous Supplementary Material records, CRC.

32. The time capsule contained press clippings from June 1944 covering D-Day.

33. Transcript of CBS News Special "Some Friends of General Eisenhower," March 29, 1969, Folder—Eisenhower, President, Death of, Robert S. Anderson Papers, DDEL.

34. Eisenhower had insisted to the staff, "Be sure to include the viewpoint of the man who did the fighting." John E. Wickam [director of the library], introduction, *D-Day 1944: Combat Art* (Abilene, KS: Dwight D. Eisenhower Library, 1969), 3. Both AHEC and DDEL hold copies of this booklet.

35. The Eisenhower Foundation, *D-Day: The Normandy Invasion in Retrospect,* foreword by Omar N. Bradley (Lawrence: University Press of Kansas, 1971), 9, 42, 53.

36. Hammond, *Reporting Vietnam,* 121. Although by late 1967 most Americans opposed the war, the opposition split between those refuting the war outright and those still hoping to win and only opposing to faulty policies.

37. Richard Nixon, "D-Day Twenty-fifth Anniversary Day: By the President of the United States of America, A Proclamation," May 31, 1969, Folder—D-Day, 25th Anniversary of Proclamation by President Richard Nixon, Dwight D. Eisenhower Library Collections, DDEL.

38. "Men Who Freed Normandy Come Back to Mark D-Day," *Baltimore Sun,* June 7, 1969.

39. The American Legion, *6 June 1944: Twenty Fifth Anniversary of the Normandy Landings at Omaha and Utah Beaches* (Paris: American Legion, Department of France, 1969), 7, 23, 29.

40. Marcel Wallenstein, "Omaha Beach Graves Mark Invasion Site," *Chicago Tribune,* June 6, 1969.

41. MacDonald, *The Mighty Endeavor,* 257–79.

42. *Patton,* dir. Franklin J. Schaffner, 172 min., Twentieth Century-Fox, 1970 (Twentieth Century-Fox Home Entertainment, 2008, DVD).

43. Suid, *Guts & Glory,* 273–77. Appy, *American Reckoning,* 90 indicates that President Nixon viewed this movie at least five times during the late spring of 1970.

44. Lieutenant General George S. Patton Jr. missed the D-Day invasion. After slapping shell-shocked soldiers under his command in Sicily in August 1943, Patton nearly went home in disgrace. He had temporarily lost command, but his misfortune panned out for Allied deception efforts concerning the Normandy invasion. In the months leading up to the June landings, Patton led a fictitious army that helped confuse the German defenders worried about multiple Allied invasions. With forces stationed more in the Pas de Calais region, where Patton supposedly hoped to attack, the Allies confronted only a fraction of German units in Normandy during the initial weeks of the invasion. Patton's allure as a successful battlefield leader may have convinced the German high command that without him in Normandy, the Allies had yet to shoot their main amphibious bolt. Carlo D'Este, *Patton: A Genius for War* (New York: HarperCollins, 1995), 585–600.

45. On the Cambodian operation, see John Shaw's insightful account, *The Cambodian Campaign: The 1970 Offensive and America's Vietnam War* (Lawrence: University Press of Kansas, 2005). For details on violence in the United States during 1970, see Appy, *American Reckoning,* 183–93, 201–6.

46. For more on the negotiation and ceasefire, see Gareth Porter, *A Peace Denied: The United States, Vietnam, and the Paris Agreement* (Bloomington: Indiana University Press, 1975).

47. Taylor Downing, "History on Television: The Making of *Cold War,* 1998," in *The Historical Film: History and Memory in Media,* ed. Marcia Landy (New Brunswick, NJ: Rutgers University Press, 2001), 295.

48. *The World at War,* dir. John Pett, 1,352 min., Thames Television and the Imperial War Museum, 1973–74 (A&E Home Video, 2004, DVD). For more on the series, see the official website, http://www.theworldatwar.com/. While largely a standard recounting of the invasion, *The World at War* did include scenes of the horrendous destruction the Allies wrought on the French countryside in the name of liberation. Although the few French people interviewed expressed nothing but gratitude, the screen showed a landscape destroyed by the inferno of war.

49. See Folder—Thomas North Papers, Documents pertaining to his retirement 1968, Thomas North Papers, AHEC.

50. "Last Rites for General Wyman," *Bridgehead Sentinel,* Winter 1970, 3–4, 28, Box—Bridgehead Sentinel, 1953–1978, Smith 1996.113, CFDM.

51. Arthur L. Chaitt, "Clarence R. Huebner Lieutenant General USA (Retired) 1888–1972," *Bridgehead Sentinel* (Spring 1973), 1–23, Box—Bridgehead Sentinel, 1973–1974, CFDM.

52. Brinkley, *Boys of Pointe du Hoc,* 98.

53. "'Mike' Kelty Dies," *Bridgehead Sentinel,* Summer 1973, 7, Box—Bridgehead Sentinel, 1973–1974, CFDM.

54. The Cornelius Ryan Collection in the Ohio University library holds a scrapbook full of newspaper articles and obituaries written upon Ryan's death. Almost every excerpt referenced *The Longest Day* as one of the author's key works, many listing the book title in the headline. Scrapbook #10, "The Longest Day" records, CRC.

55. For instance, hemorrhaging financial reserves led American leaders to halt the Bretton Woods international finance order based on U.S. currency listed at a fixed value of gold. Harold James, *International Monetary Cooperation since Bretton Woods* (New York: Oxford University Press, 1996), 205.

56. Edwards, "War and Collective Memory," 242–45.

57. Jonathan C. Randall, "D-Day 30 Years Later," *Washington Post,* June 7, 1974; American Battle Monuments Commission, Annual Report for Fiscal Year 1974, June 30, 1974, Folder—Annual Report—1974, Records of the American Battle Monuments Commission, RG 117, NACP.

58. Veterans of Foreign Wars, *1944–74: Thirty Years After . . . Commemorative Album . . . .* (Paris: Veterans of Foreign Wars, 1974), 8, 22, 32, 38, 42. AHEC collections hold a copy of this booklet.

59. *Overlord,* dir. Stuart Cooper, 84 min., National Film Trustee Co., 1975 (Waltzing Clouds, Inc., Criterion Collection, 2007, DVD).

60. As quoted in "'Overlord' Gets D-Day U.S. Release," *USA Today,* June 7, 2006.

61. Memorandum, Lt. Col. DFC Hartman, OiC Eur (ABMC), Disrepair of Pointe du Hoc site, 18 February 1976, Folder—Pointe du Hoc Correspondence, Records of the American Battle Monuments Commission, RG 117, NACP.

62. Piehler, *Remembering War the American Way,* 132. These activities commemorated sacrifice and assured a continued American presence in Europe.

63. Michael Bilton and Kevin Sim, *Four Hours in My Lai* (New York: Viking, 1992), 20.

64. Jimmy Carter, "Address to the Nation on Energy and National Goals," July 15, 1979, American Presidency Project, http://www.presidency.ucsb.edu/ws/index.php?pid=32596&st=crisis+of+confidence&st (accessed January 2, 2011).

65. David Farber, *Taken Hostage: The Iran Hostage Crisis and America's First Encounter with Radical Islam,* new ed. (Princeton: Princeton University Press, 2006), 1–4.

66. Jimmy Carter, "Meeting with Chancellor Helmut Schmidt of the Federal Republic of Germany Remarks to Reporters Following the Meeting," June 6, 1979, American Presidency Project, http://www.presidency.ucsb.edu/ws/index.php?pid=32442&st=&st1 (accessed January 2, 2011).

67. American Battle Monuments Commission, Annual Report for Fiscal Year 1978, November 7, 1979, Folder—Annual Report—1978, Records of the American Battle Monuments Commission, RG 117, NACP; Jimmy Carter, *White House Diary* (New York: Farrar, Straus and Giroux, 2010), 162.

68. Extolling an ally's defeat in a press conference would have been provocative. Yet D-Day celebrations could include Germans in charitable ways. Carter, however, neglected to release *any* major anniversary statement in 1979. His diary for the preceding week listed many challenges while Americans faced "despair, hopelessness, discouragement, and fear." Carter, *White House Diary,* 323–24, 527.

69. "Bradley Revisits Normandy Beach," *Washington Post,* June 7, 1979.

70. Letter, Brigadier General John W. Donaldson, OiC Eur (ABMC) to Major A. J. Adams (ABMC), June 11, 1979, Folder—Pointe du Hoc Correspondence, Records of the American Battle Monuments Commission, RG 117, NACP.

71. For consumption and brand identity in historical memorabilia, I have drawn on de Groot, *Consuming History,* 241–42.

72. Ronald Smelser and Edward J. Davies II, *The Myth of the Eastern Front: The Nazi-Soviet War in American Popular Culture* (New York: Cambridge University Press, 2008), 187.

73. *D-Day,* Avalon Hill, 1961, 1977. Strategic Simulations Incorporated followed suit with *The Atlantic Wall,* its version of a D-Day board game, in 1978; and Avalon returned with the massive 1980 game, *The Longest Day.* The latter game required set-up times upwards of eight to ten hours and played out over several days: these were games for serious, mature players—not young children.

74. de Groot, *Consuming History,* 141–45.

75. Fuller wrote notices and gave interviews for the *Bridgehead Sentinel* in various issues through 1977–78. Copies of these reside in Box—Bridgehead Sentinel, 1953–1978, Smith 1996.113, CFDM.

76. *The Big Red One,* dir. Samuel Fuller, 113 min., United Artists, 1980 (Warner Home Video, 1999, DVD).

77. The (likely) second version of the script Fuller wrote in 1958 did not have that opening line. See Samuel Fuller, "Script for *The Big Red One,*" March 20 1958, Folder 1991.25, Box 1991.25, Script for *The Big Red One,* CFDM.

78. Suid, *Guts & Glory,* 425–27.

79. Basinger, *World War II Combat Film;* Dombrowski, *Films of Samuel Fuller,* 184–91.

80. Suid, *Guts & Glory,* 295–423; William Hagen, "*Apocalypse Now* (1979): Joseph Conrad and the Television War," in *Hollywood as Historian: American Film in a Cultural Context,* ed. Peter C. Rollins (Lexington: University Press of Kentucky, 1983), 230-45; Peter C. Rollins and John E. O'Connor, eds., *Why We Fought: America's Wars in Film and History* (Lexington: University Press of Kentucky, 2008), chapters 17–19; Michael Anderegg, ed., *Inventing Vietnam: The War in Film and Television* (Philadelphia: Temple University Press, 1991).

81. For the junior-level initiative argument, see Ambrose, *D-Day, June 6, 1944;* and Lewis, *Omaha Beach.*

82. Comparisons to *The Longest Day* surfaced frequently in reviews of this new production. The *New York Times* film reviewer Vincent Canby observed, "The movie's battle footage is mostly

small-scale but terrifically effective, especially in a sequence devoted to the 1944 landings at Omaha Beach in Normandy, which is as good as anything in 'The Longest Day.'" Vincent Canby, "Film: 'The Big Red One,' 5 G.I.'s in World War II," *New York Times,* July 18, 1980.

83. R. M. M. Wiener, "Ex-soldier Fuller's dreams realized in 'Big Red One,'" *Boxoffice,* July 21, 1980.

84. For more on the film, see Fuller, *A Third Face,* 219, 324, 382–83, 473–84.

85. Dombrowski, *Films of Samuel Fuller,* 190-91.

86. George Stevens directed the 1959 film version of *The Diary of Anne Frank.* Stevens served with the U.S. Army as a lieutenant colonel in charge of a film unit on D-Day. This unit captured some of the iconic images of the battle. Following the Second World War, after seeing so many horrors, Stevens would only work on somber films. *George Stevens: A Filmmaker's Journey,* dir. George Stevens, Jr., 111 min., Creative Film Center, 1984 (Warner Home Video, 2004, DVD).

87. Jeffrey Shandler, "Aliens in the Wasteland: American Encounters with the Holocaust on 1960s Science Fiction Television," in *The Americanization of the Holocaust,* ed. Hilene Flanzbaum (Baltimore: Johns Hopkins University Press, 1999), 33–44.

88. Peter Novick, *The Holocaust in American Life* (New York: Houghton Mifflin, 1999), 161–69, 187–220.

89. Peter Ehrenhaus, "Why We Fought: Holocaust Memory in Spielberg's *Saving Private Ryan,*" *Critical Studies in Media Communication* 18 (2001): 328–32.

90. Beth Bailey and David Farber, introduction, *America in the Seventies,* ed. Bailey and Farber (Lawrence: University Press of Kansas, 2004), 1–2; Bruce Schulman, *The Seventies: The Great Shift in American Culture, Society, and Politics* (2001; repr., New York: Da Capo Press, 2002), xii–xvi, 254–57.

91. John Bodnar, *Remaking America: Public Memory, Commemoration, and Patriotism in the Twentieth Century* (Princeton, NJ: Princeton University Press, 1992), 206, 227–43.

CHAPTER 5

1. David E. Hoffman, *The Dead Hand: The Untold Story of the Cold War Arms Race and Its Dangerous Legacy* (New York: Doubleday, 2009), 40-45.

2. Ronald Reagan, "Radio Address to the Nation on the Federal Budget and the Western Alliance," May 29, 1982, American Presidency Project, http://www.presidency.ucsb.edu/ws/index.php?pid=42584 (accessed November 22, 2009).

3. Attachment I, Binder titled "American Battle Monuments Commission 102nd Meeting," June 24, 1982, Folder—ABMC Commission Meeting—102nd, June 24, 1982, Records of the American Battle Monuments Commission, Record Group (RG) 117, NACP.

4. Copies of these working drafts reside in Folder 06/06/1982, D-Day Taping for French TV, White House Office of Speechwriting files, Ronald Reagan Presidential Library, Simi Valley, CA. Hereafter referred to as RRL.

5. The speech transcript is located in the binder "American Battle Monuments Commission 102nd Meeting."

6. Enid Nemy, "Mrs. Reagan Visits U.S. Cemetery in Normandy on D-Day Anniversary," *New York Times,* June 7, 1982.

7. Ronald Reagan, "Radio Address to the Nation on the Trip to Europe," June 5, 1982, American Presidency Project, http://www.presidency.ucsb.edu/ws/index.php?pid=42605 (accessed November 22, 2009).

8. Farber, *Rise and Fall of Modern American Conservatism,* 160, 193.

9. Tom Morganthtau, Thomas M. DeFrank, and John Walcott, "The Upstaged Summit," *Newsweek,* June 21, 1982, 34–36.

10. Ronald Reagan, "Address of the President to the United Nations," June 17, 1982, Folder—United Nations Speech (Maseng), June 17, 1982 (1), White House Office of Speechwriting files, RRL.

11. WHORM: Alpha File, Appreciation Letters, Complaints-Criticism, and Support, RRL. D-Day did not appear in Reagan's diary until 1984. Douglas Brinkley, ed., *The Reagan Diaries* (New York: HarperCollins, 2007), 245.

12. Hagopian, *Vietnam War in American Memory,* 11.

13. James T. Patterson, *Restless Giant: The United States from Watergate to* Bush v. Gore (New York: Oxford University Press, 2005), 146–53.

14. Christy Richardson and Judith Waldrop, *Veterans: 2000, Census 2000 Brief,* U.S. Census Bureau (Washington, DC: Government Printing Office, 2003), 2.

15. Edwards, "War and Collective Memory," 245–50.

16. Ibid., 250. The U.S. Eighth Air Force, commanded by Lieutenant General James Doolittle, had conducted preinvasion bombardment operations and bombing sorties on D-Day.

17. Hill, "Memorializing Community Grief," 117.

18. See the folders pertaining to research for E Company, variously labeled, in the boxes named "Winters memories," Richard D. Winters Papers, AHEC.

19. Figures come from the ABMC's Annual Report for Fiscal Year 1979, August 14, 1980, 103; Annual Report for Fiscal Year 1980, September 30, 1980, 92; Annual Report for Fiscal Year 1981, September 30, 1981, 60; and Annual Report for Fiscal Year 1983, September 30, 1983. Each of these reports remains in a separate folder with that report's title, Records of the American Battle Monuments, RG 117, NACP.

20. Thomas Carhart, as quoted in Hagopian, *Vietnam War in American Memory,* 102–4. Hagopian subjected the Wall to thorough analysis throughout this book. For more on the Wall, see Hass, *Carried to the Wall.*

21. Bodnar, *"Good War" in American Memory,* 85–98.

22. The monument dedications came in 1982 for Vietnam, in 1995 for Korea, and in 2004 for the Second World War. A small gazebo listing the names of local people killed in the First World War stands on one side of the Mall.

23. "37 Years Later, D-Day Is Marked in Normandy," *New York Times,* June 7, 1981.

24. Weigley, *Eisenhower's Lieutenants,* 46–52, 85–89.

25. John Keegan, *The Face of Battle* (New York: Viking, 1976).

26. Keegan, *Six Armies in Normandy,* 314–17, 329, 332.

27. See D'Este, *Decision in Normandy,* 13, 17, 66–68, 120, 146, 195, and 476–507 on Montgomery's failings.

28. John Buckley, introduction, *The Normandy Campaign 1944,* 2.

29. Records of Proceedings One Hundred Third Meeting American Battle Monuments Commission, June 9, 1983, Folder—ABMC Commission Meeting—103rd, June 9, 1983, Records of the American Battle Monuments Commission, RG 117, NACP.

30. Gene Krzyzynski, "D-Day '84: Map Strategy Now," *Philadelphia Inquirer,* May 29, 1983.

31. *The Ranger,* November 1983, Folder—Louis F. Lisko, 2d Ranger BN, Ranger BN. Veteran Association Letters/Newsletters, 1963–1993, Louis Lisko Papers, AHEC.

32. Charles Cawthon, "On Omaha Beach," *American Heritage,* October/November 1983, 49.

33. Ronald Reagan, "Remarks at the Annual Convention of the National Association of Evangelicals in Orlando, Florida," March 8, 1983, RRL, http://www.reagan.utexas.edu/archives/speeches/1983/30883b.htm (accessed January 7, 2011).

34. Immerman, *Empire for Liberty,* 204.

35. Ronald Reagan, "Address to the Nation on Events in Lebanon and Grenada," October 27, 1983, RRL, http://www.reagan.utexas.edu/archives/speeches/1983/102783b.htm (accessed January 6, 2011).

36. Terkel, *"The Good War,"* 3, 254–93.

37. Studs Terkel with Sydney Lewis, *Touch and Go: A Memoir* (New York: New Press, 2007), 110.

38. Milton Dank, *D-Day* (New York: Franklin Watts, 1984), 7, 80.

39. de Groot, *Consuming History,* 31.

40. Wood, *Purpose of the Past,* 20.

41. Ronald Reagan, "Presidential Remarks: Departure for Europe," June 1, 1984, Folder—Europe: S lawn Departure—Fri, June 1, 84, White House Office of Speechwriting files, RRL.

42. Ronald Reagan, "Presidential Radio Talk: European Trip," June 2, 1984, Folder—Radio: European Trip, June 2, 1984, Ben/Elizabeth, White House Office of Speechwriting files, RRL.

43. With this point, a serious disagreement emerges between my research and Douglas Brinkley's book on Reagan's 1984 speeches. Brinkley ignored all the memory work on D-Day that appeared before Reagan's speeches. The author simplified a vast, complex, and multiheaded development. Brinkley, *Boys of Pointe du Hoc,* 8.

44. Clark DeLeon, editorial, *Philadelphia Inquirer,* May 28, 1984.

45. Michael E. Ruane, "A Tribute—Remembering 'These Young Heroes' of D-Day," *Philadelphia Inquirer,* June 3, 1984.

46. Otto Friedrich, "D-Day: Every Man was a Hero," *Time,* May 28, 1984, http://www.time.com/time/magazine/article/0,9171,951086,00.html (accessed December 23, 2009).

47. Lance Morrow, "D-Day: Fiftieth Anniversary of June 6, 1944," *Time,* May 28, 1984, http://www.time.com/time/magazine/article/0,9171,951085,00.html (accessed December 23, 2009).

48. Brinkley, *Cronkite,* 572–73.

49. Brinkley, *The Boys of Pointe du Hoc,* 8.

50. See Peggy Noonan, *What I Saw at the Revolution: A Political Life in the Reagan Era* (New York: Random House, 1990), esp. 83–90.

51. Excerpts from both appear in the research materials for the speech found in Folder—President's Trip to Normandy (1), White House Office of Speechwriting files, RRL.

52. Memorandum, "Preserving Peace and Prosperity: The President's Trip to Europe, June 1984 Themes," May 17, 1984, Folder—President's Trip to Normandy (5), White House Office of Speechwriting files, RRL.

53. Brinkley, *Boys of Pointe du Hoc,* 137–38; John Ehrman, *The Eighties: America in the Age of Reagan* (New Haven, CT: Yale University Press, 2005), 84.

54. Reagan admired the pageantry of military forces and French president Mitterrand's speech at Utah Beach, describing that ceremony "the biggest affair." Americans, however, paid more attention then and since to Reagan's speeches. Through exclusion, Utah Beach remained in the background. Brinkley, *The Reagan Diaries,* 245.

55. Brinkley provided a full copy of Reagan's speech in *Boys of Pointe du Hoc,* 225–32. For an audio recording of this speech, see "Ronald Reagan on the 40th Anniversary of D-Day,"

The History Place, n.d., http://www.historyplace.com/speeches/reagan-d-day.htm (accessed March 9, 2007).

56. "Remarks of the President at U.S.-French Ceremony Commemorating D-Day," June 6, 1984, Box—D-Day Anniversary, VOF Dawson, Gen. Smith/Gen. Allen & Gen. Huebner, CFDM.

57. For instance, the *New York Times* reprinted the majority of Reagan's Omaha Beach speech the next day. "Remarks by Reagan in Normandy," *New York Times,* June 7, 1984.

58. Brinkley, *Boys of Pointe du Hoc,* 6, 148.

59. See, for instance, Farber, *Rise and Fall of Modern American Conservatism;* and McGirr, *Suburban Warriors.*

60. Brinkley, *Boys of Pointe du Hoc,* 99–100, 196, 214.

61. See, for instance, Michael E. Ruane, "To Them, D-Day is Forever Fresh," *Philadelphia Inquirer,* June 6, 1984.

62. Edwin Guthman, "Lest We Forget the Rows at the Normandy Cemetery," *Philadelphia Inquirer,* June 10, 1984.

63. Martin Blumenson, "D-Day: Launching the 'Great Crusade,'" *Army* 34 (June 1984): 23, AHEC.

64. *D-Day Plus 40 Years,* 52 min., National Broadcasting Company, 1984, VHS, CFDM.

65. Brokaw, *The Greatest Generation,* xvii–xix. Ted Koppel of ABC recorded a reimagining of D-Day. The broadcast, D-Day Revisited, consisted of a reenacted June 6, 1944, newscast that employed 1980s media technology. The attention remained on the American sectors. Koppel offered his own thoughts in a wrap-up to this bizarre program, which delivered an incongruous rant against media influence on society. Evoking common understandings of Vietnam, he wondered what present media capabilities and approaches would have done to public morale on D-Day. *D-Day Revisited,* 23 min., ABC News, 1984, VHS, DDEL.

66. Mosse, *Fallen Soldiers,* 126.

67. de Groot, *Consuming History,* 10.

68. "Reagan Honors the Heroes of Normandy," *Philadelphia Inquirer,* June 7, 1984.

69. John D. Bulkeley, "Role that PT Boats Played in the Invasion of Normandy on 6 June 1944," n.d., Folder—1984 Fortieth Anniversary of Normandy Invasion, John D. Bulkeley Papers, DDEL. Bulkeley earned the Congressional Medal of Honor for deeds in the Pacific before D-Day, including General MacArthur's 1942 evacuation from Corregidor.

70. Letter, Edward S. Evans to LTG David Grange (Dept. of Army), June 11, 1984, Folder—PA 002 Memorials-Monuments (216001–220000), WHORM: Alpha File, RRL.

71. Letter, Lester H. Terry to Ronald Reagan, July 26, 1984, Folder—PA 002 Memorials-Monuments (240001–245000), WHORM: Alpha File, RRL.

72. Steve Twomey, "Soldiers of Germany Return for D-Day, Too," *Philadelphia Inquirer,* June 5, 1984.

73. Roger Thurow, "Normandy Snub Rankles in West Germany," *Wall Street Journal,* June 6, 1984.

74. The uncertainty provoked by Reagan's Strategic Defense Initiative (SDI, or the "Star Wars" space defense system) and a new round of European-based nuclear weapons deployments by the United States and the Soviet Union added to the sense of mistrust evident on both sides of the divide.

75. Charles Maier, *The Unmasterable Past: History, Holocaust, and German National Identity* (Cambridge, MA: Harvard University Press, 1997), 10-16; Robert G. Moeller, "What Has

'Coming to Terms with the Past' Meant in Post-World War II Germany? From History to Memory to the 'History of Memory,'" *Central European History* 35 (Spring 2002): 229.

76. See Blight, *Race and Reunion.*

77. One reporter writing in Russia noted, "The commemorations in Normandy . . . have been mocked here as an American propaganda show designed to drum into Western Europeans their dependence on United States military might and to further American might for nuclear war in Europe." Ad hominem attacks on Reagan derided him for making training films in the safety of the United States during the Second World War. John F. Burns, "As Allies Recall D-Day, Russians Say It Was Just a Sideshow to Their War," *New York Times,* June 2, 1984.

78. Ehrman, *The Eighties,* 70.

79. Ibid., 84; Brinkley, *Boys of Pointe du Hoc,* 198.

80. Brinkley, *Boys of Pointe du Hoc,* 9–10, 214–16.

81. Letter, Sid Cornell, chairman of San Diego Historical Society's Institute of History, to Michael Deaver, May 18, 1984, Folder—Omaha Beach Remarks, June 6, 1984 (1), White House Office of Speechwriting files, RRL.

CHAPTER 6

1. Memorandum for the record, John Votaw, Discussion of New Museum with Sister Sylvia, October 5, 1988, Folder—Misc Museum 1997.37.4, Box 291, CFDM.

2. Kammen, *Mystic Chords of Memory,* 701.

3. Memorandum, John Votaw, "Future Operation of First Division Museum," May 2, 1986, Folder—References, Box 1997.37.1, CFDM.

4. Transcript of presentation, "To Examine the Research/Archive Function of the Cantigny First Division Museum," 16 May 1988, Folder—Research Center Discussion, CFDM.

5. "Cantigny, Executive Summary," n.d. [June 1988], Folder—New Museum Assessment—June 1988, CFDM.

6. Letter, John Votaw to LTG Frederic J. Brown [CO of the U.S. 4th Army and Ft. Sheridan, IL], August 2, 1988, Folder—New Museum Notes, CFDM.

7. de Groot, *Consuming History,* 236–37.

8. Letter, John Votaw to the Board of Directors, January 22, 1988, Folder—New Museum Notes, CFDM. An article in the *Chicago Tribune* the day after the museum's reopening in 1992 praised the innovative exhibits while favorably commenting upon the museum's success in avoiding war glorification. Glenna Holloway, "A Living Legacy: New Military Museum Highlights the Growing Visibility of Cantigny," *Chicago Tribune,* August 28, 1992.

9. These details come from personal visits to the museum. Melissa Tyre, conversation with author, Wheaton, IL, January 8, 2007; Eric Gillespie, conversation with author, May 14, 2009, Wheaton, IL.

10. Sam Roberts, "Percentage of Veterans Dwindles in Nation," *New York Times,* May 30, 2005.

11. National World War II Glider Pilots website, "Purpose," n.d., http://www.ww2gp.org/purpose.htm (accessed February 3, 2011).

12. Hill, "Memorializing Community Grief," 118–19.

13. Alexander Cochran, "Night Jump Over Normandy: Interview with General James M. Gavin," *Military History,* August 1984, 34–40.

14. Mike Bruton, "A 'D-Day' in the Desert: DeLeon to Defend Title Against Ex-Marine," *Philadelphia Inquirer,* June 5, 1985.

15. United States Government Accountability Office, *Battle of Normandy Foundation: Uncertainties Surround Its Future Viability,* (Washington, DC: General Accounting Office, 1994), 2.

16. Stephen E. Ambrose, *To America: Personal Reflections of an Historian* (New York: Simon and Schuster, 2002), 93–100.

17. See Peter Charles Hoffer, *Past Imperfect: Facts, Fictions, Fraud; American History from Bancroft and Parkman to Ambrose, Bellesiles, Ellis, and Goodwin* (Cambridge, MA: PublicAffairs, 2004), 177–206.

18. Ambrose, *To America,* 123 (quote), 103, 116–17, 126, 132–33, 139–40, 160, 165.

19. Stephen E. Ambrose, *Crazy Horse and Custer: The Parallel Lives of Two American Warriors* (Garden City, NY: Doubleday, 1975).

20. Ambrose, *To America,* 168–72.

21. Ambrose, *Pegasus Bridge,* 9–14, 183.

22. Balkoski, *Beyond the Beachhead,* xiii–xiv, 6, 62–63, 134–35, 218.

23. Patterson, *Restless Giant,* 202.

24. Paul Kennedy, *The Rise and Fall of the Great Powers* (New York: Random House, 1987), 439. Emphases in original.

25. Transcript, Ronald Reagan, "D-Day Message," May 14, 1987, White House Office of Speechwriting files, RRL.

26. Michael Schaller, *Right Turn: American Life in the Reagan-Bush Era, 1980–1992* (New York: Oxford University Press, 2006), 60.

27. See, for instance, the series of letters between ABMC officials and Lou Lisko, Ranger Association Historian, in 1986–87, Folder—Pointe du Hoc Monument, Priv. Spons., Foreign & Other Govt. Facilities Maintenance (FAM) 5–7, Records of the American Battle Monuments, Record Group (RG) 117, NACP.

28. Letter, James Eric Pierce, Chaplain in the Chapel of Four Chaplains, to Ronald Reagan, March 6, 1987, Folder—05/14/1987 Taping: D-Day Memorial Service, White House Office of Speechwriting files, RRL.

29. Following the 1984 TV extravaganza in Normandy, Walter Cronkite experienced a similar transformation into a champion of the veterans. See Brinkley, *Cronkite,* 572.

30. Major General Albert H. Smith, USA (ret.), "Draft Transcript of a Guest Lecture, Operation Overlord," April 18, 1985, Folder—D-Day Info '93–'94, Smith Lecture, CFDM.

31. See the series of letters between Orwin C. Talbott, John Donaldson (ABMC), Joseph Dawson, and Albert Smith, February–April 1988, Folder—First (1st) Division, WWII, 1967–1968, Priv Spon, Foreign & Other Govt Facilities Maintenance (FAM) 5–7, Records of the American Battle Monuments, RG 117, NACP. The quotes come from Letter, Joseph G. Dawson III to Orwin C. Talbott and Albert H. Smith, March 29, 1988. Emphases in original.

32. Transcript of Interview, Lt. JG William M. Harvin by Robert A. Rowe, August 27, 1988, Folder—Robert A. Rowe—Naval Opns—Jefferson Boat Group—Harvin, William M., Robert A. Rowe papers, AHEC.

33. TNT News Release, September 16, 1988, Folder—The Americanization of Emily Metro-Goldwyn-Mayer, 1964, Turner Entertainment Source: THE AMERICANIZATION OF EMILY, Core Collections, MHL.

34. Herman Wouk, *War and Remembrance* (Boston: Little, Brown, 1978); "May–June 1944," *War and Remembrance,* dir. Dan Curtis, 120 min., American Broadcasting Company, 1988 (MPI Home Video, 2003, DVD). The ninth of the twelve episodes depicted the Normandy invasion.

35. Bodnar, *"Good War" in American Memory,* 192.

36. For details on these meetings between Ambrose and the veterans of E Company, see Folder 1—Start of Band of Brothers—May 1989 Reunion [January 15, 1984, March 7, 1990, February 24,

2004, n.d.], Richard D. Winters Papers, AHEC. Richard Winters felt the historical record had slighted the actions of his company on D-Day. In particular, he questioned one book: S. L. A. Marshall, *Night Drop: The American Airborne Invasion of Normandy* (Boston: Little, Brown, 1962).

37. Sydney Rubin, "Memories by the Sea: Tears for the Boys of D-Day," *Philadelphia Inquirer,* June 7, 1989.

38. George H. W. Bush, "Statement on the 45th Anniversary of D-Day," June 6, 1989, American Presidency Project, http://www.presidency.ucsb.edu/ws/index.php?pid=17117&st=&st1 (accessed January 10, 2011).

39. Joseph G. Dawson III, "Omaha Beach, Normandy," June 6, 1989, Folder—Andrus Bio, Box 1994.126, Mason Papers, CFDM.

40. *Twenty-Niner,* July 1989; Meredith L. Butterton, "Omaha Remembered 'Normandy: D-Day Reflections,'" *Twenty-Niner,* November 1989, 11–12, Folder—Robert A. Rowe—Published Material—The Twenty Niner, Robert A. Rowe Papers, AHEC.

41. Orwin Talbott, "The Big Red One Led the Way," June 6, 1989, Folder 1989.115, Box 1989.115, Bernice Hensel + Normandy Time Capsule, Box 385 1989.116, First Division Museum, CFDM.

42. Thomas A. Bailey, *The American Pageant: A History of the Republic,* 1st ed. (Boston: D. C. Heath, 1956), 880–902; Thomas A. Bailey and David M. Kennedy, *The American Pageant: A History of the Republic,* 8th ed., vol. 2 (Boston, D. C. Heath, 1987), 880–902.

43. Hoffer, *Past Imperfect,* 98–115.

44. George H. W. Bush, "Statement on the 45th Anniversary of D-Day."

45. Patterson, *Restless Giant,* 255, 337.

46. For an international comparative perspective on D-Day remembrance, see Michael Dolski, "To Set Free a Suffering Humanity," 388–414; Dolski, Edwards, and Buckley, *D-Day in History and Memory.*

47. Adams, *The Best War Ever,* 2–14, 69–70, 157–58.

48. Hoffman, *The Dead Hand,* 313, 337.

49. George Bush and Brent Scowcroft, *A World Transformed* (New York: Alfred A. Knopf, 1998), 565–66.

50. Adam Kelliher, "Steaming Towards Normandy and an Eisenhower Celebration," *Philadelphia Inquirer,* June 6, 1990.

51. Ellen O'Brien, "Honoring the Legacy of D-Day," *Philadelphia Inquirer,* June 6, 1990.

52. de Groot, *Consuming History,* 34.

53. Transcript, Eldon Wiehe oral history, n.d. (1990-93?), Folder—Wiehe, Eldon, Eisenhower Center, Box—Transcripts, Oral History Interviews, Eisenhower Center, Ru–Z, CFDM.

54. Bodnar, *"Good War" in American Memory,* 234–36.

55. Transcript, John B. Ellery oral history, n.d. [1990–93?], Folder—Ellery, John B., Eisenhower Center, Box—Transcripts, Oral History Interviews, Eisenhower Center, A–Ro, CFDM.

56. Transcript, Buddy Mazzara oral history, n.d. [1990–93?], Folder Mazzara, Buddy, Eisenhower Center, Box—Transcripts Oral History Interviews Eisenhower Center, A–Ro, CFDM.

57. Transcript, Ralph R. Burnett oral history, n.d. [1990–93?], Folder Burnett, Ralph, Eisenhower Center, Box—Transcripts Oral History Interviews Eisenhower Center, A–Ro, CFDM.

58. As quoted in Russell Miller, *Nothing Less Than Victory: The Oral History of D-Day* (New York: William Morrow, 1993), 304.

59. Ibid., 410–12.

60. Alberto Bin, Richard Hill, and Archer Jones, *Desert Storm: A Forgotten War* (Westport, CT: Praeger, 1998), 32.

61. Rick Atkinson, *Crusade: The Untold Story of the Persian Gulf War* (Boston: Houghton Mifflin, 1993), 54–55, 189, 191–95.

62. "29ers Attend Commissioning of U.S.S. Normandy," *Twenty-Niner,* March 1990, Folder Robert A. Rowe—Published Material—The Twenty Niner, Robert A. Rowe Papers, AHEC.

63. Adams, *The Best War Ever,* 4–5, and throughout; Geoffrey Wawro, *Quicksand: America's Pursuit of Power in the Middle East* (New York: Penguin, 2010), 419.

64. Bush and Scowcroft, *A World Transformed,* 486–87.

65. Atkinson, *Crusade,* 4, 476, 497.

66. Fact sheet on "Operation 'Rangers Lead the Way' to 50th Anniversary Commemoration of Ranger Units in 20th Century Ft. Benning, Georgia 17, 18, 19 June 1992," n.d., Folder—Louis F. Lisko, 2d Ranger BN, Ranger BN, Veteran Association Letters/Newsletters 1963–1993, Louis Lisko Papers, AHEC. The operation's name referenced Brigadier General Norman Cota's inspirational command to the Rangers huddled on Omaha Beach.

67. Charles R. Cawthon, *Other Clay: A Remembrance of the World War II Infantry* (Niwot: University Press of Colorado, 1990), 52–67.

68. Stephen E. Ambrose, *Band of Brothers: E Company, 506th Regiment, 101st Airborne from Normandy to Hitler's Eagle's Nest* (1992; repr., New York: Pocket Books, 2002), 3.

69. Ibid., 11, 74. See also, Ambrose, *To America,* 189–92.

70. Stephen E. Ambrose, *D-Day June 6, 1944,* 45–47.

71. Ambrose, *To America,* 201–11. The museum has since changed its name to the National World War II Museum in an effort to acknowledge all d-days throughout the war.

72. Stephen E. Ambrose, "D-Day Revisited," *Military History Quarterly,* Winter 1993, 26–33. The concrete wall stood until well into the afternoon. Because of the size of this double wall, engineers used ten *cases* of TNT to bring it down. Mitchum's ride to glory over the shattered wall in the movie, however, serves as the emotional uplift right before Zanuck ends with a cautionary take on the costs of war. "Longest Day: A Salute to Courage," *History vs. Hollywood,* 50 min., The History Channel, 2001 (Twentieth Century–Fox Home Entertainment, 2006, DVD). Ambrose also appeared in a documentary filmed in 1993, which first aired on the A&E television network the following year. This episode, "D-Day Normandy," formed part of the *Eye on History* series. "D-Day Normandy," *Eye on History,* dir. Don Horan, 45 min., Lou Reda Productions with the U.S. Naval Institute, 1993, VHS, CFDM.

73. United States Government Accountability Office, *Battle of Normandy Foundation,* 1–4.

74. Frances Fukuyama, "The End of History?" *National Interest,* Summer 1989, http://www.wesjones.com/eoh.htm (accessed February 3, 2011); Fukuyama, *The End of History and the Last Man* (New York: Free Press, 1992).

75. Patrick McDowell, "Anticipating the 50th D-Day Anniversary," *Philadelphia Inquirer,* June 6, 1993.

76. "Next June," *Atlanta Daily World,* October 24, 1993.

CHAPTER 7

1. The rereleased books included Bliven, *Story of D-Day;* D'Este, *Decision in Normandy;* Keegan, *Six Armies in Normandy;* and Ryan, *The Longest Day.*

2. Donald M. Goldstein, Katherine V. Dillon, and J. Michael Wenger, introduction, *D-Day Normandy: The Story and Photographs* (New York: Brassey's, 1994), n.p [x].

3. Winter, *Remembering War,* 1. Compare Kammen, *Mystic Chords of Memory,* 533, 625–28, 655–58; and Rosenberg, *A Date Which Will Live,* 116–38.

4. Ambrose, *D-Day, June 6, 1944,* 10, 25–26, 167, 195, 238, 256–57, 344, 579; "Ambrose Backlist Soars," *Publishers Weekly,* August 17, 1998, http://www.publishersweekly.com/pw/print/19980817/21721-pw-ambrose-backlist-soars-.html (accessed March 24, 2011). Several problems appeared in Ambrose's *D-Day.* Citing Alexander Werth's *Russia at War,* Ambrose claimed that even the people of Moscow rejoiced upon hearing of D-Day (507–8). Werth, however, presented no such picture in his book. Soviet officials commented on D-Day at the time, but the battle failed to produce popular celebration. See Werth, *Russia at War, 1941–1945* (New York: E. P. Dutton, 1964), 852–55. Ambrose (417) condemned unnamed "authors," read as Cornelius Ryan, for faulty analyses of the assault at Pointe du Hoc by U.S. Army Rangers. He lambasted claims that the Rangers had conducted a pointless assault because of the German battery's absence from the top of the cliffs. Ryan, however, correctly explained that the Rangers had found the battery and completed their mission in his book *The Longest Day.*

5. Stephen E. Ambrose, "The Meaning of D-Day,"169; H. P. Wilmott, "The Lessons to Be Learned: Perspectives and Reflections," in Weingartner, *Greatest Thing We Have Ever Attempted,* 177–83.

6. Hoffer, *Past Imperfect,* 2, 197, 205–6. Hoffer also demonstrated that Ambrose had plagiarized content, borrowing without due attribution from Balkoski's 1989 book, *Beyond the Beachhead.* Plagiarism plagued Ambrose's entire body of scholarship, but such problems failed to unsettle the man or his growing fan base.

7. de Groot, *Consuming History,* 6, 17–23, 31.

8. Tom Infield, "A D-Day Veterans' Reunion," *Philadelphia Inquirer,* April 26, 1994.

9. Alan Riding, "Ex-G.I.'s Relive Drama on Normandy's Beaches," *New York Times,* May 23, 1994.

10. *Military History Quarterly,* Summer 1994; *American Heritage,* May–June 1994. For details on sales figures, see Deirdre Carmody, "The Media Business," *New York Times,* May 30, 1994.

11. Martin Blumenson, "'Superb Account' of That Fateful Day," review of Ambrose's *D-Day, June 6, 1944,* in *Army* 44 (June 1994): 73; Gen. Gordon R. Sullivan, "D-Day Plus 50 Years," *Army* 44 (June 1994): 26, AHEC. Emphasis added.

12. For one such example, see Douglas Jehl, "Clinton Bids Navy Graduates Heed World War II Lessons," *New York Times,* May 26, 1994. Adding to this atmosphere of rereleased D-Day content, Twentieth Century–Fox decided to profit by issuing a new VHS version of *The Longest Day* for the anniversary. Stephen Hunter, "War Movie Still Falls Far Short, But Hollywood Brings It Back for a Victorious Stand on Video," *Baltimore Sun,* June 6, 1994.

13. Walter Goodman, "Remembering D-Day 50 Years Later," *New York Times,* May 25, 1994.

14. *D-Day: Carolina Liberators,* 90 min., CBS and Spartan Radiocasting, 1994, VHS, CFDM.

15. Jehl, "Clinton Bids Navy Graduates Heed World War II Lessons."

16. Peter Novick, *That Noble Dream: The "Objectivity Question" and the American Historical Profession* (New York: Cambridge University Press, 1988).

17. William J. Clinton, "The President's Radio Address," May 28, 1994, American Presidency Project, http://www.presidency.ucsb.edu/ws/index.php?pid=50255, (accessed November 22, 2009).

18. William J. Clinton, "Remarks at a Memorial Day Ceremony in Arlington, Virginia," May 30, 1994, American Presidency Project, http://www.presidency.ucsb.edu/ws/index.php?pid=50258&st=&st1 (accessed January 14, 2011). Clinton also cited Eisenhower's "fury of an aroused democracy."

19. Transcript, "Interview with Sam Donaldson of ABC News," June 5, 1994, American Presidency Project, http://www.presidency.ucsb.edu/ws/index.php?pid=50293&st=&st1 (accessed January 14, 2011).

20. Transcript, "Interview with Tom Brokaw of NBC News," June 5, 1994, American Presidency Project, http://www.presidency.ucsb.edu/ws/index.php?pid=50294&st=&st1, (accessed January 14, 2011).

21. William J. Clinton, "Remarks Honoring the Role of the United States Navy in the Normandy," June 6, 1994, Folder—MG Albert Smith, Jr., D-Day Anniversary, Box—Rare Books—Research Historian, Normandy, CFDM.

22. William J. Clinton, "Remarks on the 50th Anniversary of D-Day at Pointe du Hoc in Normandy," June 6, 1994, Folder—MG Albert Smith, Jr., D-Day Anniversary, Box—Rare Books—Research Historian, Normandy, CFDM.

23. William J. Clinton, "Remarks on the 50th Anniversary of D-Day at Utah Beach in Normandy," June 6, 1994, Folder—MG Albert Smith, Jr., D-Day Anniversary, Box—Rare Books—Research Historian, Normandy, CFDM.

24. William J. Clinton, "Remarks on the 50th Anniversary of D-Day at the United States Cemetery in Colleville-sur-Mer, France," June 6, 1994, Folder—MG Albert Smith, Jr., D-Day Anniversary, Box—Rare Books—Research Historian, Normandy, CFDM.

25. Naturally, the argument for bold action remained highly selective in application. For a critical discussion of the failure by U.S. officials and the international community at large to halt genocide in the Balkans in this period, see Sarah E. Wagner, *To Know Where He Lies: DNA Technology and the Search for Srebernica's Missing* (Berkeley: University of California Press, 2008), 21–57; and David Kieran, *Forever Vietnam: How a Divisive War Changed American Public Memory* (Amherst: University of Massachusetts Press, 2014), 127–29, 144–45.

26. Significant anniversary celebrations also took place in the United States. Chicago held a June 5 D-Day reenactment on the city's Montrose Beach. An audience of seven hundred thousand stared as re-created Higgins boats discharged nearly five hundred reenactors garbed as American infantrymen. The French ambassador to the United States, Jacques Andreani, hosted a celebratory dinner that evening at Chicago's plush Hotel Sofitel. Pamphlet, *A Grateful Nation Remembers . . . D-Day June 6, 1994,* 1994, Folder 1995.67, D-day, Box 258, CFDM; Robert Becker and Jan Ferris, "City Gives Big 'Thanks' For D-Day Mock Invasion Brings It Home For Thousands," *Chicago Tribune,* June 5, 1994; Pamphlet, *D-day 50th Anniversary Dinner, Hotel Sofitel, 1994,* Folder 1994.152.2, John Franz, Box 236, CFDM.

27. R. W. Apple Jr., "The D-Day Tour: Overview," *New York Times,* June 6, 1994.

28. "Remarks by Walter D Ehlers, MOH on Omaha Beach, Normandy France June 6, 1994," June 6, 1994, Folder 1995.27, Box 255, CFDM. For the citation, see U.S. Army, "Medal of Honor Recipients, WWII (A-F)," 2010, http://www.history.army.mil/html/moh/wwII-a-f.html (accessed January 14, 2011). Compare Whitlock, *The Fighting First,* 346.

29. Joseph T. Dawson, "Introduction of President Clinton at the 50th Anniversary of D-Day," June 6, 1994, Folder—MG Albert Smith, Jr., D-Day Anniversary, Box—Rare Books—Research Historian, Normandy, CFDM.

30. Brinkley, *Cronkite,* 620.

31. Terril Jones, "Heroes Revisit a Decisive Day of Sacrifice and Deliverance," *Philadelphia Inquirer,* June 7, 1994.

32. Hugh Sidey, "Still Brave at Heart," *Time,* June 20, 1994, http://www.time.com/time/printout/0,8816,980933,00.html (accessed January 14, 2011).

33. Linenthal and Engelhardt, *History.*

34. Weingartner, *The Greatest Thing,* 7–17, 169, 177–83.

35. Mansoor, *GI Offensive in Europe,* 1, 133. D-Day also appeared in numerous memoirs, such as Peter Masters's 1997 description of his commando service with the British Army. Peter Masters, *Striking Back: A Jewish Commando's War Against the Nazis,* foreword by Stephen E. Ambrose (Novato, CA: Presidio Press, 1997). Donald Burgett rereleased his 1967 memoir on Allied airborne experiences, *Currahee!,* in 1999. Martin Blumenson's original foreword extolled a story he felt avoided morality lessons, which made "this account of World War II relevant in these days of Vietnam." Thirty years later, however, Stephen Ambrose found a lesson in morality: "Wherever they [Americans] went they brought liberation, freedom, and democracy." Donald R. Burgett, *Currahee! A Screaming Eagle at Normandy,* foreword by Stephen E. Ambrose and introduction by Martin Blumenson (1967; repr., Novato, CA: Presidio Press, 1999), vii, xi.

36. Tom Brokaw, *The Greatest Generation* (New York: Random House, 1998), xviii–xix, xxx, 17–18.

37. Andy Rooney, *My War,* foreword by Tom Brokaw (New York: PublicAffairs, 2000), xiii-xiv.

38. Ibid., 5, 71, 155–61, 310–13.

39. JoAnna McDonald, ed., *The Faces of D-Day* (Redondo Beach, CA: Rank and File Publications, 1998). This book consisted entirely of a series of photographs, some only loosely connected to D-Day.

40. Brian Knowlton, "New Battle of Normandy Rages over U.S. Memorial," *New York Times,* March 1, 1997, http://www.nytimes.com/1997/03/01/news/01iht-wall.t.html?pagewanted=1&pagewanted=print (accessed May 13, 2010).

41. "Tom Hanks," *Inside the Actors Studio,* dir. Jeff Wurtz, 60 min., Bravo Channel, 1999 (December 12), VHS, UFTA.

42. Basinger, *World War II Combat Film,* xii–xiii.

43. Lacy McCrary, "Watching 'Private Ryan,' Veterans Relive the Horrors Years from Omaha Beach, Pain Lingers," *Philadelphia Inquirer,* August 6, 1998. Historian Thomas Childers described an Omaha Beach veteran's reaction to hearing details of one D-Day film in 1999. "Suddenly nightmarish memories came howling up from the catacombs of his long-buried past. He began to shake; he burst into tears and could not stop. The war had returned, and he could not turn it off." Childers, *Soldier from the War Returning,* 272.

44. Carrie Rickey, "Spielberg's Private Battle In 'Saving Private Ryan,'" *Philadelphia Inquirer,* July 19, 1998.

45. Ambrose, *D-Day,* 316–17. The family received a death notice for the third Niland fighting in Burma, along with the two D-Day fatalities. The Niland in Burma, however, survived capture and returned home after the war. For more on the Niland brothers, see Ruggero, *The First Men In,* 321; Roger J. Spiller, "War in the Dark," *American Heritage,* February/March 1999, http://www.americanheritage.com/articles/magazine/ah/1999/1/1999_1_41.shtml (accessed September 2, 2009).

46. Robert Rodat, "'Saving Private Ryan' Production Notes & Synopsis," n.d., Folder—Saving Private Ryan, DreamWorks 1998 (Credits, Synopsis, Productions Notes) (Music Cue Sheet), Core Collections, MHL.

47. "Steven Spielberg," *Inside the Actors Studio,* dir. Jeff Wurtz, 60 min., Bravo Channel, 1999, VHS, UFTA.

48. "Saving Private Ryan Nomination Sheet for the 1998 Academy Awards," Core Collections, MHL.

49. As quoted in John Meroney and Sean Coons, "The Man Who Brought War to Hollywood," TheAtlantic.com, August 27, 2010, http://www.theatlantic.com/culture/archive/2010/08/the-man-who-brought-war-to-hollywood/62070/1/# (accessed January 18, 2011). Compare John Lippman, "Hollywood's Drill Sergeant to the Stars is a Busy Man," *Wall Street Journal*, July 10, 1998.

50. David Ansen, "Celluloid Soldiers," *Newsweek*, July 13, 1998, http://www.newsweek.com/id/93119 (accessed July 27, 2008).

51. "Saving Private Ryan Nomination Sheet for the 1998 Academy Awards."

52. "Steven Spielberg," *Inside the Actors Studio.*

53. Suid, *Guts & Glory*, 636. Emphasis in original.

54. Rickey, "Spielberg's Private Battle."

55. Bill Higgins, "'Ryan' Leaves Them Speechless," *Los Angeles Times*, July 23, 1998.

56. Stephen E. Ambrose, "The Moment of the Century," *American Heritage*, May/June 1998, http://www.americanheritage.com/articles/magazine/ah/1998/3/1998_3_14.shtml (accessed September 2, 2009). The cover of this issue merged a still image from *Saving Private Ryan* alongside one from *The Longest Day.*

57. Jennifer Napier-Pearce, "D-Day Becomes Popular Subject on TV," *Los Angeles Times*, July 24, 1998.

58. Allen, *Until the Last Man Comes Home*, 302–3.

59. A. Susan Owen, "Memory, War and American Identity: *Saving Private Ryan* as Cinematic Jeremiad," *Critical Studies in Media Communication* 19 (2002): 259–65.

60. Basinger, *World War II Combat Film*, 262.

61. Captain John Miller (Tom Hanks) mirrors the main character in the 1950 film *Breakthrough*. Both characters are soft-spoken junior officers and citizen-soldiers who had taught high school English. Several American soldiers in *Saving Private Ryan* shoot and kill German soldiers who attempt to surrender while raising their hands and crying out, "Bitte! Bitte!" (Please! Please!). A similar scene appears in *The Longest Day* (1962).

62. The vaunted realism of *Saving Private Ryan* did not compensate for a variety of problems in the film. Questionable squad tactics, an overage Ranger captain, inept German defenders with incorrect defensive preparations, the overly melodramatic injunction to "earn this" sacrifice right after the cavalry (via air support) arrive to save the day—all countered the assertions of authenticity from the filmmakers. Doherty, *Projections of War*, 308–10; Suid, *Guts & Glory*, 627–37.

63. Andrew Hindes, "'Private Ryan's' Saving Grace," *Variety*, July 20, 1998.

64. As quoted in Higgins, "'Ryan' Leaves Them Speechless."

65. See, for instance, Tom Infield, "Rating 'Private Ryan,'" *Philadelphia Inquirer*, July 26, 1998.

66. In the *Dagwood Dispatch*, the newsletter for the 16th Infantry Regiment Association, a veteran of that 1st Infantry Division component contended that *Saving Private Ryan* "is a movie that every American should see. It depicts better than any words ever could, the Price of Freedom." He argued, "It is a story of sacrifice, duty, honor and country. It is a story of courage, bravery and heroism. It is a story about soldiers. It is a story about America." "Freedom Isn't Free," *Dagwood Dispatches*, October 1998, Box—Dagwood Dispatches, 18th [*sic*] Infantry Regiment Assoc., Jan 1991–, CFDM. Emphasis in original.

67. As quoted in Jon Meacham, "Caught in the Line of Fire," *Newsweek*, July 13, 1998, 50.

68. Neal Gabler, "'Private Ryan' Satisfies Our Longing for Unity," *Los Angeles Times*, August 9, 1998.

69. Instructors at the United States Military Academy at West Point showed the film before conducting a staff ride in Normandy. Craig Mullaney, *The Unforgiving Minute: A Soldier's Education* (New York: Penguin, 2009), 68.

70. For a brief review of some critical assessments, see Ehrenhaus, "Why We Fought," 322–25.

71. John Votaw, "The Ordeal on Omaha Beach," *Bridgehead Sentinel,* Fall 1998, 12, Box—Bridgehead Sentinel, Spring 1997–Fall/Winter 2003, CFDM.

72. William H. Smith, "Saving Private Ryan: A Missed Opportunity for Healing Racial Wounds," *Atlanta Daily World,* August 27, 1998. Compare Ronald Takaki, *Double Victory: A Multicultural History of America in World War II* (New York: Little, Brown, 2000), 31. African Americans had served as coxswains in a barrage balloon unit and as logisticians for the Normandy invasion.

73. Paul Fussell, "Hell and High Water," *London Observer,* August 2, 1998.

74. Spiller, "War in the Dark."

75. David Horton, "Old WWII Films Were No 'Slap in the Face,'" *Los Angeles Times,* July 27, 1998; Fuller, *A Third Face,* 122–23. Fuller wrote, "See, there's no way you can portray war realistically. . . . For moviegoers to get the idea of real combat, you'd have to shoot at them every so often from either side of the screen."

76. See Folder—SAVING PRIVATE RYAN, DreamWorks 1998 (CREDITS, SYNOPSIS, PRODUCTIONS NOTES) (MUSIC CUE SHEET), Core Collections, MHL.

77. Paul Keegan, "Video Games: The Latest Format for Screen Violence," in *Violence in Film and Television,* ed. James D. Torr (San Diego, CA: Greenhaven Press, 2002), 96–98.

78. Spielberg directed and DreamWorks developed the first game in the series: *Medal of Honor,* Electronic Arts, 1999. Dale Dye served as a consultant for this production.

79. de Groot, *Consuming History,* 133–41.

80. Lawrence and Jewett, *Myth of the American Superhero,* 217.

81. Ian Zack, "A New Battle for D-Day Veterans," *New York Times,* March 28, 1999. Analysis of the new Bedford memorial appears in chapter 8.

82. "The Making of the National D-Day Museum," *Save Our History,* 50 min., A&E Television, 1996, VHS, CFDM.

83. Jua Nyla Hutcheson, "A Home for D-Day Memories," *Philadelphia Inquirer,* June 7, 2000. Spielberg and Hanks both attended the ceremonies as well.

84. Stephen E. Ambrose, "The D-Day Museum," *American Heritage,* May/June 2000, http://www.americanheritage.com/articles/magazine/ah/2000/3/2000_3_38.shtml (accessed September 2, 2009).

85. Torgovnick, *The War Complex,* 2–3.

86. Stuart Elliot, "The Media Business: Advertising," *New York Times,* June 2, 1994.

87. Jim Abrams, "Normandy Foundation Is Torn, Short of Cash," *Philadelphia Inquirer,* June 8, 1994.

88. Adams, *Best War Ever,* xiii, 2–5.

CHAPTER 8

1. "Bush a Convert to Nation Building," *Washington Times,* April 7, 2008, http://www.washingtontimes.com/news/2008/apr/7/bush-a-convert-to-nation-building/# (accessed March 10, 2011).

2. Hill, "Memorializing Community Grief," 90–91, 126–65. Compare Alex Kershaw, *The Bedford Boys,* 231–32. On Charles Schulz, see David Michaelis, *Schulz and Peanuts: A Biography* (New York: HarperCollins, 2007), xii–xiii, 143, 151.

3. As one example, only the plaques covering American forces delve down to the regimental level.

4. Details come from a personal visit to the site. Pamphlet, *The National D-Day Memorial* (National D-Day Memorial Foundation, n.d. [2002?]); Hill, "Memorializing Community Grief," 150–53, 165–68.

5. "Sol Education Packet," The National D-Day Memorial Foundation, 2002.

6. *National D-Day Memorial.*

7. James W. Morrison, *Bedford Goes to War: The Heroic Story of a Small Virginia Community in World War II,* 2nd ed. (Lynchburg, VA: Warwick House Publishing, 2006), 232.

8. George W. Bush, "Remarks at the Dedication of the National D-Day Memorial in Bedford, Virginia," June 6, 2001, American Presidency Project, http://www.presidency.ucsb.edu/ws/index.php?pid=45818 (accessed April 23, 2010).

9. Morrison, *Bedford Goes to War,* 231–32.

10. Lewis also echoed popular understandings of the Second World War. D-Day remained a key moment. The Allies fought for just purposes. Lewis instructed Americans to honor their country's soldiers: "In war, it is the soldier who pays the cost for leadership failures, and it is frequently the soldier who makes right on the battlefield failed plans, flawed doctrine, poorly designed equipment, and inadequate leadership." Even academics sustained central features of the D-Day morality tale. Adrian Lewis, *Omaha Beach: A Flawed Victory* (Chapel Hill: University of North Carolina Press, 2001), x, 32, 305–6.

11. Alan Riding, "A Normandy Landing, This One for a Film," *New York Times,* June 7, 2001.

12. Patterson, *Restless Giant,* 12.

13. Robin Wright, *Sacred Rage: The Wrath of Militant Islam,* 3rd ed. (New York: Simon and Schuster, 2001), 244–45. This blow came at a cost to the terrorists of at most a few hundred thousand dollars. U.S. Congress, *Report of the Joint Inquiry into the Terrorist Attacks of September 11, 2001—By the House Permanent Select Committee on Intelligence and the Senate Select Committee on Intelligence,* 107th Congress, 2nd session (Washington, DC: Government Printing Office, 2002), 140.

14. Rosenberg, *A Date Which Will Live,* 2, 7, 12–14, 174–75.

15. Transcript, Ronald Reagan, "D-Day Message," May 14, 1987, White House Office of Speechwriting files, RRL.

16. William Safire, "On Language," *New York Times,* September 30, 2001.

17. A point made even by Bush's first secretary of defense, Donald Rumsfeld, in his generally self-serving memoir. Donald Rumsfeld, *Known and Unknown: A Memoir* (New York: Sentinel, 2011), 353.

18. Lisa Morales, "We Love Lucy AND Private Ryan," *Washington Post,* November 14, 2001.

19. Richard Huff, "No Cuts for 'Ryan' on ABC," *New York Daily News,* November 9, 2001; Nicholas Wapshott, "Hollywood Moguls Enlisted to Bolster War Effort," *London Times,* November 10, 2001.

20. Wapshott, "Hollywood Moguls"; Bob Clark, editorial, *Financial Planning,* November 1, 2001; Anita Gates, "Movies: Critic's Choice," *New York Times,* November 11, 2001; Mark Sappenfield, "US Soldiers Recapture a Peak in Public Esteem," *Christian Science Monitor,* November 9, 2001.

21. D'Este, *Eisenhower,* 1–3.

22. Paul Fussell, *The Boys' Crusade: The American Infantry in Northwestern Europe, 1944–1945* (New York: Modern Library, 2003), xii, 34–35.

23. Balkoski, *Omaha Beach,* x–xi, 4–6; Whitlock, *The Fighting First,* xi–xii; John C. McManus, *The Americans at D-Day: The American Experience at the Normandy Invasion* (New York: Forge, 2004), 13.

24. Albert H. Smith Jr., *The Big Red One at D-Day, 6 June 1944: Recollections of the Normandy Campaign and Beyond* (Blue Bell, PA: Society of the First Infantry Division, 2003).

25. Romeiser, *"Beachhead Don."* Cawthon's *Other Clay* was originally published in 1990.

26. See, for instance, Brett Martel, "'D-Day' Author Ambrose, 66, Dies," *Philadelphia Inquirer,* October 14, 2002. Douglas Brinkley, as quoted here, postulated that Ambrose "was the great populist historian of America. He didn't write for intellectuals; he wrote for everyday people."

27. *D-Day, the Sixth of June,* dir. Henry Koster, 106 min., Twentieth Century–Fox, 1956 (Twentieth Century–Fox Home Entertainment, 2002, DVD).

28. "The National D-Day Museum: Triumph of the Spirit," *Great Museums for Social Studies,* 30 min., Cambridge Educational and Echo Productions, 2003, DVD, Ball State University Library, Muncie, IN.

29. Michael Sherry questioned the tendency to declare "war" on all sorts of problems. See Sherry, *In the Shadow of War,* ix–x, 16–19, 123–24, 430, 496–500.

30. Piehler, *Remembering War the American Way,* 158.

31. George W. Bush, "Remarks at the Sainte Mere Eglise Church in Sainte Mere Eglise, France," May 27, 2002, American Presidency Project, http://www.presidency.ucsb.edu/ws/index.php?pid=62943&st=&st1 (accessed February 11, 2011).

32. George W. Bush, "Remarks at a Memorial Day Ceremony in Colleville-sur-Mer, France," May 27, 2002, American Presidency Project, http://www.presidency.ucsb.edu/ws/index.php?pid=73018&st=&st1 (accessed February 11, 2011). While lauding Bush's speech, *USA Today* erroneously described Omaha Beach as the "site of the bloodiest battle of World War II." The paper asserted that the Normandy Memorial Day ceremony "served as a reminder to Europeans, some of whom are increasingly skeptical of the war on terrorism, of U.S. efforts to liberate them from the Nazis." "In Normandy, Bush Talks of Old, New Sacrifices," *USA Today,* May 28, 2002.

33. George W. Bush, "Commencement Address at the United States Military Academy in West Point, New York," May 27, 2002, American Presidency Project, http://www.presidency.ucsb.edu/ws/index.php?pid=62730&st=&st1 (accessed February 11, 2011). Emphases added.

34. George W. Bush, *Decision Points* (New York: Crown Publishers, 2010), 228. Emphasis added.

35. Boyer, *By the Bomb's Early Light,* 334.

36. Farber, *Rise and Fall of Modern American Conservatism,* 213, 247. Compare Andrew Bacevich, *The Limits of Power: The End of American Exceptionalism* (New York: Metropolitan Books, 2008), 74–75.

37. Immerman, *Empire for Liberty,* 209–10.

38. Letter, George H. W. Bush to Cornelius Ryan, June 15, 1960, Folder—Ryan, Cornelius Letters and Correspondence—Fan Mail A-J 1959-63, Miscellaneous Supplementary Material records, CRC.

39. John King, "Bush: Join 'Coalition of Willing,'" CNN.com, November 20, 2002, http://edition.cnn.com/2002/WORLD/europe/11/20/prague.bush.nato/ (accessed April 1, 2011).

40. Bush, *Decision Points,* 229–32.

41. Dick Cheney, transcript of interview by Tim Russert, *Meet the Press,* NBC, March 16, 2003, http://www.mtholyoke.edu/acad/intrel/bush/cheneymeetthepress.htm (accessed September 5, 2011).

42. On the invasion of Iraq, see Williamson Murray and Robert H. Scales, Jr., *The Iraq War: A Military History* (Cambridge, MA: Belknap Press of Harvard University Press, 2003).

43. Thomas E. Ricks, *Fiasco: The American Military Adventure in Iraq,* with a new postscript (New York: Penguin, 2007), 111, 151, 290-91.

44. Bacevich, *Limits of Power,* 8, 59, 75. In another essay, Bacevich argued, "As applied to Iraq, 'liberation' was a code word; the real aim was more akin to pacification and control." Andrew Bacevich, "Gulliver at Bay: The Paradox of the Imperial Presidency," in Gardner and Young, *Iraq and the Lessons of Vietnam,* 128, 133.

45. Peter R. Mansoor, *Baghdad at Sunrise: A Brigade Commander's War in Iraq* (New Haven, CT: Yale University Press, 2008), 26.

46. A point that even Rumsfeld (later) acknowledged in *Known and Unknown,* 498–99.

47. Kevin Hecteman, "The D-Day + 60 Cruise of the S.S. *Jeremiah O'Brien,*" National Liberty Ship Memorial, n.d., http://www.ssjeremiahobrien.org/d-day-pixs-2004.html (accessed May 12, 2009).

48. *Bridgehead Sentinel,* Spring 2004, Box—Bridgehead Sentinel Spring 1997–Fall/Winter 2003, CFDM.

49. *Military History Quarterly,* Summer 2004, Special Section, D-Day 60th Anniversary.

50. Martin Blumenson, "D-Day: Launching the 'Great Crusade,'" *Army* 54 (June 2004): 22–37, AHEC.

51. Schickel had written a review of this production in 1980 that praised its mixture of irony, terror, and camaraderie. Richard Schickel, "Belated Victory: *The Big Red One,*" *Time,* July 21, 1980.

52. The full commendation appears in Fuller, *A Third Face,* 176–77.

53. Kent Jones, "Battle Fatigue," *Film Comment,* May/June 2004, 22–24.

54. *Ike: Countdown to D-Day,* dir. Robert Harmon, 89 min., A&E Television Networks, 2004, DVD.

55. Seymour M. Hersh, *Chain of Command: The Road from 9/11 to Abu Ghraib* (New York: HarperCollins, 2004), 11. Compare David Elliott, "Parallel Wars?: Can 'Lessons of Vietnam' Be Applied to Iraq?" in Gardner and Young, *Iraq and the Lessons of Vietnam,* 22.

56. George W. Bush, "Remarks at the Dedication of the National World War II Memorial," May 29, 2004, American Presidency Project, http://www.presidency.ucsb.edu/ws/index.php?pid=72638&st=memorial+day&st1 (accessed August 14, 2010).

57. George W. Bush, "The President's Radio Address," May 29, 2004, American Presidency Project, http://www.presidency.ucsb.edu/ws/index.php?pid=25147 (accessed November 22, 2009). One historian scathingly argued that this memorial reduced 400,000 war dead to 4,000 pleasant gold stars: "Its aim is to uphold myths of national power and innocence that have long been central to America's collective identity." Bodnar, *"Good War" in American Memory,* 91.

58. George W. Bush, "The President's Radio Address," June 5, 2004, American Presidency Project, http://www.presidency.ucsb.edu/ws/index.php?pid=25146 (accessed November 22, 2009).

59. "Bush Honors Men Who Stormed Normandy," *USA Today,* June 7, 2004.

60. George W. Bush, "Remarks on the 60th Anniversary of D-Day in Colleville-sur-Mer, France," June 6, 2004, American Presidency Project, http://www.presidency.ucsb.edu/ws/index.php?pid=72648&st=&st1 (accessed June 28, 2009).

61. Roger Cohen, "On Omaha Beach Today, Where's the Comradeship?" *New York Times,* June 5, 2004. Compare Samuel Hynes, "D-Day, in History and Memory," *New York Times,* June 6, 2004; and Elisabeth Bumiller, "How a Quiet Observance Evolved into a Day of Drama," *New York Times,* June 7, 2004.

62. Alessandra Stanley, "Once Again, Reagan Lands the Big Television Moment," *New York Times,* June 7, 2004. See also the serialized stories on Reagan, D-Day, and a local veteran in the

Orange County [CA] *Register*, June 6–11, 2004, Independent Folder 2005.241.1.1–6, CFDM; as well as Jon Meacham, "American Dreamer," *Newsweek*, June 14, 2004, http://www.newsweek.com/id/54017 (accessed July 27, 2008).

63. On approval ratings and the 2004 campaign, see Michael J. Gerson, *Heroic Conservatism: Why Republicans Need to Embrace America's Ideals (and Why They Deserve to Fail If They Don't)* (New York: HarperCollins, 2007), 201.

64. Vladimir Isachenkov, "For First Time, Russia Joins D-Day Observance," *Philadelphia Inquirer*, May 30, 2004.

65. Bumiller, "How a Quiet Observance."

66. Nancy Gibbs, "D-Day: 60th Anniversary: The Greatest Day," *Time*, May 31 2004, http://www.time.com/time/magazine/article/0,9171,994282,00.html (accessed May 28, 2009).

67. "Comparison Between D-Day, Iraq is 'Flawed, Insulting,'" *USA Today*, June 4, 2004.

68. Veteran William Mayer posited a likely report of failure by a liberal, anti-American American media. William Mayer, "If D-Day were Reported Today," *Dagwood Dispatches*, October 2004, 10–11, Box—Dagwood Dispatches, 18th [*sic*] Infantry Regiment Assoc., Jan 1991–, CFDM. Internet blog sites often presented similar arguments.

69. Peggy Noonan, "The D-Day Generation," *Washington Monthly*, June 1994, 2–3.

70. *Home of the Brave*, dir. Irwin Winkler, 106 min., Metro-Goldwyn-Mayer, 2006.

71. "'Overlord' Gets D-Day U.S. Release," *USA Today*, June 7, 2006. The "director-approved" DVD of *Overlord* was released by the Criterion Collection; for details, see Criterion website, http://www.criterion.com/films/550-overlord (accessed March 5, 2015).

72. Included on the list of programs were "D-Day Minesweeper" (2004), "The Lost Tanks of D-Day" (2004), "D-Day Destroyer" (2005), "D-Day Troops: Lost at Sea" (2005), from the *Deep Sea Detectives* series (released on DVD as *D-Day: The Total Story DVD Set*, 370 min., The History Channel, 2004).

73. David Gates, "War and Remembrance," *Newsweek*, September 24, 2007, http://www.newsweek.com/id/40994 (accessed July 27, 2008).

74. *The War*, dir. Ken Burns and Lynn Novick, 900 min., Florentine Films and Public Broadcasting Service, 2007, DVD.

75. Geoffrey C. Ward and Ken Burns, *The War: An Intimate History, 1941–1945* (New York: Alfred A. Knopf, 2007).

76. Norman Davies, *No Simple Victory: World War II in Europe, 1939–1945* (New York: Viking, 2006), 429–68.

77. Ken Ford and Steven J. Zaloga, *Overlord: The D-Day Landings*, introduction by Stephen Badsey (Westminster, MD: Osprey, 2009).

78. Jeff Shaara, *The Steel Wave: A Novel of World War II* (New York: Ballantine Books, 2008).

79. Cole Kingseed, ed., *From Omaha Beach to Dawson's Ridge: The Combat Journal of Captain Joe Dawson* (Annapolis, MD: Naval Institute Press, 2005).

80. Dick Winters with Cole Kingseed. *Beyond Band of Brothers: The War Memoirs of Major Dick Winters* (New York: Penguin, 2006).

81. Bodnar, *"Good War" in American Memory*, 202.

82. Marcus Brotherton, *We Who are Alive and Remain: Untold Stories from the Band of Brothers* (New York: Berkley Caliber Books, 2009), 235–36, 240-46; Marcus Brotherton and Lynn "Buck" Compton, *Call of Duty: My Life Before, During and After the Band of Brothers* (New York: Berkley Caliber, 2006); Marcus Brotherton, *A Company of Heroes: Personal Memories about the Real Band of Brothers and the Legacy They Left Us* (New York: Berkley Caliber, 2010); Marcus Brotherton, *Shifty's War: The Authorized Biography of Sergeant Darrell "Shifty" Powers, the Legendary Sharpshooter from the Band of Brothers* (New York: Berkley Caliber, 2011).

83. Larry Alexander, *Biggest Brother: The Life of Major D. Winters, The Man Who Led the Band of Brothers* (New York: NAL Caliber, 2005); Alexander, *In the Footsteps of the Band of Brothers: A Return to Easy Company's Battlefields with Sergeant Forrest Guth* (New York: NAL Caliber, 2010).

84. See also William "Wild Bill" Guarnere and Edward "Babe" Heffron with Robyn Post, *Brothers in Battle, Best of Friends: Two WWII Paratroopers from the Original Band of Brothers Tell Their Story,* foreword by Tom Hanks (New York: Berkley Caliber, 2007); Don Malarkey with Bob Welch, *Easy Company Soldier: The Legendary Battles of a Sergeant from World War II's "Band of Brothers"* (New York: St. Martin's Griffith, 2008).

85. Childers, *Soldier from the War Returning,* 4–5.

86. Davies, *No Simple Victory,* 468, 471.

87. Wood, *Purpose of the Past,* 194, 261.

88. See, for instance, *Dagwood Dispatches,* October 2009, Box—Dagwood Dispatches 18th [*sic*] Infantry Regiment Assoc., Jan 1991–, CFDM.

89. For just one recent example, see Edward Olshaker, "If D-Day Had Been Reported by Today's MSM," *American Thinker,* June 6, 2010, http://www.americanthinker.com/blog/2010/06/if_dday_had_been_reported_by_t.html (accessed February 15, 2011).

90. de Groot, *Consuming History,* 91.

91. "D-Day" search results, Ebay.com, http://shop.ebay.com/?_from=R40&_trksid=p5197.m570.l1313&_nkw=D-Day&_sacat=See-All-Categories (accessed February 15, 2011).

92. I base this paragraph on my personal observations while attending the conference and the Bedford memorial service. Something similar, though reduced in size to several hundred attendees, took place in June 2014 at the National World War II Museum in New Orleans. These remembrance sites often end up vying with one another for popular attention and the precious funding it brings.

93. Karl Weissenbach, director of the Eisenhower Presidential Library and Museum, and Samantha Kenner, public programs specialist, conversation with author, December 7, 2009, Abilene, KS.

94. Keith Gill, director of CFDM, conversation with author, May 14, 2009, Wheaton, IL; "65th Anniversary of D-Day and LCVP Dedication at Cantigny Park," Cantigny First Division Museum, May 19, 2009, http://www.mccormickfoundation.org/news/2009/FDMatCantigny/pr051909.aspx (accessed February 15, 2011); "65th Anniversary of D-Day and LCVP Dedication at Cantigny Park," *Chicago Tribune,* June 8, 2009.

95. Transcript, "The President's News Conference with President Nicolas Sarkozy of France in Caen, France," June 6, 2009, American Presidency Project, http://www.presidency.ucsb.edu/ws/index.php?pid=86254&st=&st1 (accessed February 15, 2011).

96. Barack Obama, "Remarks on the 65th Anniversary of D-Day in Normandy, France," June 6, 2009, American Presidency Project, http://www.presidency.ucsb.edu/ws/index.php?pid=86253&st=&st1 (accessed February 15, 2011).

97. Transcript, "The President's Weekly Address," June 6, 2009, American Presidency Project, http://www.presidency.ucsb.edu/ws/index.php?pid=86232&st=&st1 (accessed February 15, 2011).

CONCLUSION

1. Robert B. Strassler, ed., *The Landmark Thucydides: A Comprehensive Guide to the Peloponnesian War,* introduction by Victor Davis Hanson (New York: Free Press, 1996), 111–17.

2. Ibid., 115.

3. Winter, *Remembering War,* 4.

4. Ibid., 17–18. On the point of national identity, I draw on the fictional bonds, or "mystic chords of memory," that tie large groups together into an "imagined community." Benedict Anderson's pathbreaking work set the scope of discussion for this phenomenon, a project that has attracted many other scholars like Michael Kammen (cited frequently throughout this work). See Anderson, *Imagined Communities;* and Kammen, *Mystic Chords of Memory.* Michael Howard argued, "The United States indeed, virtually alone among nations, found and to some extent still finds its identity not so much in ethnic community or shared historical experience as in dedication to a value system; and the reiteration of these values, the repeated proclamation of and dedication to the liberal creed, has always been a fundamental element in the cohesion of American society." Howard, *War and the Liberal Conscience,* 116. Compare Logevall, *Embers of War*, 317; Appy, *American Reckoning*, 13, 334.

5. Michael Geyer and Sheila Fitzpatrick, eds., *Beyond Totalitarianism: Stalinism and Nazism Compared* (New York: Cambridge University Press, 2009).

6. Hagopian, *Vietnam War in American Memory,* 402–8.

7. Edwards, "War and Collective Memory," 312.

8. Mark Deimel, "The Americanization of Canadian Director Hiller," *Bruin Index* (UCLA), February 26, 1980, Folder Hiller, Arthur (magazine articles), Core Collections, MHL.

9. McDougall, *Promised Land, Crusader State,* 128, 146; Ninkovich, *The Wilsonian Century,* 16; Lloyd Gardner and Marilyn Young, introduction, Gardner and Young, *Iraq and the Lessons of Vietnam,* 8. See also, from Gardner and Young, David Elliott, "Parallel Wars?: Can 'Lessons of Vietnam' Be Applied to Iraq?," 42–44.

10. Rosenberg, *A Date Which Will Live,* 2.

11. Chalres Esdaile, "Spain 1808–Iraq 2003: Some Thoughts on the Use and Abuse of History," *Journal of Military History* 74 (January 2010): 174.

12. "As D-Day for iPad Nears, So Do Questions," CBS News.com, March 31, 2010, http://www.cbsnews.com/stories/2010/03/31/tech/main6351534.shtml (accessed November 18, 2010).

13. "Raw Data: Transcript from Obama, Sarkozy Press Conference," FoxNews.com, March 30, 2010, http://www.foxnews.com/politics/2010/03/30/raw-data-transcript-obama-sarkozy-press-conference/ (accessed April 4, 2010).

14. Amanda Terkel, "60 Plus Association Ad Compares Repealing Health Care Reform to D-Day," *Huffington Post,* October 29, 2010, http://www.huffingtonpost.com/2010/10/29/60-plus-association-ad-repeal-health-care-d-day_n_776292.html?view=screen (accessed November 18, 2010).

15. Kammen, *Mystic Chords of Memory,* 700. For a detailed comparison of American D-Day remembrance with that of other countries, see Dolski, "To Set Free a Suffering Humanity," 388–414; and Dolski, Edwards, and Buckley, *D-Day in History and Memory.*

16. On official assistance to filmmakers, see Suid, *Guts & Glory,* 168–210, 425–27, 625–37.

17. Piehler, *Remembering War the American Way,* 187.

18. Morrison, *Bedford Goes to War,* 215, 228–34.

19. Linenthal, *Sacred Ground,* 11–40.

20. Again, see Dolski, "To Set Free a Suffering Humanity," or Dolski, Edwards, Buckley, *D-Day in History and Memory,* for further development of this comparative argument.

21. McDougall, *Promised Land, Crusader State,* 4–5, 128, 173, 205–8. Emphasis in original.

22. Brinkley, *Boys of Pointe du Hoc,* 7.

23. Kaushik Roy, "Military Loyalty in the Colonial Context: A Case Study of the Indian Army during World War II," *Journal of Military History* 73 (April 2009): 515. On Allied logistical problems in general, see Kevin Smith, "Constraining OVERLORD: Civilian Logistics, TORCH, and

the Second Front," in *D-Day 1944,* ed. Theodore A. Wilson, (Lawrence: University Press of Kansas, 1994), 42–62.

24. Several letters passed between Huebner, Wyman, and Frances Ward (at *Reader's Digest*) in early 1958. See Folder—Huebner, Lt Gen C. R., NY 11 No Interview, and Folder—Wyman, General W. G., Va 5 Fort Monroe, "The Longest Day" records, CRC.

25. D'Este, *Decision in Normandy;* Ambrose, *D-Day June 6, 1944,* 440; Antony Beevor, *D-Day: The Battle for Normandy* (New York: Viking, 2009), 109. Beevor misspells the last name as "Weyman" in the brief passage.

26. Gerhard L. Weinberg, "D-day: Analysis of Costs and Benefits," in Wilson, *D-Day 1944,* 337.

27. Bodnar, *"Good War" in American Memory,* 2 and throughout.

28. Lance Morrow, "D-Day: Fiftieth Anniversary of June 6, 1944," *Time,* May 28, 1984, http://www.time.com/time/magazine/article/0,9171,951085,00.html (accessed December 23, 2009).

29. Winter, *Remembering War,* 140, 198, 276.

30. Ibid., 285.

31. Edward W. Wood Jr., *Worshipping the Myths of World War II: Reflections on America's Dedication to War* (Washington, DC: Potomac Books, 2006), x–xi, 4, 77–84, 132.

32. For an example of a recent book on D-Day, see John McManus, *The Dead and Those About to Die: The Big Red One at Omaha Beach* (New York: New American Library, 2014).

33. For video footage of remarks by President Obama at the ceremonies, see "D-Day 70th Anniversary Ceremony," 2014, C-Span website, http://www.c-span.org/video/?319649–1/president-obama-dday-70th-anniversary (accessed October 11, 2014).

BIBLIOGRAPHY

PRIMARY SOURCES

Archives, Memorials, and Museums

CANTIGNY FIRST DIVISION MUSEUM, WHEATON, ILLINOIS (CFDM)

Main Exhibit Hall
Robert R. McCormick Research Center

DWIGHT D. EISENHOWER LIBRARY AND ARCHIVES, ABILENE, KANSAS (DDEL)

Anderson, Robert S., Papers Collection
Benedict, Stephen, Papers Collection
Bulkeley, John, Papers Collection
Collins, J. Lawton, Papers Collection
Cota, Norman, Papers Collection
Eisenhower, Dwight D., Library Collections
Eisenhower, Dwight D., Papers Collection
Harlow, Bryce N., Papers Collection
Jackson, C. D., Papers Collection
Principal Files
Quesada, Elwood R., Papers Collection
World War II Participants and Contemporaries Collection
Huch, William, Papers
Shyrock, William, Papers
Young and Rubicam Papers Collection

FRANKLIN D. ROOSEVELT LIBRARY AND ARCHIVES, HYDE PARK, NEW YORK

President's Personal File Speeches
Rosenman, Samuel I., Papers

MARGARET HERRICK LIBRARY, THE ACADEMY OF MOTION PICTURE ARTS AND SCIENCES, BEVERLY HILLS, CALIFORNIA (MHL)

Core Collection
The Americanization of Emily Material
The Big Red One Material

D-Day, the Sixth of June Material
Hanks, Tom, Material
Hiller, Arthur, Material
The Longest Day Material
Saving Private Ryan Material
Selleck, Tom, Material
Zanuck, Darryl F., Material
Special Collections
Brackett, Charles, Papers
Grace, Henry, Papers
Huie, William B., Papers
Peckinpah, Sam, Papers
Production Code Administration Records
Stevens, George, Papers
Weiser, Marty, Papers
Zanuck, Darryl F., Papers
Zinnemann, Fred, Papers

NATIONAL ARCHIVES AND RECORDS ADMINISTRATION, COLLEGE PARK, MARYLAND (NACP)
Record Group 117, Records of the American Battle Monuments Commission [ABMC]
Administrative History
General Records
General Records, 1923–65
Records Relating to Cemeteries and Memorials, 1918–93
Records Relating to Construction and Maintenance
Records Relating to Dedications
Record Group 208, Records of the Office of War Information
Records of the News Bureau
Record Group 331, Records of Allied Operational and Occupation Headquarters, World War II
Supreme Headquarters Allied Expeditionary Forces (SHAEF) Special Staff Adjutant General's Division Executive Section
Supreme Headquarters Allied Expeditionary Forces (SHAEF) Special Staff Psychological Warfare Division Executive Section
Record Group 338, Records of U.S. Army Operational, Tactical, and Support Organizations (World War II and Thereafter)
Records of European Theater of Operations U.S. Army (ETOUSA)/U.S. Forces European Theater (USFET)
Record Group 407, Records of the Adjutant General's Office, 1917– [AGO]
Reports Relating to World War II and Korean War Combat Operations and to Activities in Occupied Areas, 1940–54

NATIONAL D-DAY MONUMENT, BEDFORD, VIRGINIA
Memorial Area

NATIONAL WORLD WAR II MUSEUM, NEW ORLEANS, LOUISIANA
Main Exhibit Hall

NORMANDY AMERICAN CEMETERY, COLLEVILLE-SUR-MER, FRANCE

Cemetery and Memorial Area

ROBERT E. AND JEAN R. MAHN CENTER FOR ARCHIVES AND SPECIAL COLLECTIONS, OHIO UNIVERSITY LIBRARY, ATHENS, OHIO

Ryan, Cornelius, Collection of World War II Papers (CRC)
- The "Longest Day" Records
- Miscellaneous Supplementary Material Records

RONALD W. REAGAN PRESIDENTIAL LIBRARY AND ARCHIVES, SIMI VALLEY, CALIFORNIA (RRL)

White House Office of Records Management, Alpha File
- Administration Appreciation Letters Collection
- Administration Complaints–Criticism Collection
- Administration Support Collection
- Memorials and Monuments Collection

White House Office of Speechwriting Files

UCLA FILM AND TELEVISION ARCHIVE, LOS ANGLES, CALIFORNIA (UFTA)

Motion Picture Collection

U.S. ARMY HERITAGE AND EDUCATION CENTER, CARLISLE BARRACKS, PENNSYLVANIA (AHEC)

Manuscript Collection
- Daniel, Derril M., Papers Collection
- Lisko, Lou, Papers Collection
- North, Thomas, Papers Collection
- Rowe, Robert A., Papers Collection
- Winters, Richard D., Papers Collection

Government Publications

Richardson, Christy, and Judith Waldrop. *Veterans: 2000, Census 2000 Brief.* Washington, DC: Government Printing Office, 2003.

Shulimson, Jack, and Charles M. Johnson. *U.S. Marines in Vietnam: The Landing and the Buildup, 1965.* Washington, DC: Government Printing Office, 1978.

U.S. American Battle Monuments Commission. *Normandy American Cemetery and Memorial.* Washington, DC: American Battle Monuments Commission, 1957.

U.S. Armed Forces Staff College. *The Invasion of Normandy: Operation Neptune.* n.p., 1949, 1950.

U.S. Census Bureau. *2000 Census of Population and Housing, Summary Social, Economic, and Housing Characteristics,* Washington, DC: Government Printing Office, 2003.

———. *Historical Statistics of the United States, 1789–1945,* Washington, DC: Government Printing Office, 1949.

———. *Statistical Abstract of the United States,* Washington, DC: Government Printing Office, 2000.

U.S. Congress, House, Committee on Veterans' Affairs. *D-Day Plus 20 Years: June 6, 1944–June 6, 1964,* 88th Congress, 2nd session, Washington, DC: Government Printing Office, 1964.

———. *D-Day Plus 40 Years,* 98th Congress, 2nd session, Washington, DC: Government Printing Office, 1984.

———. *D-Day Plus 50 Years,* 103rd Congress, 2nd session, Washington, DC: Government Printing Office, 1994.

U.S. Congress, Joint Committee. *Report of the Joint Inquiry into the Terrorist Attacks of September 11, 2001—By the House Permanent Select Committee on Intelligence and the Senate Select Committee on Intelligence.* 107th Congress, 2nd session. Washington, DC: Government Printing Office, 2002.

U.S. Department of Defense. *Normandy Landings 6 June 1944, United States Commemorative Activities 5–6 June 1994,* Washington, DC: Department of Defense, 1994.

U.S. Government Accountability Office. *Battle of Normandy Foundation: Uncertainties Surround Its Future Viability.* Washington, DC: General Accounting Office, November 1994.

Published Primary Sources

6 June 1944: Twenty Fifth Anniversary of the Normandy Landings at Omaha and Utah Beaches. Paris: American Legion, Department of France, 1969.

Campaign Statements of Dwight D. Eisenhower: A Reference Index, n.p., n.d. [1976?].

D-Day 1944: Combat Art. Abilene, KS: Dwight D. Eisenhower Library, 1969.

Public Papers of the Presidents of the United States: Dwight D. Eisenhower, 1956. Washington, DC: Government Printing Office, 1958.

Public Papers of the Presidents of the United States: Lyndon B. Johnson, 1963–64. Washington, DC: Government Printing Office, 1967.

Pyle, Ernie. *Brave Men.* Introduction by G. Kurt Piehler. New York: Henry Holt, 1944. Reprint, Lincoln: University of Nebraska Press, 2001.

Romeiser, John B., ed. *"Beachhead Don": Reporting the War from the European Theater, 1942–1945.* New York: Fordham University Press, 2004.

Veterans of Foreign Wars. *6 June 1944: Twentieth Anniversary of the Normandy Landings at Omaha and Utah Beaches.* Paris: S.P.E.I., 1964.

———. *1944–74: Thirty Years After . . . Commemorative Album . . . .* Paris: Veterans of Foreign Wars, 1974.

Memoirs/Diaries

Baumgarten, Harold. *Eyewitness on Omaha Beach.* Jacksonville, FL: Halrit Publishing, 1994.

Bradley, Omar N. *A Soldier's Story.* New York: Henry Holt, 1951.

Brinkley, Douglas, ed. *The Reagan Diaries.* New York: HarperCollins, 2007.

Brotherton, Marcus. *A Company of Heroes: Personal Memories about the Real Band of Brothers and the Legacy They Left Us.* New York: Berkley Caliber, 2010.

———. *Shifty's War: The Authorized Biography of Sergeant Darrell "Shifty" Powers, The Legendary Sharpshooter from the Band of Brothers.* New York: Berkley Caliber, 2011.

———. *We Who are Alive and Remain: Untold Stories from the Band of Brothers.* New York: Berkley Caliber Books, 2009.

Brotherton, Marcus, and Lynn "Buck" Compton. *Call of Duty: My Life Before, During and After the Band of Brothers.* New York: Berkley Caliber, 2006.

Burgett, Donald R. *Currahee! A Screaming Eagle at Normandy.* Foreword by Stephen E. Ambrose and introduction by Martin Blumenson. Boston: Houghton Mifflin, 1967; Novato, CA: Presidio Press, 1999.

Bush, George, and Brent Scowcroft. *A World Transformed.* New York: Alfred A. Knopf, 1998.

Bush, George W. *Decision Points.* New York: Crown Publishers, 2010.

Capa, Robert. *Slightly Out of Focus.* New York: Henry Holt, 1947.

Carter, Jimmy. *White House Diary.* New York: Farrar, Straus and Giroux, 2010.

Cawthon, Charles R. *Other Clay: A Remembrance of the World War II Infantry.* Niwot: University Press of Colorado, 1990; Lincoln: University of Nebraska, 2004.

Eisenhower, Dwight D. *Crusade in Europe.* New York: Doubleday, 1948.

Fuller, Samuel, with Christa Lang Fuller, and Jerome Henry Rudes. *A Third Face: My Tale of Writing, Fighting, and Filmmaking.* New York: Alfred A. Knopf, 2002.

Guarnere, William "Wild Bill." and Edward "Babe" Heffron, with Robyn Post. *Brothers in Battle, Best of Friends: Two WWII Paratroopers from the Original Band of Brothers Tell Their Story.* Foreword by Tom Hanks. New York: Berkley Caliber, 2007.

Kingseed, Cole, ed. *From Omaha Beach to Dawson's Ridge: The Combat Journal of Captain Joe Dawson.* Annapolis, MD: Naval Institute Press, 2005.

Malarkey, Don, with Bob Welch. *Easy Company Soldier: The Legendary Battles of a Sergeant from World War II's "Band of Brothers."* New York: St. Martin's Griffith, 2008.

Mansoor, Peter. *Baghdad at Sunrise: A Brigade Commander's War in Iraq.* New Haven, CT: Yale University Press, 2008.

Masters, Peter. *Striking Back: A Jewish Commando's War Against the Nazis.* Foreword by Stephen E. Ambrose. Novato, CA: Presidio Press, 1997.

Montgomery, Bernard Law. *The Memoirs of Field-Marshal the Viscount Montgomery of Alamein.* London: World Publishing, 1958.

Mullaney, Craig. *The Unforgiving Minute: A Soldier's Education.* New York: Penguin, 2009.

Noonan, Peggy. *What I Saw at the Revolution: A Political Life in the Reagan Era.* New York: Random House, 1990.

Rooney, Andy. *My War.* Foreword by Tom Brokaw. New York: PublicAffairs, 2000.

Rumsfeld, Donald. *Known and Unknown: A Memoir.* New York: Sentinel, 2011.

Terkel, Studs, with Sydney Lewis. *Touch and Go: A Memoir.* New York: New Press, 2007.

Winters, Dick, with Cole Kingseed. *Beyond Band of Brothers: The War Memoirs of Major Dick Winters.* New York: Penguin, 2006.

Novels

Faulkner, William. *Requiem for a Nun* (1951). In *William Faulkner: Novels 1942–1954.* Ed. Joseph Blotner and Noel Polk. New York: Library of America, 1994.

Heller, Joseph. *Catch-22.* New York: Simon and Schuster, 1961.

Huie, William Bradford. *The Americanization of Emily.* New York: Dutton, 1959. Reprint, New York: Signet, 1964.

———. *The Klansman.* New York: Delacorte Press, 1967.

———. *The Revolt of Mamie Stover.* New York: Duell, Sloan and Pearce, 1951.

Shaara, Jeff. *The Steel Wave: A Novel of World War II.* New York: Ballantine Books, 2008.

Shapiro, Lionel. *The Sixth of June: A Novel of World War II.* New York: Doubleday, 1955.

Shaw, Irwin. *The Young Lions.* Foreword by James Salter. New York: Random House, 1948; Chicago: University of Chicago Press, 2000.

Vonnegut, Kurt. *Slaughterhouse-five; or, The Children's Crusade, a Duty-Dance with Death.* New York: Delacorte Press, 1969.

Wouk, Herman. *War and Remembrance.* Boston: Little, Brown, 1978.

Miscellaneous Media

AMERICAN HERITAGE
ATLANTA DAILY WORLD
THE ATLANTIC
BALTIMORE SUN
BEDFORD DEMOCRAT
BOXOFFICE
BRUIN INDEX (UCLA)
CBS.COM
CHICAGO DAILY TRIBUNE
CHRISTIAN SCIENCE MONITOR
CNN.COM
C-SPAN
COLLIER'S
DAILY BOSTON GLOBE
FILM COMMENT
FOXNEWS.COM
HUFFINGTON POST
LONDON OBSERVER
LONDON TIMES
LOS ANGELES TIMES
MILITARY HISTORY
MILITARY HISTORY QUARTERLY
NATIONAL INTEREST
NEW YORK DAILY NEWS
NEW YORK TIMES
NEWSWEEK
ORANGE COUNTY (CALIF.) REGISTER
PHILADELPHIA INQUIRER
PUBLISHER'S WEEKLY
SATURDAY EVENING POST
TIME
TV GUIDE
USA TODAY
VARIETY
WALL STREET JOURNAL
WASHINGTON MONTHLY
WASHINGTON POST
WASHINGTON TIMES
WORLD WAR II

Veterans' Association Newsletters

BRIDGEHEAD SENTINEL
DAGWOOD DISPATCHES
THE IVY LEAVES
THE RANGER
THE TWENTY-NINER

Films, Documentaries, and Television Shows

An American in Normandy: D-Day Revisited by Samuel Fuller. Dir. Jean-Louis Comolli. 55 min. La Sept/Arte and GMT Productions, 1994.

The Americanization of Emily. Dir. Arthur Hiller. 115 min. Metro-Goldwyn-Mayer, 1964.

Band of Brothers. Dir. David Frankel, Mikael Salomon, Tom Hanks, David Leland, Richard Loncraine, David Nutter, Phil Alden Robinson, and Tony To. HBO in association with DreamWorks Pictures, 2001.

The Big Red One—The Reconstruction. Dir. Samuel Fuller. 162 min. United Artists, 1980; Warner Brothers, 2004.

Breakthrough. Dir. Lewis Seiler. 91 min. Warner Brothers Pictures, 1950.

Crusade in Europe. 519 min. March of Time and Twentieth Century–Fox, 1949.

"D-Day." *Victory at Sea.* Dir. M. Clay Adams. 27 min. National Broadcasting Company, 1953.

"D-Day." *You Are There.* 30 min. CBS Television Network Production, 1955 (March 6).

D-Day: Carolina Liberators. 90 min. CBS and Spartan Radiocasting, 1994.

"D-Day Destroyer." *Deep Sea Detectives.* 50 min. The History Channel, 2005.

"D-Day Minesweeper." *Deep Sea Detectives.* 50 min. The History Channel, 2004.

"D-Day Normandy." *Eye on History.* Dir. Don Horan. 45 min. Lou Reda Productions with the U.S. Naval Institute, 1993.

D-Day: The Normandy Invasion. Dir. Frank Capra. 51 min. U.S. Coast Guard, 1944.

"D-Day . . . The Normandy Invasion." *World War II: The War Chronicles.* Dir. Don Horan. 25 min. A&E Television Networks, 1983.

D-Day Plus 20 Years: Eisenhower Returns to Normandy. 123 min. CBS Reports, Columbia Broadcasting Systems, 1964.

D-Day Plus 40 Years. 52 min. National Broadcasting Company, 1984.

D-day Remembered. 53 min. Charles Guggenheim and Direct Cinema Limited, 1994.

D-Day Revisited. 23 min. ABC News, 1984.

D-Day Revisited. Dir. Darryl F. Zanuck. 52 min. Twentieth Century–Fox Film Corporation, 1968. Broadcast May 30, 1969.

D-Day, the Sixth of June. Dir. Henry Koster. 106 min. Twentieth Century–Fox, 1956.

D-Day: The Total Story DVD Set. 3 vol. 370 min. The History Channel, 2004.

"D-Day Troops: Lost at Sea." *Deep Sea Detectives.* 50 min. The History Channel, 2005.

Fighter Squadron. Dir. Raoul Walsh. 96 min. Warner Brothers Pictures, 1948.

George Stevens: A Filmmaker's Journey. Dir. George Stevens, Jr. 111 min. Creative Film Center, 1984.

Home of the Brave. Dir. Irwin Winkler. 106 min. Metro-Goldwyn-Mayer, 2006.

Ike: Countdown to D-Day. Dir. Robert Harmon. 89 min. Sony Pictures, 2004.

The Longest Day. Dir. Ken Annakin, Andrew Marton, Bernhard Wicki, and Darryl F. Zanuck. 178 min. Darryl F. Zanuck Productions and Twentieth Century–Fox Film Corporation, 1962.

"Longest Day: A Salute to Courage." *History vs. Hollywood.* 50 min. The History Channel, 2001.

"The Lost Tanks of D-Day." *Deep Sea Detectives.* 50 min. The History Channel, 2004.

"The Making of the National D-Day Museum." *Save Our History.* 50 min. A&E Television, 1996.

"May–June 1944." *War and Remembrance.* Dir. Dan Curtis. 120 min. American Broadcasting Company, 1988.

"The National D-Day Museum: Triumph of the Spirit." *Great Museums for Social Studies.* 30 min. Cambridge Educational and Echo Productions, 2003.

News of the Day, D-Day Tribute to Americans Overseas. Vol. 17, no. 280. 10 min. Metro-Goldwyn-Mayer, 1946.

News of the Day, Invasion Extra! Vol. 15, no. 280. 10 min. Metro-Goldwyn-Mayer, 1944.

Overlord. Dir. Stuart Cooper. 84 min. National Film Trustee Co., 1975.

Patton. Dir. Franklin J. Schaffner. 172 min. Twentieth Century–Fox, 1970.

Saving Private Ryan. Dir. Steven Spielberg. 169 min. DreamWorks Pictures and Paramount Pictures, 1998.

The Steel Helmet. Dir. Sam Fuller. 85 min. Lippert Pictures, 1951.

"Steven Spielberg." *Inside the Actors Studio.* Dir. Jeff Wurtz. 60 min. Bravo Channel, 1999.

"Tom Hanks." *Inside the Actors Studio.* Dir. Jeff Wurtz. 60 min. Bravo Channel, 1999.

The True Glory. Dir. Garson Kanin. 87 min. Ministry of Information (UK) and U.S. Office of War Information, 1945.

The War. Dir. Ken Burns and Lynn Novick. 900 min. Florentine Films and Public Broadcasting Service, 2007.

The World at War. Dir. John Pett. 1,352 min. Thames Television in cooperation with the Imperial War Museum, 1973–74.

The Young Lions. Dir. Edward Dmytryk. 167 min. Twentieth Century–Fox, 1958.

Games

The Atlantic Wall. Strategic Simulations, 1978.

Call of Duty 2. Activision, 2005.

Call of Duty 2: Big Red One. Activision, 2005.

D-Day. Avalon Hill, 1961, 1977.

Medal of Honor. Electronic Arts, 1999.

Medal of Honor: Allied Assault. Electronic Arts, 2002.

Medal of Honor: Frontline. Electronic Arts, 2002.

SECONDARY SOURCES

Books

Adams, Michael C. C. *The Best War Ever: America and World War II.* Baltimore: Johns Hopkins University Press, 1994.

Alexander, Larry. *Biggest Brother: The Life of Major D. Winters, The Man Who Led the Band of Brothers.* New York: NAL Caliber, 2005.

———. *In the Footsteps of the Band of Brothers: A Return to Easy Company's Battlefields with Sergeant Forrest Guth.* New York: NAL Caliber, 2010.

Allen, Michael J. *Until the Last Man Comes Home: POWs, MIAs, and the Unending Vietnam War.* Chapel Hill: University of North Carolina Press, 2009.

Ambrose, Stephen E. *Band of Brothers: E Company, 506th Regiment, 101st Airborne from Normandy to Hitler's Eagle's Nest.* New York: Simon and Schuster, 1992.

———. *Citizen Soldiers: The U.S. Army from the Normandy Beaches to the Bugle to the Surrender of Germany, June 7, 1944–May 7, 1945.* New York: Simon and Schuster, 1997.

———. *Crazy Horse and Custer: The Parallel Lives of Two American Warriors.* Garden City, NY: Doubleday, 1975.

———. *D-Day, June 6, 1944: The Climactic Battle of World War II.* New York: Simon and Schuster, 1994.

———. *Pegasus Bridge: June 6, 1944.* New York: Simon and Schuster, 1985.

———. *To America: Personal Reflections of an Historian.* New York: Simon and Schuster, 2002.

Anderegg, Michael, ed. *Inventing Vietnam: The War in Film and Television.* Philadelphia: Temple University Press, 1991.

Anderson, Benedict. *Imagined Communities: Reflections on the Origin and Spread of Nationalism.* Rev. ed. New York: Verso, 1991.

Anderson, Terry H. *The Movement and the Sixties: Protest in America from Greensboro to Wounded Knee.* New York: Oxford University Press, 1995.

Appy, Christian G. *American Reckoning: The Vietnam War and our National Identity.* New York: Viking, 2015.

Ashplant, T. G., Graham Dawson, and Michael Roper, eds. *The Politics of War Memory and Commemoration.* New York: Routledge, 2000.

Atkinson, Rick. *An Army at Dawn: The War in North Africa, 1942–1943.* New York: Henry Holt, 2002.

———. *Crusade: The Untold Story of the Persian Gulf War.* Boston: Houghton Mifflin, 1993.

Bacevich, Andrew. *The Limits of Power: The End of American Exceptionalism.* New York: Metropolitan Books, 2008.

———. *The New American Militarism: How Americans are Seduced by War.* New ed. New York: Oxford University Press, 2006.

Bailey, Beth, and David Farber, eds. *America in the Seventies.* Lawrence: University Press of Kansas, 2004.

Bailey, Thomas A. *The American Pageant: A History of the Republic.* 1st ed. Boston: D. C. Heath, 1956.

Bailey, Thomas A., and David M. Kennedy. *The American Pageant: A History of the Republic.* 8th ed. Vol. 2. Boston, D. C. Heath, 1987.

Balkoski, Joseph. *Beyond the Beachhead: The 29th Infantry Division in Normandy.* Foreword by Stephen E. Ambrose. 1989. Reprint, Mechanicsburg, PA: Stackpole Books, 1999.

———. *Omaha Beach: D-Day: June 6, 1944.* Mechanicsburg, PA: Stackpole Books, 2004.

———. *Utah Beach: The Amphibious Landing and Airborne Operations on D-Day.* Mechanicsburg, PA: Stackpole Books, 2005.

Bando, Mark. *Vanguard of the Crusade: The 101st Airborne Division in World War II.* Bedford, PA: Aberjona Press, 2003.

Barris, Theodore. *Victory at Vimy: Canada Comes of Age, April 9–12, 1917.* Toronto: Thomas Allen Publishers, 2007.

Barthes, Roland. *Mythologies.* Ed. and trans. Annette Lavers. Paris: Editions du Seuil, 1957. Reprint, New York: Noonday Press, 1972.

Bartov, Omer. *Germany's War and the Holocaust: Disputed Memories.* Ithaca, NY: Cornell University Press, 2003.

———. *Hitler's Army: Soldiers, Nazis, and War in the Third Reich.* New York: Oxford University Press, 1991.

Bartov, Omer, Atina Grossman, and Mary Nolan, eds. *Crimes of War: Guilt and Denial in the Twentieth Century.* New York: New Press, 2002.

Basinger, Jeanine. *The World War II Combat Film: Anatomy of a Genre.* With an updated filmography by Jeremy Arnold. New York: Columbia University Press, 1986; Middletown, CT: Wesleyan University Press, 2003.

Beevor, Antony. *D-Day: The Battle for Normandy.* New York: Viking, 2009.

Beidler, Philip D. *The Good War's Greatest Hits: World War II and American Remembering.* Athens: University of Georgia Press, 1998.

Berman, William C. *America's Right Turn: From Nixon to Clinton.* Baltimore, MD: Johns Hopkins University Press, 1998.

Bilton, Michael, and Kevin Sim. *Four Hours in My Lai.* New York: Viking, 1992.

Bin, Alberto, Richard Hill, and Archer Jones. *Desert Storm: A Forgotten War.* Westport, CT: Praeger, 1998.

Blight, David W. *Race and Reunion: The Civil War in American Memory.* Cambridge, MA: Harvard University Press, 2001.

Bliven, Bruce, Jr. *The Story of D-Day: June 6, 1994.* 50th Anniversary ed. 1956. Reprint, New York: Random House, 1994.

Blum, John Morton. *V Was for Victory: Politics and American Culture during World War II.* New York: Harcourt Brace Jovanovich, 1976.

Bodnar, John E. *The "Good War" in American Memory.* Baltimore: Johns Hopkins University Press, 2010.

———. *Remaking America: Public Memory, Commemoration, and Patriotism in the Twentieth Century.* Princeton: Princeton University Press, 1992.

Boyer, Paul S. *By the Bomb's Early Light: American Thought and Culture at the Dawn of the Atomic Age.* New York: Pantheon, 1985.

Braudel, Fernand. *The Mediterranean and the Mediterranean World in the Age of Philip II.* 2nd ed. Vol. 1. Trans. Siân Reynolds. Librairie Armand Colin, 1966; New York: Harper and Row, 1972.

Brinkley, Douglas. *The Boys of Pointe du Hoc: Ronald Reagan, D-Day, and the U.S. Army 2nd Rangers Battalion.* New York: HarperPerennial, 2005.

———. *Cronkite.* New York: HarperCollins, 2012.

Brokaw, Tom. *The Greatest Generation.* New York: Random House, 1998.

Buckley, John, ed. *The Normandy Campaign 1944: Sixty Years On.* New York: Routledge, 2006.

Burrell, Robert S. *The Ghosts of Iwo Jima.* College Station: Texas A&M University Press, 2006.

Campbell, Joseph. *The Hero with a Thousand Faces.* 3rd ed. New York: Pantheon Books, 1949. Reprint, Novato, CA: New World Library, 2008.

Canfield, Leon H., and Howard B. Wilder. *The Making of Modern America.* Boston: Houghton Mifflin, 1954.

Chambers, John Whiteclay, II, and David Culbert, eds. *World War II, Film, and History.* New York: Oxford University Press, 1996.

Childers, Thomas. *Soldier from the War Returning: The Greatest Generation's Troubled Homecoming from World War II.* New York: Houghton Mifflin Harcourt, 2009.

Connelly, Mark. *We Can Take It!: Britain and the Memory of the Second World War.* New York: Pearson, 2004.

Considine, Shaun. *Mad as Hell: The Life and Work of Paddy Chayefsky.* New York: Random House, 1994.

Dank, Milton. *D-Day.* New York: Franklin Watts, 1984.

Davies, Norman. *No Simple Victory: World War II in Europe, 1939–1945.* New York: Viking, 2006.

de Groot, Jerome. *Consuming History: Historians and Heritage in Contemporary Popular Culture.* New York: Routledge, 2009.

D'Este, Carlo. *Decision in Normandy.* Old Saybrook, CT: Konecky and Konecky, 1983; New York: HarperPerennial, 1994.

———. *Eisenhower: A Soldier's Life.* New York: Henry Holt, 2002.

———. *Patton: A Genius for War.* New York: HarperCollins, 1995.

Dolski, Michael, Sam Edwards, and John Buckley, eds., *D-Day in History and Memory: The Normandy Landings in International Remembrance and Commemoration.* Denton: University of North Texas Press, 2014.

Doherty, Thomas. *Projections of War: Hollywood, American Culture, and World War II.* Revised and updated. New York: Columbia University Press, 1999.

Dombrowski, Lisa. *The Films of Samuel Fuller: If You Die, I'll Kill You!* Middletown, CT: Wesleyan University Press, 2008.

Dower, John W. *War without Mercy: Race and Power in the Pacific War.* New York: Pantheon Books, 1986.

Drez, Ronald J., ed. *Voices of D-Day: The Story of the Allied Invasion Told by Those Who Were There.* With a foreword by Stephen E. Ambrose. Baton Rouge: Louisiana State University Press, 1994.

Dupuy, Trevor N. *A Genius for War: The German Army and General Staff, 1807–1945.* Englewood Cliffs, NJ: Prentice-Hall, 1977.

Ehrman, John. *The Eighties: America in the Age of Reagan.* New Haven, CT: Yale University Press, 2005.

The Eisenhower Foundations. *D-Day: The Normandy Invasion in Retrospect.* Foreword by Omar N. Bradley. Lawrence: University Press of Kansas, 1971.

Engelhardt, Tom. *The End of Victory Culture: Cold War America and the Disillusioning of a Generation.* New York: Basic Books, 1995.

Evans, Martin, and Ken Lunn, eds. *War and Memory in the Twentieth Century.* New York: Berg, 1997.

Fahs, Alice, and Joan Waugh, eds. *The Memory of the Civil War in American Culture.* Chapel Hill: University of North Carolina Press, 2004.

Farber, David R. *The Age of Great Dreams: America in the 1960s.* New York: Hill and Wang, 1995.

———. *The Rise and Fall of Modern American Conservatism: A Short History.* Princeton, NJ: Princeton University Press, 2010.

———. *Taken Hostage: The Iran Hostage Crisis and America's First Encounter with Radical Islam.* New ed. Princeton, NJ: Princeton University Press, 2006.

Faust, Drew Gilpin. *The Republic of Suffering: Death and the American Civil War.* New York: Alfred A. Knopf, 2008.

Flamm, Michael. *Law and Order: Street Crime, Civil Unrest, and the Crisis of Liberalism in the 1960s.* New York: Columbia University Press, 2005.

Flanzbaum, Hilene, ed. *The Americanization of the Holocaust.* Baltimore: Johns Hopkins University Press, 1999.

Foner, Eric. *The Story of American Freedom.* New York: W. W. Norton, 1998.

Ford, Ken, and Steven J. Zaloga. *Overlord: The D-Day Landings.* Introduction by Stephen Badsey. Westminster, MD: Osprey, 2009.

François, Dominique. *Normandy Breaching the Atlantic Wall: From D-Day to the Breakout and Liberation.* Trans. Gayle Wurst. Minneapolis, MN: Zenith Press, 2008.

Frei, Norbert. *Adenauer's Germany and the Nazi Past: The Politics of Amnesty and Integration.* Trans. Joel Golb. New York: Columbia University Press, 2002.

Fukuyama, Frances. *The End of History and the Last Man.* New York: Free Press, 1992.

Fuller, Samuel. *The Big Red One: The Magnificent Saga of World War II's Incredible First Infantry Division.* New York: Bantam Books, 1980.

Fussell, Paul. *The Boys' Crusade: The American Infantry in Northwestern Europe, 1944–1945.* New York: Modern Library, 2003.

———. *The Great War and Modern Memory.* New York: Oxford University Press, 1975.

———. *Wartime: Understanding and Behavior in the Second World War.* New York: Oxford University Press, 1989.

Gardner, Lloyd, and Marilyn Young, eds. *Iraq and the Lessons of Vietnam: Or, How Not to Learn from the Past.* New York: New Press, 2007.

Gerson, Michael J. *Heroic Conservatism: Why Republicans Need to Embrace America's Ideals (and Why They Deserve to Fail If They Don't).* New York: HarperCollins, 2007.

Geyer, Michael, and Sheila Fitzpatrick, eds. *Beyond Totalitarianism: Stalinism and Nazism Compared.* New York: Cambridge University Press, 2009.

Gienapp, William E. *Abraham Lincoln and Civil War America: A Biography.* New York: Oxford University Press, 2002.

Gillis, John R., ed. *Commemorations: The Politics of National Identity.* Princeton, NJ: Princeton University Press, 1994.

Goldberg, Harold J. *D-Day in the Pacific: The Battle of Saipan.* Bloomington: Indiana University Press, 2007.

Goldstein, Donald M., Katherine V. Dillon, and J. Michael Wenger. *D-Day Normandy: The Story and Photographs.* New York: Brassey's, 1994.

Goldstein, Richard. *America at D-Day: A Book of Remembrance.* Preface by Matthew B. Ridgway. New York: Dell, 1994.

Gussow, Mel. *Don't Say Yes Until I Finish Talking: A Biography of Darryl F. Zanuck.* New York: Doubleday, 1971. Reprint, New York: Pocket Books, 1972.

Hagopian, Patrick. *The Vietnam War in American Memory: Veterans, Memorials, and the Politics of Healing.* Amherst: University of Massachusetts Press, 2009.

Halberstam, David. *The Coldest Winter: America and the Korean War.* New York: Hyperion, 2007.

Halbwachs, Maurice. *On Collective Memory.* Ed. and trans. Lewis Coser. Chicago: University of Chicago Press, 1992.

Hammond, William M. *Reporting Vietnam: Media and Military at War.* Lawrence: University Press of Kansas, 1998.

Harrison, Gordon A. *Cross-Channel Attack.* U.S. Army in World War II: European Theater of Operations. Washington, DC: United States Army Center of Military History, 1951. Reprint, New York: BDD, 1993.

Hass, Kristin Ann. *Carried to the Wall: American Memory and the Vietnam Veterans Memorial.* Berkeley: University of California Press, 1998.

Herring, George C. *America's Longest War: The United States and Vietnam, 1950–1975I.* 4th ed. Boston: McGraw Hill, 2002.

———. *From Colony to Superpower: U.S. Foreign Relations since 1776.* New York: Oxford University Press, 2008.

———. *LBJ and Vietnam: A Different Kind of War.* Austin: University of Texas Press, 1994.

Hersh, Seymour M. *Chain of Command: The Road from 9/11 to Abu Ghraib.* New York: HarperCollins, 2004.

Hitchcock, William I. *The Bitter Road to Freedom: A New History of the Liberation of Europe.* New York: The Free Press, 2008.

———. *The Struggle for Europe: The Turbulent History of a Divided Continent 1945–2002.* New York: Doubleday, 2003.

Hobsbawm, Eric, and Terence Ranger, eds. *The Invention of Tradition.* New York: Cambridge University Press, 1983.

Hoffer, Peter Charles. *Past Imperfect: Facts, Fictions, Fraud; American History from Bancroft and Parkman to Ambrose, Bellesiles, Ellis, and Goodwin.* New York: PublicAffairs, 2004.

Hoffman, David E. *The Dead Hand: The Untold Story of the Cold War Arms Race and Its Dangerous Legacy.* New York: Doubleday, 2009.

Hogan, Michael, ed. *The Ambiguous Legacy: U.S. Foreign Relations in the "American Century."* New York: Cambridge University Press, 1999.

Howard, Michael. *Strategic Deception in the Second World War: British Intelligence Operations against the German High Command.* New York: W. W. Norton, 1995.

———. *War and the Liberal Conscience.* New ed. New Brunswick, NJ: Rutgers University Press, 2004.

Howarth, David. *Dawn of D-Day: These Men Were There, 6 June 1944.* London: Collins, 1959; London: Greenhill and Mechanicsburg, PA: Stackpole Books, 2001.

Huie, William Bradford. *The Execution of Private Slovik: The Hitherto Secret Story of the Only American Soldier since 1864 to Be Shot for Desertion.* New York: Duell, Sloan and Pearce, 1954.

Hunt, Michael H. *Ideology and U.S. Foreign Policy.* New Haven: Yale University Press, 1987.

Immerman, Richard H. *Empire for Liberty: A History of American Imperialism from Benjamin Franklin to Paul Wolfowitz* (Princeton, NJ: Princeton University Press, 2010).

Isserman, Maurice, and Michael Kazin. *America Divided: The Civil War of the 1960s.* 2nd ed. New York: Oxford University Press, 2003.

Jacobsen, Hans-Adolf, and Jürgen Rohwer, eds. *Decisive Battles of World War II: The German View.* Trans. Edward Fitzgerald, introduction by Cyril Falls. Frankfurt am Main: Verlag für Wehrwesen Bernard & Graefe, 1960; New York: G. P. Putnam's Sons, 1965.

James, Harold. *International Monetary Cooperation since Bretton Woods.* New York: Oxford University Press, 1996.

Jeffries, John W. *Wartime America: The World War II Home Front.* Chicago: Ivan R. Dee, 1996.

Judt, Tony. *Postwar: A History of Europe Since 1945.* New York: Penguin Press, 2005.

Kammen, Michael G. *Mystic Chords of Memory: The Transformation of Tradition in American Culture.* New York: Vintage Books, 1991.

Keegan, John. *The Face of Battle.* New York: Viking, 1976.

———. *Six Armies in Normandy: From D-Day to the Liberation of Paris.* With a new introduction for the 50th anniversary of D-Day. 1982. Reprint, New York: Penguin Books, 1994.

Kennedy, Paul. *The Rise and Fall of the Great Powers.* New York: Random House, 1987.

Keren, Michael, and Holger H. Herwig, eds. *War Memory and Popular Culture: Essays on Modes of Remembrance and Commemoration.* Jefferson, NC: McFarland, 2009.

Kershaw, Alex. *The Bedford Boys: One American Town's Ultimate D-Day Sacrifice.* Cambridge, MA: Da Capo Press, 2003.

Kershaw, Robert. *D-Day: Piercing the Atlantic Wall.* Annapolis, MD: Naval Institute Press, 1994.

Kieran, David. *Forever Vietnam: How a Divisive War Changed American Public Memory.* Amherst: University of Massachusetts Press, 2014.

Korda, Michael. *Ike: An American Hero.* New York: HarperCollins, 2007.

Kruse, Kevin M. *White Flight: Atlanta and the Making of Modern Conservatism.* Princeton, NJ: Princeton University Press, 2005.

Landy, Marcia, ed. *The Historical Film: History and Memory in Media.* New Brunswick, NJ: Rutgers University Press, 2001.

Lawrence, John Shelton, and Robert Jewett. *The Myth of the American Superhero.* Grand Rapids, MI: William B. Eerdmans, 2002.

Lebow, Richard Ned, Wulf Kansteiner, and Claudio Fogu, eds. *The Politics of Memory in Postwar Europe.* Durham, NC: Duke University Press, 2006.

Leffler, Melvyn. *For the Soul of Mankind: The United States, the Soviet Union, and the Cold War.* New York: Hill and Wang, 2007.

Le Goff, Jacques. *History and Memory.* Trans. Steven Rendall and Elizabeth Claman. New York: Columbia University Press, 1992.

Lewis, Adrian R. *The American Culture of War: The History of U.S. Military Force from World War II to Operation Iraqi Freedom.* New York: Routledge, 2007.

———. *Omaha Beach: A Flawed Victory.* Chapel Hill, NC: University of North Carolina Press, 2001.

Linenthal, Edward Tabor. *Sacred Ground: Americans and Their Battlefields.* Urbana: University of Illinois Press, 1991.

Linenthal, Edward Tabor, and Tom Engelhardt, eds. *History Wars: The Enola Gay and Other Battles for the American Past.* New York: Metropolitan Books, 1996.

Linn, Brian M. *The Echo of Battle: The Army's Way of War.* Cambridge, MA: Harvard University Press, 2007.

Lockenour, Jay. *Soldiers as Citizens: Former Wehrmacht Officers in the Federal Republic of Germany, 1945–1955.* Lincoln: University of Nebraska Press, 2001.

Logevall, Frederick. *Choosing War: The Lost Chance for Peace and the Escalation of War in Vietnam.* Berkeley: University of California Press, 1999.

———. *Embers of War: The Fall of an Empire and the Making of America's Vietnam.* New York: Random House, 2012.

MacDonald, Charles B. *The Mighty Endeavor: American Armed Forces in the European Theater in World War II.* New York: Oxford University Press, 1969.

Maier, Charles. *The Unmasterable Past: History, Holocaust, and German National Identity.* Cambridge, MA: Harvard University Press, 1997,

Mansoor, Peter. *The GI Offensive in Europe: The Triumph of American Infantry Divisions, 1941–1945.* Lawrence: University Press of Kansas, 1999.

Marling, Karal Ann, and John Wetenhall. *Iwo Jima: Monuments, Memories, and the American Hero.* Cambridge, MA: Harvard University Press, 1991.

Marshall, S. L. A. *Night Drop: The American Airborne Invasion of Normandy.* Boston: Little, Brown, 1962.

McDonald, JoAnna, ed. *The Faces of D-Day.* Redondo Beach, CA: Rank and File Publications, 1998.

McDougall, Walter A. *Promised Land, Crusader State: The American Encounter with the World since 1776.* New York: Houghton Mifflin, 1997.

McGirr, Lisa. *Suburban Warriors: The Origins of the New American Right.* New ed. Princeton, NJ: Princeton University Press, 2002.

McManus, John C. *The Americans at D-Day: The American Experience at the Normandy Invasion.* New York: Tom Doherty Associates, LLC, 2004.

———. *The Dead and Those About to Die: The Big Red One at Omaha Beach.* New York: New American Library, 2014.

Michaelis, David. *Schulz and Peanuts: A Biography.* New York: HarperCollins, 2007.

Miller, Russell. *Nothing Less than Victory: The Oral History of D-Day.* New York: William Morrow, 1993.

Millett, Allan, and Peter Maslowski. *For the Common Defense: A Military History of the United States of America.* Rev. ed. New York: Free Press, 1994.

Moreno, Barry. *The Statue of Liberty Encyclopedia.* New York: Simon and Schuster, 2000.

Morison, Samuel Eliot. *History of United States Naval Operations in World War II.* Vol. 9. *The Invasion of France and Germany, 1944–1945.* Boston: Little, Brown, 1957; Edison, NJ: Castle Books, 2001.

Morrison, James W. *Bedford Goes to War: The Heroic Story of a Small Virginia Community in World War II.* 2nd ed. Lynchburg, VA: Warwick House Publishing, 2006.

Mosse, George. *Fallen Soldiers: Reshaping the Memory of the World Wars.* New York: Oxford University Press, 1990.

Müller, Jan-Werner, ed. *Memory and Power in Post-War Europe: Studies in the Presence of the Past.* New York: Cambridge University Press, 2002.

Murray, Williamson, and Allan R. Millett. *A War to be Won: Fighting the Second World War.* Cambridge, MA: Harvard University Press, 2000.

Murray, Williamson, and Robert H. Scales, Jr. *The Iraq War: A Military History.* Cambridge, MA: Belknap Press of Harvard University Press, 2003.

Ninkovich, Frank. *The Wilsonian Century: U.S. Foreign Policy since 1900.* Chicago: University of Chicago Press, 1999.

Nora, Pierre, ed. *Realms of Memory: Rethinking the French Past.* 3 vols. Ed. Lawrence Kritzman, trans. Arthur Goldhammer. New York: Columbia University Press, 1996–1998.

Novick, Peter. *The Holocaust in American Life.* New York: Houghton Mifflin, 1999.

———. *That Noble Dream: The "Objectivity Question" and the American Historical Profession.* New York: Cambridge University Press, 1988.

Overy, Richard J. *Why the Allies Won.* New York: W. W. Norton, 1995.

Patterson, James T. *Restless Giant: The United States from Watergate to* Bush v. Gore. New York: Oxford University Press, 2005.

Penrose, Jane, ed. *The D-Day Companion: Leading Historians Explore History's Greatest Amphibious Assault.* New York: Osprey Press, 2004.

Piehler, G. Kurt. *Remembering War the American Way.* 1995. Reprint, Washington, DC: Smithsonian Institution Press, 2004.

Porch, Douglas. *The Path to Victory: The Mediterranean Theater in World War II.* New York: Farrar, Straus and Giroux, 2004.

Porter, Gareth. *A Peace Denied: The United States, Vietnam, and the Paris Agreement.* Bloomington: Indiana University Press, 1975.

Prados, Edward F., U.S. Navy Memorial Foundation, ed. *Neptunus Rex: Naval Stories of the Normandy Invasion, June 6, 1944.* Novato, CA: Presidio Press, 1998.

Quétel, Claude. *A Memorial for Peace.* Foreword by Jean-Marie Girault, trans. John Lee. Caen, France: Editions du Regard, 1993.

Record, Jeffrey. *The Specter of Munich: Reconsidering the Lessons of Appeasing Hitler.* Sterling, VA: Potomac Books, 2006.

Ricks, Thomas E. *Fiasco: The American Military Adventure in Iraq.* With a new postscript. New York: Penguin, 2007.

Roberts, Mary Louise. *What Soldiers Do: Sex and the American GI in World War II France.* Chicago: University of Chicago Press, 2013.

Robin, Ron. *Enclaves of America: The Rhetoric of American Political Architecture Abroad, 1900–1965.* Princeton, NJ: Princeton University Press, 1992.

Rollins, Peter C., ed. *Hollywood as Historian: American Film in a Cultural Context.* Lexington: University Press of Kentucky, 1983.

Rollins, Peter C., and John E. O'Connor. *Why We Fought: America's Wars in Film and History.* Lexington: University Press of Kentucky, 2008.

Rose, Kenneth D. *Myth and the Greatest Generation: A Social History of Americans in World War II*. New York: Routledge, 2007.

Rosenberg, Emily S. *A Date Which Will Live: Pearl Harbor in American Memory*. Durham, NC: Duke University Press, 2003.

Rousso, Henry. *The Vichy Syndrome: History and Memory in France since 1944*. Trans. Arthur Goldhammer. Cambridge, MA: Harvard University Press, 1991.

Ruggero, Ed. *The First Men In: U.S. Paratroopers and the Fight to Save D-Day*. New York: HarperCollins, 2006.

Ryan, Cornelius. *The Longest Day: June 6, 1944*. New York: Simon and Schuster, 1959.

Schaller, Michael. *Right Turn: American Life in the Reagan-Bush Era, 1980–1992*. New York: Oxford University Press, 2006.

Schmitz, Helmut, ed. *A Nation of Victims? Representations of German Wartime Suffering from 1945 to the Present*. New York: Rodopi B.V., 2007.

Schrecker, Ellen. *Many Are the Crimes: McCarthyism in America*. Princeton, NJ: Princeton University Press, 1999.

Schulman, Bruce. *The Seventies: The Great Shift in American Culture, Society, and Politics*. 2001. Reprint, New York: Da Capo Press, 2002.

Shaw, John. *The Cambodian Campaign: The 1970 Offensive and America's Vietnam War*. Lawrence: University of Kansas Press, 2005.

Sheehan, Neil. *A Bright Shining Lie: John Paul Vann and America in Vietnam*. New York: Vintage Books, 1988.

Sherry, Michael S. *In the Shadow of War: The United States since the 1930's*. New Haven, CT: Yale University Press, 1995.

———. *The Rise of American Air Power: The Creation of Armageddon*. New York: Yale University Press, 1987.

Slotkin, Richard. *The Fatal Environment: The Myth of the Frontier in the Age of Industrialization, 1800–1890*. New York: Atheneum, 1985.

———. *Regeneration Through Violence: The Mythology of the American Frontier, 1600–1860*. Middletown, CT: Wesleyan University Press, 1973.

Smelser, Ronald, and Edward J. Davies II. *The Myth of the Eastern Front: The Nazi-Soviet War in American Popular Culture*. New York: Cambridge University Press, 2008.

Smith, Albert H., Jr. *The Big Red One at D-Day, 6 June 1944: Recollections of the Normandy Campaign and Beyond*. Blue Bell, PA: Society of the First Infantry Division, 2003.

Smith, Richard Norton. *The Colonel: The Life and Legend of Robert R. McCormick, 1880–1955*. Boston: Houghton Mifflin, 1997.

Spayd, P. A., and Gary Wilkins, eds. *Bayerlein: After Action Reports of the Panzer Lehr Division Commander; From D-Day to the Ruhr*. Atglen, PA: Schiffer, 2005.

Speidel, Hans. *Invasion 1944*. Trans. Theo R. Crevenna, introduction Truman Smith. New York: Henry Regnery, 1950. New York: Paperback Library, 1968. Originally published as *Invasion 1944, Ein Beitrag zu Rommels und des Reiches Schicksal*. Tubingen und Stuttgart: Rainer Wunderlich Verlag Hermann Leins, 1949.

Stillwell, Paul, ed. *Assault on Normandy: First-Person Accounts from the Sea Services*. Annapolis, MD: Naval Institute Press, 1994.

Strassler, Robert B., ed. *The Landmark Thucydides: A Comprehensive Guide to the Peloponnesian War*. Introduction by Victor Davis Hanson. New York: Free Press, 1996.

Suid, Lawrence H. *Guts & Glory: The Making of the American Military Image in Film*. Rev. ed. Lexington: University Press of Kentucky, 2002.

Takaki, Ronald. *Double Victory: A Multicultural History of America in World War II.* New York: Little, Brown, 2000.

Terkel, Studs. *"The Good War": An Oral History of World War II.* New York: New Press, 1984.

Tobin, James. *Ernie Pyle's War: America's Eyewitness to World War II.* Lawrence: University Press of Kansas, 1997.

Torgovnick, Marianna. *The War Complex: World War II in Our Time.* Chicago: University of Chicago Press, 2005.

Torr, James D., ed. *Violence in Film and Television.* San Diego, CA: Greenhaven Press, 2002.

Trouillot, Michel-Rolph. *Silencing the Past: Power and the Production of History.* Boston: Beacon Press, 1995.

Tsouras, Peter. *Disaster at D-Day: The Germans Defeat the Allies, June 1944.* London: Greenhill Books. Mechanicsburg, PA: Stackpole Books, 1994.

van Creveld, Martin. *Fighting Power: German and U.S. Army Performance.* Westport, CT: Greenwood Press, 1982.

van der Vat, Dan. *D-Day: The Greatest Invasion – A People's History.* Toronto: Black Walnut Books, 2003.

Voss, Frederick S. *Reporting the War: The Journalistic Coverage of World War II.* Washington, DC: Smithsonian Institution Press for the National Portrait Gallery, 1994.

Wagner, Sarah E. *To Know Where He Lies: DNA Technology and the Search for Srebernica's Missing.* Berkeley: University of California Press, 2008.

Ward, Geoffrey C., and Ken Burns. *The War: An Intimate History, 1941–1945.* New York: Alfred A. Knopf, 2007.

Wawro, Geoffrey. *Quicksand: America's Pursuit of Power in the Middle East.* New York: Penguin, 2010.

Weeks, Jim. *Gettysburg: Memory, Market and an American Shrine.* Princeton, NJ: Princeton University Press, 2003.

Weigley, Russell F. *Eisenhower's Lieutenants: The Campaign of France and Germany, 1944–1945.* Bloomington: Indiana University Press, 1981.

Weinberg, Gerhard L. *A World at Arms: A Global History of World War II.* New York: Cambridge University Press, 1994.

Weingartner, Steven, ed. *The Greatest Thing We Have Ever Attempted: Historical Perspectives on the Normandy Campaign.* Wheaton, IL: Cantigny First Division Foundation, 1998.

Werth, Alexander. *Russia at War, 1941–1945.* New York: E. P. Dutton, 1964.

Whelan, Richard. *Robert Capa.* New York: Alfred A. Knopf, 1985.

Whiting, Charles. *Hemingway Goes to War.* Phoenix Mill, UK: Alan Sutton Press, 1999.

Whitlock, Flint. *The Fighting First: The Untold Story of the Big Red One on D-Day.* Boulder, CO: Westview Press, 2004.

Wieviorka, Olivier. *Normandy: The Landings to the Liberation of Paris.* Trans. M. B. DeBevoise. Cambridge, MA: Harvard University Press, 2008.

Wilson, Theodore A., ed. *D-Day 1944.* With a foreword by John S. D. Eisenhower. Lawrence: University Press of Kansas, 1994.

Winter, Jay. *Remembering War: The Great War between Memory and History in the Twentieth Century.* New Haven: Yale University Press, 2006.

Wood, Edward W., Jr. *Worshipping the Myths of World War II: Reflections on America's Dedication to War.* Washington, DC: Potomac Books, 2006.

Wood, Gordon S. *The Purpose of the Past: Reflections on the Uses of History.* New York: Penguin, 2008.

Wright, Robin. *Sacred Rage: The Wrath of Militant Islam.* 3rd ed. New York: Simon and Schuster, 2001.

Wunthnow, Robert. *The Restructuring of American Religion: Society and Faith since World War II.* Princeton, NJ: Princeton University Press, 1988.

Articles

Ambrose, Stephen E. "D-Day Revisited." *Military History Quarterly,* Winter 1993, 26–33.

———. "Why We Won the War: The Politics of WWII." *Army* 44 (June 1994): 13–18.

Ambrosius, Lloyd E. "Woodrow Wilson and George W. Bush: Historical Comparisons of Ends and Means in Their Foreign Policies." *Diplomatic History* 30 (June 2006): 509–54.

Anthony, Constance G. "American Democratic Interventionism: Romancing the Iconic Woodrow Wilson." *International Studies Perspectives* 9 (2008): 239–53.

Blumenson, Martin. "D-Day: Launching the 'Great Crusade.'" *Army* 34 (June 1984): 22–37.

———. "D-Day: Launching the 'Great Crusade.'" *Army* 54 (June 2004): 24–38.

———. "DDay in Retrospect: Could the Germans Have Won?" *Army* 14 (June 1964): 69–75.

———. "'Superb Account' of That Fateful Day." Review of Stephen Ambrose's *D-Day, June 6, 1944: The Climactic Battle of World War II.*" *Army* 44 (June 1994): 73.

Confino, Alon. "Collective Memory and Cultural History: Problems of Method." *American Historical Review* 102 (December 1997): 1386–1403.

Ehrenhaus, Peter. "Why We Fought: Holocaust Memory in Spielberg's *Saving Private Ryan.*" *Critical Studies in Media Communication* 18 (2001): 321–37.

Esdaile, Chalres. "Spain 1808–Iraq 2003: Some Thoughts on the Use and Abuse of History." *Journal of Military History* 74 (January 2010): 173–88.

Friedman, Hal M. "Reactions and Non-Reactions: Lessons of the Korean War and the Public Debate over Containment and American National Military Strategy, 1950–1955." *U.S. Military History Review* 1 (December 2014): 3–24.

Moeller, Robert G. "What Has 'Coming to Terms with the Past' Meant in Post–World War II Germany?: From History to Memory to the 'History of Memory.'" *Central European History* 35 (Spring 2002): 223–56.

Nora, Pierre. "Between Memory and History: Les Liuex de Memoire." Trans. Marc Roudebush. *Representations* 26 (Spring 1989): 7–26.

Owen, A. Susan. "Memory, War and American Identity: *Saving Private Ryan* as Cinematic Jeremiad." *Critical Studies in Media Communication* 19 (2002): 249–82.

Roy, Kaushik. "Military Loyalty in the Colonial Context: A Case Study of the Indian Army during World War II." *Journal of Military History* 73 (April 2009): 497–529.

Sullivan, Gordon R. "D-Day Plus 50 Years." *Army* 44 (June 1994): 21–26.

Unpublished Papers, Dissertations, or Presentations

Dolski, Michael. "'Dead Man's Nothin' but a Corpse': Forgetting the Korean War." Presentation at Society of Military History annual conference, Army Historical Foundation, Arlington, VA, May 12, 2012.

———. "'To Set Free a Suffering Humanity': D-Day in American Remembrance." PhD diss., Temple University, 2012.

Edwards, Sam. "The Beginning of the End: D-Day in British Cultural Memory." Presentation at Society of Military History annual conference, Virginia Military Institute, Lexington, VA, May 22, 2010.

———. "War and Collective Memory: American Military Commemoration in Britain and France, 1943 to the Present." PhD diss., Lancaster University, 2007.

Hill, Roger H. "Memorializing Community Grief: Bedford, Virginia, and the National D-Day Memorial." DA diss., George Mason University, 2006.

Weinberg, Gerhard. "Keynote Address." Overlord Echoes conference, Liberty University, Lynchburg, VA, June 4, 2009.

Websites

American Battle Monuments Commission. www.abmc.gov

American D-Day. www.americandday.org

American Presidency Project, University of California, Santa Barbara. www.presidency.ucsb.edu

American Thinker. www.americanthinker.com

Canadian War Museum online exhibit. www.museedelaguerre.ca/cwm/exhibitions

History Place. www.historyplace.com

Internet Movie Database. www.IMDb.com

Cantigny First Division Museum. www.firstdivisionmuseum.org

Criterion Collection, www.criterion.com

Dwight D. Eisenhower Memorial Commission, Directory of Speeches. www.eisenhowermemorial.org

Miller Center of Public Affairs, University of Virginia, Presidential Speech Archive. www.millercenter.org

National Liberty Ship Memorial. www.ssjeremiahobrien.org

National World War II Glider Pilots. www.ww2gp.org

Radio Days. www.otr.com

U.S. Army Military History Institute. www.carlisle.army.mil

The World at War. www.theworldatwar.com

INDEX

Entries in **boldface** refer to illustrations.